Study Guide
to accompany

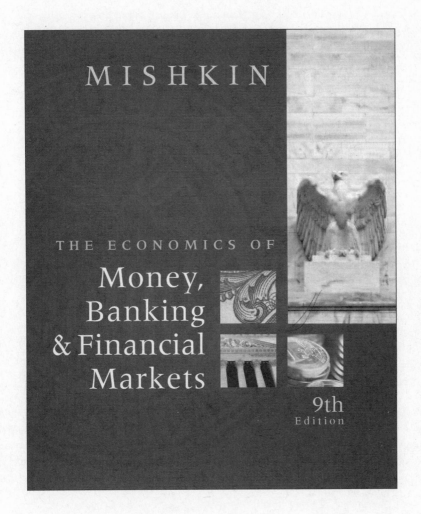

MISHKIN

THE ECONOMICS OF
Money,
Banking
& Financial
Markets

9th
Edition

Edward Gamber
Lafayette College

David Hakes
University of Northern Iowa

Pearson Addison-Wesley

Boston San Francisco New York
London Toronto Sydney Tokyo Singapore Madrid
Mexico City Munich Paris Cape Town Hong Kong

Acquisitions Editor: Noel Kamm Seibert
Project Manager: Kerri McQueen
Production Editor: Alison Eusden
Manufacturing Buyer: Carol Melville

Pearson Addison-Wesley™ is a trademark of Pearson Education, Inc.

Addison-Wesley
is an imprint of

www.pearsonhighered.com

1 2 3 4 5 6 BB 12 11 10 09

ISBN-13: 978-0-321-60001-1
ISBN-10: 0-321-60001-0

CONTENTS

HOW TO USE THIS STUDY GUIDE

This *Study Guide* will help you learn the concepts in *The Economics of Money, Banking, and Financial Markets*. As you work your way through each chapter, you will actively review the important definitions, details of financial institutions, and economic principles from your textbook. You will also actively apply the economic models to graphical and numerical problems. This reinforcement of the important textbook ideas will allow you to more quickly master the concepts and will better prepare you for exams.

Each chapter corresponds with your textbook and contains the following learning tools.

- *Chapter Review:* Each chapter begins with a summary of the chapter. The chapter review is divided into sections based on the section headings provided in the text.

- *Helpful Hints:* This section provides some additional suggestions and examples to help clarify the more difficult material.

- *Terms and Definitions:* Students match key terms from the text to their definitions. This section is particularly important because a working economic and financial vocabulary is necessary in order for the student to advance through the material.

- *Problems and Short-Answer Questions:* We provide a number of multi-step problems that require numerical, graphical, or written solutions. The problems are based on the larger issues developed in the chapter. Smaller issues are addressed with approximately ten short-answer questions.

- *Critical Thinking:* This section provides a single multi-step problem that is an application of one of the major issues developed in the chapter.

- *Self-Test:* The self-test section provides fifteen true/false and twenty multiple-choice questions to validate areas of successful learning and to highlight areas needing improvement.

- *Solutions:* Detailed solutions for all problems and questions are provided at the end of each chapter.

You should experiment with different ways to use this *Study Guide* to better help you learn. Most students should work through each section of the *Study Guide* in order. However, if you feel *very* comfortable with the text material, then you might want to proceed directly to the Self-Test section. If you are happy with your performance, then you can begin the next chapter.

Edward N. Gamber
David R. Hakes

1 Why Study Money, Banking, and Financial Markets?

Chapter Review

PREVIEW

The study of money, banking, and financial markets is of value because it provides answers to everyday financial questions such as: How will an increase in interest rates affect my purchase of a new car or my decision to save for retirement? This chapter establishes the importance of learning about money, banking, and financial markets. Events in the financial markets will have direct effects on your financial well-being. Financial institutions in the economy have an impact on how efficiently funds are moved from savers to borrowers. Money and monetary policy influence inflation, interest rates, and national output.

WHY STUDY FINANCIAL MARKETS?

Financial markets allow funds to move from people with an excess of funds to those with a shortage. In the bond market, firms borrow by issuing securities (claims on the issuer's income or assets) called bonds. Bonds require the issuer to make periodic payments to the purchaser. These payments are known as interest. The interest rate is the cost of borrowing expressed as a percent per year. The interest rate is determined in the bond market. Since different interest rates tend to move together, economists often simply refer to "the" interest rate. In the stock market, firms issue securities called common stock. Stock represents a share of ownership of the company.

WHY STUDY FINANCIAL INSTITUTIONS AND BANKING?

Financial institutions are necessary in order for financial markets to function efficiently. Financial intermediaries borrow from one group and lend to another. Banks are financial intermediaries that accept deposits and make loans. Financial crises are major disruptions in financial markets characterized by sharp declines in asset prices and the failure of many firms. Other related financial institutions are insurance companies, mutual funds, finance companies, and investment banks. Banks are still the largest group of financial intermediaries, but the other financial institutions are growing in importance. A recent financial innovation is the delivery of financial services electronically, which is known as e-finance.

WHY STUDY MONEY AND MONETARY POLICY?

Money, or the money supply, is defined as anything that is generally accepted in payment for goods and services or the repayment of debt. Changes in the money supply have an impact on many economic variables. Money affects the business cycle, the upward and downward movements in aggregate output. Output is usually measured by GDP. Reductions in the growth rate of the money supply have preceded every period of declining output, known as recessions, since the beginning of the 20th century. Not every reduction in the money supply, however, is followed by a recession. The unemployment rate usually rises during recessions. The money supply also has an effect on the price level and the inflation rate. There is a positive relationship between inflation and the growth rate of the money supply. Generally, high growth rates of the money supply are associated with high interest rates on long-term bonds, and low growth rates of the money supply with low long-term bond rates, but this relationship is too complex to address here. Monetary policy is the management of money and interest rates. Monetary policy is conducted by a country's central bank. The U.S. central bank is known as the Federal Reserve System. Fiscal deficits may result in a financial crisis, an increase in the growth rate of the money supply, a higher rate of inflation, and higher interest rates.

WHY STUDY INTERNATIONAL FINANCE?

Financial markets have become increasingly integrated throughout the world. In the foreign exchange market, currencies of one country are exchanged for currencies of another. The price of one country's currency in terms of another's is known as the foreign exchange rate.

HOW WE WILL STUDY MONEY, BANKING, AND FINANCIAL MARKETS

This textbook stresses the economic way of thinking by developing a unifying framework for the study of money, banking, and financial markets. The text emphasizes the following basic concepts:

- A simplified approach to the demand for assets

- The concept of equilibrium

- Basic supply and demand to explain behavior in financial markets

- The search for profits

- An approach to financial structure based on transaction costs and asymmetric information

- Aggregate supply and demand analysis

This text focuses on tools rather than simple facts, so your knowledge will not become obsolete. The analytical framework focuses on changes in one variable at a time, holding all other variables constant.

Helpful Hints

1. Be prepared to rely on the model of supply and demand. This text, along with most economics texts, uses the model of supply and demand where applicable to illuminate the workings of the market. If you have forgotten the basics of supply and demand analysis, it might be to your advantage to improve your understanding of the model by reading the supply and demand chapter in the introduction of any principles of economics text.

2. Throughout the text, when dealing with supply and demand in the financial markets, always identify each side of the market as either the borrow or the lender of the funds. For example, in the bond market, the supplier of the bond is the borrower, and the demander of the bond is the lender. Then, after you have solved the analytical problem at hand, you can ask yourself, does this result make sense in term of the borrowers and lenders?

3. Aggregate income and aggregate output are considered equal because the purchase of final goods and services (output) generates an equivalent value of payments to the factors of production that produced the output (income).

4. The term "business cycle" mistakenly suggests that the movements in output are smooth and predictable. In reality, business cycles are irregular, unpredictable, and of varying duration. For this reason, business cycles are sometimes referred to as "economic fluctuations," which highlights their unpredictable nature.

Terms and Definitions

Choose a definition for each key term.

Key Terms:

_____aggregate output

_____aggregate price level

_____bond

_____budget deficit

_____business cycles

_____Federal Reserve System (the Fed)

_____financial intermediaries

_____financial markets

_____foreign exchange market

_____foreign exchange rate

_____inflation

_____inflation rate

_____interest rate

_____monetary policy

_____money (money supply)

_____security

_____stock

_____unemployment rate

Definitions:

1. the market in which one currency is exchanged for another

2. a debt security that promises to make periodic payments for a specified period of time.

3. the upward and downward movements of aggregate output in the economy

4. a claim on the borrower's future income that is sold by the borrower to the lender

5. the management of the money supply and interest rates

6. institutions that borrow from people who have saved and then lend to others

7. the percentage of the labor force not working

8. the total production of final goods and services in the economy

9. the U.S. central bank responsible for monetary policy

10. an excess of government expenditure over tax revenues

11. the condition of a continuously rising price level

12. a security that is a claim on the earnings and assets of a company

13. the rate of change of the price level

14. markets in which funds are transferred from people who have a surplus of funds to those who have a shortage of funds.

15. the average price of goods and services in an economy

16. anything that is generally accepted in payment for goods and services or in the repayment of debt

17. the cost of borrowing or the price paid for the rental of funds expressed as a percent per year

18. the price of one currency in terms of another

Problems and Short-Answer Questions

PRACTICE PROBLEMS

1. Suppose you are the Chief Financial Officer (CFO) of a large corporation. For each of the following situations, which of the following financial markets would your company use: the bond market, the stock market, or the foreign exchange market? Explain.
    a. Your company has $100 million that it would like to use to construct a factory in Germany.

    _____

    _____

    b. Your company wishes to borrow $100 million to construct a factory in the United States.

    _____

    _____

    c. Your company wishes to raise $100 million to construct a factory by selling additional shares of ownership in the company. That is, your company wishes to take on new partners.

    _____

    _____

2. Suppose that you are the head of the central bank of the United States.
    a. What is the name of the organization that you direct?

    _____

    _____

    b. Suppose the United States is experiencing a high rate of inflation. Is the money supply likely to be growing slowly or quickly? Explain.

    _____

    _____

    c. If you wished to reduce the rate of inflation, what would you do to the growth rate of the money supply? Explain.

    _____

    _____

d. What is the likely effect of your anti-inflationary monetary policy on aggregate output and unemployment? Explain.

_____

_____

_____

SHORT-ANSWER QUESTIONS

1. Suppose that Ford Motor Company imports very little of steel from foreign countries but exports a great number of cars to foreigners. Would Ford prefer that the dollar be strong on the foreign exchange markets (the dollar buys much foreign currency) or weak? Explain.

   _____

   _____

2. Suppose that you are going to travel in Europe for the summer after you graduate from college. Would you prefer that the dollar be strong on the foreign exchange markets or weak? Explain.

   _____

   _____

3. In which of the following markets is the interest rate determined—the bond market, stock market, or the foreign exchange market?

   _____

4. Look at the graph in Chapter 1 of your text that shows the exchange rate of the U.S. dollar over the last 35 years. During which year would you think that exporters would have had the greatest difficulty selling their goods overseas? Why?

   _____

   _____

5. What are financial intermediaries? Why is a bank considered a financial intermediary? Why do you think an insurance company is also considered a financial intermediary?

   _____

   _____

   _____

   _____

6. In addition to commercial banks, what other institutions are considered to be banks?

    _____

    _____

7. Suppose that the economy is in a recession. Just prior to the recession, what likely happened to the growth rate of money? In what direction is aggregate output likely to be moving? Unemployment? Inflation? Long–term bond interest rates?

    _____

    _____

    _____

8. Monetary policy is the management of which two monetary variables? What institution is responsible for monetary policy in the United States?

    _____

    _____

Critical Thinking

You are watching a business news report on television with your roommate. The news reporter states that the Fed is raising interest rates and reducing the growth rate of the money supply in order to reduce the risk of future inflation. Your roommate says, "We need to take a bigger course load next semester and graduate early, because there is always a recession following a reduction in the growth rate of money. If we wait too long, it will be much harder to find a job."

1. Is it true that a recession always follows a reduction in the growth rate of the money supply? Explain.

    _____

    _____

2. If there is a recession, will it be more difficult to find a job when you graduate? Explain.

    _____

    _____

3. If the Fed reduces the growth rate of money, what will likely happen to the inflation rate? Explain.

_____

_____

Self-Test

TRUE/FALSE QUESTIONS

_____1.   The interest rate is determined in the stock market.

_____2.   An increase in the value of the dollar relative to foreign currency (a strong dollar) means that foreign goods have become less expensive to U.S. residents, and U.S. goods have become more expensive to foreigners.

_____3.   Insurance companies are financial intermediaries because they borrow from their depositors and loan those funds to others.

_____4.   A financial intermediary is an institution that borrows from people who have saved and then loans those funds to others.

_____5.   Banks are the largest financial intermediaries in the U.S. economy.

_____6.   Since different interest rates tend to move together, economists often refer to "the" interest rate.

_____7.   An increase in the growth rate of money has preceded every recession in the United States since the beginning of the 20th century.

_____8.   A recession is a sudden expansion in Gross Domestic Product.

_____9.   An increase in the growth rate of the money supply is associated with an increase in the rate of inflation.

_____10. Monetary policy is the management of fiscal deficits and surpluses.

MULTIPLE-CHOICE QUESTIONS

1.   The foreign exchange market is where
   a.   the interest rate is determined.
   b.   the price of one country's currency in terms of another's is determined.
   c.   the inflation rate is determined.
   d.   bonds are sold.

2. Stock prices, as measured by the Dow Jones Industrial Average,
   a. have not unchanged much over time.
   b. have risen smoothly over time.
   c. have been extremely volatile over time.
   d. have declined substantially since they peeked in the mid 1980s.

3. Which of the following is an example of a debt security that promises to make payments periodically for a specified period of time?
   a. bond
   b. stock
   c. financial intermediary
   d. foreign exchange

4. Which of the following is likely to occur if the stock market has been rising quickly?
   a. Consumers are willing to spend more on goods and services.
   b. Firms will increase their investment spending on new equipment.
   c. Firms will sell newly issued stock to raise funds for investment spending.
   d. all of the above

5. If the dollar becomes weaker on the foreign exchange market (the value of the dollar falls relative to the value of foreign currency), which of the following is true?
   a. A trip to Europe is going to be less expensive in terms of dollars.
   b. Ford will export more cars to Mexico.
   c. A BMW automobile produced in Germany will cost less to import into the United States.
   d. U.S. citizens will import more goods and services from abroad.

6. When a firm issues stock, it
   a. has borrowed from the public.
   b. has taken on additional partners that own part of the assets of the firm and share in the firm's earnings.
   c. has purchased foreign currency.
   d. has agreed to make periodic payments for a specific period of time to the owner of the security.

7. Which of the following is an example of financial intermediation?
   a. A saver makes a deposit in a credit union, and the credit union makes a loan to a member for a new car.
   b. IBM issues a bond that is sold to a retired person.
   c. IBM issues common stock that is sold to a college student.
   d. All of the above are examples of financial intermediation.

8. Which of the following are the largest financial intermediaries in the U.S. economy?
   a. insurance companies
   b. finance companies
   c. banks
   d. mutual funds

9. The term "bank" generally includes all of the following institutions except
   a. commercial banks.
   b. credit unions.
   c. savings and loan associations.
   d. finance companies.

10. A decrease in the growth rate of the money supply is most likely to be associated with
    a. a decrease in both aggregate output and the inflation rate.
    b. an increase in both aggregate output and the inflation rate.
    c. a decrease in aggregate output and an increase in the inflation rate.
    d. an increase in aggregate output and a decrease in the inflation rate.

11. If inflation is higher in Canada than in the United States, it is likely that
    a. aggregate output is larger in Canada than in the United States.
    b. the Canadian money supply is growing faster than in the U.S. money supply.
    c. the United States has a larger fiscal deficit.
    d. the United States has higher interest rates.
    e. all of the above are true.

12. Monetary policy is the management of
    a. budget surpluses and deficits.
    b. government spending and taxation.
    c. the money supply and interest rates.
    d. unemployment and aggregate output.

13. Fiscal policy involves decisions about
    a. the money supply and interest rates.
    b. unemployment and inflation.
    c. government spending and taxation.
    d. central banking and the Federal Reserve System.

14. Low growth rates in the money supply are most likely to be associated with
    a. a high rate of inflation and high long-term bond rates.
    b. a high rate of inflation and low long-term bond rates.
    c. a low rate of inflation and high long-term bond rates.
    d. a low rate of inflation and low long-term bond rates.

15. An increase in the growth rate of the money supply is most likely to be followed by
    a. a low point in the business cycle.
    b. a recession.
    c. a reduction in inflation.
    d. an increase in inflation.

Solutions

Terms and Definitions

 8   aggregate output

15   aggregate price level

 2   bond

10   budget deficit

 3   business cycles

 9   Federal Reserve System (the Fed)

 6   financial intermediaries

14   financial markets

 1   foreign exchange market

18   foreign exchange rate

11   inflation

13   inflation rate

17   interest rate

 5   monetary policy

16   money (money supply)

 4   security

12   stock

 7   unemployment rate

Practice Problems

1. a. The foreign exchange market, because that is where dollars can be exchanged for euros.

    b. The bond market, because that is where firms sell debt securities, known as bonds, to borrow large sums of money for capital construction.

    c. The stock market, because that is where firms sell ownership shares of the company, known as common stock.

2. a. Federal Reserve System

    b. Quickly, because the growth rate of the money supply and the rate of inflation have a positive association.

    c. Reduce the growth rate of the money supply, because a lower growth rate of the money supply is associated with a lower inflation rate.

    d. Often, but not always, a reduction in the growth rate of money is leads to a reduction in aggregate output (recession)

and a corresponding increase in the unemployment rate.

Short-Answer Questions

1. Ford would like a weak dollar (the dollar buys less foreign currency or foreign currency buys more dollars). This makes Fords appear cheap to foreigners, and they buy more.

2. You would like a strong dollar (the dollar buys a large amount of foreign currency). This makes your European trip cost less in terms of dollars.

3. The bond market.

4. Around 1985, because the value of the dollar hit its peak. Thus, U.S. goods were very expensive in terms of foreign currencies.

5. Institutions that borrow from one group and lend to another. Banks accept deposits (borrow from depositors) and lend those funds to loan customers. Insurance companies collect premiums (borrow from their insured customers) and lend those funds to loan customers (usually corporations).

6. Savings and loan associations, mutual savings banks, and credit unions.

7. Money growth decreased, output is decreasing, and it is likely that unemployment is rising, inflation is decreasing, and long-term bond rates are falling.

8. Money and interest rates. Federal Reserve System (or simply the Fed).

Critical Thinking

1. No. It is true that all recession since the beginning of the 20th century have been preceded by a reduction in the growth rate of money. However, sometimes a reduction in the growth rate of money is not followed by a recession, making recessions hard to predict.

2. Yes. When output falls, unemployment usually rises, making it more difficult to find a job.

3. Inflation will go down in the future because inflation rates and growth rates of the money supply have a positive association.

True/False Questions

1. F
2. T
3. F
4. T
5. T
6. T
7. F
8. F
9. T
10. F

Multiple-Choice Questions

1. b
2. c
3. a
4. d
5. b
6. b
7. a
8. c
9. d
10. a
11. b
12. c
13. c
14. d
15. d

2 An Overview of the Financial System

Chapter Review

PREVIEW

Financial markets (bond and stock markets) and financial intermediaries (banks, insurance companies, pension funds) move funds from lender-savers to borrower-spenders.

FUNCTION OF FINANCIAL MARKETS

Financial markets channel funds from those who have saved to those who wish to spend more than their income. This movement of funds can be accomplished by direct finance, where borrowers borrow directly from lenders by selling lenders securities. Securities are also known as financial instruments. This movement of funds improves efficiency by channeling funds to those with productive uses for the funds from those with no investment opportunities, producing an efficient allocation of capital (wealth that is used to produce more wealth). It also allows consumers to better time their purchases.

STRUCTURE OF FINANCIAL MARKETS

Financial markets can be categorized as debt and equity markets, primary and secondary markets, exchanges and over-the-counter markets, and money and capital markets. In a debt market, the borrower issues a debt instrument in which the borrower agrees to pay interest and principal payments until maturity. Alternatively, in an equity market, firms issue stock, which are claims to share the net income and assets of the firm. The owner may also receive dividends. Primary markets are where new issues of a security are sold, often to investment banks that underwrite the securities. Secondary markets are where existing issues are resold. Secondary markets can be exchanges, where buyers and sellers meet in a central location, or over-the-counter where dealers at different locations have an inventory of securities. The money market is where short-term securities (maturity of less than one year) are traded. The capital market is where longer-term debt and equity instruments are traded.

FINANCIAL MARKET INSTRUMENTS

The main money market instruments are U.S. Treasury bills, negotiable bank certificates of deposit, commercial paper, repurchase agreements, federal funds, and Eurodollars. U.S. Treasury bills are the most liquid instruments because they are most actively traded and have essentially no default risk. Federal funds are loans from one bank to another, usually overnight. The interest rate in this market, the federal funds rate, is important because it is a measure of the stance of monetary policy. The main capital market instruments are stocks, mortgages, corporate bonds, U.S. government securities, U.S. government agency securities, state and local government bonds (municipal bonds), and consumer and commercial loans. For corporate finance, the value of stocks outstanding exceeds the value of corporate bonds outstanding, but each year the volume of new issues of bonds exceeds the volume of new issues of stock. Interest payments on municipal bonds are exempt from federal income taxation.

INTERNATIONALIZATION OF FINANCIAL MARKETS

Foreign bonds are sold in a foreign country and are denominated in the currency of the country in which the bonds are sold. Eurobonds are bonds denominated in a currency other than the country in which it is sold. Eurodollars are dollar denominated deposits in foreign banks outside the United States or in foreign branches of U.S. banks. Eurodollars are an important source of funds to U.S. banks. Foreign stock markets have also grown in importance.

FUNCTION OF FINANCIAL INTERMEDIARIES: INDIRECT FINANCE

A second route by which funds can move from lenders to borrowers is known as indirect finance because an intermediary is between the lenders and the borrowers. A financial intermediary borrows funds from one group and lends to another in a process known as financial intermediation. Financial intermediaries reduce transactions costs, allow for risk sharing, and solve problems caused by adverse selection and moral hazard.

- Transaction costs associated with borrowing and lending are reduced because banks exploit economies of scale when writing loan contracts. This gain in efficiency allows intermediaries to provide liquidity services to their customers.

- Risk sharing allows intermediaries to sell assets with less risk than the risk of the assets they purchase, which is known as asset transformation. Risk sharing also allows individuals to diversify their assets.

- Financial transactions suffer from asymmetric information because the borrower knows more about the probability of repayment than the lender. Before the transaction, adverse selection may occur because borrowers most unlikely to repay are most eager to borrow. After the transaction, moral hazard may occur if the borrower engages in immoral behavior by using the loan in a way that reduces the probability of repayment. Financial intermediaries screen out bad credit risks to reduce adverse selection, and monitor borrowers to reduce moral hazard.

TYPES OF FINANCIAL INTERMEDIARIES

The primary financial intermediaries are:

- *Depository institutions, or banks:* Commercial banks, savings and loan associations, mutual savings banks, and credit unions.

- *Contractual savings institutions:* Life insurance companies, fire and casualty insurance companies, and pension funds.

- *Investment intermediaries:* Finance companies, mutual funds, money market mutual funds, and investment banks.

REGULATION OF THE FINANCIAL SYSTEM

The government regulates financial markets for two main reasons: to increase the information available to investors and to ensure the soundness of the financial system. To avoid the problems of asymmetric information, the Securities and Exchange Commission (SEC) requires corporations that issue securities to disclose information about their sales, assets, and earnings, and restricts insider trading. To avoid a financial panic that could lead to a collapse of financial intermediaries, the government restricts who can enter into the financial intermediary industry, sets reporting requirements for financial intermediaries, restricts the activities of banks (banks could not be involved in the securities industry – repealed in 1999), and restricts the assets that financial intermediaries can hold (banks can't hold common stock). It also provides deposit insurance. In the past, the government has limited competition by limiting branching (recently repealed) and by setting the maximum interest rates that could be paid on checking and savings deposits, known as Regulation Q (repealed in 1986).

Helpful Hints

1. A financial instrument, such as a corporate bond, is a liability to the firm that issued it and an asset to the person that buys it. Therefore, if the question is asked, "Is a corporate bond an asset or a liability?" the response must be, "to whom?" That is, the same instrument will appear on different sides of the balance sheet for the issuer and the buyer.

2. When a security is traded in a secondary market, the firm receives no funds. Yet the secondary market is important to the firm because it makes their securities more liquid, making the securities more desirable and raising their price. In addition, the secondary market also sets the price of the security that the issuing firm receives in the primary market should the firm issue additional securities.

3. The problems of asymmetric information affect a loan transaction both before and after the loan is made. *Before* the loan is made, adverse selection may occur because risky borrowers have the greatest incentive to borrow. *After* the loan has been made, moral hazard occurs if borrowers use the borrowed money in a riskier fashion that was agreed to in the loan contract. To avoid this problem, banks screen and monitor borrowers.

Terms and Definitions

Choose a definition for each key term.

Key Terms:

_____adverse selection

_____asymmetric information

_____capital market

_____diversification

_____economies of scale

_____equities

_____Eurodollars

_____exchanges

_____federal funds rate

_____financial intermediation

_____investment banks

_____money market

_____moral hazard

_____over-the-counter (OTC) market

_____primary market

_____secondary market

_____transaction costs

_____underwriting

Definitions:

1. a financial market in which only short-term debt instruments are traded

2. a secondary market in which dealers at different locations who have an inventory of securities stand ready to buy and sell securities to anyone who comes to them and is willing to accept their prices

3. the reduction in transaction costs per dollar of transaction as the scale of transactions increases

4. the unequal knowledge that each party to a transaction has about the other party

5. U.S. dollars deposited in foreign banks outside the United States or in foreign branches of U.S. banks

6. guaranteeing prices on securities to corporations and then selling the securities to the public

7. the problem created by asymmetric information before a transaction occurs when the people who are most undesirable from the other party's point of view are the ones who are most likely to want to engage in the financial transaction

8. investing in a portfolio whose returns do not always move together, with the result that overall risk is lower than for individual assets

9. a financial market in which longer-term debt and equity instrument are traded

10. the process of indirect finance whereby financial intermediaries link lender-savers and borrower-spenders

11. the risk that one party to a transaction will engage in behavior that is undesirable from the other party's point of view

12. secondary markets in which buyers and sellers of securities meet in one central location to conduct trades

13. claims to share in the net income and assets of a corporation, such as common stock

14. the time and money spent trying to exchange financial assets, goods, or services

15. a financial market in which new issues of a security are sold to initial buyers

16. firms that assist in the initial sale of securities in the primary market

17. a financial market in which securities that have previously been issued can be resold

18. the interest rate banks charge other banks on overnight loans

Problems and Short-Answer Questions

PRACTICE PROBLEMS

1. For each of the following financial transactions, determine whether the transaction represents a case of *direct finance* or a case of *indirect finance*.

   a. You deposit $10,000 in your savings account at Wells Fargo Bank and Mary Smith borrows $10,000 from Wells Fargo Bank to buy a car.

   _____

   b. You purchase stock in IBM through your Merrill Lynch stockbroker.

   _____

   c. You pay your life insurance premiums and your life insurance company makes a mortgage to a homebuyer.

   _____

   d. You buy shares in a Fidelity mutual fund, and Fidelity buys stock in General Motors.

   _____

   e. You purchase bonds issued by General Electric through your Piper Jaffray broker.

   _____

   f. You borrow $10,000 from your parents to help pay for college tuition.

   _____

   g. You purchase a U.S. government bond on an over-the-counter market.

   _____

   h. You pay $1,000 per month into your pension fund. The pension fund purchases stock in Pearson Addison-Wesley Publishing Company.

   _____

2. For each of the following financial transactions, determine whether the transaction involves debt or equity markets, primary or secondary markets, exchanges or over-the-counter markets, and money or capital markets.

   a. You buy a U.S. Government Treasury Bill that matures in six months from your Morgan Stanley broker.

   _____

   _____

   b. You buy stock in Microsoft from your UBS broker.

   _____

   c. The investment banking division of Edward Jones underwrites Microsoft's new issue of stock.

   _____

   _____

   d. You buy a bond issued by Hewlett Packard that matures in 20 years from your local bond dealer.

   _____

   _____

   e. You buy stock in Ford Motor Company through discount broker Charles Swab.

   _____

3. For each of the following financial intermediaries, identify the primary liabilities (sources of funds) and assets (uses of funds) from the following lists.

   Sources of funds (assets):
   a. commercial paper, stocks, and bonds
   b. employer and employee contributions
   c. premiums from policies
   d. shares
   e. deposits

   Uses of funds (liabilities):
   f. mortgages
   g. corporate bonds and mortgages
   h. stocks, bonds
   i. business and consumer loans, mortgages, U.S. government securities, and municipal bonds
   j. corporate bonds and stocks
   k. consumer loans
   l. consumer and business loans

	Sources	Uses
Commercial banks	_____	_____
Savings and loan associations	_____	_____
Credit unions	_____	_____
Life insurance companies	_____	_____
Pension funds, government retirement funds	_____	_____
Finance companies	_____	_____
Mutual funds	_____	_____

4. The following questions address the soundness of financial intermediaries.
    a. What is a financial panic?

    _____

    _____

    b. What are the six types of regulations the government employs in an attempt to ensure the soundness of our financial intermediaries? Explain.

    _____

    _____

    _____

    _____

    _____

    _____

    c. What regulations have been reduced or repealed. Explain.

    _____

    _____

    _____

    _____

SHORT-ANSWER QUESTIONS

1. Explain the difference between direct and indirect finance.

    _____

    _____

    _____

2. Explain the difference between debt and equity markets, primary and secondary markets, exchanges and over-the-counter markets, and money and capital markets.

    _____

    _____

    _____

    _____

    _____

3. Which money market instrument is considered most liquid? Why? Which capital market instrument has the greatest dollar amount outstanding? On an annual basis, which capital market instrument do firms use most to acquire additional capital funds?

    _____

    _____

4. Other things being the same, which of the following instruments are the least risky to own: short-term bonds, long-term bonds, or equities? Why?

    _____

    _____

    _____

    _____

5. What is the difference between a *foreign bond* and a *Eurobond*? What is the relationship between a Eurobond and European currency known as the euro?

    _____

    _____

    _____

    _____

6. Suppose that after John receives an auto loan from his credit union, he takes the money to a casino and gambles instead of using the money to buy a car. What type of asymmetric information problem have we witnessed: adverse selection or moral hazard? Explain.

_____

_____

_____

7. Name three reasons why a financial intermediary might be able to move funds from lenders to borrowers efficiently?

_____

_____

_____

_____

8. What are the main categories of depository institutions? What is their main source of funds (liabilities)? Which category of depository institution is the largest in terms of assets?

_____

_____

_____

9. What type of investment intermediary sells shares and buys money market instruments? What is the most unusual feature of these funds?

_____

_____

_____

10. Which institutions are subject to Federal Deposit Insurance Corporation (FDIC) regulations, and what is the nature of the regulations?

_____

_____

_____

Critical Thinking

Your grandmother dies and bequeaths to you $10,000. When you receive the check, your best friend accompanies you to the bank in which you plan to deposit the money. Once inside the bank, your friend notices that the rate the bank pays on savings deposits is 3% while the rate the bank charges on auto loans is 9%. Your friend suggests, "Why don't you just stand by the door to the auto loan office and offer the next auto loan customer a loan directly from you? You could charge much more than the 3% you would get on your deposit and cut out the middleman."

1. Explain why it would likely be unprofitable for you to make such a loan?

    _____

    _____

    _____

    _____

    _____

    _____

2. Why is it more likely that the bank is able to make the loan profitably?

    _____

    _____

    _____

    _____

Self-Test

TRUE/FALSE QUESTIONS

_____1. Financial markets improve efficiency by channeling funds to those with productive uses for them from those with no investment opportunities.

_____2. When an individual buys a bond issued by General Motors through a Merrill Lynch bond dealer, we have seen a demonstration of indirect finance.

_____3. Securities are liabilities for the person that buys them, but assets for the individual or company that issues them.

_____4. The primary market is where new issues of securities are sold, and the secondary market is where previously issued securities are resold.

_____5. Bonds are sold in the equity market while stocks are sold in the debt market.

_____6. Stocks are a less risky investment for savers than bonds because stockholders are residual claimants.

_____7. Commercial paper is considered to be the most liquid money market instrument.

_____8. Eurodollars are dollar denominated deposits in foreign banks that are outside the United States or in foreign branches of U.S. banks.

_____9. Individuals may find it efficient to save their funds in a financial intermediary because financial intermediaries have lower transactions costs when making loans due to economies of scale in making loans.

_____10. Moral hazard occurs when risky individuals that are least likely to repay their loans and therefore have the most to gain from getting the loan are the ones that tend to actively seek loans.

_____11. Asymmetric information in financial markets exists because borrowers know more about the true likelihood of the repayment of the loan than do lenders.

_____12. More funds flow to corporations through the corporate bond market than through financial intermediaries.

_____13. Life insurance companies are the largest financial intermediaries in the United States when measured by the size of their assets.

_____14. Mutual funds sell shares and use the funds to buy diversified portfolios of stocks and bonds.

_____15. To increase information available to investors and to insure the soundness of the financial system, the government heavily regulates the financial system.

MULTIPLE-CHOICE QUESTIONS

1. Which of the following would be considered direct finance?
    a. You pay life insurance premiums to Franklin Life and Franklin Life makes a mortgage to a homebuyer.
    b. You buy a bond issued by General Electric through a broker at Smith Barney.
    c. You deposit $100,000 in First National Bank and First National Bank lends $100,000 to Ace Hardware.
    d. None of the above would be considered direct finance.

2. Which of the following statements regarding direct finance is true?
    a. Direct finance occurs when borrowers sell securities directly to lenders.
    b. Direct finance requires the use of financial intermediaries.
    c. In the United States, more funds flow through the direct financial channels than through indirect financial channels.
    d. Securities are assets for the firm that issues them and liabilities for the individual that buys them.

3. Which of the following is true regarding primary and secondary markets?
    a. Primary markets are for stocks while secondary markets are for bonds.
    b. Primary markets are for long-term securities while secondary markets are for short-term securities.
    c. Primary markets are where new issues of securities are sold while secondary markets are where previously issued securities are resold.
    d. Primary markets are exchanges while secondary markets are over-the-counter.

4. Investment banks facilitate the sale of securities in the
    a. over-the-counter market.
    b. stock exchange.
    c. secondary market.
    d. primary market.

5. Which of the following is an example of a money market instrument?
    a. a mortgage
    b. a share of stock in IBM
    c. a John Deere bond with 20 years to maturity
    d. U.S. government treasury bill with 6 months to maturity

6. Which of the following is likely to generate the least risk to the purchaser?
    a. a 30-year mortgage
    b. a share of stock in IBM
    c. a short-term bond
    d. a long-term bond

7. Which of the following is true regarding the characteristics of debt and equity?
    a. Equity holders are residual claimants.
    b. Bond holders receive dividends.
    c. Equity securities are considered short term.
    d. A bond is an asset to the firm that issues it.

8. When a bond denominated in dollars is sold in Great Britain, it is known as
    a. a foreign bond.
    b. a Eurobond.
    c. Eurodollars.
    d. foreign exchange.

9. Financial intermediaries
    a. reduce transactions costs for lender-savers and borrower-spenders.
    b. allow for risk sharing for the lender-savers.
    c. solve some of the problems caused by asymmetric information.
    d. achieve all of the above.

10. Which of the following is an example of indirect finance?
    a. You pay life insurance premiums to Franklin Life, and Franklin Life makes a mortgage to a homebuyer.
    b. You buy a bond issued by General Electric through a broker at Smith Barney.
    c. You buy stock in Microsoft through a local OTC dealer.
    d. None of the above would be considered indirect finance.

11. In a given year, corporations raise the greatest amount of funds through which of the following instruments?
    a. corporate stocks
    b. commercial paper
    c. corporate bonds
    d. repurchase agreements

12. Before a loan is made, banks screen their prospective loan customers to avoid the problem of
    a. risk sharing.
    b. adverse selection.
    c. moral hazard.
    d. asset transformation.

13. Rick Smith just received an auto loan for $5,000. After he received the loan, he decided to gamble with the money at a nearby casino instead of buying a car. This is an example of
    a. diversification.
    b. asset transformation.
    c. adverse selection.
    d. moral hazard.

14. When a financial intermediary such as a bank borrows from one person and lends to another, we have observed a demonstration of
    a. indirect finance.
    b. direct finance.
    c. foreign finance.
    d. investment banking.

15. When lenders have inferior knowledge relative to borrowers about the potential returns and risks associated with an investment project, it gives rise to the problem known as
    a. financial intermediation.
    b. transaction costs.
    c. asset transformation.
    d. asymmetric information.

16. Which of the following is a depository institution?
    a. pension fund
    b. life insurance company
    c. credit union
    d. finance company

17. Which of the following institutions holds mortgages as their primary asset?
    a. banks
    b. savings and loan associations
    c. money market mutual funds
    d. credit unions

18. Mutual funds
    a. collect deposits and lend for mortgages.
    b. are organized around some common bond, usually employment.
    c. sell shares and use the proceeds to buy diversified portfolios of stocks and bonds.
    d. receive premiums from policies and purchase corporate bonds and stock.

19. Which of the following regulatory agencies protects depositors from bank failures by guaranteeing repayment of deposits up to $100,000 per depositor at a bank?
    a. Securities and Exchange Commission (SEC)
    b. Federal Reserve System
    c. Office of Thrift Supervision
    d. Federal Deposit Insurance Corporation (FDIC)

20. Prior to 1986, Regulation Q gave the Federal Reserve the power to
    a. limit competition between banks by placing a ceiling on the interest rates banks could pay on savings deposits.
    b. limit competition between banks by restricting interstate branching.
    c. increase competition among banks by expanding entry into the banking industry.
    d. increase competition among banks by imposing stringent reporting requirement for disclosure of information to the public.

Solutions

Terms and Definitions

<u>7</u>   adverse selection
<u>4</u>   asymmetric information
<u>9</u>   capital market
<u>8</u>   diversification
<u>3</u>   economies of scale
<u>13</u> equities
<u>5</u>   Eurodollars
<u>12</u> exchanges
<u>18</u> federal funds rate
<u>10</u> financial intermediation
<u>16</u> investment banks
<u>1</u>   money market
<u>11</u> moral hazard
<u>2</u>   over-the-counter (OTC) market
<u>15</u> primary market
<u>17</u> secondary market
<u>14</u> transaction costs
<u>6</u>   underwriting

Practice Problems

1. a. Indirect finance
    b. Direct finance
    c. Indirect finance
    d. Indirect finance
    e. Direct finance
    f. Direct finance
    g. Direct finance
    h. Indirect finance

2. a. debt, secondary, over-the-counter (all bonds are sold OTC), money
    b. equity, secondary, over-the-counter (Microsoft is traded on NASDAQ, an OTC market), capital
    c. equity, primary, no exchange or OTC market is involved yet, capital
    d. debt, secondary, over-the-counter, capital
    e. equity, secondary, exchange (Ford is traded on the NYSE), capital

3.

	Sources	Uses
Commercial banks	e	i
Savings and loan associations	e	f
Credit unions	e	k
Life insurance companies	c	g
Pension funds, government retirement funds	b	j
Finance companies	a	l
Mutual funds	d	h

4. a. A collapse of financial intermediaries because the providers of funds doubt the health of the intermediaries and pull their funds out of both sound and unsound institutions.
    b. *Restrictions on entry*: the government provides a charter only to upstanding, well capitalized individuals.
        Disclosure: intermediaries are subject to stringent reporting requirements.
        Restrictions on assets and activities: there are limits on the riskiness of the assets held by intermediaries.
        Deposit insurance: People suffer less of a financial loss when a depository institution fails.
        Limits on Competition: branching restrictions limit competition which was believed to cause failures.
        Restrictions on interest rates: Regulation Q set the ceiling on interest rates that banks could pay, limiting their ability to compete.
    c. Banks can again be involved in the securities industry (investment banking activities). Branching restrictions have been reduced or eliminated. Regulation Q was abolished and banks can now pay the interest rate they choose.

Short-Answer Questions

1. With direct finance, borrowers acquire funds directly from lenders by selling them securities. With indirect finance, a financial intermediary stands between the lender and borrower and helps transfer the funds from one to the other.

2. A debt security is for borrowing while an equity security is for ownership. The primary market is where new issues are sold, and the secondary market is where existing issues are resold. An exchange is centralized while an OTC market is decentralized and linked by computers. The money market is for short-term debt, and the capital market is for long-term funds.

3. U.S. Treasury bills, because they are the most actively traded security and have no default risk. Corporate stocks. Corporate bonds.

4. Equity holders are residual claimants, so in the event of a bankruptcy, they receive funds only after all of the debt holders have been paid. Short-term debt securities have smaller fluctuations in prices than long-term securities do. Therefore, short-term bonds have the least risk.

5. Foreign bonds are sold in a foreign country and denominated in that country's currency. Eurobonds are denominated in a currency other than the currency of the country in which it is sold. There is no relationship between a Eurobond and the euro. That is, Eurobonds are not denominated in euros.

6. Moral hazard. Moral hazard is the risk that the borrower will engage in activities that are immoral from the lender's point of view. In this case, the borrower is using the money in a riskier manner than was agreed to in the loan contract.

7. They have lower transactions costs due to economies of scale. They provide risk sharing. They reduce the problems associated with asymmetric information by screening and monitoring borrowers.

8. Commercial banks, savings and loan associations and mutual savings banks, and credit unions. Deposits are the main liability. Commercial banks are the largest.

9. Money market mutual funds. Since they buy such safe and liquid instruments with the funds they have acquired, they are able to allow shareholders to write checks against the value of their share holdings.

10. Commercial bank, mutual savings banks, and savings and loan associations. The FDIC provides insurance of up to $100,000 for each depositor at a bank, examines the books of insured banks, and imposes restrictions on assets that banks can hold.

Critical Thinking

1. The transaction costs would be prohibitive because it would be expensive to pay a lawyer to write a loan contract that would be used only once. It would be risky because you would be putting all of your eggs in one basket by lending all of your money to one person. Finally, you are unlikely to know how to avoid the problems of asymmetric information. There could be adverse selection in that risky borrowers desire to borrow. There could be moral hazard in that the borrow may take the loan money and use it to gamble instead of buying a car.

2. Banks make many similar loans, so they pay the lawyer only once for a contract that can be used many times. Banks make a variety of different loans whose returns do not always move together, which reduces their risk on the group of loans. Banks know how to screen and monitor loan customers to reduce adverse selection and moral hazard.

True/False Questions

1. T
2. F
3. F
4. T
5. F
6. F
7. F
8. T
9. T
10. F
11. T
12. F
13. F
14. T
15. T

Multiple-Choice Questions

1. b
2. a
3. c
4. d
5. d
6. c
7. a
8. b
9. d
10. a
11. c
12. b
13. d
14. a
15. d
16. c
17. b
18. c
19. d
20. a

3   What Is Money?

Chapter Review

PREVIEW

Money has always been important to the economy because it promotes economic efficiency. Here we develop a current definition of money by addressing the functions of money, and learning about the different forms of money through history.

MEANING OF MONEY

Money is anything that is generally accepted in payment for goods or services or in the repayment of debts. The definition of money includes currency (notes and coins) and checking account deposits. Money is not the same as wealth or income. A person's wealth includes the person's money, but it also includes other assets such as bonds, stock, art, land, and houses. Income is a flow of earnings per unit of time while money is a stock, which is measured at a given point in time.

FUNCTIONS OF MONEY

Money has three primary functions. Money serves as a

- *medium of exchange*. Money is used to pay for goods and services. The use of a medium of exchange is efficient for two reasons: It reduces transactions costs (the time spent exchanging goods or services), and it allows for specialization and the division of labor. In a barter economy -- an economy without money -- goods and services are exchanged directly for other goods and services. Transaction costs are high because an exchange requires a "double coincidence of wants."

- *unit of account*. Money is used to measure value in the economy. As a result, all prices are in terms of money. The use of money as a unit of account is efficient because it reduces transactions costs. In a barter economy, where all goods must be valued in terms of all other goods, the exchange of just a small number of goods requires an enormous number of prices. When money is a unit of account, there is only one price per good and transaction costs are small.

- *store of value*. Money is used as a repository of purchasing power. This allows people to earn money today, and spend it at a later date. Other assets are a store of value, and they may provide a greater rate of return, but people still hold money because of its liquidity. During inflation, when prices are rising rapidly, people are reluctant to hold money because its value is falling.

EVOLUTION OF THE PAYMENTS SYSTEM

The payments system has evolved. Most economic systems first employed *commodity money*, usually a valuable commodity or precious metal such as gold or silver. Because metals are difficult to transport, societies developed paper currency that was fully convertible into precious metals. More recently, paper currency has evolved into *fiat money*, money decreed by governments as legal tender but not convertible into the precious metal. Since coins and paper currency are easily stolen and hard to transport, modern banking has invented *checks*. Checks instruct your bank to transfer money from your bank account to another person's account. Checks are efficient because some payments cancel each other out so no currency need be physically moved; checks can be easily written for large amounts; checks reduce loss from theft; and checks provide receipts for purchases. But checks take time to move from place to place, so the money is not available immediately when deposited, and checks are expensive to process. Computers now allow for *electronic payment* of bills over the Internet. *E-money* is money that exists only in electronic form, in the form of debit cards, stored-value cards, and e-cash. Each type of money is more efficient than its predecessor because it lowers transactions costs.

MEASURING MONEY

Since there is no single measure of money that is accurate for all times and for all purposes, the Federal Reserve defines two measures of the money supply, known as monetary aggregates.

- M1 = currency + traveler's checks + demand deposits + other checkable deposits
- M2 = M1 + small-denomination time deposits + savings deposits and money market deposit accounts + money market mutual fund shares (retail)

All of the assets in M1 are perfectly liquid. M2 includes some assets that are not quite as liquid as those in M1. These two measures of the money supply do not always move together, so the proper choice of a measure of money by policymakers does matter for the conduct of monetary policy.

HOW RELIABLE ARE THE MONEY DATA?

It is difficult to measure money for two reasons: It is hard to decide which monetary aggregate is best, and the Fed substantially revises earlier estimates of the monetary aggregates. The Fed revises earlier estimates because small depository institutions only report their deposits infrequently, and seasonal variation is revised as new data comes in. Revisions in the growth rates of the monetary aggregates are great enough that we should not be too concerned with short-run movements in the money supply and should only be concerned with longer-run movements.

Helpful Hints

1. One of the functions of money is to serve as a unit of account. When serving in this capacity, money expresses the relative value between all goods. That is, when all prices are established in terms of money, money is the common denominator across all goods. If an apple costs 25 cents, while an orange costs 50 cents, we know that it takes two apples to get an orange. The relative value between the goods has been established.

2. The M1 monetary aggregate includes demand deposits and other checkable deposits. Note that it is not the check that is part of the money supply. It is the balance in the account that is money. A fresh checkbook with 25 checks is of no value unless there is a positive balance in the account.

3. As we move from M1 to M2, we include slightly less liquid assets. M1 only includes perfectly liquid assets in that the items in M1 don't need to be converted into anything else in order to be exchanged for goods and services. The additional assets in M2 are highly liquid, but they require some small expense or effort to convert them into cash.

Terms and Definitions

Choose a definition for each key term.

Key Terms:

_____commodity money

_____currency

_____fiat money

_____liquidity

_____medium of exchange

_____monetary aggregates

_____payments system

_____store of value

_____unit of account

_____wealth

Definitions:

1. the method of conducting transactions in the economy

2. anything used to measure value in an economy

3. money made of precious metals or another valuable commodity

4. paper currency decreed by a government as legal tender but not convertible into coins or precious metal

5. all resources owned by an individual, including all assets

6. paper money and coins

7. the relative ease and speed with which an asset can be converted into cash

8. the two measures of the money supply used by the Federal Reserve System (M1 and M2)

9. a repository of purchasing power over time

10. anything that is used to pay for goods and services

Problems and Short-Answer Questions

PRACTICE PROBLEMS

1. Which of the three functions of money (medium of exchange, unit of account, store of value) is illustrated by each of the following situations?
   a. Susan purchases a case of soda at the grocery store with a check.

   _____

   b. Bryce puts $3,000 in his checking account and plans to spend it next month when he pays his college tuition.

   _____

   c. To avoid confusion, prisoners in a POW camp value all of their tradable items in terms of cigarettes.

   _____

d. Joe goes shopping for meat. At the meat counter, he notices that fresh fish is priced at $10 per pound while frozen fish is priced at $5 per pound. He immediately recognizes that he could get twice as much frozen fish as fresh fish for the same expenditure.

_____

e. Lisa is willing to specialize as an economics professor and receive payment in dollars because she is confident that she can go to the market and spend those dollars for food, clothing, and shelter.

_____

f. A prisoner in a POW camp keeps 100 cigarettes in his locker even though he does not smoke, because he believes that he will be able to buy chocolates with them next week when packages from home arrive.

_____

g. For tax purposes Jennifer's Flower Shop values the store's inventory, which includes a variety of different types of flowers, at $40,000.

_____

h. Joe buys ten gallons of gasoline with a $20 bill.

_____

2. Suppose there are four goods produced in an economy—apples, oranges, pears, and bananas.
   a. If this is a barter economy, list the prices needed in order to exchange any good for any other good. How many are there?

   _____

   _____

   b. Suppose dollars are introduced into the economy and universally circulate as money. What are the prices needed in order to exchange any good for any other good? How many are there?

   _____

   _____

    c.   Which system has lower transactions costs, the barter system or the one with money? Does the difference in transactions costs increase or decrease as the economy expands? Explain.

_____

_____

_____

3. What type of payment (commodity money, fiat money, checks, electronic payment, e-money) is employed in each of the following situations?

    a.   While in France, you use a 100 euro note to purchase a bottle of wine.

_____

    b.   On the island of Yap, stone wheels are used to purchase all goods and services.

_____

    c.   You have your mortgage and life insurance premiums automatically paid each month by your bank directly out of your checking account.

_____

    d.   One hundred fifty years ago, your great great grandfather purchased a new suit with a $20 gold piece.

_____

    e.   You write a check each month on your NOW account at your savings and loan and mail it your auto insurance company to pay your premium.

_____

    f.   You buy a new lawnmower at Sears and pay directly out of your checking account with your debit card.

_____

    g.   You buy a soda at a Quick Shop with a ten dollar bill.

_____

    h.   You purchase $20 worth of subway rides in Washington, D.C. Instead of tickets, you receive a disposable paper card with a magnetic strip on the back (similar to the back of a credit card). You feed it into the turnstile each time you ride the train, and you continue to use it until the $20 has been used up.

_____

4. List the monetary aggregates (M1 and/or M2) in which each of the following assets belongs. If the asset does not belong in either of the monetary aggregates, write "none."

    a.   currency _____

    b.   Eurodollars_____

    c.   government bonds_____

    d.   demand deposits _____

    e.   savings deposits _____

    f.   large denomination time deposits_____

    g.   checkable deposits_____

    h.   stocks _____

    i.   money market deposit accounts (retail _____

    j.   small denomination time deposits _____

SHORT-ANSWER QUESTIONS

1. What is income? What is wealth? Does someone who has a high income or is wealthy necessarily have a lot of money? Explain.

    _____

    _____

    _____

    _____

2. What is a barter economy? What are transactions costs? What are two reasons why transactions costs are high in a barter system?

    _____

    _____

    _____

    _____

3. What are the necessary characteristics of a commodity if it is to function effectively as money?

   _____

   _____

4. Why do people hold money as a store of value when there are many other assets, such as houses and bonds, that earn a greater rate of return and are also a store of value?

   _____

   _____

5. What are some advantages of using checks as a means of payment? What are some shortcomings?

   _____

   _____

   _____

   _____

6. What are the assets included in M1? What separates them from the assets in M2?

   _____

   _____

   _____

7. Which is the larger monetary aggregate, M1 or M2? Why?

   _____

   _____

8. Does it matter what definition of money policy makers use as the true measure of money when making monetary policy decisions? Why?

   _____

   _____

9. Why does the Fed revise its earlier estimates of the monetary aggregate?

   _____

   _____

   _____

10. Are short-run movements in the money supply important? Explain.

_____

_____

Critical Thinking

You are with your best friend at the bank when she cashes her paycheck for cash. She takes the $500 of currency and, with a frown on her face, she says, "Money is just becoming paper these days. I should go the United States Treasury and demand that they give me gold in exchange for this paper. Then I'd have some real money."

1. Explain to your friend what type of money she received.

_____

_____

2. What are some of the advantages and disadvantages of this type of money?

_____

_____

_____

3. What type of money does your friend think she wants? Explain. Would the U.S. Treasury redeem her currency in gold? Why or why not?

_____

_____

_____

4. In the modern high-technology world, has money moved beyond paper? Explain.

_____

_____

_____

Self-Test

TRUE/FALSE QUESTIONS

_____1. Money is anything that is generally accepted in payment for goods and services or in the repayment of debt.

_____2. Income is the same thing as money, because if someone has a high income, that person earns a lot of money.

_____3. Of the three functions of money, the function that separates money from all other assets is that money serves as a medium of exchange.

_____4. Barter is inefficient because it requires that there be a "double coincidence of wants" in order for an exchange to take place.

_____5. Barter is inefficient because barter requires an enormous number of prices for each good to be valued in terms of all other goods.

_____6. Money is the most liquid store of value in the economy.

_____7. Money is an excellent store of value during inflationary times.

_____8. Fiat money evolved into commodity money because commodity money is less likely to be stolen and is easier to transport.

_____9. Fiat money is paper money that the government has guaranteed to redeem in terms of a particular precious metal.

_____10. The driving force behind the movement from checks toward electronic payment is the time and high cost of transporting and processing checks.

_____11. Savings deposits are included in the monetary aggregate known as M1.

_____12. M1 contains only perfectly liquid financial assets.

_____13. Policy makers can use either M1 or M2 as a guide for monetary policy and get the same results because the movements of these monetary aggregates always closely track each other.

_____14. The Fed rarely revises its first estimates of the monetary aggregates because its first estimates usually turn out to be very accurate.

_____15. The Fed should not concern itself too much with short-run movements in the money supply because there are significant revisions in the monetary aggregates due to small depository institutions reporting their deposits infrequently and revisions in seasonal variation as new data comes in.

MULTIPLE-CHOICE QUESTIONS

1. Which of the following is measured as a flow per unit of time?
    a. money
    b. wealth
    c. income
    d. all of the above

2. Which of the following economies has the least efficient payments system?
    a. an economy using gold as a commodity money
    b. a barter economy
    c. an economy using fiat money
    d. an economy using currency and deposit money

3. In which of the following economies are goods and services traded directly for other goods and services?
    a. an economy using gold as a commodity money
    b. a barter economy
    c. an economy using fiat money
    d. an economy using currency and deposit money

4. Which of the following is not a purpose or function of money?
    a. store of value
    b. medium of exchange
    c. protection against inflation
    d. unit of account

5. A payments system based on money is
    a. more efficient than a barter economy because transactions costs are lower.
    b. more efficient than a barter economy because fewer prices are needed to establish relative values between all commodities.
    c. less efficient than a barter economy because a money economy requires that there be a double coincidence of wants in order for there to be an exchange.
    d. less efficient than a barter economy because money is costly to transport.
    e. Both (a) and (b) are correct.

6. With a payments system based on money, John can specialize as a medical doctor and use the money earned from his efforts to buy all of the things he needs. Which of the functions of money has been most clearly demonstrated by the scenario above?
    a. store of value
    b. medium of exchange
    c. protection against inflation
    d. unit of account

7. Which of the following is not a characteristic of an effective commodity money?
    a. It must be widely accepted.
    b. It must be standardized.
    c. It must be divisible.
    d. It should be able to be easily reproduced by everyone in the economy.
    e. All of the above are characteristics of an effective commodity money.

8. An asset with great liquidity is one that
    a. can be converted into a medium of exchange with relative ease and speed.
    b. generates high transactions costs when liquidating.
    c. is an excellent store of value.
    d. acts as a unit of account.
    e. all of the above

9. Which of the following is an example of a commodity money?
    a. a five dollar bill
    b. a check drawn on a bank account in the United States
    c. a credit card
    d. cigarettes in a POW camp
    e. all of the above

10. Which of the following is an example of fiat money?
    a. a five dollar bill
    b. a twenty dollar gold piece
    c. sea shells used as money in a primitive society
    d. cigarettes in a POW camp
    e. all of the above

11. Which of the following forms of payment is least efficient because it generates the highest transactions costs?
    a. checks
    b. commodity money
    c. fiat money
    d. electronic payment

12. Which of the following is <u>not</u> an example of electronic money?
    a. debit card
    b. stored-value card
    c. smart card
    d. credit card

13. Which of the following statements about fiat money is false?
    a. Fiat money is paper currency decreed by government as legal tender.
    b. Fiat money is easier to transport than commodity money.
    c. Fiat money is redeemable into a particular precious metal such as gold.
    d. Fiat money should be made difficult to counterfeit.

14. When prices are rising rapidly, money does not act as a good
    a. unit of account.
    b. medium of exchange.
    c. liquid asset.
    d. store of value.

15. Which of the following is not included in the M1 monetary aggregate?
    a. money market deposit accounts
    b. currency
    c. demand deposits
    d. NOW accounts
    e. traveler's checks

16. Checkable deposits are included in which of the following monetary aggregates?
    a. M1 only.
    b. M2 only.
    c. M1 and M2.
    d. Checkable deposits are not included in either of the monetary aggregates.

17. Which of the following is not included in M2?
    a. currency
    b. large-denomination time deposits
    c. small-denomination time deposits
    d. savings deposits

18. Which of the following statements about the monetary aggregates is true?
    a. M1 is greater than M2.
    b. The growth rates of M1 and M2 always track each other very closely.
    c. The Fed is more concerned with long-run movements in the monetary aggregates rather than short-run movements.
    d. The Fed rarely revises its estimates of the monetary aggregates.

19. Which of the following statements about the liquidity of the assets in the monetary aggregates is true?
    a. The assets in M1 are more liquid than the assets in M2.
    b. The assets in M2 are more liquid than the assets in M1.
    c. All of the assets in the monetary aggregates have equal liquidity because they are all considered money.
    d. The only liquid asset in the monetary aggregates is currency.

20. Which of the following is not a characteristic of barter economies?
    a. Barter requires that there be a double coincidence of wants in order for there to be an exchange.
    b. Barter requires an enormous number of prices in order for every good to be valued in terms of every other good.
    c. In a barter economy, it is difficult for people to specialize in the production of just one item.
    d. Barter generates very low transactions costs.
    e. In a barter economy, goods are exchanged directly for other goods.

Solutions

Terms and Definitions

 3 commodity money
 6 currency
 4 fiat money
 7 liquidity
10 medium of exchange
 8 monetary aggregates
 1 payments system
 9 store of value
 2 unit of account
 5 wealth

Practice Problems

1. a. medium of exchange
   b. store of value
   c. unit of account
   d. unit of account
   e. medium of exchange
   f. store of value
   g. unit of account
   h. medium of exchange

2. a. apples/orange, apples/pear, apples/banana, orange/pear, orange/banana, pears/banana. $[n(n-1)]/2 = (4 \times 3)/2 = 12/2 = 6$.
   b. dollars/apple, dollars/orange, dollars/pear, dollars/banana. Four.
   c. The system with money needs fewer prices so transactions costs are lower. The difference in transactions costs increases as the economy expands because the number of prices needed in a barter economy explodes as the number of goods increases.

3. a. fiat money
   b. commodity money
   c. electronic payment
   d. commodity money
   e. checks
   f. e-money
   g. fiat money
   h. e-money (stored-value card)

4. a. M1, M2
   b. None
   c. None
   d. M1, M2
   e. M2
   f. None
   g. M1, M2
   h. None
   i. M2
   j. M2

Short-Answer Questions

1. Income is a flow of earnings per unit of time. Wealth is a total collection of property that serves to store value. Money is the asset that is generally accepted in payment for goods or services. It is not necessary that high income or wealthy people have a great deal of money. High income may spend it all, and wealthy people may hold their wealth in forms other than money.

2. System without money where goods and services are exchanged directly for other goods and services. Transaction cost is the time spent trying to exchange goods and services. Barter requires a "double coincidence of wants," and an enormous number of prices to establish relative values.

3. It must be easily standardized, widely accepted, easily divisible, easy to carry, and it must not deteriorate quickly.

4. Money is perfectly liquid because it is a medium of exchange. Other assets involve transaction costs when converting them into a medium of exchange.

5. Advantages are that checks increase efficiency since some payments cancel each other out. Checks can be written for large amounts, there is little loss from theft, and checks provide a receipt. Some problems are that it takes time to get checks from one place to another so you do not have access to your money immediately when you deposit a check, and checks are expensive to process.

6. Currency, traveler's checks, demand deposits, and other checkable deposits. All of the assets

in M1 are a medium of exchange (perfectly liquid).

7. M2, because M2 includes all of M1 plus additional slightly less liquid assets.

8. Yes, because while the monetary aggregates tend to often move together, sometimes their growth rates diverge greatly.

9. Because the Fed must estimate deposits in small depository institutions because they report data infrequently, and because the adjustment of the data for seasonal variation is revised as more data become available.

10. Probably not. Since the monetary aggregates are substantially revised over time, the initially released data are not reliable.

Critical Thinking

1. Fiat money. It is money that is decreed by government as legal tender but it is not convertible into a particular precious metal.

2. It is lighter and, therefore, easier to transport. However, it will only be accepted if people trust that the authorities will not print too much of it, and that the paper money is difficult to counterfeit.

3. Commodity money, which is a precious metal or another valuable commodity. No. Modern money is fiat money and it is not redeemable in any particular precious metal.

4. Yes. People can electronically transfer their account balances to pay their bills. Recurring bills can be paid automatically. E-money exists in the form of debit cards, stored-value cards and smart cards, and e-cash.

True/False Questions

1. T
2. F
3. T
4. T
5. T
6. T
7. F
8. F
9. F
10. T
11. F
12. T
13. F
14. F
15. T

Multiple-Choice Questions

1. c
2. b
3. b
4. c
5. e
6. b
7. d
8. a
9. d
10. a
11. b
12. d
13. c
14. d
15. a
16. c
17. b
18. c
19. a
20. d

Understanding Interest Rates

Chapter Review

PREVIEW

This chapter establishes what interest rates are and addresses the ways in which they are measured. The most accurate measure of *interest rates* is *yield to maturity*. The concept of yield to maturity reveals that bond prices and interest rates are negatively related, and the longer the maturity of the bond, the greater the change in the price of the bond from a given change in the interest rate. Interest rates are important because they affect how much people and firms wish to save or borrow. The terms defined in this chapter will be employed throughout the book.

MEASURING INTEREST RATES

Present value (or present discounted value) is today's value of a future cash payment given an interest rate of i. The basic present value formula is:

$$PV(1+i)^n = CF \text{ or } PV = CF/(1+i)^n$$

where PV = present value, CF = future cash flow, and n = number of years to maturity.

For example, a simple loan of $100 (the present value) at 6% for one year (n = 1) generates a future cash flow payment of $100(1.06) = $106 one year from today. Alternatively, the present value of a future cash payment of $106 to be received one year from today is $106/1.06 = $100 today.

There are four basic types of credit market instruments: a simple loan, a fixed-payment loan (also known as a fully amortized loan), a coupon bond, and a discount bond (also known as a zero-coupon bond). A simple loan and a discount bond require the borrower to make one payment at the end of the loan, which includes both the principle and interest. Fixed-payment loans (installment loans such as auto loans and mortgages) and coupon bonds require the borrower to make periodic payments to the lender until a maturity date. The payments on a fixed-payment loan are all the same size and each payment includes a combination of interest and principle. The periodic payments on a coupon bond are interest payments alone, and the final payment at maturity includes the face-value or principle of the bond.

The most important and accurate way to calculate the interest rate is *yield to maturity*, which is the interest rate that equates the present value of cash flow payments received from a debt instrument with its price or value today. The price or value today of any instrument is equal to the sum of the present value of all of its future cash flow payments. Since a simple loan and a discount bond generate only one future cash flow payment, yield to maturity on each of those instruments can be calculated with the present value formula provided above. If the value today and the future cash flow values are known, one can use the formula above to solve for i, which is the yield to maturity. For the simple one year case, $i = (CF - PV)/PV$, which is also our formula for simple interest.

We follow the same general process for finding the yield to maturity for fixed-payment loans and coupon bonds, but since they generate periodic future cash flow payments, we must sum the present value of each future cash flow payment and equate it to the value or price of the instrument today. The general formula for an instrument generating annual payments until some future maturity date is:

$$\text{Value today (price)} = CF/(1 + i) + CF/(1 + i)^2 + CF/(1 + i)^3 + \ldots + CF/(1 + i)^n$$

If the price of the instrument and the future cash flow payments are known, we can solve for i and get the yield to maturity. Because this calculation is not easy, many pocket calculators have been programmed to solve this problem.

When the formula above is applied to a coupon bond the following facts emerge:

- If the yield to maturity equals the coupon rate (coupon/face value), the price of the bond equals its face value.

- If the yield to maturity is above the coupon rate, the price of the bond is below its face value, and vice versa.

- The price of the bond and its yield to maturity are negatively related. This is also true for a discount bond.

A consol or perpetuity is a coupon bond with no maturity. For a perpetuity, $P = C/i$, or $i = C/P$, where P is the price of the perpetuity, C = annual coupon, and i = yield to maturity. This formula is also an approximation of yield to maturity for any long-term coupon bond, and it is know as *current yield* when used in this manner. The greater the maturity of the bond, the better current yield approximates yield to maturity.

THE DISTINCTION BETWEEN INTEREST RATES AND RETURNS

The actual *rate of return* earned by the holder of a coupon bond includes the capital gains or losses on the bond from fluctuations in the price of the bond. The formula for the *return* on a bond held from time t to $t + 1$ is:

$$\text{Return} = (C + P_{t+1} - P_t)/P_t$$

where C = coupon payment, P_t = price of the bond at t, and P_{t+1} = price of the bond at $t + 1$. General findings from this concept include:

- The return on a bond equals the yield to maturity if the holding period is equal to maturity (the bond is held to maturity).

- An increase in interest rates causes the price of a bond to fall, resulting in a capital loss on bonds with maturity greater than the holding period.

- The longer to maturity, the greater is the change in price (and capital gain or loss) from a change in interest rates, and the greater is the impact on the return on the bond.

- Thus, a bond with a high yield to maturity can have negative returns if interest rates rise and the bond is sold before maturity (has a short holding period).

Prices (and therefore returns) are more volatile on long-term bonds than short-term bonds. This volatility in returns that results from changes in the interest rate is known as *interest rate risk*.

THE DISTINCTION BETWEEN REAL AND NOMINAL INTEREST RATES

The *nominal interest rate* has not been corrected for the effects of inflation. The *real interest rate* has been adjusted for inflation so that it more accurately reflects the true cost to borrowers and true return to lenders. The Fisher equation shows the necessary adjustment,

$$i_r = i - \pi^e$$

where i = nominal interest rate, i_r = real interest rate, and π^e = expected inflation. Borrowers and lenders respond to real interest rates. When real rates are low, there are greater incentives to borrow and fewer incentives to lend.

Helpful Hints

1. We can use the present value formulas in this chapter to solve for the yield to maturity (interest rate) on an instrument if we know the price (value today) of the instrument and its future cash flow payments. Alternatively, and equally important, we can use the present value formulas in this chapter to solve for the price of an instrument given the interest rate and its future cash flow payments. Using the formulas in this alternative way, one can clearly see the main points developed in this chapter. When interest rates rise, the present value of future cash flows decrease and the price of existing instruments fall. Longer-term instruments have more terms to be discounted at higher powers, so the longer to maturity, the greater is the change in the price of an instrument from the same size change in the interest rate. Thus, long-term bonds can generate greater capital gains and losses when held for short holding periods, demonstrating that long-term bonds are not considered to generate a sure return when held for short periods.

2. *Yield to maturity* is the return the owner of an instrument would realize if the owner held the instrument to maturity. If the holding period is less than

maturity, the return to the holder may differ from the yield to maturity. If the yield to maturity on comparable instruments rises (the interest rate rises), then the price of the bond will fall and the returns to the holder of the bond will fall below the bond's original yield to maturity if the holder of the bond sells it before maturity.

Terms and Definitions

Choose a definition for each key term.

Key Terms:

_____coupon bond

_____coupon rate

_____current yield

_____discount bond (zero-coupon bond)

_____face value (par value)

_____interest-rate risk

_____nominal interest rate

_____present discounted value

_____real interest rate

_____return (rate of return)

_____simple loan

_____yield to maturity

Definitions:

1. a specified final amount paid to the owner of a coupon bond at the maturity date

2. an approximation of the yield to maturity that equals the yearly coupon payment divided by the price of a coupon bond

3. the payments to the owner of a security plus the change in the security's value, expressed as a fraction of its purchase price

4. today's value of a payment to be received in the future when the interest rate is i

5. the interest rate that equates the present value of payments received from a credit market instrument with its value today

6. a credit market instrument that is bought at a price below its face value and whose face value is repaid at the maturity date

7. a credit market instrument that pays the owner a fixed interest payment every year until the maturity date, when a specified final amount is repaid

8. the interest rate adjusted for expected inflation so that it more accurately reflects the true cost of borrowing

9. the possible reduction in returns associated with changes in interest rates

10. an interest rate that does not take inflation into account

11. a credit market instrument providing the borrower with an amount of funds that must be repaid to the lender at the maturity date along with an additional payment of interest

12. the dollar amount of the yearly coupon payment expressed as a percentage of the face value of a coupon bond

Problems and Short-Answer Questions

PRACTICE PROBLEMS

1. Calculate the present value of each of the following.
   a. $1,000, to be received one year from today, and the interest rate is 4%.

   _____

   b. $1,000, to be received one year from today, and the interest rate is 8%.

   _____

   c. $1,000, to be received two years from today, and the interest rate is 4%.

   _____

   d. Compare your answers to *a* and *b* above. What happens to the present value of a future cash flow if the interest rate rises? Why?

   _____

   _____

   _____

   e. Compare your answers to *a* and *c* above. What happens to the present value of a future cash flow as the future cash flow is received farther into the future? Why?

   _____

   _____

   _____

2. The following questions are based on a $1,000 face value coupon bond with a coupon rate of 10%.

    a. Suppose the bond has one year to maturity and you buy it for $1,018.52. What is the yield to maturity on the bond? Is the yield to maturity above or below the coupon rate of 10%? Why?

    _____

    _____

    _____

    b. Since the equation is often considered too difficult to solve, simply write down the equation that one would have to solve to find the yield to maturity if the bond has two years to maturity, and you paid $965 for the bond. If this equation were solved, would the resulting yield to maturity be above or below the coupon rate of 10%? Why?

    _____

    _____

    _____

    c. What price would the bond sell for if it had two years to maturity and the interest rate (and therefore the yield to maturity) on the bond is 7%?

    _____

    d. What price would the bond sell for if it had two years to maturity and the interest rate (and therefore the yield to maturity) on the bond is 8%?

    _____

    e. Compare c and d above. What happens to the price of a bond if the interest rate rises? Make a general statement with regard to the price of any coupon bond and the interest rate?

    _____

    _____

    f.   What price would the bond sell for if it had one year to maturity and the interest rate is 7%? What is the price of the bond if the interest rate is 8%? Using your results from *c* and *d* above, how much did the price change on the two-year bond when the interest rate rose to 8% from 7%? How much did the price change for the one-year bond when the interest rate rose to 8% from 7%? Make a general statement with regard to the sensitivity of bond prices to changes in interest rates.

_____

_____

_____

_____

3.   Suppose you purchase a coupon bond with 20 years to maturity for $1,000. It pays coupons of $70 per year.

    a.   Suppose after one year, you must sell the bond to help pay for tuition. Further suppose that interest rates have risen so that the price of the bond has fallen to $950. What is the rate of return that you earned for holding the bond one year?

_____

_____

    b.   What was the size of the capital gain or loss on the bond?

_____

    c.   Is it possible to make negative returns on a long-term U.S. government bond if the holding period is less than maturity? Explain.

_____

_____

    d.   Do long-term U.S. government bonds generate a sure return if you will need to sell them before maturity? Explain.

_____

_____

    e.   What name do we apply to the type of risk long-term bond holders bear when the holding period is less than maturity?

_____

4. What is the value of the real interest rate in each of the following situations.
   a. The nominal interest rate is 15%, and the expected inflation rate is 13%.

   _____

   b. The nominal interest rate is 12%, and the expected inflation rate is 9%.

   _____

   c. The nominal interest rate is 10%, and the expected inflation rate is 9%.

   _____

   d. The nominal interest rate is 5%, and the expected inflation rate is 1%.

   _____

   e. In which of the above situations would you prefer to be the lender? Why?

   _____

   f. In which of the above situations would you prefer to be the borrower? Why?

   _____

SHORT-ANSWER QUESTIONS

1. If a lender makes a simple loan of $500 for one year and charges 6%, how much will the lender receive at maturity? If a lender makes a simple loan of $500 for one year and charges $40 interest, what is the simple interest rate on that loan?

   _____

   _____

2. What is the alternative name for a fixed-payment loan? How is it similar to a coupon bond? How is it different?

   _____

   _____

   _____

   _____

3. What is a bond's coupon rate? Does it change over the life of the bond? If a bond's yield to maturity exceeds its coupon rate, what is its price compared to par (or face value)? Why?

    _____

    _____

    _____

    _____

4. What is a consol or perpetuity? What is the price of a perpetuity if it pays an annual coupon of $70, and its yield to maturity is 7%? What is its price if the yield to maturity rises to 14%?

    _____

    _____

5. What is the yield to maturity on a consol that pays an annual coupon of $70, and it sells for $700? What is the *current yield* of the consol? Explain the relationship between yield to maturity and current yield on a consol.

    _____

    _____

    _____

6. What are the characteristics of a bond for which current yield is a good estimate of yield to maturity? (Hint: Look at question 5 above.) Why?

    _____

    _____

    _____

7. If you lend money at a 10% nominal interest rate, but you expect inflation to be 6% over the life of the loan, at what rate do you expect your purchasing power to grow? What is the real interest rate on the loan?

    _____

    _____

8. Suppose the interest rate (and therefore the yield to maturity) increases by the same amount on Treasury bills and bonds. Which would you prefer to be holding when the increase in the interest rate takes place: a one-year Treasury bill or a 20-year Treasury bond? Why?

    _____

    _____

9. If the holder of a bond sells the bond before maturity, will the rate of return on the bond equal its yield to maturity? Why or why not?

    _____

    _____

    _____

10. Suppose long-term U.S. Treasury bonds have no default risk. Does this mean that long-term U.S. Treasury bonds are risk free? Explain.

    _____

    _____

Critical Thinking

Your friend just won a state lottery that claims to pay the winner $30,000. The lottery actually pays the holder of the winning ticket $10,000 per year for the next three years. The first $10,000 payment arrives immediately. The second arrives one year from today. And the third arrives two years from today. Your friend excitedly says to you, "I need all the money right now because I want to make a down payment on a house. Since you have saved some money, why don't you just give me the $30,000 and I'll give you the ticket. Then you can collect the $30,000 and we'll be even."

1. Should you give your friend $30,000 for the winning lottery ticket? Why or why not?

    _____

    _____

2. Suppose the interest rate is 5%. What price would you pay for the winning lottery ticket?

    _____

    _____

3. Suppose the interest rate is 8%. What price would you pay for the winning lottery ticket?

    _____

    _____

4. Which interest rate implies a greater present value for the lottery ticket? Why?

_____

_____

Self-Test

TRUE/FALSE QUESTIONS

_____1. Most people would prefer to receive $100 one year from today than receive $100 today because the present discounted value of a future cash flow is greater than the future cash flow.

_____2. A fixed-payment loan requires the borrower to make a single payment to the lender when the loan matures, and that single payment includes both the principle and interest.

_____3. The coupon rate on a bond is the coupon divided by the face value (par) of the bond.

_____4. Yield to maturity is what economists mean when they use the term "interest rate."

_____5. If a $1,000 face value bond pays annual coupons of $50, has two years to maturity, and has a yield to maturity of 7%, it will sell for $963.84.

_____6. If the yield to maturity on a bond exceeds its coupon rate, the price of the bond will be above its face value.

_____7. The price of a bond and its yield to maturity are negatively related.

_____8. The yield to maturity on a U.S. Treasury bill that sells for $9,500 today, has a face value of $10,000, and matures in one year, is 5%.

_____9. If the nominal interest rate is 7% and expected inflation is 2%, then the real interest rate is 9%.

_____10. Current yield is a better estimate of yield to maturity for short-term bonds than for long-term bonds.

_____11. Current yield and yield to maturity on a perpetuity are the same.

_____12. If a bondholder pays $1,000 for a 20-year bond that pays $40 annual coupons, holds the bond for one year and than sells the bond for $1,050, the rate of return for that year for the bondholder is 9%.

_____13. A security that pays the holder $500 five years from today is preferred to a security that pays the holder $100 per year for the next five years.

_____14. If the interest rate falls the same amount for both short-term and long-term bonds, bondholders would prefer to be holding short-term bonds.

_____15. Borrowers have a greater desire to borrow when the nominal interest rate is 15% and the expected inflation rate is 13% than when the nominal interest rate is 6% and the expected inflation rate is 2%.

MULTIPLE-CHOICE QUESTIONS

1. The most accurate measure of interest rates is
   a. the coupon rate.
   b. yield to maturity.
   c. current yield.
   d. discounted present value.

2. If the interest rate is 5%, the present value of $1,000 to be received five years from today is
   a. $783.53.
   b. $866.66.
   c. $952.38.
   d. $1,000.00.
   e. $1,050.00.

3. If a borrow must repay $106.50 one year from today in order to receive a simple loan of $100 today, the simple interest on this loan is
   a. 65%.
   b. 5.0%.
   c. 6.1%.
   d. 6.5%.
   e. none of the above.

4. You are in a car accident, and you receive an insurance settlement of $5,000 per year for the next three years. The first payment is to be received today. The second payment is to be received one year from today, and the third payment two years from today. If the interest rate is 6%, the present value of the insurance settlement is
   a. $15,000.00.
   b. $14,166.96.
   c. $13,365.06.
   d. $13,157.98.

5. Which of the following instruments pays the holder of the instrument a fixed interest payment every year until maturity, and then at maturity pays the holder the face value (principle) of the instrument?
   a. simple loan
   b. fixed-payment loan
   c. coupon bond
   d. discount bond

6. A U.S. Treasury bill is an example of a
   a. simple loan
   b. fixed-payment loan
   c. coupon bond
   d. discount bond

7. A coupon bond with a face value of $1,000 that pays an annual coupon of $100 has a coupon rate of
   a. $100.
   b. $1,100.
   c. 10%.
   d. 9.1%.
   e. none of the above.

8. What is the approximate yield to maturity on a coupon bond that matures one year from today, has a par value of $1,000, pays an annual coupon of $70, and whose price today is $1,019.05?
   a. 4%
   b. 5%
   c. 6%
   d. 7%
   e. 8%

9. What price will a coupon bond sell for if it has two years to maturity, a coupon rate of 8%, a par value of $1,000, and a yield to maturity of 12%?
   a. $920.00
   b. $924.74
   c. $932.40
   d. $1,035.71
   e. $1,120.00

10. Which of the following bonds has the highest yield to maturity?
    a. a 20-year, $1,000 par, 5% coupon bond selling for $900.
    b. a 20-year, $1,000 par, 5% coupon bond selling for $1,000.
    c. a 20-year, $1,000 par, 5% coupon bond selling for $1,100.
    d. There is not enough information to answer this question.

11. Which of the following statements is true?
    a. If the yield to maturity on a bond exceeds the coupon rate, the price of the bond is below its face value.
    b. If the yield to maturity on a bond exceeds the coupon rate, the price of the bond is above its face value.
    c. If the yield to maturity on a bond exceeds the coupon rate, the price of the bond is equal to its face value.
    d. None of the above is true.

12. Suppose you purchase a perpetuity for $1,000 that pays coupons of $50 per year. If the interest rate changes and becomes 10%, what will happen to the price of the perpetuity?
    a. The price will not change and will always equal $1,000 because this bond always pays $50 per year.
    b. The price will rise by $50.
    c. The price will fall by $50.
    d. The price will rise by $500.
    e. The price will fall by $500.

13. What is the approximate yield to maturity on a discount bond that matures one year from today with a maturity value of $10,000, and the price today is $9,174.31?
    a. 92%
    b. 10%
    c. 9.2%
    d. 9%
    e. 8%

14. With regard to a coupon bond, the coupon divided by the face value of the bond is known as the
    a. yield to maturity.
    b. current yield.
    c. face value rate.
    d. coupon rate.

15. If market participants expect there to be some inflation in the future,
    a. real interest rates will exceed nominal interest rates.
    b. nominal interest rates will exceed real interest rates.
    c. nominal and real interest rates will be the same.
    d. there will be no relationship between nominal and real interest rates.

16. If the interest rate falls by the same amount on all bonds regardless of the length to maturity, which of the following bonds would you prefer to be holding?
    a. a $10,000 U.S. Treasury bill with one year to maturity
    b. a $10,000 U.S. Treasury note with 10 years to maturity
    c. a $10,000 U.S. Treasury bond with 20 years to maturity
    d. It does not matter which instrument is held because there is no risk associated with any of them.

17. What is the rate of return on a long-term, 5% coupon rate bond that was purchased at its face value of $1000, held for one year, and because interest rates rose sold after one year for $920?
    a. −8%
    b. −3.3%
    c. −3%
    d. 5%
    e. 13%

18. Which of the following statements is true?
    a. Current yield is a better approximation of yield to maturity for long-term bonds when compared to short-term bonds.
    b. Bond prices vary inversely with the interest rate for both coupon bonds and discount bonds.
    c. The longer to maturity, the greater is the change in the price of a bond from the same size change in the interest rate.
    d. The coupon rate on a coupon bond is fixed once the bond is issued.
    e. All of the above are true.

19. Bondholders are displeased when interest rates rise because, on the bonds they currently hold,
    a. the prices will fall.
    b. the coupon payments will fall.
    c. the yield to maturity will fall.
    d. all of the above are true.

20. If the nominal interest rate is 4% and the expected rate of inflation is 2%, then the real interest rate is
    a. −2%
    b. 2%
    c. 4%
    d. 6%
    e. 8%

Solutions

Terms and Definitions

_7_   coupon bond

_12_   coupon rate

_2_   current yield

_6_   discount bond (zero-coupon bond)

_1_   face value (par value)

_9_   interest-rate risk

_10_   nominal interest rate

_4_   present discounted value

_8_   real interest rate

_3_   return (rate of return)

_11_   simple loan

_5_   yield to maturity

Practice Problems

1. a. $1,000/1.04 = $961.54

   b. $1,000/1.08 = $925.93

   c. $1,000/(1.04)^2 = $924.56

   d. The present value falls because a larger interest rate means that a value today would grow into a larger value in the future so a value in the future must be discounted to a greater degree to find its value today.

   e. The present value falls because a value today would grow larger if allowed to grow farther into the future so a value farther into the future must be discounted to a greater degree to find its value today.

2. a. $1,018.52 = $1,100/1 + i. Solve for i = $1,100 − ($1,018.52/$1,018.52) = 0.08 = 8%. It would be below. If the price is above the face value (or par), then the yield to maturity must be below the coupon rate.

   b. $965 = $100/(1 + i) + $100/(1 + i)^2 + $1,000/(1 + i)^2 and solve for i. It would be above. If the price is below the face value (or par), then the yield to maturity must be above the coupon rate.

   c. P = $100/1.07 + $1,100/(1.07)^2 = $93.46 + $960.78 = $1,054.24

   d. P = $100/1.08 + $1,100/(1.08)^2 = $92.59 + $943.07 + $1,035.66

e. The price of the bond falls. Bond prices and interest rates are negatively related.

f. If i = 7%, P = $1,100/1.07 = $1,028.04. If i = 8%, P = $1,100/1.08 = $1,018.52. For the two year case, the price changes is $1,054.24 − $1,035.66 = $18.58. For the one-year case, the price change is $1,028.04 − $1,018.52 = $9.52. The longer to maturity, the greater is the change in the price of a bond from the same size change in the interest rate.

3. a. *Return* = ($70 + $950 − $1,000)/$1,000 = $20/$1,000 = 2%.

   b. Capital loss of $50.

   c. Yes. If interest rates rise causing a capital loss greater than the gains from the coupons, then the returns could be negative.

   d. No. Although the coupons are sure, the price of the bond can be volatile.

   e. Interest rate risk.

4. a. 15% − 13% = 2%

   b. 12% − 9% = 3%

   c. 10% − 9% = 1%

   d. 5% − 1% = 4%

   e. *d* above, because it generates the largest real interest rate.

   f. *c* above, because it generates the smallest real interest rate.

Short-Answer Questions

1. $500 × 1.06 = $530.

   $40/$500 = 0.08 = 8%

2. Fully amortized loan. Both require the borrower to make periodic payments to the lender until maturity. The payments on a fixed-payment loan are all the same size and each is part principle and interest. The payments on a coupon bond are each just interest payments and the last one at maturity is the principle.

3. Yearly coupon/face value. No, because the coupon and face value are fixed. Its price must be below par because the fixed coupons and principle are discounted to the present using a larger interest rate. In addition, the only way to make a bond with fixed coupons

and par pay a higher yield to maturity is to have it sell for a lower price (a discount).

4. A coupon bond with no maturity. $P = \$70/0.07 = \$1000$. $P = \$70/0.14 = \$500$.

5. $i = C/P = \$70/\$700 = 0.10 = 10\%$. $i = C/P = \$70/\$700 = 0.10 = 10\%$. They are the same.

6. Current yield is a good estimate for yield to maturity for very long-term bonds (and becomes a perfect estimate for bonds with no maturity, known as perpetuities.) This is because the discounted present value of the many coupons of long-term bonds is similar to a perpetuity, and the principle payment is discounted to such a great degree.

7. 4%. 4%.

8. A one-year Treasury bill. When interest rates rise, the prices of existing instruments fall, but the prices of long-term instruments fall more, causing a greater capital loss on the bond.

9. Usually not. If interest rates have changed during the holding period, then the price of the bond moves inversely with the change in the interest rate, and the bond generates a capital gain or loss in addition to its current yield.

10. No. They have interest rate risk, which is the possible reduction in returns associated with changes in interest rates.

Critical Thinking

1. No. Employing any positive interest rate, the present value of the lottery ticket is less than $30,000.

2. $\$10,000 + \$10,000/1.05 + \$10,000/(1.05)^2 = \$28,594.10$

3. $\$10,000 + \$10,000/1.08 + \$10,000/(1.08)^2 = \$27,832.65$

4. 5%. A smaller interest rate causes a present value to grow more slowly over time, and therefore a future sum would require a smaller discount when it is discounted back to the present.

True/False Questions

1. F
2. F
3. T
4. T
5. T
6. F
7. T
8. F
9. F
10. F
11. T
12. T
13. F
14. F
15. T

Multiple-Choice Questions

1. b
2. a
3. d
4. b
5. c
6. d
7. c
8. b
9. c
10. a
11. a
12. e
13. d
14. d
15. b
16. c
17. c
18. e
19. a
20. b

5 The Behavior of Interest Rates

Chapter Review

PREVIEW

Interest rates fluctuate. In this chapter we employ both the bond market and the liquidity preference framework to see how a variety of shocks affects interest rates. We address how a change in the money supply affects the interest rate, both in the near term while other determinants of the interest rate are held constant, and in the long run when other determinants are allowed to adjust to the change in the money supply.

DETERMINANTS OF ASSET DEMAND

Before we address the demand for bonds, we first address the demand for assets in general, such as money, bonds, stock, and art. Holding everything else unchanged, the quantity demanded of any asset is:

1. Positively related to the wealth of the buyer.

2. Positively related to the expected return on the asset relative to that on an alternative asset.

3. Negatively related to the risk of the asset relative to that of alternative assets.

4. Positively related to the liquidity of the asset relative to that of alternative assets.

SUPPLY AND DEMAND IN THE BOND MARKET

The bond demand curve shows the relationship between the quantity demanded of bonds and the price of bonds, holding everything else constant. Recall, a high price of a bond corresponds to a low interest rate. Since the demander of bonds is a lender, at a high price of bonds (a low interest rate), the quantity demanded of bonds is low. Alternatively, at a low price of bonds (a high interest rate) the quantity demanded of bonds is relatively high. As a result, the bond demand curve has the usual downward slope when graphed in price/quantity space.

The bond supply curve shows the relationship between the quantity supplied of bonds and the price of bonds, holding everything else constant. Since the supplier of bonds is the borrower, at a high price of bonds (a low interest rate), the quantity supplied of bonds is high, and the bond supply curve has the usual positive slope when graphed in price/quantity space.

The intersection of bond supply and bond demand determines the equilibrium price and quantity of bonds. The equilibrium price generates a corresponding equilibrium interest rate.

CHANGES IN EQUILIBRIUM INTEREST RATES

Equilibrium interest rates change when there is a shift in the demand or supply of bonds.

The demand for bonds shifts right if there is an increase in wealth (often from a business cycle expansion), a decrease in the riskiness of bonds relative to other assets, an increase in the liquidity of bonds relative to other assets, or an increase in the expected return on bonds relative to other assets. The expected return on bonds could rise due to a reduction in expected inflation (which raises real returns to lenders at each price of bonds) or a decrease in the expected interest rate (which would cause an increase in the price of bonds in the future and increase real returns).

The supply of bonds shifts right if there is an increase in the expected profitability of investment opportunities (from a business cycle expansion), an increase in expected inflation (which reduces real costs of borrowing at each price of bonds), or an increase in government deficits.

A rightward shift in the demand for bonds increases the price of bonds and reduces the interest rate. A rightward shift in the supply of bonds decreases the price of bonds and increases the interest rate. An increase in expected inflation causes bond supply to shift right, bond demand to shift left, the price of bonds to fall, and interest rates to rise. This effect is known as the Fisher effect.

SUPPLY AND DEMAND IN THE MARKET FOR MONEY: THE LIQUIDITY PREFERENCE FRAMEWORK

The liquidity preference framework suggests that the interest rate is determined by the supply and demand for money. While the bond market best shows how expected inflation affects interest rates, the liquidity preference framework best shows how changes in income, the price level, and the money supply affect interest rates.

Because money earns little or no interest, the interest rate on bonds is the opportunity cost of holding money. Therefore, at high interest rates, the opportunity cost of holding money is high, and the quantity demanded of money is low. Using similar logic, at low interest rates, the quantity demanded of money is high. As a result, the demand for money has the usual negative slope when graphed in interest rate/quantity of money space. Since we assume that the central bank controls the supply of money at some fixed quantity, the supply of money is vertical line at the fixed quantity of money supplied. The intersection of money supply and money demand determines the equilibrium interest rate.

Changes in the supply or demand for money cause changes in the equilibrium interest rate. The demand curve for money shifts right if there is an increase in income or if there is an increase in the price level. An increase in the money supply will shift the money supply curve to the right. Thus, other things held constant, an increase in income during a business cycle expansion will cause interest rates to rise, an increase in the price level will cause interest rates to rise, and an increase in the money supply will cause interest rates to fall. This last result is known as the liquidity effect.

An increase in the money supply, however, might not leave "other things equal." An increase in the money supply is expansionary, so it tends to raise national income, raise the price level, and increase expected inflation. Therefore, an increase in the growth rate of the money supply generates opposing effects on the interest rate: The liquidity effect suggests that interest rates should immediately fall, while the income, price-level, and expected inflation effects suggest that the interest rate should rise. There are three possible outcomes. If the liquidity effect is larger than the other effects, an increase in the rate of money growth will cause interest rates to first fall, and then rise, but not to the level of the original interest rate. If the liquidity effect is smaller than the other effects, the interest rate will first fall, and then rise above the original interest rate. And if the liquidity effect is smaller than the other effects and we adjust quickly to expected inflation, then an increase the rate of money growth only causes interest rates to rise. Empirical evidence suggests that an increase in money growth first causes the interest rate to fall, and then rise above the original interest rate.

Helpful Hints

1. When dealing with the bond market, it is always helpful to remember that the bond suppliers are borrowers, and that the bond demanders are lenders. This distinction is particularly useful when dealing with disequilibrium. For example, if the price of bonds is above equilibrium, there is an excess supply of bonds. If there is an excess supply of bonds, then *desired borrowing exceeds desired lending*. Interest rates rise and the price of bonds falls until we reach equilibrium.

2. Supply and demand models can address both positive and negative shocks to variables that affect supply and demand. In the text and study guide, we often just explain the results of one direction of shock just to save space. For example, we show how an increase in inflation expectations in the bond market affects bond demand, bond supply, the price of bonds, and the interest rate. It is helpful (and good practice) if you address the opposite shock from that demonstrated in the text and see if you can generate the opposite result. In the case described above, since the text demonstrated the case of an increase in expected inflation, you should see if you are able to demonstrate the case of a decrease in expected inflation in the bond market.

3. The phrase, "liquidity preference" is an alternative term for "money demand." That is, our desire to hold money is our preference to be liquid, or liquidity preference. Therefore, a model that employs the supply and demand for money is termed the "liquidity preference framework."

4. The asset market approach (the bond market) and the liquidity preference framework are generally compatible. That is, they generally provide the same answer to the question of how interest rates should respond to a particular shock. We only employ both markets because each market provides a particularly clear answer for how interest rates respond to a few important shocks. Specifically, the bond market provides a clear answer to how interest rates respond to changes in expected inflation, while the liquidity preference framework (market for money) provides a clear answer to how interest rates respond to changes in income, the price level, and the money supply.

Terms and Definitions

Choose a definition for each key term.

Key Terms:

_____asset market approach

_____expected return

_____fisher effect

_____liquidity

_____liquidity preference framework

_____opportunity cost

_____risk

_____theory of asset demand

_____wealth

Definitions:

1. the amount of interest or expected return sacrificed by not holding an alternative asset

2. the outcome that when expected inflation occurs, interest rates will rise

3. Keynes's theory of the demand for money

4. an approach used to determine asset prices using stocks of assets rather than flows

5. the return on an asset expected over the next period

6. all resources owned by an individual, including all assets

7. the relative ease and speed with which an asset can be converted into cash

8. the degree of uncertainty associated with the return on an asset

9. the theory that the quantity demanded of an asset is positively related to wealth, positively related to the expected return and liquidity of the asset relative to alternatives, and negatively related to the risk of the asset compared to alternatives

Problems and Short-Answer Questions

PRACTICE PROBLEMS

1. Employ the theory of asset demand to determine whether you would increase or decrease your quantity demanded of bonds in response to the following events. Explain.
   a. Your grandmother dies and leaves you a bequest of $100,000.

   _____

   _____

   b. Your brokerage firm lowers its commissions on stock transactions but keeps its commissions the same on bond transactions.

   _____

   _____

   c. You are risk averse. You anticipate more volatility in future stock returns.

   _____

   _____

   d. You become more pessimistic about future returns in the stock market.

   _____

   _____

   e. You wreck your uninsured automobile.

   _____

   _____

   f. Your brokerage firm offers discount commissions if you use the Internet for bond transactions.

   _____

   g. U.S. brokerage firms close many Middle East offices due to threats from terrorists.

   _____

2. a. Information is provided below for the demand and supply of $1,000 face value, one-year discount bonds that pay no coupon, and are held to maturity (for the full year). Complete the table and plot demand and supply in the graph provided below. Record the corresponding interest rates on the graph in the box beside the related price. Quantities are in billions of dollars.

Price	Quantity demanded	Quantity supplied	Corresponding interest rate
$975	100	300	_____
$950	150	250	_____
$925	200	200	_____
$900	250	150	_____

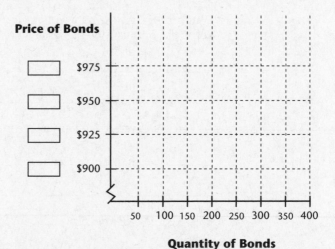

b. What is the equilibrium price, interest rate, and quantity demanded of bonds?

_____

_____

c. Suppose that the price of bonds is above the equilibrium price at, say, $950. Explain why this price is not the market-clearing price, and explain how and why the price of bonds and interest rates adjust to equilibrium.

_____

_____

d. Suppose that wealth in the economy increases causing the demand for bonds to increase by $100 billion at each price. Show this shift on the accompanying graph. What is the new equilibrium price, interest rate, and quantity of bonds?

_____

_____

3. For each of the following events, describe the shift in the supply and/or demand for bonds, and describe the impact on the price of bonds and the interest rate. Use the graph provided to help you determine the answer.

a. There is an increase peoples' wealth.

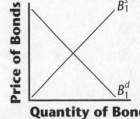

_____

_____

_____

b. An SEC ruling allows brokerage firms to reduce their commissions on bond transactions but not on stock transactions.

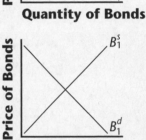

_____

_____

_____

c. The volatility of stock returns decreases.

_____

_____

_____

d. People expect higher interest rates in the future.

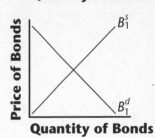

_____

_____

_____

e. There is an increase in the expected rate of inflation.

_____

_____

_____

f. People become more pessimistic about stock returns.

_____

_____

_____

g. The government runs a higher than expected budget deficit.

_____

_____

_____

h. A business cycle expansion occurs.

_____

_____

_____

4. For each of the following events, use the liquidity preference framework and shift money demand or money supply to determine the change in the equilibrium interest rate.

a. There is a higher level of income due to a business cycle expansion.

_____

_____

_____

_____

b.   There is a higher price level.

_____   **Interest Rate**

_____

_____

_____   **Quantity of Money**

c.   The Federal Reserve increases the money supply.

_____   **Interest Rate**

_____

_____

_____   **Quantity of Money**

5.   Suppose that the Federal Reserve increases the growth rate of the money supply.   Further, suppose this event causes a liquidity effect, income effect, price-level effect, and expected inflation effect.
   a.   In what direction do interest rates move in response to each of these effects?

   _____

   _____

   b.   Suppose that the liquidity effect is immediate and smaller than the other effects, and our expectations of inflation adjust slowly. Draw the time path of interest rates on the graph below from an increase in the growth rate of the money supply that occurs at time "T."

   _____

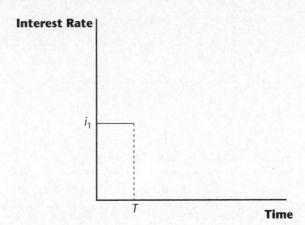

   c.   Suppose that interest rates adjust to a shock in money growth as suggested in part (b) above. If the Federal Reserve wanted to reduce interest rates over the near term, should it increase or decrease the growth rate in the

money supply?   Why? If the Fed wanted to reduce interest rates in the
long run, should it increase or decrease the growth rate in the money
supply? Why?

_____

_____

SHORT-ANSWER QUESTIONS

1. In the theory of asset demand, what are the four factors that affect whether to
    buy one asset rather than another?

    _____

    _____

2. Suppose you buy a one-year discount bond that pays no coupons, has a face
    value of $1,000, and you hold it for the entire year. If you pay $963 for it, what
    is the corresponding interest rate?

    _____

3. If there is an excess demand for bonds, is the price of bonds above or below the
    equilibrium price? Explain the price adjustment to equilibrium.

    _____

    _____

4. Suppose people expect lower interest rates in the future. Use the bond market
    to explain the impact of this event on interest rates.

    _____

    _____

5. What three events would shift the supply of bonds to the right?

    _____

    _____

6. Suppose there is a decrease in expected inflation. Use the bond market to
    explain the impact of this event on interest rates.

    _____

    _____

7. In question 6 above, the change in interest rates that results from a change in expected inflation is known as what?

   _____

8. In Keynes's liquidity preference framework, what is the opportunity cost of holding money? Why?

   _____

   _____

9. According to the liquidity preference framework, in what direction do interest rates move in response to an increase in the money supply, other things unchanging? What is the name of this effect?

   _____

   _____

10. If the Federal Reserve increases the growth rate of the money supply, which effect works in the opposite direction from the others? Explain.

    _____

    _____

Critical Thinking

You are watching the national news with your parents. The news anchor says that interest rates are higher than the historical average. Your parents know that you will begin looking to buy a house in a just few years. Your father says, "I hope that someone is appointed soon to run the Fed that will expand the money supply faster. If more money is available, borrowing rates will go down, and it will be much cheaper for you to buy a home."

1. If the liquidity effect is smaller than the income, price-level, and expected inflation effects, is it true that increasing the growth rate in the money supply will decrease interest rates? Explain for both the near term and longer run.

   _____

   _____

   _____

   _____

2. If it is going to be a significant amount of time before you buy a home, is a faster or slower growth rate in the money supply likely to create lower interest rates for you? Explain.

_____

_____

_____

_____

_____

Self-Test

TRUE/FALSE QUESTIONS

_____1. According to the theory of asset demand, an increase in expected returns in the stock market decreases the quantity demanded of bonds.

_____2. According to the theory of asset demand, an increase in the volatility of returns in the stock market decreases the quantity demanded of bonds.

_____3. A one-year discount bond for which the owner pays $937, holds it for the entire one year, and receives $1,000 at maturity, generates an interest rate of 6.7%.

_____4. The price of a bond and the interest rate are always negatively related for any type of bond, whether a discount or coupon bond.

_____5. If the price of bonds is below the equilibrium price, there will be an excess supply of bonds, and interest rates will rise.

_____6. An increase the government's budget deficit shifts the supply of bonds to the right, decreases the price of bonds, and increases the interest rate.

_____7. The asset market approach emphasizes flows rather than stocks of assets to determine asset prices.

_____8. An increase in expected inflation decreases real returns at each price of bonds causing bond demand to shift left, bond supply to shift right, the price of bonds to fall, and interest rates to rise.

_____9. When expected inflation rises causing interest rates to rise, we have seen a demonstration of the Fisher effect.

_____10. An increase in the riskiness of bonds causes bond demand to increase, the price of bonds to rise, and interest rates to fall.

_____11. The liquidity preference framework suggests that the interest rate is determined by the supply and demand for bonds.

_____12. In the liquidity preference framework, an increase in incomes, *ceteris paribus*, causes money demand to shift left and interest rates to fall.

_____13. An increase in the money supply, other things held constant, causes interest rates to fall.

_____14. If there is an increase in the growth rate of the money supply and the resulting liquidity effect is smaller than the combined income, price-level, and expected inflation effects, then the interest rate will eventually rise above the initial interest rate.

_____15. If there is an increase in the growth rate of the money supply, the resulting liquidity effect is smaller than the combined income, price-level, and expected inflation effects, and inflationary expectations adjust quickly, then the interest rate will immediately rise and rise further over time.

MULTIPLE-CHOICE QUESTIONS

1. In the theory of asset demand, which of the following will decrease the quantity demanded of an asset?
   a. an increase in the wealth of the buyer
   b. an increase in the expected return on the asset relative to alternative assets
   c. an increase in the risk of the asset relative to alternative assets
   d. an increase in the liquidity of the asset relative to alternative assets

2. What is the interest rate on a one-year discount bond that pays $1,000 at maturity, is held for the entire year, and the purchase price is $955?
   a. 4.5%
   b. 4.7%
   c. 5.5%
   d. 9.5%

3. The price of bonds and the interest rate are
   a. uncorrelated.
   b. positively correlated.
   c. negatively correlated.
   d. either positively or negatively correlated depending on whether the market participant is a bond buyer or a bond seller.

4. Along the supply curve for bonds, an increase in the price of bonds
   a. decreases the interest rate and increases the quantity of bonds supplied.
   b. decreases the interest rate and decreases the quantity of bonds supplied.
   c. increases the interest rate and increases the quantity of bonds supplied.
   d. increases the interest rate and decreases the quantity of bonds supplied.

5. If the price of bonds is below the equilibrium price, there is an excess
    a. supply of bonds, the price of bonds will fall, and the interest rate will rise.
    b. supply of bonds, the price of bonds will rise, and the interest rate will fall.
    c. demand for bonds, the price of bonds will fall, and the interest rate will rise.
    d. demand for bonds, the price of bonds will rise, and the interest rate will fall.

6. Which of the following statements about the bond market is true?
    a. Bond demand corresponds to willingness to lend.
    b. Bond supply corresponds to willingness to borrow.
    c. The supply and demand of bonds are measured in terms of "stocks" of assets, so it can be considered an asset market approach to the determination of asset prices and returns.
    d. All of the above are true.

7. If the demand for bonds shifts to the left, the price of bonds
    a. decreases and interest rates fall.
    b. decreases and interest rates rise.
    c. increases and interest rates rise.
    d. increases and interest rates fall.

8. An increase in the riskiness of stocks causes
    a. bond demand to shift right.
    b. bond demand to shift left.
    c. bond supply to shift right.
    d. bond supply to shift left.

9. A decrease in wealth in the economy causes
    a. bond demand to shift right, the price of bonds to rise, and interest rates to fall.
    b. bond demand to shift left, the price of bonds to fall, and interest rates to rise.
    c. bond supply to shift right, the price of bonds to fall, and interest rates to rise.
    d. bond supply to shift left, the price of bonds to rise, and interest rates to fall.

10. An increase in expected inflation causes
    a. bond demand to shift left, bond supply to shift right, and interest rates to fall.
    b. bond demand to shift right, bond supply to shift left, and interest rates to rise.
    c. bond demand to shift left, bond supply to shift right, and interest rates to rise.
    d. bond demand to shift right, bond supply to shift left, and interest rates to fall.

11. Which of the following would cause the demand for long-term bonds to shift right?
    a. Stocks become less risky.
    b. People expect interest rates to fall in the future.
    c. Brokerage firms reduce their commissions on stock transactions.
    d. People increase their expectations of inflation.

12. Which of the following will cause interest rates to rise?
    a. The stock market has become more volatile.
    b. Firms become pessimistic about the future profitability of new plant and equipment.
    c. People reduce their expectations of inflation.
    d. The government increases its budget deficit.

13. When an increase in expected inflation causes interest rates to rise, this is known as the
    a. liquidity effect.
    b. output effect.
    c. Fisher effect.
    d. deficit effect.

14. A business cycle expansion causes
    a. both bond demand and bond supply to shift right.
    b. both bond demand and bond supply to shift left.
    c. bond demand to shift right and bond supply to shift left.
    d. bond demand to shift left and bond supply to shift right.

15. In the liquidity preference framework, interest rates are determined by the supply and demand for
    a. bonds.
    b. stocks.
    c. output.
    d. money.

16. Which of the following effects from an increase in the money supply causes interest rates to decrease in the short run?
    a. the income effect
    b. the liquidity effect
    c. the expected inflation effect
    d. the price-level effect

17. An increase in the price level causes
    a. money demand to shift to the right and interest rates increase.
    b. money demand to shift to the left and interest rates decrease.
    a. the money supply to shift to the right and interest rates decrease.
    b. the money supply to shift to the left and interest rates decrease.

18. Suppose there is an increase in the growth rate of the money supply. If the liquidity effect is smaller than the income, price-level, and expected inflation effects, and if inflationary expectations adjust slowly, then in the <u>short run</u>, interest rates
    a. remain unchanged.
    b. rise.
    c. fall.
    d. become unpredictable.

19. Suppose there is an increase in the growth rate of the money supply. If the liquidity effect is smaller than the output, price-level, and expected inflation effects, then in the <u>long run</u>, interest rates
    a. remain unchanged when compared to their initial value.
    b. rise when compared to their initial value.
    c. fall compared to their initial value.
    d. become unpredictable.

20. In the long run, if the output, price-level, and expected inflation effects outweigh the liquidity effect, to reduce interest rates the Federal Reserve should
    a. maintain the growth rate of the money supply.
    b. increase the growth rate of the money supply.
    c. decrease the growth rate of the money supply.
    d. none of the above.

Solutions

Terms and Definitions

_4_   asset market approach

_5_   expected return

_2_   fisher effect

_7_   liquidity

_3_   liquidity preference framework

_1_   opportunity cost

_8_   risk

_9_   theory of asset demand

_6_   wealth

Practice Problems

1. a. increase, because your wealth has increased

    b. decrease, because the relative liquidity of bonds has decreased

    c. increase, because bonds are relatively less risky

    d. increase, because bonds have relatively higher expected returns

    e. decrease, because your wealth has decreased

    f. increase, because the bonds have become more liquid

    g. decrease, because bonds have become less liquid

2. a.

Price	Quantity demanded	Quantity supplied	Corresponding interest rate
$975	100	300	($1,000 – $975)/$975 = 2.6%
$950	150	250	($1,000 – $950)/$950 = 5.3%
$925	200	200	($1,000 – $925)/$925 = 8.1%
$900	250	150	($1,000 – $900)/$900 = 11.1%

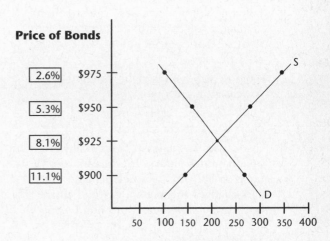

Price of Bonds

Quantity of Bonds

b. $925, 8.1%, 200 billion dollars

c. At $950 (or an interest rate of 5.3%), the quantity demanded of bonds is $150 billion while the quantity supplied is $250 billion. The excess supply of bonds means that desired borrowing exceeds desired lending, causing the price of bonds to fall to $925 and the corresponding interest rate to rise to 8.1%.

d. $950, 5.3%, 250 billion dollars.

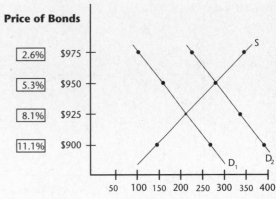

Price of Bonds

Quantity of Bonds

3. a. bond demand shifts right, price of bonds increases, interest rate falls

    b. bond demand shifts right, price of bonds increases, interest rate falls

    c. bond demand shifts left, price of bonds decreases, interest rate rises

    d. due to expected capital losses, expected returns on bonds falls so bond demand shifts left, price of bonds decreases, interest rate rises

e. for each price of bonds, the real interest rate on bonds decreases, causing bond demand to shift left, bond supply to shift right, the price of bonds to fall, interest rates to rise

f. bond demand shifts right, price of bonds increases, interest rate falls

g. bond supply right, price of bonds decreases, interest rate rises

h. this causes an increase in expected profit opportunities and an increase in wealth, bond supply right, bond demand right, and changes in bond prices and interest rates are ambiguous (but bond supply usually shifts right more so price of bonds decreases, interest rate increases)

4. a. money demand shifts right, interest rates rise

b. money demand shifts right, interest rates rise

c. money supply shifts right, interest rates fall

5. a. Liquidity effect causes interest rates to fall. Income, price-level, and expected inflation effects cause interest rates to rise.

b.

c. Increase money growth because the liquidity effect is immediate, causing interest rates to fall. Decrease money growth because the stronger income, price-level, and expected inflation effects suggest that the interest rate would fall in the long run.

Short-Answer Questions

1. Wealth, expected return relative to alternative assets, risk relative to alternative assets, and liquidity relative to alternative assets.

2. ($1,000-$963)/$963 = 3.8%

3. The price of bonds is below equilibrium. An excess demand for bonds means that desired lending exceeds desired borrowing, the interest rate falls, and the price of bonds rises.

4. Lower interest rates in the future would mean higher bond prices in the future and an increase in expected returns on bonds purchased today, shifting bond demand to the right today. Bond prices rise and interest rates fall.

5. An increase in the expected profitability of investment opportunities, an increase in expected inflation, and an increase in the budget deficit.

6. For each price of bonds, the real interest rate on bonds increases, causing bond demand to shift right, bond supply to shift left, the price of bonds to rise, and interest rates to fall.

7. The Fisher effect.

8. The interest rate, because since he assumes that money earns no interest, the interest rate is what is sacrificed by holding money.

9. Interest rates decrease. Liquidity effect.

10. The liquidity effect suggests that interest rates should fall, but the income, price-level, and expected inflation effects all suggest that interest rates should rise.

Critical Thinking

1. Not necessarily. In the near term, if people are slow to adjust their expectations of inflation, then interest rates will first fall (liquidity effect). But in the longer run, the interest rate will rise to a point higher than the original interest rate (income, price-level, expected inflation effects). If people adjust their inflationary expectation quickly, then the liquidity effect is overwhelmed by the expected inflation effect even in the near term; interest rates rise in both the near term and long term.

2. The empirical evidence suggests that while there is a small short-term liquidity effect from a change in the growth rate of money, in the long run the liquidity effect is dominated by the income, price-level, and expected inflation effects. Therefore, after all effects

are accounted for, a reduction in money growth tends to cause interest rates to decline.

True/False Questions

1. T
2. F
3. T
4. T
5. F
6. T
7. F
8. T
9. T
10. F
11. F
12. F
13. T
14. T
15. T

Multiple-Choice Questions

1. c
2. b
3. c
4. a
5. d
6. d
7. b
8. a
9. b
10. c
11. b
12. d
13. c
14. a
15. d
16. b
17. a
18. c
19. b
20. c

6 The Risk and Term Structure of Interest Rates

Chapter Review

PREVIEW

There are many different interest rates. Due to differences in risk, liquidity, and tax treatment, bonds with the same term to maturity may have different interest rates. The relationship between these interest rates is known as the *risk structure of interest rates*. Bonds with different terms to maturity (but that are otherwise the same) also have different interest rates. The relationship between these interest rates is known as the *term structure of interest rates*.

RISK STRUCTURE OF INTEREST RATES

Bonds with the same term to maturity may have different interest rates because they have differences in

- Risk of default,
- Liquidity,
- Income tax treatment.

Default occurs when the issuer of a bond is unable to make interest payments or pay off the face value when the bond matures. U.S. Treasury bonds are considered to be *default-free bonds* because they have no risk of default. The *risk premium* is the spread between the interest rate on bonds with default risk and the interest rate on default-free bonds, both of the same maturity. It shows how much bondholders must be compensated to hold a bond with default risk. The risk premium can be demonstrated by analyzing the separate markets for default-free U.S. Treasury bonds and corporate bonds of the same maturity. Suppose the price in each market is originally the same, and therefore the interest rate is the same. Since corporations have some possibility of default, the expected return on corporate bonds is lower. The corporate bond's return is also more uncertain. Since the relative expected return is lower and the risk is higher, the theory of asset demand tells us that the demand for corporate bonds will decrease, or shift left. At the same time, the relative return on default-free government bonds is higher and their risk is lower, so the demand for Treasury bonds increases, or shifts right. The price of corporate bonds falls, and their interest rate rises. The price of Treasury bonds rises, and their interest rate falls. The difference between the two interest rates is the risk premium. An increase in default risk on corporate or municipal bonds will increase the risk premium on those bonds. *Credit-rating agencies* rate the quality of corporate and municipal bonds in terms of the probability of default. Similar risk premiums can be calculated between bonds with different bond ratings.

According to the theory of asset demand, *liquidity* is a desirable attribute. U.S. Treasury bonds are more widely traded, and thus are easier to sell quickly and at lower cost than comparable corporate bonds. Similar to the analysis of default risk described above, the difference in liquidity between U.S. Treasury securities and corporate bonds causes a further decrease in the demand for corporate bonds and a further increase in the demand for U.S. Treasury bonds. Thus, differences in liquidity across bonds increase the "risk and liquidity premium," which is simply called the *risk premium* by convention.

Interest payments received from holding municipal bonds are exempt from federal income tax. Other things being the same, if a bondholder were in the 35% tax bracket, a 10% return on taxable U.S. Treasury bonds would net the holder 6.5% after tax. The bondholder might prefer a similar municipal security even though it pays less than 10% as long as it pays more than 6.5%. Alternatively, applying the analysis from above, the tax exempt status of municipal bonds increases the demand for municipal bonds, which increases their price and decreases their interest rate. The taxable status of Treasury bonds decreases their demand and increases their interest rate. Thus, municipal bonds usually pay lower rates than U.S. Treasury bonds.

TERM STRUCTURE OF INTEREST RATES

Bonds that are otherwise the same may have different interest rates if the time to maturity is different. A *yield curve* is a plot of interest rates for a particular type of bond with different terms to maturity. That is, a yield curve shows the term structure of interest rates. A theory of the term structure must explain the following three empirical facts:

- Interest rates on bonds of different maturities move together over time.

- When short-term rates are low, yield curves tend to be upward sloping; when short-term rates are high, yield curves tend to be downward sloping, or inverted.

- Yield curves almost always slope upward.

There are three theories of the term structure of interest rates. The *expectations theory* argues that, if bonds of different maturities are perfect substitutes, then the interest rate on a long-term bond is the average of short-term interest rates that people expect to prevail over the life of the bond. For example, if the one-year interest rate is 6%, and next year's expected one-year rate is 7%, the current two-year rate must be (6% + 7%)/2 = 6.5%. As a result, a bondholder would be indifferent between holding sequential one-year bonds earning first 6% and then 7%, and holding a two-year bond earning 6.5%. This theory can explain the first two empirical facts listed above. However, since short-term rates are as likely to rise as fall, the expectations theory suggests that yield curves should generally be flat.

The *segmented markets theory* of the term structure argues that, if bonds of different maturities are not substitutes at all, then interest rates for different maturity bonds are completely separate, and the interest rate for each maturity is determined by the supply and demand for bonds of that maturity. Since the demand for short-term bonds is greater than for long-term bonds, the prices of short-term bonds will be higher and their interest rates lower than long-term bonds. This theory can explain the third empirical fact listed above.

The *liquidity premium theory* of the term structure combines components of the previous two theories. This theory suggests that bonds of different maturities are substitutes, but not perfect substitutes. As a result, the liquidity premium theory argues that the interest rate on long-term bonds is an average of short-term interest rates expected to occur over the life of the long-term bond (from the expectations theory) plus a positive term that represents the liquidity premium (from the segmented markets theory). Since people prefer short-term to long-term bonds, the liquidity premium is larger on long-term bonds. The *preferred habitat theory* is the same as the liquidity premium theory if bondholders prefer short-term bonds. While the expectations theory and the segmented markets theories can each explain some of the three empirical facts about the term structure of interest rates, the liquidity premium theory and preferred habitat theories can explain all three. In addition, the liquidity premium/preferred habitat theories allow us to infer future movements in short-term interest rates from the yield curve as follows:

- A steeply upward-sloping yield curve indicates that short-term rates are expected to rise.

- A mildly upward-sloping yield curve suggests that short-term rates are expected to stay the same.

- A flat curve indicates that short-term rates are expected to decline slightly.

- An inverted curve (downward sloping) indicates that short-term rates are expected to decline substantially.

Helpful Hints

1. The segmented markets theory of the term structure is based on the argument that bonds of different maturities are not substitutes. This will be true if people won't accept any interest rate risk. If people won't accept any interest rate risk, they will only buy bonds of a maturity that perfectly matches their expected holding period. If you are saving for next year's vacation, you will only buy bonds in the market for one-year bonds. If you are saving for your retirement, you will only buy bonds in the market for 30-year bonds, and so on. As such, the interest rate for any particular maturity bond is unrelated to the interest rate for any other maturity bond.

2. The preferred habitat theory is a more general theory of the term structure than the liquidity premium theory. The preferred habitat theory leaves open what

length to maturity bondholders might prefer. If we argue that, other things the same, bondholders would always prefer short-term bonds, then long-term bonds require an interest rate premium in order to get people to buy them, and the preferred habitat theory and the liquidity premium theory become the same.

Terms and Definitions

Choose a definition for each key term.

Key Terms:

_____credit-rating agencies

_____default

_____default-free bonds

_____expectations theory

_____inverted yield curve

_____liquidity premium theory

_____risk premium

_____risk structure of interest rates

_____segmented markets theory

_____term structure of interest rates

_____yield curve

Definitions:

1. A theory of the term structure that argues that markets for different-maturity bonds are completely separate so that the interest rate for bonds of any given maturity is determined solely by supply and demand for bonds of that maturity

2. Bonds with no default risk, such as U.S. Treasury bonds

3. The proposition that the interest rate on a long-term bond will equal the average of short-term interest rates that people expect to prevail over the life of the long-term bond

4. The spread between the interest rate on bonds with default risk and the interest rate on default-free bonds

5. A plot of the interest rates for particular types of bonds with different terms to maturity

6. The relationship among the various interest rates on bonds with the same term to maturity

7. Investment advisory firms that rate the quality of corporate and municipal bonds in terms of the probability of default

8. The proposition that the interest rate on a long-term bond will equal the average of short-term interest rates that people expect to prevail over the life of the long-term bond plus a positive term that represents the liquidity premium

9. A situation in which the party issuing a debt instrument is unable to make interest payments or pay off the face value when the instrument matures

10. The relationship among interest rates on bonds with different terms to maturity

11. A yield curve that is downward sloping

Problems and Short-Answer Questions

PRACTICE PROBLEMS

1. Suppose that the health of the economy improves so that the probability of corporations defaulting on their bonds decreases.

    a. Use the diagrams below to show the shifts in the supply and demand for corporate bonds and U.S. Treasury bonds from the event described above. Describe and explain the shifts in the curves.

    _____

    _____

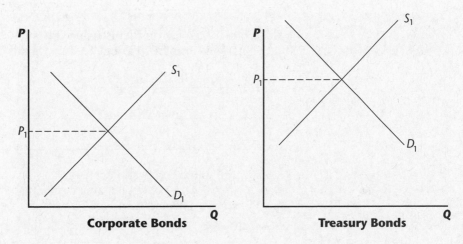

    b. What happens to the price and interest rate on corporate bonds?

    _____

    c. What happens to the price and interest rate on Treasury bonds?

    _____

    d. What happens to the risk premium? Explain.

    _____

    _____

2. Describe the shifts in supply and demand in the financial markets that would result from each of the following events, and then describe the impact on the relevant spread or risk premium.

   a. A major AAA-rated corporation defaults on its bonds. What happens in the markets for corporate bonds and U.S. Treasury bonds, and the spread?

   _____

   _____

   _____

   b. The volume of transactions in the corporate bond market increases so that corporate bondholders are more confident that they can find a buyer easily should they decide to sell their corporate bonds. What happens in the markets for corporate bonds and U.S. Treasury bonds, and the spread?

   _____

   _____

   _____

   c. The top marginal tax bracket is reduced from 40% to 30%. What happens in the markets for municipal and Treasury bonds and the spread?

   _____

   _____

   _____

   d. A major BBB-rated corporation defaults on its bonds. What happens in the markets for bonds rated BBB and corporate bonds rated AAA and the spread between BBB and AAA bonds?

   _____

   _____

   _____

3. Suppose your marginal tax rate is 30%.

   a. What is your after-tax return from holding (to maturity) a one-year corporate bond with a yield to maturity of 10%?

   _____

   b. What is your after-tax return from holding (to maturity) a one-year municipal bond with a yield to maturity of 8%?

   _____

c. If both of these bonds have the same degree of risk and liquidity, which one would you prefer to own?

_____

d. What does this example suggest about the relationship between the interest rates on municipal bonds versus other bonds?

_____

_____

4. The following questions address the term structure of interest rates.
    a. Suppose people expect the interest rate on one-year bonds for each of the next four years to be 4%, 5%, 6%, and 7%. Calculate the implied interest rate on bonds with a maturity of one-year, two-years, three-years, and four-years if the expectations theory of the term structure of interest rates is correct.

_____

_____

    b. Plot the yield curve generated by this data if the expectations theory of the term structure of interest rates is correct.

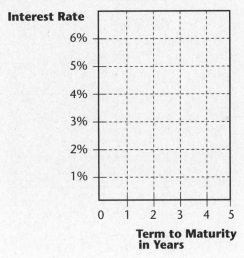

    c. Can the yield curve you derived in *b* above be used to explain why yield curves almost always slope upward? Explain.

_____

_____

d. Since short-term interest rates are just as likely to rise as fall, in the long run people on average expect short-term interest rates to be steady. Suppose that people expect the one-year bond rate to remain at 4% for each of the next four years. If the liquidity premium theory of the term structure is correct, what are the liquidity premiums implied by a yield curve that looks like the one you plotted in *b* above?

_____

_____

5. For each of the following descriptions of a yield curve, what is the market predicting about movements in future short-term interest rates, assuming that the liquidity premium theory of the term structure is correct? Explain.
a. The yield curve is perfectly flat.

_____

_____

b. The yield curve is moderately upward sloping.

_____

_____

c. The yield curve is inverted.

_____

_____

d. The yield curve is steeply upward sloping.

_____

_____

SHORT-ANSWER QUESTIONS

1. What is the risk premium?

_____

_____

2. What three characteristics of a bond are collectively embedded in the risk structure of interest rates? How does a change in each affect the spread or risk premium?

    _____

    _____

    _____

3. Suppose a corporate bond pays an interest rate of 10%. What interest rate would you expect an identical (same maturity, risk, liquidity,...) municipal bond to pay if the marginal tax rate is 25%?

    _____

4. What are the two main credit-rating agencies? What are these firms advising investors about? What name do we attach to bonds rated Baa (or BBB) or higher? What name to we attach to bonds rated below Baa (or BBB)?

    _____

    _____

    _____

5. Why are interest rates on U.S. Treasury bonds usually higher than on municipal bonds when U.S. Treasury bonds are default-free and municipal bonds have some default risk?

    _____

    _____

6. How does the expectations theory of the term structure of interest rates explain the fact that interest rates on bonds of different maturities move together over time?

    _____

    _____

7. How does the expectations theory of the term structure of interest rates explain the fact that yield curves almost always slope upward?

    _____

8. How does the segmented markets theory of the term structure of interest rates explain the fact that yield curves almost always slope upward?

    _____

    _____

    _____

9. Suppose that the Fed has tightened monetary policy and has temporarily pushed short-term interest rates unusually high. People expect the Fed to sharply lower short-term rates in the future. According to the liquidity premium theory of the term structure, what is the likely shape of the yield curve in this situation?

_____

10. If rising interest rates are associated with economic booms and falling interest rates with recessions, what would most likely follow a steeply upward-sloping yield curve – inflation or recession? Why?

_____

_____

Critical Thinking

You are presented with two alternatives: You can buy a three-year bond with a yield to maturity of 7%, or you can buy a one-year bond with a yield to maturity of 6%, then purchase another one-year bond with a yield to maturity of 7%, and when the second bond matures, purchase another one-year bond with a yield to maturity of 8%.

1. What is your expected annual rate of return for the first strategy?

_____

2. What is your expected annual rate return for the second strategy?

_____

3. What can you say about the two expected returns?

_____

4. If the liquidity premium theory of the term structure of interest rates is correct, which one of these choices would you pick? Why?

_____

_____

_____

Self-Test

TRUE/FALSE QUESTIONS

_____1. The spread between the interest rate on a one-year U.S. Treasury bond and a 20-year U.S. Treasury bond is known as the risk premium.

_____2. If General Motors Corporation unexpectedly defaults on a bond issue, the spread between U.S. Treasury bonds and corporate bonds will widen.

_____3. When U.S. marginal income tax rates were very low, municipal bonds generally paid higher interests than U.S. Treasury bonds of the same maturity.

_____4. If more people are participating in the corporate bond market so that corporate bonds are considered to be more liquid, bondholders will increase their demand for corporate bonds, decrease their demand for U.S. Treasury bonds, and the risk premium will fall.

_____5. The difference in the default risk among bonds is the sole determinant of the risk premium.

_____6. When there is a "flight to quality" in the bond market, the spread between bonds rated BBB and U.S. Treasury bonds narrows.

_____7. If a corporate bond pays 10% while a municipal bond pays 7.5%, a bondholder in a 15% marginal income tax bracket would prefer to hold the municipal bond, given that the bonds are otherwise identical.

_____8. The term structure of interest rates is the relationship among interest rates on bonds with different terms to maturity.

_____9. A plot of the interest rates on default-free government bonds with different terms to maturity is known as a term structure curve.

_____10. Yield curves almost always slope downward.

_____11. The expectations theory of the term structure of interest rates assumes that bonds of different maturities are prefect substitutes.

_____12. The segmented markets theory of the term structure of interest rates cannot explain why yield curves usually slope upward.

_____13. If the expectations theory of the term structure of interest rates is true, and if the one-year bond rate is 4% and the two-year bond rate is 5%, then participants in the bond market must think that next year's one-year bond rate will be 6%.

_____14. According to the liquidity premium theory of the term structure of interest rates, people prefer to hold short-term bonds, so they must be compensated with a higher interest rate in order to be induced to hold long-term bonds.

_____15. According to the liquidity premium theory of the term structure of interest rates, a flat yield curve indicates that short-term interest rates are expected to stay the same.

MULTIPLE-CHOICE QUESTIONS

1. The risk premium on a bond may be affected by all of the following except the bond's
    a. liquidity.
    b. risk of default.
    c. income tax treatment.
    d. term to maturity.

2. Which of the following bonds tends to pay the highest interest rate?
    a. U.S. Treasury bonds
    b. corporate Aaa bonds
    c. municipal Aaa bonds
    d. They all pay the same interest rate.

3. Which of the following would cause the risk premium on corporate bonds to fall?
    a. There are fewer participants in the bond markets causing a reduction in the daily volume of transactions.
    b. There is an increase in brokerage commissions.
    c. Forecasters predict that the economy will grow more quickly for the next few years.
    d. U.S. Treasury bonds become more liquid.

4. If the default risk on corporate bonds increases, the demand for corporate bonds shifts
    a. right, the demand for U.S. Treasury bonds shifts left, and the risk premium rises.
    b. left, the demand for U.S. Treasury bonds shifts right, and the risk premium falls.
    c. right, the demand for U.S. Treasury bonds shifts left, and the risk premium falls.
    d. left, the demand for U.S. Treasury bonds shifts right, and the risk premium rises.

5. If the risk premium on corporate bonds increases, then
    a. the price of corporate bonds has increased.
    b. the price of default-free bonds has decreased.
    c. the spread between the interest rate on corporate bonds and the interest rate on default-free bonds has become greater.
    d. the spread between the interest rate on corporate bonds and the interest rate on default-free bonds has become smaller.

6. Municipal bonds tend to pay lower interest rates than U.S. Treasury bonds because
    a. interest payments received from holding municipal bonds are exempt from federal income tax.
    b. municipal bonds are default-free.
    c. municipal bonds are more liquid than U.S. Treasury bonds.
    d. all of the above are true.

7. A reduction in income tax rates shifts the demand for municipal bonds to the
    a. left, shifts the demand for U.S. Treasury bonds to the right, and increases interest rates on municipal bonds relative to U.S. Treasury bonds.
    b. left, shifts the demand for U.S. Treasury bonds to the right, and decreases interest rates on municipal bonds relative to U.S. Treasury bonds.
    c. right, shifts the demand for U.S. Treasury bonds to the left, and increases interest rates on municipal bonds relative to U.S. Treasury bonds.
    d. right, shifts the demand for U.S. Treasury bonds to the left, and decreases interest rates on municipal bonds relative to U.S. Treasury bonds.

8. Suppose your marginal income tax rate is 25%. If a corporate bond pays 10%, what interest rate would an otherwise identical municipal bond have to pay in order for you to be indifferent between holding the corporate bond and the municipal bond?
    a. 12.5%
    b. 10%
    c. 7.5%
    d. 2.5%

9. In which of the following situations would you choose to hold the corporate bond over the municipal bond, assuming that corporate and municipal bonds have the same maturity, liquidity, and default risk?
    a. The corporate bond pays 10%, the municipal bond pays 7%, and your marginal income tax rate is 35%.
    b. The corporate bond pays 10%, the municipal bond pays 7%, and your marginal income tax rate is 25%.
    c. The corporate bond pays 10%, the municipal bond pays 8%, and your marginal income tax rate is 25%.
    d. The corporate bond pays 10%, the municipal bond pays 9%, and your marginal income tax rate is 20%.

10. Which of the following would be considered to be "high-yield bonds"?
    a. junk bonds
    b. speculative-grade bonds
    c. bonds rated Caa
    d. All of the above are correct.

11. A plot of the yields on bonds with different terms to maturity but the same risk, liquidity, and tax considerations is known as
    a. a term-structure curve.
    b. a yield curve.
    c. a risk-structure curve.
    d. an interest-rate curve.

12. Which of the following statements is not true?
    a. Interest rates on bonds of different maturities tend to move together over time.
    b. Yield curves almost always slope upward.
    c. When short-term interest rates are high, yield curves tend to be downward sloping.
    d. When short-term interest rates are low, yield curves tend to be inverted.

13. The expectations theory of the term structure of interest rates implies that yield curves should usually be
    a. upward sloping.
    b. downward sloping.
    c. flat.
    d. vertical.

14. According to the expectations theory of the term structure of interest rates, if the one-year bond rate is 3%, and the two-year bond rate is 4%, next year's one-year rate is expected to be
    a. 3%.
    b. 4%.
    c. 5%.
    d. 6%.

15. The segmented markets theory of the term structure of interest rates is based on the assumption that
    a. bonds of different maturities are not substitutes.
    b. bonds of different maturities are perfect substitutes.
    c. long-term bonds are preferred to short-term bonds.
    d. long-term interest rates are an average of expected short-term rates.

16. According to the segmented markets theory of the term structure of interest rates, if bondholders prefer short-term bonds to long-term bonds, the yield curve will be
    a. flat.
    b. upward sloping.
    c. downward sloping.
    d. vertical.

17. According to the liquidity premium theory of the term structure of interest rates, if the one-year bond rate is expected to be 4%, 5%, and 6% over each of the next three years, what is the interest rate on a three-year bond if the liquidity premium on a three-year bond is 0.5%?
    a. 4%
    b. 4.5%
    c. 5%
    d. 5.5%
    e. 6%

18. According to the liquidity premium and preferred habitat theories of the term structure of interest rates, a flat yield curve indicates that
    a. future short-term interest rates are expected to rise.
    b. future short-term interest rates are expected to stay the same.
    c. future short-term interest rates are expected to fall.
    d. bondholders no longer prefer short-term bonds to long-term bonds.

19. Which of the following theories of the term structure of interest rates best explains the observed empirical facts about the relationship among interest rates on bonds with different terms to maturity?
    a. the liquidity premium theory
    b. the expectations theory
    c. the segmented markets theory
    d. the risk premium theory

20. According to the liquidity premium theory of the term structure of interest rates, a mildly upward-sloping yield curve suggests that
    a. short-term interest rates are expected to rise.
    b. short-term interest rates are expected to fall.
    c. short-term interest rates are expected to stay the same.
    d. bondholders prefer long-term bonds to short-term bonds.

Solutions

Terms and Definitions

_7_ credit-rating agencies

_9_ default

_2_ default-free bonds

_3_ expectations theory

_11_ inverted yield curve

_8_ liquidity premium theory

_4_ risk premium

_6_ risk structure of interest rates

_1_ segmented markets theory

_10_ term structure of interest rates

_5_ yield curve

Practice Problems

1. a. The demand for corporate bonds increases while the demand for default-free bonds decreases as funds move from Treasury bonds to corporate bonds.

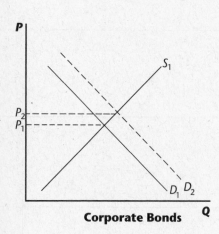

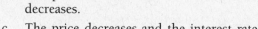
Corporate Bonds   Q   **Treasury Bonds**   Q

  b. The price increases and the interest rate decreases.

  c. The price decreases and the interest rate increases.

  d. The risk premium decreases because corporate bonds have less default risk.

2. a. The demand for corporate bonds shifts left and the demand for U.S. Treasury bonds shifts right. Interest rates increase on corporate bonds and interest rates fall on Treasury bonds, so the risk premium or spread increases.

  b. The demand for corporate bonds shifts right and the demand for U.S. Treasury bonds shifts left. Interest rates decrease on corporate bonds and interest rates increase on Treasury bonds, so the risk premium or spread decreases.

  c. The tax advantage of municipals decreases, so the demand for municipals shifts left, the demand for Treasury bonds shifts right. Interest rates on municipals increase and interest rates on Treasury bonds decrease. If municipals were paying lower interest rates than Treasuries, then interest rates on municipals will rise toward Treasuries or could even rise above Treasuries, causing the spread to increase.

  d. The demand for BBB corporate bonds shifts left and the demand for AAA corporate bonds shifts right. This causes interest rate increase on BBB bonds and decrease on AAA bonds, causing the spread between BBB and AAA bonds to increase.

3. a. After paying taxes, you get to keep 70% of the 10%, or 7%.

  b. The interest is tax exempt, so you keep all 8%.

  c. The municipal bond.

  d. Municipal bonds will pay a lower interest rate than corporate or Treasury bonds of similar risk, liquidity, and maturity.

4. a. 1 year = 4%, 2 years = (4% + 5%)/2 = 4.5%, 3 years = (4% + 5% + 6%)/3 = 5%, 4 years = (4% + 5% + 6% + 7%)/4 = 5.5%.

b.

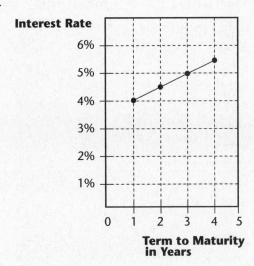

c. No. The expectations theory of the term structure can only explain an upward-sloping yield curve if short-term rates are expected to rise, but rates can't always be expected to rise.

d. 1 year = 4% − 4% = 0%, 2 year = 4.5% − 4% = 0.5%, 3 year = 5% − 4% = 1%, 4 year = 5.5% − 4% = 1.5%.

5. a. Future short-term rates are expected to fall slightly, because if interest rates were expected to be stable, the curve would slope up slightly due to the liquidity premium.

b. Future short-term rates are expected to stay the same, because a stable interest rate plus an increasing liquidity premium will cause a moderately upward slope.

c. Future short-term interest rates are expected to fall sharply. If long-term rates are sharply below short-term rates even with a liquidity premium attached, short-term rates must be expected to fall sharply.

d. Future short-term rates are expected to rise. If the curve is rising faster than can be explained by the liquidity premium, it must be because short-term rates are expected to rise.

Short-Answer Questions

1. The amount of additional interest people must earn in order to be willing to hold a risky bond.

2. Risk of default, liquidity, and income tax treatment. An increase in the risk of default or a decrease in liquidity of a corporate bond causes the risk premium to increase. A decrease in the tax rate causes an increase in the interest rate on tax-exempt bonds (municipals), which can be considered an increase in the risk premium on municipals.

3. After tax interest rate on corporate = interest rate on municipal. 10%(1 − 0.25) = 7.5%.

4. Moody's Investor Service and Standard and Poor's Corporation. They advise investors about the probability of default on corporate and municipal bonds. Investment-grade securities. Speculative-grade or junk bonds.

5. The tax-exempt status of the municipal bond outweighs the lower risk of the Treasury bond.

6. If long-term rates are an average of expected short-term rates, then an increase in short-term rates and expected future short-term rates will increase long-term rates too.

7. It can't explain it. The expectations theory alone suggests that yield curves should be flat on average.

8. The theory argues that bonds of different maturities are not substitutes and people have a greater demand for short-term bonds than long-term bonds. Thus, the prices are higher on short-term bonds and their interest rates are lower.

9. If people expect short-term rates to fall sharply in the future, the yield curve will be downward sloping.

10. Inflation. An upward-sloping yield curve means people expect future short-term rates to rise, so people expect a boom. Prices tend to rise during an economic boom.

Critical Thinking

1. 7%.
2. (6% + 7% + 8%)/3 = 7%.
3. The expected returns are the same.
4. The three one-year bonds are preferred. Other things the same, people prefer short-term securities. Thus, people require a liquidity premium (a higher interest rate) in order to be induced to hold longer-term bonds, and this three-year bond does not pay a liquidity premium.

True/False Questions

1. F
2. T

3. T
4. T
5. F
6. F
7. F
8. T
9. F
10. F
11. T
12. F
13. T
14. T
15. F

Multiple-Choice Questions

1. d
2. b
3. c
4. d
5. c
6. a
7. a
8. c
9. b
10. d
11. b
12. d
13. c
14. c
15. a
16. b
17. d
18. c
19. a
20. c

7 The Stock Market, the Theory of Rational Expectations, and the Efficient Markets Hypothesis

Chapter Review

PREVIEW

There are a variety of fundamental theories that underlie the valuation of stocks and other securities. These theories require that we understand how expectations affect stock market behavior, because to value a stock, people must form expectations about a firm's future dividends and the rate to discount future values. The *theory of rational expectations*, when applied to financial markets, implies the *efficient market hypothesis*.

COMPUTING THE PRICE OF COMMON STOCK

Stockholders have voting rights within the firm and are *residual claimants* on the firm's *cash flows*. Stockholders also receive *dividends* from the net earnings of the corporation. The value of any investment is the present discounted value of all expected cash flows the investment will generate over its life. A one-period model of stock price determination would suggest that $P_0 = [Div/(1 + ke)] + [P_1/(1 + ke)]$, where P_0 = the current price of the stock, Div = the dividend paid at the end of the year, k_e = the required return on investments on equities, and P_1 = the price of the stock at the end of the period. The *generalized dividend model* extends the single period model by discounting all future expected cash flows. Since the sale price is so far in the future, it is discounted to such a degree that its value can be ignored. Thus, the generalized dividend model says that the current price of a stock is the sum of the present value of the future dividends. This is difficult to calculate because it requires that we estimate all future dividends. The *Gordon growth model* is a simplified version of generalized dividend model that assumes a constant growth rate of dividends. Thus, $P_0 = Div_0(1 + g)/(k_e - g) = Div_1/(k_e - g)$, where Div_0 = the most recent past dividend, Div_1 = the next future dividend, and g = the expected constant growth rate of dividends.

HOW THE MARKET SETS STOCK PRICES

On a day-to-day basis, stock prices are set by the interaction of traders in the stock market. As with an auction, the price of a stock is determined by the buyer who values the stock the greatest. Based on the Gordon growth model, the trader who values the stock the greatest either has less uncertainty regarding its future cash flows or estimates its cash flows to be greater than other traders do. New information that causes even small changes in expectations about dividend growth rates or required returns causes large changes in stock prices, so stock markets are often volatile. Monetary policy affects stock prices by altering the required rate of return on equities (k_e) and by altering the performance of the economy, which alters the expected growth rate of dividends (g).

THE THEORY OF RATIONAL EXPECTATIONS

The evaluation of stock prices requires that people form expectations about firms' future cash flows and the discount rate. An older theory, called *adaptive expectations*, suggests that expectations of a variable are based on an average of past values of that variable. A more modern theory, called *rational expectations*, suggests that expectations are identical to *optimal forecasts* (the best guess of the future), which uses all available information. This does not mean that rational expectations are perfectly accurate. Expectations can still be rational even if an additional factor is important in the prediction but was not available to the forecaster. It would be irrational if additional information were available but the forecaster ignored it or was unaware of it.

It is logical that people form rational expectations because there is a cost to people whose expectations are not based on the optimal forecast. As a result:

- If there is a change in the way a variable moves, the way in which expectations of this variable are formed will change as well.

- The forecast errors of expectations will on average be zero, and they cannot be predicted ahead of time.

THE EFFICIENT MARKET HYPOTHESIS: RATIONAL EXPECTATIONS IN FINANCIAL MARKETS

The application of the theory of rational expectations to financial markets is called the *efficient market hypothesis*. It suggests that prices of securities fully reflect all available information. The above statement is derived from the following: Since the expected return on a security equals the equilibrium return, and if rational expectations hold the expected return equals the optimal forecast of the return, then it follows that the optimal forecast of the return equals the equilibrium return. Therefore, current prices in a financial market are set so that the optimal forecast of a security's return equals the equilibrium return.

In an efficient market, since prices of securities fully reflect all available information, all *unexploited profit opportunities* will be eliminated by arbitrage. For example, if the optimal forecast of tomorrow's price of a stock is higher than today's price, buying today at the lower price would generate abnormally high returns. This would cause people to buy the stock, driving its price up and its returns down until the optimal forecast of the returns is reduced and equals the equilibrium return. This does not require that all market participants be well informed. "Smart money" will eliminate the profit opportunities.

The stronger version of the efficient market hypothesis suggests that not only are the prices of securities the result of optimal forecasts, they reflect the true fundamental value of the securities, or what is known as the *market fundamentals* (the items that have a direct impact on future income streams of the securities). If this is true, one investment is as good as any other.

The efficient market hypothesis suggests that hot tips and investment advisor's published recommendations cannot help an investor outperform the market because this information is already fully incorporated into the price of securities. One would need to have the information before others have it in order to outperform the market. In addition, stock prices will respond to announcements only when the information being announced is unexpected. Most investors should engage in a "buy and hold" strategy, which will generate the average market return in the long run but with lower costs due to fewer brokerage commissions.

Some economists think that stock market crashes are evidence that the stronger version of efficient markets is not true. However, other economists use *rational bubbles* to explain crashes. A *bubble* is when the price of an asset differs from its fundamental market value. It may not be irrational to hold an asset when its price exceeds its fundamental value if you think that the price will go even higher before it falls.

BEHAVIORAL FINANCE

Behavioral finance applies concepts from other social sciences like psychology to understand securities prices. Loss aversion may stop smart money from engaging in *short sales* even when a stock is overvalued. In addition, investor overconfidence and social contagion can explain why trading volume is so high, why stocks get overvalued, and why speculative bubbles occur.

Helpful Hints

1. When most people hear the phrase "rational expectations," they think that it cannot be true because they know some very irrational people. However, the theory of rational expectations does not require that all or even most people are rational. It only requires that enough people are rational, what we call *smart money*, that their behavior removes all profit opportunities by moving securities prices to their equilibrium values. This also helps explains why studies employing survey data will find that many people engage in irrational behavior while stock market studies usually show that market outcomes support the theory of rational expectations.

2. Rational bubbles are related to the "greater fool" theory. The greater fool theory suggests that an investor will buy an asset at a price that exceeds the fundamental value of the asset if the investor thinks that there will be an even greater fool who will pay even more for it in the future. Therefore, if an

investor believes that the fundamental value of a stock is $50, he will be willing to buy it at $100 if he thinks he can sell it $150 before its value falls back to $50.

Terms and Definitions

Choose a definition for each key term.

Key Terms:

_____adaptive expectations

_____bubble

_____cash flows

_____dividends

_____efficient market hypothesis

_____gordon growth model

_____market fundamentals

_____optimal forecast

_____rational expectations

_____stockholders

_____unexploited profit opportunity

_____short sales

_____arbitrage

Definitions:

1. The application of rational expectations to financial markets

2. The manner by which market participants eliminate unexploited profit opportunities

3. A situation in which the price of an asset differs from its fundamental market value

4. Periodic payments made by equities to shareholders

5. Selling borrowed shares of stock that must be replaced at a later date, thus betting that the stock price will go down

6. A situation in which an investor can earn a higher than normal return

7. Expectations of a variable based on an average of past values of the variable

8. Items that have a direct impact on future income streams of a security

9. Expectations that reflect optimal forecasts using all available information

10. The difference between cash receipts and cash expenditures

11. Those who hold stock in a corporation

12. The best guess of the future using all available information

13. A model of stock price valuation that assumes a constant growth rate of dividends

Problems and Short-Answer Questions

PRACTICE PROBLEMS

1. Suppose that a stock is expected to pay a $1 dividend at the end of this year and that your required return on equity investments is 9%.

   a. Using a one-period model of stock price determination, what would you pay for the stock if you expect to sell it in one year for $17.50?

   _____

   b. Using the Gordon growth model, what would you pay for the stock if you expected the dividends to grow at 3% per year?

   _____

   c. Suppose that you meet the CEO of the firm and you are so impressed that you consider the company to be of lower risk that you previously thought, and so you reduce your required return on this equity investment to 7%. Using the Gordon growth model, what would you pay for this stock?

   _____

   d. Suppose the CEO provides you with inside information that the dividends are going to grow at 4% per year. Using the Gordon growth model, if your required return on this equity investment remains at 7%, what price would you pay for the stock?

   _____

   e. Compare your answers from *b*, *c*, and *d*. According to the Gordon growth model of stock price determination, for a given dividend payment, what are the only things that can increase the price of a stock?

   _____

   _____

   f. If the Fed engaged in an expansionary monetary policy by lowering interest rates, how would the variables in the Gordon growth model be affected, and what would likely happen to stock prices?

   _____

   _____

   _____

2. If the efficient market hypothesis is true, how will each of the follow events affect the relevant asset or security price? Explain your answer.

a. IBM announces profits of $100 million. Stock analysts had predicted profits of $300 million. What happens to the price of IBM stock?

_____

_____

b. IBM announces profits of $300 million. Stock analysts had predicted profits of $300 million. What happens to the price of IBM stock?

_____

_____

c. IBM announces a merger with Dell Computer. The deal is so complex that only financial analysts and other financially sophisticated people can correctly assess that it will make both firms much more efficient and profitable. The average person is simply confused. What happens to the price of IBM stock?

_____

_____

d. The price of IBM stock has risen each day for the past three days. What should happen to the price of IBM stock on the fourth day?

_____

_____

e. Your investment advisor calls you and tells you that IBM stock is significantly undervalued, and that you should buy it. What will likely happen to the price of IBM stock in the future?

_____

_____

f. Your investment advisor calls you and tells you that the price of IBM stock has risen significantly each of the past two Fridays. He suggests that you should buy IBM stock on Thursday. What will likely happen to the price of IBM stock on Friday?

_____

_____

g. A new Federal Reserve chairman is appointed and will take office in three months. The future chairman announces that when he takes over, he plans to tighten monetary policy and raise interest rates. Three months later, the new Fed chair takes his position. What happens to the stock market on the day he takes over?

_____

_____

SHORT-ANSWER QUESTIONS

1. John values ABC stock at $10 per share. Susan values it at $15 per share, and Bill values it at $20 per share. In a free-market auction, who will buy ABC stock? Why? What is the range for the price of ABC stock? Explain.

_____

_____

_____

2. Suppose a person has better information about a firm than others and so has greater certainty regarding the future cash flows of the firm. Other things being the same, will that person be willing to pay more, the same, or less than others for stock in that firm? Explain.

_____

_____

3. Are rational expectations always perfectly accurate? Why or why not?

_____

_____

_____

4. Suppose there is a change in the way a variable moves. If adaptive expectations accurately represent how people form expectations, are forecast errors zero on average, and unpredictable? Explain.

_____

_____

_____

5. Suppose there is a change in the way a variable moves. If rational expectations accurately represent how people form expectations, are forecast errors zero on average, and unpredictable? Explain.

   _____

   _____

   _____

6. If the optimal forecast of tomorrow's stock price is higher than today's price, are there unexploited profit opportunities? If the efficient market hypothesis is correct, how does the behavior of market participants eliminate the unexploited profit opportunity?

   _____

   _____

   _____

7. If the stronger version of the efficient market hypothesis is true so that stock prices reflect the true fundamental value of the stock, what strategy should most investors use when investing? Explain.

   _____

   _____

   _____

8. If the efficient market hypothesis is true, can stock prices be predicted? Explain.

   _____

   _____

   _____

9. Can a stock market bubble be rational? Explain.

   _____

   _____

10. If the efficient market hypothesis is correct, what investment strategy is best for most investors?

   _____

   _____

Critical Thinking

You are watching a broadcast of the Financial Market Report on CNN with a friend. The host reports that a tropical storm in the Gulf of Mexico named Katrina has just been upgraded to hurricane status. It is expected to hit the entire gulf coast of the United States and destroy most of the sugar beet farms. Your friend says, "We should purchase stock in C&H Sugar because they produce only pure cane sugar from outside the gulf region, and its stock price will surely rise after the storm damages its competitors."

1. Is it likely that you can make abnormally high returns by using this information to buy stock in C&H Sugar? Why or why not?

    _____

    _____

    _____

2. Suppose that a friend of your works for the U.S. Weather Bureau. She calls you late at night, and in casual conversation tells you that weather satellites have detected cloud movements that suggest that an enormous storm is in the process of forming. The weather bureau has not yet reported this information. It is afraid of causing panic because there are no evacuation plans in place. Can you earn abnormally high returns using this information? Why or why not?

    _____

    _____

    _____

3. What will happen to the price and returns to stock in C&H Sugar as you (and later others) buy stock in C&H Sugar? Can abnormally high returns be maintained? Explain.

    _____

    _____

    _____

Self-Test

TRUE/FALSE QUESTIONS

____1. Using the one-period valuation model of stock prices, if a share of stock pays an annual dividend of $3, you require a 13% return on equity investments, and if you believe that you can sell the stock next year for $50, then you would be willing to pay $46.90 for the share of stock today.

_____2.   Using the Gordon growth model of stock price determination, if a share of stock will pay a $2 dividend next year, dividends are expected to grow 3%, and people require an 11% return on equity investments, then the price of the stock is $14.29.

_____3.   According to the Gordon growth model of stock price valuation, the trader that values a stock higher than other traders must have less uncertainty regarding the stock's future cash flows or the trader estimates its cash flows to be greater than other traders do.

_____4.   According to the Gordon growth model of stock price determination, a monetary policy that raises interest rates reduces stock prices by increasing the discount rate and reducing the growth rate of the economy and therefore dividends.

_____5.   Other things being the same, if people reduce their required rate of return on investments in equities, stock prices will fall.

_____6.   If adaptive expectations accurately represent how people form their expectations, then people's expectations will be identical to optimal forecasts.

_____7.   Rational expectations are perfectly accurate.

_____8.   The efficient market hypothesis suggests that the prices of securities fully reflect all available information, so the average investor cannot find unexploited profit opportunities.

_____9.   Everyone in a financial market must be will informed and have rational expectations in order for the price of a security to be driven to the optimal forecast of the price of that security.

_____10.   According to the stronger version of the efficient market hypothesis (which argues that prices of securities are driven to their fundamental values), one investment is as good as any other because security prices are correct.

_____11.   The efficient market hypothesis suggests that published reports of financial analysts will help investors that use this information outperform the market.

_____12.   According to the efficient market hypothesis, the most profitable investment strategy requires the continuous buying and selling of stock.

_____13.   Some evidence suggests that investors tend to be overconfident and mistakenly attribute the profits they earn to their trading skills, leading them to trade too often.

_____14.   According to the efficient market hypothesis, stock prices will respond to an announcement only when the information being announced is new and unexpected.

_____15.   The existence of stock market bubbles proves that people are irrational, and thus the theory of rational expectations is incorrect.

MULTIPLE-CHOICE QUESTIONS

1. Using the one-period model of stock price determination, at what price should a stock sell for if the required return on equity investments is 8%, the stock pays a dividend of $0.50 next year, and the stock is expected to sell next year for $30?
   a. $27.78
   b. $28.24
   c. $30
   d. $30.50

2. According to the Gordon growth model of stock price determination, at what price should a stock sell for if the required return on equity investments is 12%, the stock will pay a dividend of $1.80 next year, and dividends are expected to grow at a constant rate of 3%?
   a. $12
   b. $15
   c. $18
   d. $20
   e. A price cannot be calculated because the future selling price of the stock is unknown.

3. If a company called Advanced Technologies has yet to pay a dividend on its stock, the generalized dividend model predicts that the company's stock may still have value because
   a. the required return on investment for high technology companies is zero.
   b. all companies are legally required to pay dividends within ten years of the initial public offering of stock.
   c. people expect Advanced Technologies to pay dividends in the future.
   d. all companies that have any physical assets have value.

4. According to the Gordon growth model of stock price determination, other things being the same, if the required return on equity investment were to rise, stock prices should
   a. rise.
   b. fall.
   c. be unaffected.
   d. rise or fall because stock prices are unpredictable.

5. Which of the following is true regarding the pricing of assets?
   a. The price is set by the buyer willing to pay the highest price.
   b. The price is set by the buyer who can take best advantage of the asset.
   c. Other things being the same, the price is set by buyers with the best information because the reduced uncertainty allows them to discount cash flows at a lower rate.
   d. All of the above are correct.
   e. None of the above is correct.

6. Suppose that the Fed engages in an expansionary monetary policy, which reduces interest rates. Which of the following statements best describes the impact of this event on the stock market?
    a. There will be a decrease in the required rate of return on equities, an increase in the growth rate on dividends, and stock prices will rise.
    b. There will be an increase in the required rate of return on equities, a decrease in the growth rate on dividends, and stock prices will fall.
    c. There will be a decrease in the required rate of return on equities, a decrease in the growth rate on dividends, and stock prices will fall.
    d. There will be an increase in the required rate of return on equities, a decrease in the growth rate on dividends, and stock prices will rise.

7. The efficient market hypothesis is an application of the theory of
    a. adaptive expectations.
    b. perfect expectations.
    c. rational expectations.
    d. efficient expectations.

8. Interest rates have been at 5% for the past four years. The economy goes into a recession causing the Fed chairperson to announce an expansionary monetary policy with an interest rate target of 3%. You forecast interest rates for next year to be 5%. This is an example of a theory called
    a. adaptive expectations.
    b. rational expectations.
    c. fundamental expectations.
    d. forecast expectations.

9. Which of the following statements about rational expectations is true?
    a. Rational expectations are the same as adaptive expectations.
    b. Rational expectations are always accurate.
    c. Rational expectations are identical to optimal forecasts.
    d. Rational expectations theory suggests that forecasts errors of expectations are sizable and can be predicted.
    e. All of the above are true.

10. If stock markets are efficient, then
    a. hot tips are valuable.
    b. a well-diversified mutual fund may be the best investment strategy for the average investor.
    c. investors need the advice of financial analysts in order to make an average return.
    d. the optimal investment strategy is to buy and sell often in order to profit from price swings.

11. An "optimal forecast" is best defined as the
    a. correct forecast.
    b. best guess using all available information.
    c. actual outcome.
    d. best possible forecast using past values of the variable.

12. Which of the following is not true regarding efficient markets.
    a. The prices of securities reflect all available information.
    b. Smart money eliminates unexploited profit opportunities.
    c. Everyone in the market must be well informed.
    d. Hot tips in the stock market are unlikely to bring exceptional returns.

13. Ford Motor Company announces quarterly profits of $200 million. Its stock price immediately falls based on this news. It is likely that
    a. the pre-announcement price reflected higher profit expectations.
    b. expectations are not rational.
    c. markets are not efficient.
    d. stock prices are a biased measures of future corporate earnings.

14. According to the efficient market hypothesis, paying a financial analyst for investment advice
    a. will increase your expected returns substantially.
    b. will not affect on your returns.
    c. may decrease your returns somewhat due to high brokerage commissions.
    d. will have no predictable effect on your returns.

15. If the efficient market hypothesis is true,
    a. stock prices should rise every year.
    b. hot tips help investors earn abnormally high returns.
    c. the advice of financial analysts is useful.
    d. a buy and hold investment strategy is best.

16. Unexploited profit opportunities
    a. are often available.
    b. are quickly eliminated by arbitrage.
    c. help investors generate abnormally high returns in the long run.
    d. none of the above

17. According the efficient market hypothesis, in order to earn abnormally high returns, an investor would need to
    a. read many published reports of stock analysts.
    b. buy mutual funds that have performed exceptionally well in the past.
    c. have better information than other market participants.
    d. all of the above

18. Announcements of already-known information
    a. generate unexploited profit opportunities.
    b. improve forecasts of stock prices.
    c. reduce stock returns.
    d. fail to affect stock prices.

19. Stock market bubbles
    a. can occur even if market participants are rational.
    b. prove that the efficient market hypothesis is incorrect.
    c. occur when stock prices move directly with the fundamental value of the stock.
    d. should be able to be predicted by stock analysts.

20. Evidence from studies in behavioral finance suggest that
    a. investors do not fear losing money so they engage in too much short selling.
    b. investors are overconfident so they buy and sell too often.
    c, investment fads cause stock prices to be undervalued most of the time.
    d. all of the above

Solutions

Terms and Definitions

_7_ adaptive expectations

_3_ bubble

_10_ cash flows

_4_ dividends

_1_ efficient market hypothesis

_13_ Gordon growth model

_8_ market fundamentals

_12_ optimal forecast

_9_ rational expectations

_11_ stockholders

_6_ unexploited profit opportunity

_5_ short sales

_2_ arbitrage

Practice Problems

1. a. $P = \$1/1.09 + \$17.50/1.09 = \$18.50/1.09$
         $= \$16.97$

    b. $P = \$1/(9\% - 3\%) = \$1/0.06 = \$16.67$

    c. $P = \$1/(7\% - 3\%) = \$1/0.04 = \$25.00$

    d. $P = \$1/(7\% - 4\%) = \$1/0.03 = \$33.33$

    e.   A reduction in the required return on equities or an increase in the growth rate of dividends.

    f.   Interest rates on bonds would fall causing investors to accept lower returns in the stock market (k_e would fall). The economy would grow more quickly causing the growth rate of dividends to rise (g would rise). Stock prices would rise.

2. a.   The price falls. Even though profits appear high, the stock price had fully reflected the greater expected profits, so this was bad news.

    b.   The price stays the same (if no other events take place). Expectations were realized. The stock price had fully reflected the correct profits, so the announcement was not news.

    c.   The price rises. It is not necessary that everyone in a financial market be well informed for unexploited profit opportunities to be eliminated. Smart money can move the market.

d.   The price could rise or fall because stock prices have incorporated all available public information.

e.   The price could rise or fall because the current price is the best guess of the true value of the stock.

f.   The price could rise or fall because regular patterns will be acted upon to remove the unexploited profit opportunities.

g.   There should be no impact on the stock market because the Fed Chairman's comments are already fully reflected in the stock prices.

Short-Answer Questions

1. Bill, because assets go to the person who values them the most. The price will exceed $15 and could range up to $20. The price is set by the one that values the asset the most, and that person will bid something greater than the next highest bidder.

2. More. The individual with superior information and certainty will discount the future cash flows at a lower interest rate, increasing the valuation of the stock.

3. No. Forecasts will be accurate on average, but unpredictable events will cause the actual event to randomly deviate from the optimal forecast.

4. No. If an event makes the average value of a random variable permanently larger, adaptive expectations will fail to fully adjust and will under-predict the variable, making forecast errors non-zero and predictable.

5. Yes. If an event makes the average value of a random variable permanently larger, rational expectations will fully reflect the new information, making forecast errors zero on average, and unpredictable.

6. Yes. If the price is below the optimal forecast, the return to the stock will exceed the equilibrium return. Smart money will engage in arbitrage, buying the stock and causing the price to increase until the optimal forecast of the return equals the equilibrium return. The unexploited profit opportunity is eliminated.

7. Since there are no unexploited profit opportunities and the price reflects

fundamental value, one stock is as good another. Buy and hold a diversified set of stocks to generate the average market return and avoid excessive brokerage commissions.

8. No. If stock prices reflect all publicly available information, then no unexploited profit opportunities exist.

9. Yes. Rational people may hold an asset whose price exceeds its fundamental value because they believe someone else will pay a higher price in the future.

10. Use a "buy and hold" strategy to generate an average market return at low cost.

Critical Thinking

1. No. If markets are efficient, the current price of the stock incorporates all available information. Since information about the storm is public, the price of the stock will already have risen before you can buy it.

2. Yes. Since the information is not publicly available, it will not be incorporated into the price. You can buy at the low price and make abnormally high returns as the price appreciates.

3. The price will rise, and the returns will return to the equilibrium return. Abnormally high returns cannot be maintained in the long run. The behavior of smart money eliminates the unexploited profit opportunity.

True/False Questions

1. T
2. F
3. T
4. T
5. F
6. F
7. F
8. T
9. F
10. T
11. F
12. F
13. T
14. T
15. F

Multiple-Choice Questions

1. b
2. d
3. c
4. b
5. d
6. a
7. c
8. a
9. c
10. b
11. b
12. c
13. a
14. c
15. d
16. b
17. c
18. d
19. a
20. b

8 An Economic Analysis of Financial Structure

Chapter Review

PREVIEW

The financial structure is designed to promote economic efficiency. The efficiency of the financial system affects the performance of the macroeconomy.

BASIC FACTS ABOUT FINANCIAL STRUCTURE THROUGHOUT THE WORLD

There are eight basic facts about the financial structure that this chapter will explain.

- *Stocks are not the most important source of external financing for businesses.* In the United States, only 11% of external financing comes from stock. In other developed countries it is much less.

- *Issuing marketable debt and equity securities is not the primary way in which businesses finance their operations.* Stocks and bonds combined only add up to 43% of the external source of funds to U.S. businesses, even less in other countries.

- *Indirect finance, which involves the activities of financial intermediaries, is many times more important than direct finance, in which businesses raise funds directly from lenders in financial markets.* Since most of the newly issued securities of firms are sold to financial intermediaries, less than 10% of external funding is truly direct finance.

- *Financial intermediaries, particularly banks, are the most important source of external funds used to finance businesses.* While this is true for the United States, it is even more the case in developing nations.

- *The financial system is among the most heavily regulated sectors of the economy.* Regulations promote the provision of information and stability of the system.

- *Only large, well-established corporations have easy access to securities market to finance their activities.* Small firms obtain their funding from banks.

- *Collateral is a prevalent feature of debt contracts for both households and businesses.* Collateralized debt, known as *secured debt*, requires the borrower to pledge an asset to the lender to guarantee payment of the debt.

- Debt contracts typically are extremely complicated legal documents that place substantial restrictions on the behavior of the borrower. Loan contracts usually contain restrictive covenants that restrict the activities in which the borrower can engage.

Understanding transaction costs and information costs will help explain the eight facts above.

TRANSACTION COSTS

People with only a small amount to loan cannot lend through the financial markets because the brokerage fees are too large and the denominations of issues may be too large. To lower transaction costs, mutual funds take advantage of *economies of scale* by combining many small savers' funds and buying a widely diversified portfolio. Financial intermediaries also gain *expertise* in carrying out customer transactions, which reduces transaction costs further. This cost reduction allows money market mutual funds to provide *liquidity services*.

ASYMMETRIC INFORMATION: ADVERSE SELECTION AND MORAL HAZARD

Asymmetric information is when each party to a transaction has unequal knowledge about the other party. This leads to two problems: *adverse selection* before the transaction, and *moral hazard* after the transaction. Adverse selection occurs when bad credit risks are the ones who most desire to borrow. Moral hazard occurs when borrowers engage in activities that are undesirable from the lender's point of view. The analysis of how asymmetric information affects economic behavior is known as *agency theory*.

THE LEMONS PROBLEM: HOW ADVERSE SELECTION INFLUENCES FINANCIAL STRUCTURE

If a buyer can't determine if a product for sale is a lemon, he will pay only a low value. Sellers of good products won't want to sell at the lower price. The market becomes small and inefficient at moving goods from sellers to buyers. In financial markets, the adverse selection problem suggests that risky firms benefit more from borrowing. If lenders can't distinguish between good and bad firms, they will pay only low prices for securities (that is, charge high interest rates). Good firms won't bother to sell securities at the low price, so the market is small and inefficient. This is a reason why stocks and bonds are not the primary source of financing for businesses.

There are tools to help reduce the asymmetric information problem that caused the lemons problem. These tools help lenders distinguish good firms from bad.

- *Private production and sale of information.* Standard and Poor's, Moody's, and Value Line gather information and sell it. However, the *free-rider problem* (those not paying for the information still benefit from it) reduces the production of private information.

- *Government regulation to increase information.* The Securities and Exchange Commission (SEC) requires firms to have independent audits, use standard accounting principles, and disclose information about sales, assets, and earnings. Thus, the financial system is heavily regulated. This reduces the asymmetric information problem, but does not eliminate it.

- *Financial intermediation.* Since it is so hard for individuals to acquire enough information to make completely informed loans, most people lend to financial intermediaries, such as a bank, who then lend to the ultimate borrower. The bank becomes an expert in sorting good credit risks from bad. There is no free-rider problem because the bank makes private, nontraded loans rather than buying securities. The larger and more established the firm, the more likely it is that they will issue securities rather than borrow from an intermediary.

- *Collateral and net worth. Collateral* is property promised to the lender if the borrower defaults, which reduces the consequences to the lender of a default. *Net worth,* or equity capital, is the difference between a firm's assets and liabilities. Large net worth lowers the probability of default, and acts as collateral in the event of default.

HOW MORAL HAZARD AFFECTS THE CHOICE BETWEEN DEBT AND EQUITY CONTRACTS

The *principal-agent problem* causes a particular type of moral hazard in equity contracts. Managers (agents) act in their own interests rather than the interests of the stockholders (principals). The following are tools that help solve the principal-agent problem.

- *Production of information: monitoring.* Stockholders can engage in *costly state verification,* which is the monitoring of the firm through auditing and observing management. It is expensive and suffers from the free-rider problem.

- *Government regulation to increase information.* Governments impose standard accounting principles and punish fraud.

- *Financial intermediation.* Venture capital firms pool resources of their partners and help entrepreneurs start new businesses. In exchange they receive equity and membership on the board of directors, which provides lower-cost verification activities.

- *Debt contracts.* Since a lender receives a fixed amount of interest as opposed to a portion of the profits, the principal-agent problem is much smaller with debt finance when compared to equity finance. This explains why debt contracts are more prevalent than equity contracts.

HOW MORAL HAZARD INFLUENCES FINANCIAL STRUCTURE IN DEBT MARKETS

Although debt contracts suffer from moral hazard less than equity contracts, there is still an incentive for the borrower to behave in a more risky fashion than the lender wants. The following tools help solve the moral hazard problem in debt contracts by making the contracts *incentive compatible*.

- *Net worth and collateral.* When borrowers have more to lose, moral hazard is reduced.

- *Monitoring and enforcement of restrictive covenants.* Covenants can discourage undesirable behavior (avoid risky behavior), encourage desirable behavior (require life insurance for the borrower), keep collateral valuable, and provide information (periodic accounting reports).

- *Financial intermediation.* Monitoring and restrictive covenants still suffer from the free-rider problem. Financial intermediaries make private loans that don't have this problem, which explains why financial intermediaries are predominate.

CONFLICTS OF INTEREST

Financial institutions achieve economies of scope by offering many services that utilize the same information resource. Conflicts of interest occur, however, when financial service providers serve multiple interests and misuse or conceal information needed for funds to be channeled to those with productive investment opportunities. Three major types of financial services suffer from conflicts of interest, causing firms to distort information and reduce efficiency.

- *Underwriting and research in investment banking:* An investment bank serves the firm for whom it is issuing the securities and the investors to whom it sells the securities. Issuers benefit from optimist research while investors want unbiased research. If revenue from underwriting exceeds brokerage commissions, the information about the firm may be overly favorable. *Spinning* occurs when investment banks allocate profitable *initial public offerings* to executives of other companies to gain their investment banking business.

- *Auditing and consulting in accounting firms:* Accounting firms offer auditing services and *management advisory services*—advice on taxes, accounting or management information systems, and business strategies. Auditors feel pressure to make favorable reports to avoid losing management advisory services business, to avoid criticizing the management advice given to the client from the nonauditing portion of the accounting firm, and to retain the clients auditing business.

- *Credit assessment and consulting in credit-rating agencies:* Since firms pay to have their debt rated, credit-rating agencies have an incentive to provide a favorable rating while investors and regulators want an impartial rating. Also, there is pressure for credit-rating agencies to provide favorable ratings because they wish to secure consulting contracts to advise firms on the structure of debt issues.

Two major policy measures have been implemented to reduce conflicts of interest: the Sarbanes-Oxley Act of 2002 and the Global Legal Settlement of 2002 against the ten largest investment banks.

Helpful Hints

1. Transaction costs and information costs explain the proportion of external finance done through stocks, bonds, and intermediation. High transaction costs suggest that only large borrowers and lenders use the direct financial markets, so most people and firms use intermediaries. Information costs due to adverse selection and moral hazard further explain why most external finance is through intermediaries. Information costs also explain why most of the remaining direct finance is done with debt rather than equity.

2. Markets are efficient when all mutually beneficial transactions take place. Therefore, markets become inefficient when there are impediments to trade that reduce the number of participants in the market. In the case of the financial markets, transaction costs and information costs reduce the amount of participants in the direct finance markets, reducing the efficiency of the direct finance markets and providing an opportunity for financial intermediaries to improve efficiency.

Terms and Definitions

Choose a definition for each key term.

Key Terms:

_____agency theory

_____collateral

_____economies of scale

_____economies of scope

_____free-rider problem

_____incentive-compatible

_____principle-agent problem

_____restrictive covenants

_____secured debt

_____unsecured debt

_____venture capital firm

Definitions:

1. Debt guaranteed by collateral

2. The reduction in transaction costs per dollar of transaction as the size of transactions increases

3. The ability to use one resource to provide many different products and services

4. Property that is pledged to the lender to guarantee payment in the event that the borrower is unable to make debt payments

5. A moral hazard problem that occurs when managers act in their own interest rather than in the interests of the owners due to having different sets of incentives

6. A financial intermediary that pools the resources of its partners and uses the funds to help entrepreneurs start up new businesses

7. The problem that arises when people who do not pay for information take advantage of the information that others have paid for

8. Provisions that restrict and specify certain activities that a borrower can engage in

9. The analysis of how asymmetric information problems affect economic behavior

10. Debt not guaranteed by collateral

11. Having the incentives of both parties to a contract in alignment

Problems and Short-Answer Questions

PRACTICE PROBLEMS

1. Firms can seek funds through bank and nonbank loans (added together), bonds, and stock. Answer the following questions regarding the preferred method of external finance chosen in different countries.
   a. For the United States, rank the sources of funds from most utilized to least.

   _____

   _____

   b. Rank the sources of funds from most utilized to least for other industrialized countries and for developing countries.

   _____

   _____

   c. Compare the sources of funds for U.S. firms to the sources of funds for firms from other industrialized and developing countries. Explain the similarities and differences.

   _____

   _____

   _____

   _____

2. The following questions refer to the adverse selection problem generated by asymmetric information known as the "lemons problem."
   a. In general, what is the "lemons problem?"

   _____

   _____

   _____

b. What is the lemons problem as it applies to the direct financial markets?

_____

_____

_____

c. What tools have been developed to reduce the lemons problem in direct financial markets?

_____

_____

_____

d. Have these tools completely solved the problem? Explain.

_____

_____

_____

3. The following questions are based on the principal-agent problem.
    a. What is the principal-agent problem?

_____

_____

b. What tools have been developed to reduce the principal-agent problem in direct financial markets?

_____

_____

_____

_____

c. Have these tools completely solved the problem? Explain.

_____

_____

_____

4. Which of the following, transaction costs, adverse selection, or moral hazard, help explain the eight facts about financial structure below? Explain.

   a. Stocks are not the most important source of finance for businesses.

   _____

   _____

   b. Issuing marketable securities is not the primary way businesses finance their operations.

   _____

   _____

   c. Indirect finance is many times more important than direct finance.

   _____

   _____

   d. Financial intermediaries, particularly banks, are the most important source of external funds to business.

   _____

   _____

   e. The financial system is heavily regulated.

   _____

   _____

   f. Only large, well-established corporations have access to securities markets to finance their activities.

   _____

   _____

   g. Collateral is a prevalent feature of debt contracts.

   _____

   _____

   h. Debt contracts are complicated documents often placing restrictions on the behavior of borrowers.

   _____

   _____

5. The following questions address conflicts of interest.
    a. What two major policy measures have been implemented to reduce conflicts of interest?

    _____

    _____

    b. What measures are in the Sarbanes-Oxley Act to improve the quality of information provided to the financial markets?

    _____

    _____

    c. Does separating a business's functions always improve the quality of information provided to the market? Why or why not?

    _____

    _____

SHORT-ANSWER QUESTIONS

1. Why are transaction costs high for small savers/lenders?

    _____

    _____

2. How are financial intermediaries able to lower transaction costs?

    _____

    _____

3. How does the free-rider problem reduce efficiency in financial markets?

    _____

    _____

    _____

    _____

4. Is adverse selection a problem before or after a loan transaction? Is moral hazard a problem before or after a loan transaction? Explain each.

_____

_____

_____

5. How does government regulation help reduce adverse selection in stock and bond markets?

_____

_____

6. Which are more important sources of external funds to businesses, stocks and bonds or banks? Are banks becoming more or less important over time? Why?

_____

_____

7. When lenders require a borrower to have a high net worth and collateral, are they trying to reduce adverse selection or moral hazard or both? Explain.

_____

_____

8. Why do debt contracts have fewer principal-agent problems than equity contracts?

_____

_____

9. What are the types of restrictive covenants in a debt contract?

_____

_____

_____

10. What three financial services suffer the most from conflicts of interest? Explain.

_____

_____

_____

Critical Thinking

Suppose that you have worked all summer and accumulated $5000. You would like to save it, but you might need it one year from this fall for tuition payments. Your friends all have ideas about where you should save it.

1. One friend says, "Lend it to my brother. He's starting a new restaurant that is sure to make big profits." Is this a good choice? Explain.

    _____

    _____

    _____

2. Another friend says, "You should buy stocks and bonds. The market has been doing very well lately. Use my broker. Here's his card." Is this a good choice? Explain.

    _____

    _____

    _____

3. Yet another friend says, "Given your small amount of funds and your need to be liquid, you should buy either a money market mutual fund or simply deposit it in a bank. Is this a good choice? Explain.

    _____

    _____

    _____

Self-Test

TRUE/FALSE QUESTIONS

_____1. Stocks are the most important source of external funds for businesses in the United States.

_____2. In the United States, bonds are a more important source of external funds than stocks.

_____3. Although banks are the most important source of external funds to businesses worldwide, their role is shrinking slightly over time.

_____4. Over 90% of American households own securities.

_____5. Financial intermediaries, such as mutual funds, take advantage of economies of scale to reduce transaction costs by combining many small savers funds and buying a diversified portfolio.

_____6. Banks reduce the free-rider problem in information production because they make private nontraded loans rather than purchasing securities that are traded in financial markets.

_____7. Adverse selection occurs when borrowers use borrowed funds in a manner that lenders find objectionable.

_____8. Bonds create a greater moral hazard problem than stocks.

_____9. The adverse selection problem in financial markets is eliminated by the private production and sale of information about borrowers by companies such as Standard and Poor's, Moody's, and Value Line.

_____10. When lenders cannot sort good borrowers from bad ones, they lend less and the financial markets become inefficient.

_____11. The principal-agent problem occurs when managers act in their own interests rather than the interests of stockholders.

_____12. Firms with relatively low net worth and little collateral are more likely to default on their loans.

_____13. To make a debt contract more incentive compatible, lenders may include restrictive covenants requiring the borrower to keep the collateral valuable.

_____14. The Sarbanes-Oxley Act of 2002 reduced conflicts of interest in investment banking by fining the ten largest investment banks $1.4 billion for past exploitation of their conflicts of interest.

_____15. When financial institutions attempt to achieve economies of scope, their operations tend to become subject to conflicts of interest.

MULTIPLE-CHOICE QUESTIONS

1. The largest source of external finance for U.S. businesses is
   a. stocks.
   b. bonds.
   c. bank and nonbank loans.
   d. venture capital firms.

2. Which of the following statements is true?
   a. Firms raise more funds with bonds than with bank loans.
   b. Firms raise more funds with bonds than with stocks.
   c. Stocks and bonds are the largest source of external funds to businesses.
   d. Direct finance is much more important than indirect finance as a source of external funds to businesses.

3. In which country do firms use direct finance to the greatest degree when compared to the firms of the other countries?
    a. United States
    b. Germany
    c. Japan
    d. Canada

4. Small savers/lenders use intermediaries as opposed to direct lending because intermediaries
    a. reduce transaction costs of the saver.
    b. increase diversification of the saver.
    c. reduce risk of the saver.
    d. do all of the above.

5. Large, well-known companies are more likely than small companies to acquire funds through
    a. direct finance.
    b. banks.
    c. issuing collateral.
    d. nonbank financial intermediaries.

6. Which of the following demonstrates adverse selection?
    a. A borrower takes the funds from a loan to a casino and gambles.
    b. A corporate officer uses the funds from the sale of securities to buy art for his office.
    c. A scientist applies for a loan to research a possible cure for cancer with a low probability of success but a high payoff if successful.
    d. all of the above

7. Your parents loan you money to pay your tuition and you use the money to play on-line poker instead. This is an example of
    a. the free-rider problem.
    b. moral hazard.
    c. adverse selection.
    d. financial intermediation.

8. The "lemons problem" is a term used to describe the
    a. free-rider problem in financial markets.
    b. principal-agent problem in financial markets.
    c. moral hazard problem in financial markets.
    d. adverse selection problem in financial markets.

9. When bad credit risks have the most to gain from a loan so they most actively seek a loan, we have a demonstration of
    a. the free-rider problem.
    b. moral hazard.
    c. adverse selection.
    d. financial intermediation.

10. Banks reduce the free-rider problem in information production by
    a. charging others for information about the financial condition of potential borrowers.
    b. buying tradable securities with their depositors funds.
    c. buying information from firms that specialize in gathering information about smaller borrowers, such as Standard and Poor's and Moody's.
    d. making private nontraded loans so other lenders cannot benefit from the information they have collected about the borrower.

11. Which of the following is <u>not</u> a tool used to reduce adverse selection in the financial markets?
    a. Monitoring and enforcement of restrictive covenants.
    b. Government regulation to increase information about borrowers.
    c. Private production and sale of information about borrowers.
    d. Requiring collateral and a high net worth from the borrower.
    e. Financial intermediation to more efficiently produce information on borrowers.

12. The principal-agent problem arises mainly because
    a. principals find it difficult and costly to monitor agents' activities.
    b. agents' incentives are not always compatible with those of the principals.
    c. principals have incentives to free-ride off the monitoring expenditures of other principals.
    d. all of the above

13. The principal-agent problem causes
    a. the collateral problem.
    b. moral hazard.
    c. adverse selection.
    d. the lemons problem.

14. Which of the following is <u>not</u> a tool used to reduce the principal-agent problem?
    a. Stockholders engage in costly state verification by auditing and observing management.
    b. Venture capital firms provide funds to new firms in exchange for equity and membership on the board of directors.
    c. Firms issue equity instead of debt because the principal-agent problem is smaller with equity.
    d. Governments regulate firms by imposing standard accounting principles and by punishing fraud.

15. Restrictive covenants
    a. reduce adverse selection.
    b. solve the lemons problem.
    c. make debt contracts more incentive compatible.
    d. are most common in equity contracts.

16. You go into an electronics store to buy a big-screen television. A salesperson rudely tells you that he's too busy to help you now. He says you'll just have to wait. Then you watch him get a cup of coffee and take his break. You've just seen a demonstration of
    a. the principal-agent problem.
    b. adverse selection.
    c. the lemons problem.
    d. how collateral reduces moral hazard.

17. Which of the following is <u>not</u> an example of a restrictive covenant in a debt contract?
    a. requiring borrowers to keep their collateral valuable
    b. requiring borrowers to have life insurance
    c. requiring borrowers to provide periodic accounting reports
    d. requiring borrowers to pay a high interest rate

18. Which of the following reduces both adverse selection and moral hazard in a loan arrangement?
    a. requiring that the borrower provide collateral
    b. requiring that the borrower have high net worth
    c. having the borrower use an intermediary, such as a bank, for the loan
    d. all of the above

19. When an investment bank uses information it developed about a firm's credit risk to help market the firm's securities, and then its brokers use the same information to advise investors to whom it sells the securities, we have seen an example of an investment bank exploiting economies of
    a. scale.
    b. scope.
    c. finance.
    d. banking.

20. Which of the following areas is <u>not</u> generally recognized to generate excessive conflicts of interest?
    a. commercial banking
    b. credit assessment and consulting in credit-rating agencies
    c. underwriting and research in investment banking
    d. auditing and consulting in accounting firms

Solutions

Terms and Definitions

 9 agency theory

 4 collateral

 2 economies of scale

 3 economies of scope

 7 free-rider problem

11 incentive-compatible

 5 principle-agent problem

 8 restrictive covenants

 1 secured debt

10 unsecured debt

 6 venture capital firm

Practice Problems

1. a. Bank and nonbank loans (together) 56%, bonds 32%, stocks 11%.

    b. Bank and nonbank loans (together) are greatest, followed by bonds and stocks for other industrialized and developing countries.

    c. All countries utilize bank and nonbank loans the most, followed by bonds, and then stocks. The United States relies on direct finance more than other countries do. Developing countries lack the institutions to support sophisticated direct financial markets, so they rely on bank and nonbank loans more.

2. a. Sellers know more about the quality of the product than buyers. Buyers must assume the product may be a lemon (low quality) and bid a low price. At that price, only low-quality products will be offered for sale. The market is too small and is inefficient.

    b. Borrowers know more about the probability of default than lenders. If lenders can't distinguish good firms from bad, lenders bid low prices for securities (charge high interest rates). At the low price, only risky borrowers sell securities. The market is too small and is inefficient.

    c. Private firms produce and sell information; government regulates firms, requiring them to increase information to lenders; lenders require borrowers to pledge collateral against a loan and have

high net worth; financial intermediaries use their expertise to sort good firms from bad.

    d. No. The fact that financial intermediaries are larger than direct finance suggests that the adverse selection problems in direct finance have not been completely solved.

3. a. Managers act in their own interests instead of the interests of stockholders.

    b. Stockholders can produce information through audits and by monitoring management; governments can regulate to increase information to stockholders by requiring standardized accounting; funds can be supplied through debt contracts as opposed to equity contracts; financial intermediaries, such as venture capital firms, can monitor at a lower cost with no free-rider problem.

    c. No. The fact that financial intermediaries are larger than direct finance suggests that the principle-agent problems in direct finance have not been completely solved.

4. a. Adverse selection, moral hazard. Stocks suffer from the lemons problem and costly state verification so stocks are not the most important source of funding.

    b. Adverse selection: stocks and bonds suffer from the lemons problem so they are not the most important source of funding.

    c. Transaction costs, adverse selection, moral hazard. Indirect finance reduces transaction costs for small lenders and efficiently collects information to reduce adverse selection and moral hazard, while avoiding the free-rider problem.

    d. Adverse selection, moral hazard. Banks make nontraded loans so the information they collect to reduce both adverse selection and moral hazard is less subject to the free-rider problem.

    e. Adverse selection, moral hazard. Governments regulate to increase information to lenders both before the loan and after.

    f. Adverse selection. More information is known about large, well-known companies, so they have access to direct finance.

g. Adverse selection. Lenders select borrowers that provide collateral, which lowers the lender's risk.

h. Moral hazard. Debt contracts require complicated restrictive covenants to lower moral hazard.

5. a. Sarbanes-Oxley Act of 2002 and the Global Legal Settlement of 2002.

b. The CEO and CFO must certify the company's financial statements, and auditors must be truly independent.

c. No. The loss of economies of scope could more than offset the gains from a reduction in conflicts of interest.

Short-Answer Questions

1. Brokerage fees are large, and the denominations of the instruments are too large.

2. They take advantage of economies of scale by combining the funds of many small savers, and they gain expertise in carrying out repetitious transactions.

3. Due to the problems of adverse selection and moral hazard, lenders need costly information about borrowers. Individual lenders don't want to pay for gathering the information if they can use other's information for free, so little information is produced and too little is loaned.

4. Before. After. Adverse selection occurs when risky borrowers who have the most to gain are the ones who want to borrow. Moral hazard occurs when borrowers use the money they borrowed in a manner that lenders would consider undesirable.

5. The SEC requires firms to have independent audits, use standard accounting, and report information on sales, assets, and earnings.

6. Banks. Less important over time because information is getting easier to acquire, so direct finance should continue to grow.

7. Both. Both help banks select a borrower and both help make contracts incentive compatible because borrowers have more to lose.

8. The problem is smaller because debt holders receive a fixed payment of interest regardless of the performance of the firm while stockholders share in the profits.

9. Covenants can: Discourage bad behavior such as taking on risky investments, encourage good behavior such as buying insurance, require that collateral be kept valuable, and provide information in the form of quarterly reports.

10. Underwriting and research in investment banking, auditing and consulting in accounting firms, and credit assessment and consulting in credit-rating agencies. Underwriters want favorable research regarding issuing corporations while investors want unbiased research. Auditors may provide favorable audits to gain consulting business, to avoid criticizing advice previously given by their own consultants, and to retain auditing business. Credit-rating agencies want to provide favorable ratings of firms to get the firm's debt rating business and consulting business, so the ratings may not be unbiased.

Critical Thinking

1. The loan would have high transaction costs because a one-of-a-kind contract would have to be written. Your investment would not be diversified or liquid. It is a poor choice.

2. Your funds are so few and the denominations so large that you cannot buy a diversified portfolio. Transaction costs would be high due to brokerage fees. The funds would not be liquid. It is a poor choice.

3. Either choice would be diversified. Due to economies of scale and expertise of the intermediary, transaction costs are so low that the intermediary can offer liquidity services. Good choice.

True/False Questions

1. F
2. T
3. T
4. F
5. T
6. T
7. F
8. F
9. F
10. T
11. T
12. T

13. T
14. F
15. T

Multiple-Choice Questions

1. c
2. b
3. a
4. d
5. a
6. c
7. b
8. d

9. c
10. d
11. a
12. d
13. b
14. c
15. c
16. a
17. d
18. d
19. b
20. a

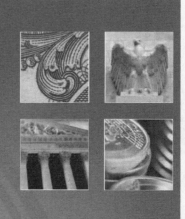

9 Financial Crises and the Subprime Meltdown

Chapter Review

PREVIEW

Financial crises are major disruptions in financial markets characterized by a decline in asset prices and the failure of many firms. This chapter explains why the most recent financial crisis occurred, why these crises are so prevalent, and why these crises tend to be followed by severe economic contractions.

FACTORS CAUSING FINANCIAL CRISES

A financial crisis occurs when a disruption in the financial system causes an increase in asymmetric information, which increases adverse selection and moral hazard problems. As a result, financial markets fail to channel funds efficiently from savers to productive investment opportunities, causing a reduction in lending and a severe contraction in economic activity. Six categories of factors cause financial crises.

- Asset market effects on balance sheets: Events that reduce the net worth of borrowing firms effectively reduce borrowing firms' collateral, increasing moral hazard and adverse selection because borrowing firms have less to lose. Things that reduce the net worth of the borrowing firm include (1) a decline in the stock market that reduces the firm's value; (2) an unanticipated decline in the price level that raises the real burden of the firm's debt payments when debt payments are fixed in nominal terms; (3) an unanticipated decline in the value of the domestic currency that raises the real burden of the firm's debt payments when debt payments are denominated in a foreign currency; and (4) asset write-downs that reduce the value of assets on the borrowing firm's balance sheet.

- Deterioration in financial institutions' balance sheets: A deterioration of a financial institution's balance sheet reduces its capital and reduces its ability to lend.

- Banking crisis: A severe deterioration in a financial institution's balance sheet will cause it to fail. Due to asymmetric information problems, depositors may remove their deposits from both risky and sound banks, causing even some sound banks to fail. A bank panic occurs when many banks fail simultaneously, which reduces lending and raises interest rates.

- Increases in uncertainty: An increase in uncertainty makes it more difficult for lenders to screen good credit risks from bad ones, which reduces lending.

- Increases in interest rates: At higher interest rates, good credit risks no longer wish to borrow, while bad credit risks are still willing to borrow, increasing the adverse selection problem and reducing lending. In addition, an increase in interest rates raises interest payments and reduces a firm's cash flow, causing it to use more borrowed funds rather than internal funds for expansion. But due to information asymmetry, lenders will not lend as much as the firm would have had internally at a lower interest rate.

- Government fiscal imbalances: If private investors fear that the government will default on its debt, private investors won't purchase government bonds and private banks may be forced to buy them. If the value of these bonds decreases, it will reduce bank capital, and bank lending will decrease. Fear of a government default may also cause a reduction in the domestic currency's value, leading to an increase in adverse selection and moral hazard problems described above.

DYNAMICS OF PAST U.S. FINANCIAL CRISES

Past financial crises in the United States have progressed in two or three stages.

Stage one: Initiation of financial crisis. A financial crisis can begin in several ways.

- A financial crisis often begins with financial liberalization, the elimination of restrictions on financial markets and institutions, or when there are financial innovations that avoid regulation. Often a credit boom results and financial firms take on excessive risk. To avoid a bank panic, governments often provide a safety net for depositors. The safety net, unfortunately, increases moral hazard, causing banks to take on even more risk. Government regulators usually lack the resources and expertise to control the risk-taking. Loan losses reduce bank capital, causing a reduction in bank lending, known as deleveraging. Depositors withdraw their funds, further reducing bank lending, and economic activity contracts.

- An asset-price bubble, caused by a credit boom, causes asset prices to rise above their fundamental values. When the bubble bursts, the net worth of borrowers is reduced, increasing asymmetric information and reducing lending. The deterioration of balance sheets of financial institutions also reduces lending. This happened in the 1990s and again with the recent housing price bubble.

- In the 19th century, spikes in interest rates caused an increase in adverse selection and moral hazard, reducing the number of credit worthy borrowers willing to borrow at the high rates.

- An increase in uncertainty due to the failure of a major financial firm or a stock market crash. The reduction in information increases adverse selection and moral hazard, reducing lending.

Stage two: Banking crisis. Due to the uncertainty about their banks' health, depositors begin to withdraw funds from banks, causing a bank panic. This increases adverse selection and moral hazard, reducing bank lending. Bank panics are a feature of all U.S. financial crises in the last 200 years.

Stage three: Debt deflation. If the resulting economic downturn leads to a sharp reduction in prices, debt deflation can result. This occurs when a substantial unanticipated decline in the price level increases firms' burden of indebtedness. This can reduce economic activity for a long time. The most significant case of debt deflation in U.S. history was the Great Depression.

THE SUBPRIME FINANCIAL CRISIS OF 2007–2008

Mismanagement of financial innovation in the subprime residential mortgage market and a bursting of a housing price bubble initiated the financial crisis of 2007–2008.

- In recent times, borrowers with less-than-perfect credit have been able to get mortgages, called subprime mortgages. Other borrowers with higher-than-average default rates could get alt-A mortgages. Through the process of securitization, these mortgages were bundled into standardized securities, called mortgage-backed securities. Further financial engineering generated sophisticated financial products called structured credit products, which are instruments based on the cash flows of underlying assets such as mortgages. Most noteworthy is a collateralized debt obligation (CDO), which paid out the cash flows from different risk subgroups within a subprime mortgage-backed security, with the highest rated group paying first, etc.

- A housing price bubble developed, aided by foreign cash flows and the expansion of subprime mortgage-backed securities. The resulting higher housing prices increased mortgage lending even more because lenders felt secure that borrowers were unlikely to default when their homes have appreciated.

- Agency problems arose because the subprime mortgage market was based on the originate-to-distribute business model. The mortgage originator had little incentive to lend to good credit risks, and risky borrowers had incentives to buy houses in a rising market. Lax regulations didn't require lenders to disclose information about the borrower's ability to repay the loan. Rating agencies were subject to conflicts of interest because they were earning fees from the clients whose mortgage-backed securities they were rating.

- Information problems surfaced because financial engineering had created structured products that were so complicated that they were hard to value correctly.

- The housing price bubble burst. Since lending standards had been weak, and borrowers had made very small down payments and now owed more than the value of the house, defaults rose sharply.

- Although the crisis originated in the United States, the crisis spread globally when European banks suffered losses on U.S. mortgage-backed securities, causing the interbank lending market to freeze up in Europe and the United States.

- Banks' balance sheet deteriorated because, as U.S. housing prices decreased, the value of mortgage-backed securities decreased. Banks had to deleverage (reduce lending). With no one else able to step in to collect information and make loans, the increase in adverse selection and moral hazard reduced loans and economic activity.

- High-profile financial firms failed, including Bear Stearns, Fannie Mae, Freddie Mac, and Lehman Brothers.

- A controversial bailout package for Wall Street was enacted, but the stock market crash accelerated, and unemployment continued to rise.

DYNAMICS OF FINANCIAL CRISES IN EMERGING MARKET ECONOMIES

Emerging market economies are economies in an earlier stage of market development that have recently opened up their markets for goods, services, and capital to the rest of the world. Financial crises in these economies develop along two paths: Mismanagement of financial liberalization/globalization or severe fiscal imbalances.

- Mismanagement of financial liberalization/globalization: Due to weaker financial supervision in emerging market economies, financial liberalization creates an even bigger lending boom in emerging market economies. High risk loans fail, causing a lending crash. The deterioration in banks' balance sheets is even more harmful here because the securities markets are less developed.

- Governments in emerging market economies with a fiscal imbalance often force their banks to buy the government's debt. When the value of the debt decreases, it causes the deterioration of the banks' balance sheets. The instability of the government also adds to uncertainty.

In response to the deterioration in the banks' balance sheets, participants in the foreign exchange markets engage in a speculative attack on the currency, selling the currency and driving its value down. The speculative attack on the domestic currency could also come from a severe fiscal imbalance where investors fear that the government cannot repay its debts.

The decline in the value of the domestic currency causes a sharp rise in the debt burden of firms, which leads to a decline in firms' net worth, causing an increase in adverse selection and moral hazard. In addition, the depreciation of the currency leads to an increase in import prices and an increase in inflation and interest rates, reducing firm's net worth even more. The inability of firm's to repay their debts to the banks and the increase in the value of the banks' foreign-currency denominated deposits causes a banking crisis, even greater adverse selection and moral hazard problems, a reduction in lending, and a severe contraction in economic activity.

The previous discussion helps explain the recent financial crises in Mexico, East Asia, and Argentina.

Helpful Hints

1. Financial crises are associated with financial liberalization or innovation, combined with a government safety net. The unregulated financial liberalization causes a lending boom, and the government safety net exaggerates the problem by making the loans appear to be less risky.

2. At some point in a financial crisis, the lending boom turns into a lending crash. Regardless of the source, in the end, an increase in adverse selection and moral hazard in the credit markets reduces lending to a point that it substantially reduces investment and economic activity and increases unemployment.

Terms and Definitions

Choose a definition for each key term.

Key Terms:

_____asset-price bubble

_____bank panic

_____credit boom

_____debt deflation

_____deleveraging

_____emerging market economies

_____financial crisis

_____mortgage-backed securities

_____originate-to-distribute model

_____securitization

_____subprime mortgages

Definitions:

1. a standardized debt security backed by mortgages

2. a situation in which asset prices are driven well above their fundamental economic values

3. a process in which a substantial unanticipated decline in the price level increases the burden of indebtedness

4. economies at an earlier stage of market development that have recently opened up to the flow of goods, services, and capital from the rest of the world

5. a situation in which financial institutions expand their lending at a rapid pace

6. when deposits are removed from banks causing multiple banks to fail simultaneously

7. the bundling of loans (such as mortgages) into standard debt securities

8. mortgages for borrowers with less-than-stellar credit records

9. when financial institutions cut back on their lending

10. a business model in which a mortgage was originated by a separate party and then distributed to an investor as an underlying asset in a security

11. a major disruption in financial markets characterized by a decline in the prices of assets and the failure of many firms

Problems and Short-Answer Questions

PRACTICE PROBLEMS

1. Explain how each of the following events affects the state of a borrowering firm's balance sheet, and thus how it affects the severity of asymmetric information problems in the financial system.
   a. A decline in the stock market

   _____

   _____

   _____

   b. An unanticipated decline in the price level

   _____

   _____

   _____

   c. An unanticipated decline in the value of the domestic currency

   _____

   _____

   _____

   d. A write-down in the value of assets

   _____

   _____

   _____

2. The following questions address debt deflation.
   a. What is debt deflation?

   _____

   _____

b.   How does debt deflation affect economic activity? Explain.

_____

_____

_____

_____

c.   What event in U.S. history is the greatest example of debt deflation?

_____

d.   How much did prices fall during this period? What was the rate of unemployment during this period?

_____

3.   The following questions address the subprime mortgage crisis.
   a.   What is a subprime mortgage?

_____

   b.   What is a mortgage-backed security?

_____

   c.   Explain the agency problem in the originate-to-distribute business model.

_____

_____

_____

   d.   How did the factors described in *a*, *b*, and *c* combine to create a housing price bubble?

_____

_____

_____

_____

e.   What happens when an asset bubble pops?

_____

_____

_____

_____

SHORT-ANSWER QUESTIONS

1.   Why does an increase in adverse selection and moral hazard reduce aggregate economic activity?

_____

_____

2.   Why do financial crises in emerging market economies tend to be more severe compared to those in developed economies?

_____

_____

_____

_____

3.   How can a government's fiscal imbalance cause a financial crisis?

_____

_____

_____

4.   How can a spike in interest rates cause a financial crisis?

_____

_____

_____

5.   What type of crisis is common to all U.S. financial crises? Why?

_____

_____

6. Why does a financial crisis often begin with financial liberalization or innovation?

_____

_____

7. Does a government safety net increase or decrease adverse selection and moral hazard? Explain.

_____

_____

8. What was the source of the recent subprime financial crisis?

_____

_____

_____

Critical Thinking

You are watching a financial news show on CNN with your roommate. The commentator is discussing the recent subprime financial crisis in the United States. Your roommate says, "I don't know why we are having difficulty figuring out the causes and cures for our financial crisis. There was a financial crisis in Russia in 1998 and in Argentina 2001-2002. Why don't we just study their crises and copy their solutions. All of these financial crises are the same."

1. What is an "emerging market economy?"

_____

_____

2. What was the main source of the financial crises in Russia and Argentina in the late 1990s and early 2000s?

_____

_____

3. What was the main source of the most recent subprime financial crises in the United States?

_____

_____

4. Are the sources of financial crises (and therefore the solutions to financial crises) the same in countries at different levels of development? Explain.

_____

_____

_____

_____

Self-Test

TRUE/FALSE QUESTIONS

_____1. An increase in adverse selection and moral hazard in the credit markets tends to increase bank lending.

_____2. An increase in interest rates tends to drive high risk borrowers from the loan market, reducing adverse selection and moral hazard.

_____3. Financial crises often begin with financial liberalization or innovation.

_____4. An unanticipated decline in the price level raises the real burden of a firm's debt payments when these debt payments are fixed in nominal terms.

_____5. An increase in adverse selection and moral hazard increases the lender's screening and monitoring costs, thereby reducing the amount of loans extended.

_____6. A government safety net in the credit markets that guarantees a borrower's repayment, causes banks to be more conservative in their lending practices, and thus reduces their risk exposure.

_____7. Sooner or later, an asset-price bubble must burst because the price of an asset cannot stay above its fundamental value forever.

_____8. The originate-to-distribute business model reduces agency problems in the mortgage market.

_____9. The securitization of mortgages reduces the risk that the securitized mortgages will default.

_____10. A subprime loan is a loan for which the interest rate is below the prime rate.

_____11. Financial crises in emerging market economies are often more severe than those in more developed economies.

_____12. In an emerging market economy, the concurrent crises of a financial crisis and a currency crisis are often referred to as the "twin crises."

_____13. Events that reduce the net worth of a borrowing firm reduce the firm's capital, effectively reducing the borrowing firm's collateral and increasing adverse selection and moral hazard.

_____14. A reduction in the value of a country's currency improves the condition of domestic firms' balance sheets and reduces the risk of default on loans.

_____15. Bank panics are a feature of all financial crises in emerging market economies, but bank panics have never been associated with a financial crisis in the United States.

MULTIPLE-CHOICE QUESTIONS

1. Borrowers with risky investment projects have the greatest desire to borrow, creating a problem known as
    a. uncertainty.
    b. interest rate risk.
    c. adverse selection.
    d. moral hazard.

2. After a borrower receives a loan, the borrower has an incentive to use the loan in a riskier fashion than specified in the loan contract, creating a problem known as
    a. financial engineering.
    b. deleveraging.
    c. adverse selection.
    d. moral hazard.

3. Which of the following does not cause a reduction in the net worth of the borrowing firm in a loan market?
    a. a decline in the stock market that reduces the value of the firm
    b. an unanticipated increase in the price level that reduces the value of the firm's liabilities
    c. an unanticipated decline in the value of the domestic currency when the firm's debt is denominated in terms of a foreign currency
    d. asset write-downs on the firm's balance sheet

4. Financial crises
    a. are prevalent in all industrial economies.
    b. only occur in emerging market economies.
    c. rarely have an impact on aggregate economic output.
    d. tend to be more severe in financially advanced countries.

5. Which of the following is an example of debt deflation?
    a. A credit boom deflates into a credit crunch.
    b. An unanticipated decrease in the price level increases the burden of indebtedness.
    c. There is a write-down in the value of assets.
    d. An asset-price bubble bursts and deflates.

6. A subprime mortgage is
   a. a loan with a lower-than-prime interest rate.
   b. a securitized loan.
   c. denominated in a foreign currency.
   d. a loan to someone with less-than-excellent credit.

7. The recent subprime financial crisis began with
   a. mismanagement of financial innovations in the subprime residential mortgage market.
   b. a spike in interest rates for subprime borrowers.
   c. an excessive government fiscal imbalance where the government forced banks to buy its subprime bonds.
   d. the bailout of subprime Wall Street firms.

8. Financial crises in emerging market economies tend to be more severe than in financially advanced economies because
   a. there is weaker financial supervision in emerging market economies.
   b. bankers in emerging market economies are less experienced with screening and monitoring for adverse selection and moral hazard.
   c. bank panics are more crippling to an emerging market economy because the financial markets are less developed.
   d. all of the above

9. Securitization is a process by which
   a. deposits are insured by the FDIC against default.
   b. loans are insured against default.
   c. loans are bundled into standardized securities.
   d. securities are rated as investment grade or less-than-investment grade.

10. The main problem with the originate-to-distribute business model for mortgage lending is that
    a. the interest rate is driven so high that borrowers default.
    b. it reduces funds flowing into the mortgage market.
    c. it is subject to a significant principle-agent problem.
    d. it only works efficiently when packaging subprime mortgages.

11. What economic process is believed to have caused the Great Depression to last so long?
    a. debt deflation
    b. securitization
    c. the stock market crash
    d. the bursting of the asset-price bubble

12. Regardless of the original source of the financial crisis, all credit booms end in a credit crash because of
    a. corruption in the mortgage industry.
    b. an increase in adverse selection and moral hazard in the loan market.
    c. massive government deficits.
    d. collateralized debt obligations.

13. Why does a financial crisis ultimately cause a substantial reduction in economic activity?
    a. The government responds to the crisis with excessive regulation.
    b. Only corrupt bankers survive the crisis.
    c. The financial crisis causes a fiscal deficit.
    d. The resulting credit crash severely reduces investment for productive activities.

14. Which of the following is unlikely to cause a reduction in lending?
    a. a decline in the stock market
    b. a bank panic
    c. a decrease in interest rates
    d. an unanticipated decline in the price level

15. In an emerging market economy, what two types of financial crises are often referred to as the "twin crises?"
    a. a banking crisis and a currency crisis
    b. a fiscal crisis and a monetary crisis
    c. an asset crisis and a liability crisis
    d. a lending crisis and a borrowing crisis

16. Which of the following is one of the main sources of a financial crisis in an emerging market economy?
    a. excessive government regulation
    b. a restriction on the extension of credit
    c. severe government fiscal imbalances
    d. all of the above

17. Which of the following has not been a source of past financial crises in the United States?
    a. severe government fiscal imbalances
    b. mismanagement of financial liberalization or innovation
    c. a spike in interest rates
    d. the bursting of an asset-price bubble

18. Deleveraging occurs when banks
    a. increase their lending.
    b. contract their lending.
    c. increase their capital.
    d. reduce the interest rates they charge on loans.

19. Which of the following statements is true when there is an increase in adverse selection and moral hazard in the loan market?
    a. Banks tend to lend more, which generates an asset-price bubble.
    b. Banks tend to reduce interest rates.
    c. Banks tend to reduce lending because fewer firms want to borrow.
    d. Banks tend to reduce lending because they cannot separate good credit risks from bad ones as efficiently.

20. Severe government fiscal imbalances may cause a financial crisis because the fiscal imbalance may cause the government to
    a. increase taxes.
    b. decrease spending.
    c. sell high-risk government securities to domestic banks.
    d. restrict financial innovations.

Solutions

Terms and Definitions

__2__ asset-price bubble

__6__ bank panic

__5__ credit boom

__3__ debt deflation

__9__ deleveraging

__4__ emerging market economies

__11__ financial crisis

__1__ mortgage-backed securities

__10__ originate-to-distribute model

__7__ securitization

__8__ subprime mortgages

Practice Problems

1. a. A decline in the stock market reduces the net worth of a borrowing firm, reducing the collateral pledged against the loan and increasing adverse selection and moral hazard.

    b. A decrease in the price level increases the real burden of a borrowing firm's debt (liabilities), reducing the net worth of a borrowing firm. As in *a* above, a firm has less to lose if it defaults on a loan, increasing adverse selection and moral hazard.

    c. A reduction in the value of the domestic currency raises the real burden of a borrowing firm's debt payments when the debt is denominated in a foreign currency, reducing the net worth of a borrowing firm. As in *a* above, a firm has less to lose if it defaults on a loan, increasing adverse selection and moral hazard.

    d. When asset prices decline, firm's write down (reduce) the value of the assets they own on their balance sheets. This reduces the net worth of the borrowing firm. As in *a* above, the firm has less to lose if it defaults on a loan, increasing adverse selection and moral hazard.

2. a. It is a process in which a substantial, unanticipated decline in the price level increases the burden of indebtedness.

    b. It reduces economic activity because the reduction in the price level reduces the value of the borrowing firm's assets but not its liabilities, causing a deterioration in the firm's balance sheet. Adverse selection and moral hazard problems increase, lending contracts sharply, and aggregate economic activity remains depressed.

    c. the Great Depression

    d. Prices fell 25% during the Great Depression. The rate of unemployment was 25%.

3. a. It is a mortgage for borrowers with less-than-excellent credit records.

    b. It is a standardized debt security back by mortgages.

    c. The originator of the loan distributes the loan to the ultimate lender (investor), and thus the mortgage originator has little incentive to make sure that the mortgage is a good credit risk.

    d. Mortgage originators loaned money to subprime borrowers, packaged the loans into mortgage-backed securities, and profitably sold them to investors around the world. So much easy credit entered the housing market that it drove housing prices above their fundamental values.

    e. When the price of housing returns to the fundamental value, it causes many borrowers to default because they owe more on their homes than the home is worth. The defaults cause financial firms to become insolvent, reducing lending and economic activity.

Short-Answer Questions

1. Because an increase in adverse selection and moral hazard makes it difficult and more costly for lenders to find low-risk borrowers, lenders contract their lending, which reduces investment and economic activity.

2. Emerging market economies have weaker bank supervision and their banks lack expertise in screening and monitoring, so the lending boom is greater and the lending crash is greater. In addition, emerging market banks borrow abroad at higher interest rates, causing a greater crisis when their balance sheets deteriorate. The financial markets are

less developed, so a banking crisis is even more harmful.

3. When the government runs a large deficit and private investors fear that the government will default on its debt, the government may force domestic banks to buy its debt. If the value of the debt decreases, it will reduce bank capital and bank lending will decrease.

4. A spike in interest rates causes an increase in adverse selection and moral hazard because only borrowers with risky projects are willing to borrow at the high rates. Bank lending decreases.

5. Banking crises. When the credit boom turns into a credit crash, the increase in defaults causes depositors to withdraw their funds from banks, causing a bank panic.

6. Financial liberalization or innovation creates a credit boom, which causes financial firms to take on excessive risk and also causes a bubble in asset prices. When the asset-price bubble pops, the credit boom turns into a credit crunch.

7. A government safety net increases adverse selection and moral hazard because it allows lenders to take on even more risk because borrowers feel secure that there is a government guarantee of the debt.

8. Mismanagement of financial innovation in the subprime residential mortgage market and a bursting of a housing price bubble was the source of the recent subprime financial crisis.

Critical Thinking

1. It is an economy at an earlier stage of market development that has recently opened up to the flow of goods, services, and capital from the rest of the world

2. Severe fiscal imbalances caused the governments in Russia and Argentina to force domestic banks to buy their government debt, which later fell in value.

3. Mismanagement of financial innovation in the subprime residential mortgage market and a bursting of the resulting housing price bubble.

4. No. The sources are different so the solutions are different. Russia and Argentina needed to more closely balance the government's budget (raise taxes or cut government spending).

The United States may need to regulate the markets for financial innovations such as mortgage-backed securities.

True/False Questions

1. F
2. F
3. T
4. T
5. T
6. F
7. T
8. F
9. F
10. F
11. T
12. T
13. T
14. F
15. F

Multiple-Choice Questions

1. c
2. d
3. b
4. a
5. b
6. d
7. a
8. d
9. c
10. c
11. a
12. b
13. d
14. c
15. a
16. c
17. a
18. b
19. d
20. c

10 Banking and the Management of Financial Institutions

Chapter Review

PREVIEW

This chapter focuses on how commercial banks are managed in order to maximize profits. We concentrate on commercial banks because they are the most important financial intermediaries.

THE BANK BALANCE SHEET

A bank's balance sheet lists its sources of funds (liabilities, such as deposits) and uses of funds (assets, such as loans). It has the characteristic that total assets = total liabilities + capital. A bank's liabilities include checkable deposits (demand deposits, NOW accounts, MMDAs), nontransactions deposits (savings deposits, time deposits or CDs), and borrowings (discount loans, federal funds borrowed, borrowing from the BHC parent, repurchase agreements, Eurodollars). Bank capital is on the liability side and is the bank's net worth. Checkable deposits have gone from over 60% of bank liabilities in 1960 to only 6% today. Nontransactions deposits are approximately 53% of bank liabilities.

A bank's assets include reserves (the bank's deposits at the Fed plus its vault cash), cash items in the process of collection, deposits at its correspondent banks (for check clearing, securities purchases, foreign exchange), securities (U.S. government and agency securities known as *secondary reserves*, and state and local government securities), loans (commercial and industrial, real estate, consumer, interbank), and other assets (physical capital). The *required reserve ratio* or *reserve requirement* sets the percent of checkable deposits that must be held as *required reserves*. It is 10% at this time. The bank may choose to hold *excess reserves*.

BASIC BANKING

Banks make profits from asset transformation. They borrow short (accept relatively short-term deposits) and lend long (make loans that are relatively longer). When a bank receives additional deposits, it gains an equal amount of reserves. When it loses deposits, it loses an equal amount of reserves. In the simplest case, banks make profits by lending the excess reserves generated from a deposit and charging a higher interest rate on the loan than they pay on the deposit.

GENERAL PRINCIPLES OF BANK MANAGEMENT

Banks engage in *liquidity management* to be prepared for *deposit outflows*. For this reason, banks hold excess reserves and secondary reserves even though they earn less interest than less liquid assets such as loans. First, when a bank faces deposit outflow, it need not change other parts of its balance sheet if it has ample excess reserves. Second, the bank could sell some of its securities with relatively low transaction costs. Third, it could get a discount loan from the Fed, but it would have to pay the *discount rate*, the interest rate charged by the Fed. Finally, it could call in loans or sell loans to another bank, but this is the costliest way to acquire funds and is to be avoided.

Banks engage in *asset management* to seek the highest returns possible, reduce risk, and provide liquidity. They do this by seeking borrowers who will pay high rates but are a low risk of default, buying securities with high returns and low risk, buying a variety of assets to lower risk through diversification, and maintaining just enough liquid assets to insure against deposit outflows. *Liability management* used to be a staid affair because 60% of their liabilities were checkable deposits for which they could not compete by paying interest, and there was no well-developed federal funds market. Post-1960, large *money center banks* began selling negotiable CDs and borrowing from other banks. Thus, banks began to actively seek funds if they found productive loan prospects.

Banks must manage the amount of capital they hold in order to lessen the chance of a bank failure (assets < liabilities) and to meet capital requirements set by regulatory authorities, which is known as *capital adequacy management*. Bank capital is the cushion for the reduction in the value of assets that results from bad loans. Other things the same, the greater the capital account, the more bad loans the bank can sustain and remain solvent (have positive net worth). However, the lower the bank capital, the higher the return on equity for the owners of the bank, causing a trade-off between safety and return to equity holders. This relationship is demonstrated by the definition of *return on equity* (ROE). ROE = net profit after taxes/equity capital. Reducing capital increases ROE. Due to the cost of holding capital, regulatory authorities enforce minimum bank capital requirements. To increase the amount of capital relative to assets, a bank can issue more common stock, reduce the bank's dividends to increase retained earnings, or reduce the bank's assets by selling off loans or securities. In a financial crisis, it is difficult for banks to raise capital, so banks usually reduce loans, causing a credit crunch.

MANAGING CREDIT RISK

Credit risk is the risk associated with the probability of default on a loan. To avoid the asymmetric information problems of adverse selection and moral hazard, banks engage in five activities. First, banks *screen and monitor* borrowers by collecting information on borrowers prior to the loan, specializing in lending to particular industries to gain expertise in screening, and monitoring and enforcing restrictive covenants to ensure that the borrower uses the loan for the prescribed activities. Second, banks develop *long-term customer relationships* to more efficiently gather information on the borrower and to provide the borrower with an incentive to reduce moral hazard for future borrowing. Third, banks issue *loan commitments*, which promotes long-term customer relationships. Fourth, banks require *collateral and compensating balances* from the borrower. Compensating balances act as collateral and help the bank monitor the spending of the loan. Finally, the bank can engage in *credit rationing*, refusing to make a loan even at a high interest rate or making a loan for a smaller amount that was originally requested.

MANAGING INTEREST-RATE RISK

Interest-rate risk is the riskiness of earnings associated with changes in interest rates. If a bank has more rate-sensitive (short-term) liabilities than assets, a rise in interest rates will reduce bank profits. This is because the increase in interest a bank pays on its liabilities will exceed the increase in interest it receives on its assets. Alternatively, a decline in interest rates will raise bank profits. Basic *gap analysis* can measure the sensitivity of bank profits to changes in interest rates. Gap = rate-sensitive assets − rate-sensitive liabilities. Gap × change in interest rate = change in bank profits. *Duration analysis* measures the interest rate sensitivity of the market value of the bank's assets and liabilities, and thus shows the change in net worth of the bank from a change in interest rates. Percent change in market value of security = − percentage-point change in interest rate × duration in years. Both measures indicate that banks with more rate-sensitive liabilities tend to suffer when interest rates rise and gain when they fall. Managing interest-rate risk can be costly if it requires changing the average duration of a bank's assets or liabilities.

OFF-BALANCE-SHEET ACTIVITIES

Off-balance-sheet activities involve trading financial instruments and generating income from fees and loan sales, which affect bank profits but don't appear on the balance sheet. A *loan sale*, or secondary loan participation, is when a bank sells all or part of a loan's cash stream. Fee income is earned from foreign exchange trades for a customer, servicing mortgage-backed securities, guaranteeing debt such as banker's acceptances, providing backup lines of credit, and creating structured investment vehicles (SIVs). Trading activities can be profitable but risky, requiring the bank to put risk assessment procedures in place and restrict employees from taking on too much risk.

Helpful Hints

1. Prior to 1960, more than 60% of a bank's liabilities were checkable deposits. Since banks could not actively compete for those deposits by paying interest on them, a bank's size was largely determined by its local source of funds. Post-1960, banks with exceptionally profitable loan opportunities can actively seek funds by borrowing in ways that didn't exist prior to the 1960s. Thus, a bank now has more influence over its size and growth rate than prior to 1960.

2. Capital protects a bank from bankruptcy or insolvency. Insolvency is when the value of a bank's assets falls below the value of its liabilities. Thus, a bank can sustain a reduction in the value of its assets by the amount of its capital. If a bank has $1 billion in capital, the value of its assets could fall by up to $1 billion and the bank would still be technically solvent.

Terms and Definitions

Choose a definition for each key term.

Key Terms:

_____asset management
_____balance sheet
_____capital adequacy management
_____compensating balance
_____credit rationing
_____credit risk
_____discount loans
_____duration analysis
_____equity multiplier (em)
_____excess reserves
_____gap analysis
_____interest-rate risk
_____liability management
_____liquidity management
_____reserve requirements
_____reserves
_____return on equity (roe)
_____secondary reserves

Definitions:

1. Regulation making it obligatory for depository institutions to keep a certain fraction of their deposits as reserves

2. A measurement of the sensitivity of the market value of a bank's assets and liabilities to changes in interest rates

3. The risk arising from the possibility that the borrower will default

4. The possible reduction in returns associated with changes in interest rates

5. The acquisition of assets that have a low rate of default and diversification of asset holdings to increase profits

6. Net profit after taxes per dollar of equity capital

7. Reserves in excess of required reserves

8. A list of the assets and liabilities of a bank that balances: total assets equal total liabilities plus capital

9. Short-term U.S. government and agency securities held by private banks

10. The acquisition of funds at low cost to increase profits

11. A bank's deposits at the Fed plus its vault cash

12. The amount of assets per dollar of equity capital

13. A bank's decision about the amount of capital if should maintain and then the acquisition of that capital

14. A lender refuses to make a loan or restricts the size of the loan to less than the full amount sought

15. The decisions made by a bank to maintain sufficient liquid assets to meet the bank's obligations to depositors

16. A bank's borrowings from the Federal Reserve System

17. A measurement of the sensitivity of bank profits to changes in interest rates calculated as rate-sensitive liabilities minus rate-sensitive assets

18. A required minimum amount of funds that a firm receiving a loan must keep in a checking account at the lending bank

Problems and Short-Answer Questions

PRACTICE PROBLEMS

1. Record each of the following events in the T-account provided below.
   a. Joe deposits his $3,000 paycheck into his checking account at Local Bank.

   Local Bank

Assets	Liabilities

   b. Local Bank deposits the check at the Fed and the Fed collects the funds for Local Bank.

   Local Bank

Assets	Liabilities

   c. What happens to a bank's reserves when it receives a deposit?

   _____

   d. Joe withdraws $500 cash and pays his rent. His landlord deposits the $500 in Landlord Bank.

   Local Bank

Assets	Liabilities

   Landlord Bank

Assets	Liabilities

e. What happens to a bank's reserves when it loses a deposit?

_____

f. Suppose the reserve requirement is 10%. Landlord bank lends out the maximum it can from the $500 deposit.

Landlord Bank

Assets	Liabilities

g. For Landlord Bank to make profits, what must be true about the interest rate it pays on deposits compared to the interest rate it receives on loans?

_____

2. Suppose that Liquidity Management Bank has the following balance sheet position and that the required reserve ratio on deposits is 20%. The numbers below are in millions.

Assets		Liabilities	
Reserves	$25	Deposits	$100
Loans	75	Bank capital	10
Securities	10		

a. Show the impact of a $5 million deposit outflow on the bank's balance sheet.

Assets	Liabilities

b. Must the bank make any adjustments in its balance sheet in order to meet its reserve requirement? Explain.

_____

_____

c. Show the impact of another $5 million deposit outflow on the bank's balance sheet (for a total of $10 million deposit outflow).

Assets	Liabilities

d. Must the bank make any adjustments in its balance sheet in order to meet its reserve requirement? Explain.

_____

_____

e. If the bank chooses to sell off securities to meet its reserve requirement, how many dollars of securities must it sell? Explain. Show the bank's balance sheet after the sale of securities.

_____

_____

Assets	Liabilities

f. Why would a bank choose to sell its securities rather than its loans to meet its liquidity needs? What might happen to the bank if there were such a great deposit outflow that it ran out of securities and no one would lend to it, so it had to sell off some of its loans?

_____

_____

_____

_____

3. Below you will find balance sheets for High Capital Bank and Low Capital Bank. Numbers are in millions.

High Capital Bank

Assets		Liabilities	
Reserves	$90	Deposits	$540
Loans	510	Bank capital	60

Low Capital Bank

Assets		Liabilities	
Reserves	$90	Deposits	$560
Loans	510	Bank capital	40

a. How many dollars of bad loans can each bank sustain before it becomes insolvent? As a result, which bank has the lower probability of becoming insolvent?

_____

_____

b. Suppose net profit after taxes is $6 million for each bank. What is each bank's return on assets (ROA)? What is each bank's return on equity (ROE)? Which bank is more profitable to its owners?

_____

_____

c. What does this example say about the relationship between safety and returns to equity holders? What is regulatory response to this situation?

_____

_____

4. Suppose that Rate-Sensitive Bank has the following balance sheet. All values are in millions of dollars.

Rate-Sensitive Bank

Assets		Liabilities	
Variable-rate Loans	$5	Variable-rate CDs	$30
Short-term Loans	10	Money Market	
Short-term Securities	15	Deposit Accounts	20
Reserves	10	Checkable Deposits	10
Long-term Loans	30	Savings Deposits	10
Long-term Securities	30	Long-terms CDs	20
		Equity Capital	10

a. Employ basic gap analysis to determine this bank's "gap."

b. If interest rates suddenly increase by two percentage points, by how much do the bank's profits change?

c. If, instead, interest rates decrease by three percentage points, by how much do the bank's profits change?

d. If a bank has more rate-sensitive liabilities than assets, how do bank profits move with respect to the interest rate?

e. Suppose the average duration of the assets of this bank is four years while the average duration of the liabilities is two years. Use duration analysis to determine the change in the net worth of the bank if interest rates rise by three percentage points.

SHORT-ANSWER QUESTIONS

1. What are secondary reserves? What purpose do they serve? What advantage do they have over excess reserves?

2. What is the largest source of funds to commercial banks? Are checkable deposits a more important or less important source of funds today when compared to 40 years ago?

   _____

   _____

3. What category of assets generates the greatest profits for commercial banks? Why would banks receive more profit from this type of asset?

   _____

   _____

4. If a bank has $1,000 in deposits and the required reserve ratio is 10%, how much are the bank's required reserves? In what form must the bank hold them?

   _____

   _____

5. When banks engage in asset management, they seek high-return, low-risk, liquid assets. Why is this difficult?

   _____

   _____

6. If a depositor withdraws $100 from his deposit at a bank, what happens to the bank's reserves?

   _____

7. How do banks reduce their exposure to credit risk?

   _____

   _____

   _____

8. What methods can a bank use to increase its capital relative to assets?

   _____

   _____

9. What are off-balance-sheet activities? Are they growing or diminishing?

   _____

   _____

10. How can a bank generate liquidity in the face of deposit outflow?

_____

_____

_____

Critical Thinking

You are watching the news with a friend. The news anchor says that the Fed has just increased the interest rate for the eighth meeting in a row. Your friend says, "I bet banks just love these increases in the interest rate. Banks must be making enormous profits charging those high interest rates. Bank stock prices must just be going through the roof."

1. Use a description of gap analysis to explain to your friend how a rising interest rate tends to affect a bank's profits.

_____

_____

_____

_____

_____

2. Use a description of duration analysis to explain to your friend how a rising interest rate tends to affect a bank's net worth.

_____

_____

_____

_____

_____

Self-Test

TRUE/FALSE QUESTIONS

_____1.   A bank's assets are its source of funds.

_____2.   Checkable deposits are the primary source of bank funds.

_____3. Bank capital is the net worth of a bank, and it equals the total assets of the bank minus the total liabilities.

_____4. Borrowings from the Fed are called discount loans, and the interest rate the borrowing bank pays on the loan is known as the discount rate.

_____5. Required reserves are a fixed percentage of a bank's total liabilities.

_____6. Loans provide banks with most of their profits.

_____7. When a bank is faced with deposit outflows, its first choice for acquiring reserves to meet the deposit outflow is to sell off loans.

_____8. Banks keep over 50% of their assets in excess reserves to insure that they are liquid enough to meet deposit outflows.

_____9. A bank fails when the value of its liabilities exceeds the value of its assets.

_____10. Negotiable CDs and bank borrowings have increased as a source of funds to banks since 1960.

_____11. Increasing a bank's capital increases the bank's safety and increases the bank's return on equity (ROE).

_____12. To reduce credit risk, banks often require collateral and compensating balances from the borrower.

_____13. If the average duration of a bank's assets exceeds the average duration of a bank's liabilities, an increase in interest rates will increase a bank's net worth.

_____14. If a bank has more rate-sensitive liabilities than assets, an increase in interest rates will reduce the bank's profits.

_____15. Off-balance-sheet activities have declined in importance for banks over the last twenty-five years.

MULTIPLE-CHOICE QUESTIONS

1. Which of the following is the greatest source of funds to commercial banks today?
    a. checkable deposits
    b. nontransactions deposits
    c. borrowings
    d. bank capital

2. Which of the following was the greatest source of funds to commercial banks in 1960?
    a. checkable deposits
    b. nontransactions deposits
    c. borrowings
    d. bank capital

3. Which of the following bank assets is the most liquid?
   a. state and local government securities
   b. commercial and industrial loans
   c. real estate loans
   d. U.S. government securities

4. Required reserves are a fixed percentage of a bank's
   a. assets.
   b. loans.
   c. checkable deposits.
   d. capital.
   e. liabilities.

5. Which of the following is true about a bank's balance sheet?
   a. A bank's liabilities are its source of funds.
   b. A bank's assets are its use of funds.
   c. Assets – liabilities = bank capital.
   d. All of the above are true.

6. The sum of a bank's vault cash plus its deposits at the Fed is the bank's
   a. capital.
   b. federal funds.
   c. reserves.
   d. cash items in the process of collection.
   e. excess reserves.

7. Which of the following is generally the least expensive way for a bank to acquire funds?
   a. checkable deposits.
   b. federal funds.
   c. nontransactions deposits.
   d. borrowings such as Eurodollars or repurchase agreements.
   e. discount loans.

8. When you deposit your $3,000 paycheck in your bank, which was written on an account at a different bank, the immediate impact on your bank's balance sheet is that your bank's deposits rise by $3,000 and your bank's
   a. reserves rise by $3,000.
   b. cash items in the process of collection rise by $3,000.
   c. loans rise by $3,000.
   d. capital rises by $3,000.
   e. None of the above is correct.

9. When a bank suffers deposit outflows, and it has no excess reserves, the bank will generally first try to raise the funds by
   a. calling in some loans.
   b. selling some loans.
   c. borrowing from the Fed.
   d. selling some of its securities.

10. Which of the following would not be considered a managed liability?
    a. negotiable certificates of deposit
    b. federal funds borrowed
    c. Eurodollar borrowings
    d. checkable deposits.

11. A bank has $100 in checkable deposits, reserves of $15, and the reserves requirement is 10%. Suppose the bank suffers a $10 deposit outflow. If the bank chooses to borrow from the Fed to meet its reserve requirement, how much does it need to borrow?
    a. $0
    b. $1.50
    c. $4
    d. $5
    e. $10

12. Which of the following is <u>not</u> true regarding how banks manage their assets? Banks seek assets that
    a. are liquid.
    b. provide diversification.
    c. have no default risk.
    d. generate high returns.

13. Suppose that a bank's balance sheet consists of the following: On the liability side it has $93 of deposits and $7 of capital, while on the asset side it has $10 of reserves and $90 of loans. How many dollars of bad loans can this bank sustain before it become insolvent?
    a. $0
    b. $7
    c. $9.30
    d. $10
    e. $93

14. Other things being the same, a bank with a greater amount of capital
    a. has a lower risk of failure.
    b. has a higher rate of return on equity to the owners.
    c. is more liquid.
    d. All of the above are true.

15. Which of the following is <u>not</u> a method by which banks reduce their <u>credit risk</u>?
    a. Collect information on prospective borrowers to screen out high-risk borrowers.
    b. Use gap analysis to help balance a bank's rate-sensitive assets and liabilities.
    c. Develop long-term relationships with borrowers.
    d. Enforce restrictive covenants in the loan contract.
    e. Engage in credit rationing.

16. Banks often specialize in providing loans to firms in a particular industry because this activity
    a. reduces the cost of acquiring and analyzing information about the borrower.
    b. reduces the bank's exposure to interest-rate risk.
    c. allows the bank to increase the diversification of its loan portfolio.
    d. is required by law.
    e. All of the above are true.

17. Suppose a bank has a "gap" of −$50 million dollars. What will happen to its profits if interest rates rise by 2%?
    a.   Profits rise by $100 million.
    b.   Profits fall by $100 million.
    c.   Profits rise by $1million.
    d.   Profits fall by $1 million.

18. Which of the following statements about interest-rate risk is true?
    a.   A commercial bank usually has a larger "gap" than an equivalent size savings and loan.
    b.   An increase in interest rates always increases commercial bank profits.
    c.   If a bank has more rate-sensitive liabilities than assets, an increase in interest rates reduces bank profits.
    d.   Banks tend to have more rate-sensitive assets than liabilities.
    e.   All of the above are true.

19. Which of the following does <u>not</u> describe an off-balance-sheet activity?
    a.   A bank guarantees a firm's debt by signing a banker's acceptance.
    b.   A bank writes a mortgage and sells it to a life insurance company.
    c.   A bank makes a loan to a large corporate customer.
    d.   A bank exchanges dollars for euros for a large corporate customer.

20. Using duration analysis, if a bank's assets have an average duration of 4 years, and if the interest rate rises by 2%, what will happen to the value of the bank's assets?
    a.   The value of the assets will rise by 8%.
    b.   The value of the assets will fall by 8%.
    c.   The value of the assets will rise by 2%.
    d.   The value of the assets will rise by 2%.

Solutions

Terms and Definitions

 5 asset management

 8 balance sheet

13 capital adequacy management

18 compensating balance

14 credit rationing

 3 credit risk

16 discount loans

 2 duration analysis

12 equity multiplier (EM)

 7 excess reserves

17 gap analysis

 4 interest-rate risk

10 liability management

15 liquidity management

 1 reserve requirements

11 reserves

 6 return on equity (roe)

 9 secondary reserves

Practice Problems

1. a.

Local Bank

Assets		Liabilities	
Cash items in process of collection	+$3000	Checkable deposits	+$3000

b.

Local Bank

Assets		Liabilities	
Reserves	+$3000	Checkable deposits	+$3000

c. Its reserves rise by precisely the size of the increase in the deposit.

d.

Local Bank

Assets		Liabilities	
Reserves	−$500	Checkable deposits	−$500

Landlord Bank

Assets		Liabilities	
Reserves	+$500	Checkable deposits	+$500

e. Its reserves fall by precisely the size of the decrease in the deposit.

f.

Landlord Bank

Assets		Liabilities	
Reserves	+$50	Checkable deposits	+$500
Loans	+$450		

g. It must pay a lower interest rate on its deposits than it receives on its loans.

2. a.

Assets		Liabilities	
Reserves	$20	Deposits	$95
Loans	75	Bank capital	10
Securities	10		

b. No. Required reserves after the deposit outflow are (0.20 × $95) = $19 million so the bank had enough excess reserves to handle the deposit outflow.

c.

Assets		Liabilities	
Reserves	$15	Deposits	$90
Loans	75	Bank capital	10
Securities	10		

d. Yes. Required reserves after the deposit outflow are (0.20 × $90 million) = $18 million, and the bank only has $15 million. The bank has a reserve deficiency of $3 million.

e. $18 million – $15 million = $3 million. The bank should sell $3 million in securities.

Assets		Liabilities	
Reserves	$18	Deposits	$90
Loans	75	Bank capital	10
Securities	7		

f. Transaction costs are small on securities held as secondary reserves. Selling off loans is costly because they usually can't be sold for full value. If the bank had to discount its loans to such a degree that the value of its assets fell below the value of its liabilities, the bank would be insolvent.

3. a. High Capital Bank: $60 million. Low Capital Bank: $40 million. High Capital Bank has a lower probability of becoming insolvent.

b. ROA for each = $6/$600 = 1%. ROE for High Capital Bank = $6/$60 = 10%. ROE for Low Capital Bank = $6/$40 = 15%. Low Capital Bank is more profitable.

c. There is a trade off between profitability and safety. As a result, bank regulations impose bank capital requirements.

4. a. $30 million – $50 million = – $20 million.

b. 0.02 × – $20 million = – $400,000.

c. – 0.03 × (– $20 million) = $600,000.

d. Interest rates and profits are inversely related.

e. Change in value of assets = – 0.03 × 4 × $100 million = – $12 million.

Change in value of liabilities = – 0.03 × 2 × $90 million = – $5.4 million.

– $12 million – (– $5.4 million) = – $6.6 million.

Short-Answer Questions

1. Short-term U.S. government securities. They provide liquidity in case of deposit outflow and they earn interest while excess reserves do not.

2. Nontransactions deposits supply about 53% of the funds. Checkable deposits are less important, going from 60% of the funds to about 6%.

3. Loans. Loans are riskier and less liquid than other bank assets.

4. $100. Reserves can be held as deposits at the Federal Reserve or as vault cash.

5. High return assets tend to be higher risk and less liquid.

6. The bank's reserves fall by $100.

7. Banks screen and monitor borrowers, specialize in lending to particular industries, monitor and enforce restrictive covenants, develop long-term customer relationships, issue loan commitments, require collateral and compensating balances, and engage in credit rationing.

8. Issue more common stock, reduce the bank's dividends to increase retained earnings, or reduce the bank's assets by selling off loans or securities.

9. The generation of income from fees and loan sales, which generate profit but don't appear on the balance sheet. They have nearly doubled since 1980.

10. A bank can hold excess reserves, sell secondary reserves, get a discount loan from the Fed or other borrowings, or sell off loans.

Critical Thinking

1. The gap is defined as: rate-sensitive assets – rate-sensitive liabilities. Gap × change in interest rate = change in bank profits. Since banks tend to have more rate-sensitive liabilities than assets, the gap tends to be negative. Thus, an increase in interest rates reduces bank profits because the increase in interest a bank pays on its liabilities exceeds the increase in interest it receives on its assets

2. Duration is the average lifetime of a security's stream of payments. The percent change in market value of security = – percentage-point change in interest rate × duration in years. Since banks tend to have longer-term assets than liabilities, there is a greater reduction in the value of the assets than the liabilities in response to an increase in the interest rate. Thus, the net worth of a bank falls when interest rates rise.

True/False Questions

1. F
2. F
3. T
4. T
5. F
6. T
7. F
8. F
9. T
10. T
11. F
12. T
13. F
14. T
15. F

Multiple-Choice Questions

1. b
2. a
3. d
4. c
5. d
6. c
7. a
8. b
9. d
10. d
11. c
12. c
13. b
14. a
15. b
16. a
17. d
18. c
19. c
20. b

11 Economic Analysis of Financial Regulation

Chapter Review

PREVIEW

In this chapter, we use economic analysis to show why financial institutions and banks are so heavily regulated. Financial regulation, however, is not always successful. Banking and financial crises cause regulators to reform existing regulations.

ASYMMETRIC INFORMATION AND FINANCIAL REGULATION

Much of banking regulation is based on the presence of asymmetric information, which causes adverse selection and moral hazard problems in banking. Banking regulations can be grouped into the following categories:

- *The government safety net*: Depositors lack information about the quality of a bank's private loans. Thus, before deposit insurance, depositors were reluctant to put funds in a bank, and even small negative shocks to the banking system could cause bank panics and the contagion effect. In response, the FDIC was established in 1934. Bank failures are handled through either the payoff method or the purchase and assumption method, which guarantees all deposits. In addition to deposit insurance, central banks can act as the "lender of last resort" to troubled institutions. A government safety net fixes one set of problems but causes a moral hazard problem (financial institutions take on excessive risk), and an adverse selection problem (risk-loving entrepreneurs may choose to enter the financial industry). Since the failure of a very big financial institution may cause a financial disruption, some institutions have been considered "too big to fail" so their insolvencies were handled by the purchase and assumption method, which further increases the moral hazard problem. The consolidation of the financial industry causes more financial institutions to be "too big to fail," and conglomerate financial firms may receive a safety net for nonbanking activities.

- *Restrictions on asset holdings*: Because depositors and creditors of financial institutions cannot easily monitor the institution's assets, regulations restrict banks from holding risky assets such as common stock and regulations require banks to diversify.

- *Capital Requirements:* Banks have capital requirements that establish a minimum *leverage ratio* (capital asset ratio) of 5%. The *Basel Accord* increases the capital-asset ratio for risky banks by establishing risk-based capital requirements for banks in over 100 countries.

- *Financial supervision: chartering and examination*: Chartering financial institutions limits adverse selection by preventing undesirable people from controlling them. On-site examinations and the application of the CAMELS rating to a bank's activities reduce moral hazard. Banks also file quarterly call reports.

- *Assessment of risk management*: Since banks can take on more risk than is apparent from their balance sheets, regulators are interested in a bank's management processes for controlling risk of fraud, risky trading activities, and interest rate risk.

- *Disclosure requirements*: Due to the free-rider problem, depositors and creditors don't create enough information about the bank's condition. Regulators respond by requiring financial institutions to adhere to standard accounting principles and to disclose substantial information. Financial firms are required to employ mark-to-market accounting (fair-value accounting) where assets are valued at what they would sell for. During a financial crisis, however, prices of financial instruments may fall below their true value, reducing a lender's capital, and causing lender's to reduce their lending, making the crisis worse.

- *Consumer protection*: As a result of asymmetric information, "truth in lending" laws require lenders to be clear about financing charges. Other laws, such as The Equal Credit Opportunity Act of 1974 and The Community Reinvestment Act of 1977, forbid discrimination in lending. Recent additions to the Truth in Lending Act of 2008 require greater information on the borrower's ability to repay and on the true terms of the loan.

- *Restrictions on competition*: Competition may increase moral hazard by causing financial institutions to assume greater risk to maintain profits. In the past, U.S. banks were restricted from branching and Glass-Steagall kept nonbank institutions from engaging in banking activities, but these restrictions caused inefficiency and higher charges to consumers.

It is difficult to successfully regulate financial institutions because financial institutions have incentives to avoid the regulations, the regulations may have unintended consequences, and regulators are subject to political pressure to regulate more easily.

Because the same types of asymmetric information problems exist in banking everywhere, financial regulation in foreign countries is similar to that in the United States—financial institutions are chartered, supervised, regulated, and insured. International financial institutions are particularly difficult to regulate because they can shift their business from one country to another.

THE 1980S SAVINGS AND LOAN AND BANKING CRISIS

Few banks and S&Ls failed from 1934 to 1980. An increase in adverse selection and moral hazard caused bank failures to increase more than tenfold from the early 1980s to the early 1990s. This happened for the following reasons. Financial innovation decreased the profitability of banks by increasing competition for both their source of funds and their use of funds, causing banks to make riskier loans to maintain profits. Deposit insurance increased moral hazard. Riskier assets like junk bonds became available. New legislation (DIDMCA of 1980) allowed S&Ls to invest in riskier activities such as commercial real estate and junk bonds, raised FDIC insurance to $100,000 per account, and removed the ceiling on interest rates that could be paid on deposits, allowing risky banks to pay higher rates and attract more funds, causing greater moral hazard. Banks and savings and loans took on additional risk and failures rose, causing losses for the FDIC. Regulators responded with FIRREA of 1989 and FDICIA of 1991, which baled out the commercial banking and savings and loan industries and re-regulated the banking industry.

BANKING CRISES THROUGHOUT THE WORLD

Extensive parallels exist between the banking crises in the United States and those in other countries, indicating that similar forces are at work. All banking crises start with financial liberalization or innovation combined with a weak bank regulatory system and a government safety net. The costs associated with the U.S. banking crisis of the 1980s appears small when taken as a percent of GDP – only 3% for the United States but over 50% for Argentina and Indonesia.

WHITHER FINANCIAL REGULATION
AFTER THE SUBPRIME FINANCIAL CRISIS?

The recent subprime financial crisis will likely lead to additional financial regulations. Future regulations to reduce the agency problems associated with the originate-to-distribute model of credit may include:

- Increased regulation of mortgage brokers to prevent them from encouraging borrowers to take on more debt than they can afford.

- Fewer subprime mortgage products will be available because these products may be too complicated for unsophisticated borrowers.

- Regulation of compensation for those involved in the distribution of mortgage-related securities.

- Higher capital requirements for financial firms to compensate for their increased risk.

- Additional regulation of privately owned, government-sponsored enterprises (such as Fannie Mae) to reduce their risk exposure.

- Heightened regulation to limit financial institutions' risk taking.

- Increased regulation of credit-rating agencies to increase the accuracy of the information provided to investors.

- Additional regulation of derivatives, particularly credit-default swaps.

There is a danger that overregulation will stifle future financial innovation.

Helpful Hints

1. Depositors face the same problems of adverse selection and moral hazard when depositing money in banks as banks face when lending depositors money. To avoid these asymmetric information problems in private financial markets, banks screen borrowers, employ restrictive covenants preventing borrowers from investing in risky activities, employ restrictive covenants requiring that their borrowers maintain a minimum net worth, and monitor borrowers. Similarly, on behalf of depositors, regulators require banks to have a charter, restrict risky asset holdings of banks, impose capital requirements on banks, and examine banks.

2. The moral hazard problem in banking increases when a bank nears insolvency. When a bank is technically insolvent, the bank is lending the depositors' money with no contribution from the owners because the bank no longer has a positive net worth. That is, the owners have nothing to lose. Thus, the incentive is for the bank to seek out the highest risk loans possible. If the loans fail to perform, the depositors or FDIC may lose, but the owners lose nothing. If the loans perform, the owners gain. It is as if the bank is allowed to gamble with someone else's money. If the gamble loses, the bank doesn't care because it's someone else's money. But if the gamble pays off, the bank gets to keep the winnings.

Terms and Definitions

Choose a definition for each key term.

Key Terms:

_____bank failure

_____financial supervision (prudential supervision)

_____Basel Accord

_____leverage ratio

_____mark-to-market accounting

_____off-balance sheet activities

Definitions:

1. Overseeing who operates banks and how they are operated

2. Bank activities that involve trading financial instruments and the generation of income from fees and loan sales, all of which affect bank profits but are not visible on the balance sheet

3. An accounting entry in which assets are valued in the balance sheet at what they would sell for in the market

4. A situation in which a bank cannot satisfy its obligations to pay its depositors and other creditors and so goes out of business

5. An agreement that required that banks hold as capital at least 8% of their risk-weighted assets

6. A bank's capital divided by its assets

Problems and Short-Answer Questions

PRACTICE PROBLEMS

1. Depositors and regulators face an adverse selection and moral hazard problem that is similar to what banks and private lenders face in their loan markets. (See Helpful Hint #1.)

   a. What are the main four ways that financial regulators reduce the adverse selection and moral hazard problems in banking? What problem does each regulation reduce – adverse selection or moral hazard?

   _____

   _____

   _____

   _____

   b. Match the answers you provided in *a* above to the solutions banks and private lenders have used to reduce the same problems in their loan markets.

   _____

   _____

   _____

   _____

   _____

   _____

2. Some banks in the United States have been considered by regulators to be "too big to fail."

   a. What two ways can the FDIC handle an insolvent bank? If a regulator decides that a bank is "too big to fail," how does the regulator handle an insolvent bank, and what does it mean to the depositors and creditors of the bank?

   _____

   _____

   _____

b. What is the purpose of a policy that designates some banks as "too big to fail?"

_____

_____

c. What problem is exaggerated by this policy? Explain.

_____

_____

d. How does financial consolidation affect the "too big to fail" policy? Explain.

_____

_____

e. There are two methods the FDIC can use to handle an insolvent bank. Which method generates the least moral hazard? Why?

_____

_____

_____

SHORT-ANSWER QUESTIONS

1. What two problems are solved by deposit insurance? Explain.

_____

_____

_____

2. What two problems are created by deposit insurance? Explain.

_____

_____

_____

3. Why do regulators require that banks maintain a minimum capital-to-asset ratio?

   _____

   _____

4. What does a CAMELS rating measure?

   _____

   _____

5. What problem is caused by too much competition in banking? How did regulators restrict competition in the past? What problems did these regulations cause?

   _____

   _____

   _____

6. Why is it difficult to regulate international banking? What did the Basel Accord attempt to do?

   _____

   _____

7. Are the sources of financial crises in other countries similar or different from those in the United States? What are the main sources of financial crises? Are the sizes of the crises similar? Explain.

   _____

   _____

8. What factors contributed to the increase in the number of bank and savings and loan failures during the 1980s?

   _____

   _____

   _____

Critical Thinking

Suppose you are watching television. An advertisement for Risky Bank suggests that it is a bank that seeks risky speculative loans and junk bonds, and it is willing to pay 10% on its certificates of deposit. Immediately following that advertisement is a commercial for Safe Bank. Safe Bank screens and monitors its borrowers so that the loans are sure to be repaid. However, it only pays 5% on its certificates of deposit.

1. If the FDIC insures all deposits, where would you choose to place your deposit? Why?

   _____

   _____

2. If there were no deposit insurance, where would you likely choose to place your deposit? Why?

   _____

   _____

3. Explain how this example shows why countries charter and supervise their banks. What problems are reduced by requiring bank charters and by supervising banks?

   _____

   _____

   _____

   _____

Self-Test

TRUE/FALSE QUESTIONS

_____1. The presence of deposit insurance from the FDIC reduces moral hazard and adverse selection problems in the banking industry.

_____2. It is usually cheaper for the taxpayer if the FDIC resolves an insolvent institution by the "purchase and assumption method."

_____3. A policy of "too big to fail" provides a competitive advantage to very large banks because the policy effectively guarantees repayment to all depositors and creditors of a large bank in the event of a bank failure rather than just the insured depositors and creditors.

_____4. Requiring banks to be chartered reduces adverse selection in banking because it reduces the chances that undesirable or risk-loving people can gain control of a bank.

_____5. The Basil Accord requires all signing countries to provide deposit insurance to their depository institutions.

_____6. A bank's balance sheet alone provides an accurate picture of the degree of risk to which the bank is exposed.

_____7. The requirement that banks employ mark-to-market accounting may cause lenders to contract lending during a financial crisis.

_____8. Capital requirements are intended to reduce moral hazard in banking by making a bank failure more costly to the owners of the bank.

_____9. The Community Reinvestment Act of 1974 was enacted to prevent "redlining."

_____10. A sharp decrease in interest rates at the beginning of the 1980s caused losses for S&Ls and many failures.

_____11. Banking crises in different countries almost always begin with embezzlement by corrupt bankers.

_____12. Future financial regulations will likely allow for the expansion of subprime mortgage lending.

_____13. In 2008, the Federal Reserve began allowing lenders to make mortgages without regard to the borrower's ability to repay but instead based solely on the value of the home.

_____14. The Federal Deposit Insurance Corporation Improvement Act of 1991 (FDICIA) instituted risk-based premiums for deposit insurance.

_____15. The cost of the banking crisis in the United States measured as a percent of GDP far exceeds comparable crises in other countries around the world.

MULTIPLE-CHOICE QUESTIONS

1. Which of the following is _not_ true of a banking system with deposit insurance?
   a. Depositors are more likely to deposit their money in a bank.
   b. Depositors are less likely to withdraw their money in the event of a crisis.
   c. Depositors are less likely to collect information about the quality of the bank's loans.
   d. The moral hazard problem in banking is reduced.

2. If a bank becomes insolvent and the FDIC reorganizes the bank by finding a willing merger partner, the FDIC resolved this insolvency problem through the
   a. payoff method.
   b. safety net method.
   c. purchase and assumption method.
   d. CAMELS method.

3. The presence of deposit insurance increases the *adverse selection* problem in banking by
   a. attracting risk-loving people into bank ownership.
   b. increasing risky loans in banking.
   c. reducing bank capital.
   d. reducing the amount of deposits in the bank.

4. If the FDIC considers an insolvent bank to be "too big to fail," it will resolve the insolvency through the
   a. payoff method, which guarantees all deposits.
   b. payoff method, which guarantees only deposits that do not exceed $100,000.
   c. purchase and assumption method, which guarantees all deposits.
   d. purchase and assumption method, which guarantees only deposits that do not exceed $100,000.

5. The "too big to fail" policy of the FDIC
   a. decreases the moral hazard incentives for large banks.
   b. increases the moral hazard incentives for large banks.
   c. decreases the moral hazard incentives for small banks.
   d. increases the moral hazard incentives for small banks.

6. Which of the following banking regulations is most focused on reducing adverse selection in banking?
   a. consumer protection laws
   b. disclosure requirements requiring banks to use standard accounting principles
   c. periodic on-site examinations
   d. bank charter requirements

7. A bank's capital-to-asset ratio is also known as its
   a. leverage ratio.
   b. profit ratio.
   c. equity ratio.
   d. liability ratio.

8. Regulators impose capital requirements on banks because a low capital-to-asset ratio dramatically
   a. increases a bank's adverse selection.
   b. increases a bank's moral hazard.

   c. increases a bank's CAMELS rating.
   d. decreases a bank's rate of return on equity.
   e. All of the above are true.

9. The McFadden Act of 1927 and the Glass-Steagall Act of 1933
   a. increased bank competition and increased efficiency in banking.
   b. reduced bank competition and reduced efficiency in banking.
   c. increased bank competition and reduced efficiency in banking.
   d. reduced bank competition and increased efficiency in banking.

10. The primary objective of the Basel Accord was to standardize
    a. deposit insurance across international boundaries.
    b. bank examinations across international boundaries.
    c. bank capital requirements across international boundaries.
    d. branching restrictions across international boundaries.

11. Savings and loans grew rapidly in the 1980s because
    a. the removal of restrictions on the interest rates depository institutions could pay on deposits.
    b. deposit insurance coverage was raised to $100,000 per account.
    c. the market for large certificates of deposit expanded.
    d. All of the above are true.

12. The Community Reinvestment Act of 1977
    a. prevented "redlining," which is when a bank refuses to lend in a particular area.
    b. put a ceiling on interest rates that banks could charge.
    c. required banks to provide information to borrowers about the true cost of their loan.
    d. did none of the above.

13. Which of the following was <u>not</u> a cause of the savings and loan and banking failures in the 1980s?
    a. Depository institutions were allowed to pay higher interest rates to attract more funds.
    b. The FDIC used the purchase and assumption method to close failed depository institutions.
    c. All restrictions on savings and loan's assets were removed.
    d. Banks and savings and loans had greater competition from junk bonds and commercial paper, and they responded by making riskier loans to maintain profits.

14. Most banking crises around the world started with
    a. corrupt bankers.
    b. financial liberalization or innovation.
    c. excessive regulation.
    d. a crisis in the United States.

15. The final cost to the taxpayer for the savings and loan bailout was approximately
    a. $20 million.
    b. $150 million.
    c. $20 billion.
    d. $150 billion.

16. With regard to the subprime financial crisis, future financial regulations will likely
    a. expand the subprime mortgage market.
    b. lower capital requirements for financial institutions.
    c. increase the size and scope of government-sponsored enterprises such as Fannie Mae and Freddie Mac.
    d. provide greater incentives for credit-rating agencies to provide reliable ratings.

17. Which of the following methods used by the FDIC to address a bank failure generates the greatest moral hazard?
    a. payoff method
    b. purchase and assumption method
    c. CAMELS method
    d. safety net method

18. Off-balance-sheet activities of a bank
    a. are illegal.
    b. reduce bank profits.
    c. increase the bank's risk.
    d. are unregulated.

19. Mark-to-market accounting
    a. helps banks lend more during a financial crisis.
    b. requires financial firms to value assets at what they would sell for.
    c. increases a bank's capital in a financial crisis.
    d. none of the above

20. Which of the following statements regarding banking crises throughout the world is true?
    a. The causes of banking crises are so unique across countries that any solution must be tailored specifically to the needs of that country.
    b. The 1980s savings and loan and banking crisis in the United States was more costly as a percent of GDP than any modern banking crisis in the rest of the world.
    c. Japan is the only industrialized country to avoid banking crises altogether in the post-WWII period.
    d. None of the above is true.

Solutions

Terms and Definitions

 _4_ bank failure

 _1_ financial supervision (prudential supervision)

 _5_ Basel Accord

 _7_ leverage ratio

 _3_ mark-to-market accounting

 _2_ off-balance-sheet activities

Practice Problems

1. a. Chartering to prevent undesirables from controlling a bank – reduces adverse selection. Restrict asset holdings of banks – reduces moral hazard. Impose capital requirements on banks – reduces moral hazard. Examine banks – reduces moral hazard.

    b. Banks screening borrowers is similar to regulators chartering banks. Banks employing restrictive covenants preventing borrowers from investing in risky activities is similar to regulators restricting asset holdings of banks. Banks employing restrictive covenants requiring borrowers to have a minimum net worth is similar to regulators imposing capital requirements. Banks monitoring borrowers is similar to regulators examining banks.

2. a. The payoff method, and the purchase and assumption method. It uses the purchase and assumption method, which provides guarantees of repayment of large uninsured depositors and creditors of the insolvent bank.

    b. To avoid the financial disruption that could occur if depositors of a large bank lost their deposits.

    c. It increases the moral hazard problem because depositors have no incentive to monitor the bank, so the bank might take on even greater risk.

    d. There are more banks that are too big to fail, and there are conglomerate firms that may accidentally receive a safety net for their non-banking activities.

    e. The payoff method. With this method depositors and creditors may not get all of their money back and stock holders lose all of their money, so all participants have a greater incentive to monitor the bank's loans more closely.

Short-Answer Questions

1. Because depositors can't judge the quality of a bank's loans, depositors were afraid to put their money in a bank, and they would withdraw it when an adverse shock hits the economy, causing a bank panic.

2. Adverse selection – risk-loving entrepreneurs may choose to enter banking. Moral hazard – banks take on excessive risk because depositors have no reason to monitor the bank.

3. To reduce moral hazard. The greater the capital-to-asset ratio (leverage ratio), the more the bank has to lose if it fails, and so it pursues less risky activities.

4. Capital adequacy, asset quality, management, earnings, liquidity, and sensitivity to market risk.

5. Competition may increase moral hazard because banks may try to maintain their profits by assuming greater risk. Branching restrictions and the Glass-Steagall Act. These restrictions reduced efficiency and raised charges to consumers.

6. Because banks that operate in different countries can shift their business from one country to another. It standardized banks' capital requirements across countries to 8% of risk-weighted assets.

7. Similar. Financial liberalization or innovation, weak banking regulations, and a government safety net. The crises in the United States have been much smaller when measured as a percent of GDP.

8. Savings and loans were allowed to take on newly available risky assets such as junk bonds and commercial real estate loans. FDIC insurance was increased. Financial institutions were allowed to pay market interest rates, which increased the cost of funds.

Critical Thinking

1. Put the deposit in Risky Bank because your deposit is guaranteed regardless of whether the bank's loans turn out to be good or not.

2. Since there is such a high chance of the bank becoming insolvent, put your money in the safe bank and accept the lower interest rate.

3. To avoid adverse selection, banks are chartered to make sure that excessively risky people and crooks are not allowed to control a bank. To avoid moral hazard, banks are supervised to make sure that they maintain significant capital and hold low-risk assets.

True/False Questions

1. F
2. F
3. T
4. T
5. F
6. F
7. T
8. T
9. T
10. F
11. F
12. F
13. F
14. T
15. F

Multiple-Choice Questions

1. d
2. c
3. a
4. c
5. b
6. d
7. a
8. b
9. b
10. c
11. d
12. a
13. c
14. b
15. d
16. d
17. b
18. c
19. b
20. d

12

Banking Industry: Structure and Competition

Chapter Review

PREVIEW

Banks are financial intermediaries in business to earn profits. Compared to other countries, the United States has many more small banks. In this chapter we see why there are so many banks in the United States, and we address the competitiveness, efficiency, and soundness of the banking system.

HISTORICAL DEVELOPMENT OF THE BANKING SYSTEM

The first commercial bank in the United States was chartered in 1782. From 1791 to 1811, the Bank of the United States was created to act as both a private bank and a *central bank*, a government institution that has responsibility for the supply of money and credit in the economy. From 1816 to 1832, the Second Bank of the United States acted as the central bank. Until 1863, commercial banks were chartered by the states, and they were called *state banks*. In 1863, the Office of the Comptroller of the Currency federally chartered banks, call *national banks*. Thus, since 1863 the United States has a *dual banking system* where state and national banks operate side by side. Our current central bank, the Federal Reserve System (the Fed), was created in 1913. In 1933, legislation created the Federal Deposit Insurance Corporation (FDIC) to prevent depositor losses from bank failures. That same year, the Glass-Steagall Act separated the activities of commercial banks from those of the securities industry. At present, the Comptroller of the Currency supervises national banks, the Fed and the state banking authorities supervise the state banks that chose to be Fed members, while the FDIC and state authorities supervise the insured non-Fed members. State authorities alone supervise the few uninsured state banks. The Fed supervises bank holding companies.

FINANCIAL INNOVATION AND THE GROWTH OF THE "SHADOW BANKING SYSTEM"

A change in the financial environment will stimulate a search by financial institutions for innovations that are likely to be profitable. The research and development of new financial products and services is known as *financial engineering*. Financial innovation has come from three basic sources that often interact with each other:

- *Responses to changes in demand conditions*: The increasing volatility of interest rates since the 1970s has increased interest-rate risk resulting in an increase in the demand for adjustable-rate mortgages and *financial derivatives* such as *futures contracts* to *hedge* interest-rate risk.

- *Responses to changes in supply conditions*: Improvements in *information technology* have lowered the cost of processing financial transactions so financial institutions can supply new products and services, and improved information acquisition making it easier for firms to issue securities. As a result, there has been an increase in the use of bank credit and debit cards and electronic banking such as the ATM, ABM, and virtual bank. Lesser-known firms are now able to issue junk bonds and commercial paper. *Securitization* has allowed illiquid loans to be bundled into standardized amounts and sold to a third party. This innovation was at the center of the subprime mortgage crisis of the mid 2000s.

- *The desire to avoid costly regulations*: Two particularly burdensome regulations that have caused loophole mining and innovation are reserve requirements, which acted as a tax on deposits, and deposit rate ceilings known as Regulation Q, which caused deposit withdrawal known as *disintermediation*. In response, we find growth in money market mutual funds and sweep accounts.

Financial innovation has reduced banks' cost advantages in acquiring funds and their income advantages on their assets. Banks' cost advantage in acquiring funds was reduced when competitive pressures caused the elimination of Regulation Q. Banks' income advantages on assets have been reduced due to competition from junk bonds, securitization, and commercial paper. As a result, banks' traditional lines of business (making loans funded by deposits) have become less profitable, leading to a decline in traditional banking and an expansion in the shadow banking system. Banks have responded by making riskier loans for real estate and for corporate takeovers and leveraged buyouts, and by pursuing off-balance-sheet activities.

STRUCTURE OF THE U.S. COMMERCIAL BANKING INDUSTRY

The United States has a much greater number of commercial banks than other countries due to anti-competitive *branching* restrictions. The McFadden Act of 1927, coupled with the Douglas Amendment of 1956, essentially eliminated branching across state lines. The Midwestern agricultural states restricted branching the most so they have the largest number of small banks. The large number of banks is evidence of a lack of competition generated from protected market areas, not evidence of competition. The growth of banks holding companies and ATMs are responses to branching restrictions that weakened the anti-competitive effects of those restrictions.

BANK CONSOLIDATION AND NATIONWIDE BANKING

After a period of stability in the number of commercial banks from 1934 to the mid-1980s, the number of banks has declined substantially. From 1985 to 1992, bank failures and consolidations both contributed to the reduction in the number of banks. During this period, banks consolidated because loophole mining reduced the effectiveness of branching restrictions. This exposed the gains of diversification, economies of scale, and *economies of scope* that could be made from allowing banks to expand their markets areas. Reciprocal agreements between groups of states allowing expansion across state lines created *superregional banks*. Bank consolidation continued in the 1990s due to the increase in information technology favoring large banks and the Riegle-Neal Interstate Banking and Branching Efficiency Act of 1994, which established a basis for a nationwide banking system through interstate branching. Most economists think that, in the future, the U.S. banking industry will have fewer but still several thousand banks, and a larger number of megabanks. Economists also think that the benefits of bank consolidation of gains in efficiency and risk reduction through diversification will outweight the costs of reduced competition and reduced lending to small businesses. Indeed, most economists see nationwide branching as increasing competition.

SEPARATION OF THE BANKING AND OTHER FINANCIAL SERVICE INDUSTRIES

The Glass-Steagall Act of 1933 separated banking from other financial services industries such as securities, insurance, and real estate. Over time, both banks and other financial institutions encroached on the other's territory. In 1987, the Fed allowed BHCs to underwrite securities as long as the revenue generated was less than a certain amount. Glass-Steagall was repealed by the Gramm-Leach-Bliley Financial Services Modernization Act of 1999 in order to put U.S. banks on an equal footing with foreign banks that have fewer restrictions on the type of business in which they can engage. This act has caused further consolidation of the banking industry. The subprime financial crisis also caused numerous mergers between banks and investment banks, quickly creating more complex banking organizations.

THRIFT INDUSTRY: REGULATION AND STRUCTURE

Regulation of structure of the thrift industry closely parallels that of the commercial bank industry. Savings and loans are primarily supervised by the Office of Thrift Supervision while their deposit insurance is administered by the FDIC. S&Ls have historically had more liberal branching laws than banks and they can get longer-term loans at lower rates from the Federal Home Loan Bank System than banks can from the Fed. Mutual savings banks are regulated by the states and usually receive insurance from the FDIC. Credit unions are organized around a common bond such as employment. They are regulated by the National Credit Union Association and get deposit insurance from the National Credit Union Share Insurance Fund. Credit unions are typically small.

INTERNATIONAL BANKING

International banking has undergone rapid growth due to three factors. First, the rapid growth of international trade and multinational corporations has caused firms to need banking services in foreign countries. Second, American banks have become involved in global investment banking. Third, American banks have become involved in the Eurodollar market. Eurodollars are dollar denominated deposits in foreign banks outside the United States or foreign branches of U.S. banks. The majority of these deposits are time deposits that are then loaned to U.S. banks in units of $1 million. U.S. banks engage in international banking by opening branches overseas, creating Edge Act corporations, and opening international banking facilities (IBFs) in the United States. Foreign banks operate in the United States by owning an agency office of the foreign bank, a subsidiary U.S. bank, or a branch of the foreign bank. Foreign banks have been very successful in the United States. The International Banking Act of 1978 removed some of the advantage of foreign banks, and put U.S. banks on a more equal footing with foreign banks with regard to reserve requirements and branching.

Helpful Hints

1. Since branching has historically been restricted in the United States, banks have expanded via bank holding companies (BHCs). A holding company is a corporation that exists to hold stock in other companies. A BHC holds stock in banks, and bank-related companies. A lead bank that wishes to expand but cannot open branch offices creates a holding company and sells its stock to the holding company. The original stockholders of the lead bank now own stock in the BHC rather than the bank itself. While the bank could not buy other banks, the BHC can purchase other banks. The banks that are owned by the holding company are considered "affiliates" of the BHC but not branches. That is, the affiliates are still technically separate corporations and the flow of funds between those affiliates is restricted. When banks are allowed to branch, funds can flow freely between branches because each branch is simply a separate office of the same bank, and deposits from one branch can be loaned out from another branch. BHCs are considered inefficient substitutes for branching, and given the option banks will expand through branching rather than through BHCs.

Terms and Definitions

Choose a definition for each key term.

Key Terms:

_____bank holding companies

_____branches

_____central bank

_____community banks

_____deposit rate ceilings

_____disintermediation

_____dual banking system

_____economies of scope

_____futures contracts

_____hedge

_____national banks

_____securitization

_____shadow banking system

_____state banks

_____superregional banks

_____sweep account

Definitions:

1. State chartered banks

2. The U.S. banking system where banks supervised by the federal government operate side by side with banks supervised by the state governments

3. Additional offices of banks that conducts banking operations

4. Restriction on the maximum interest rate payable on deposits

5. Federally chartered banks

6. An arrangement in which any balances above a certain amount in a corporation's checking account at the end of a business day are "swept out" of the account and invested in overnight repos that pay the corporation interest

7. The process of transforming illiquid financial assets into marketable capital market instruments

8. Companies that own one or more banks

9. A contract in which the seller agrees to provide a certain standardized commodity to the buyer on a specific future date at an agreed upon price

10. The government agency that oversees the banking system and is responsible for the supply of money and credit in the economy

11. To protect oneself against risk

12. The ability to use one resource to provide many different products and services

13. Bank holding companies similar in size to money center banks, but whose headquarters are not based in a money center city

14. A reduction in the flow of funds into the banking system that causes the amount of financial intermediation to decline

15. Financial system in which bank lending has been replaced by lending via the securities markets

16. Small banks

Problems and Short-Answer Questions

PRACTICE PROBLEMS

1. The following questions address financial innovation in U.S. banking.
    a. List the three main sources for financial innovation and provide examples of the banking industry's responses to each.

    _____

    _____

    _____

    _____

    _____

    _____

    _____

    b. Prior to 2008, the Fed did not pay interest on bank reserves. For every $1,000 in deposits, how much did banks lose in forgone interest (opportunity cost) because of reserve requirements if banks charged 8% on loans and the require reserve ratio was 10%?

    _____

    _____

    c. For every $1,000 in deposits, how much did banks lose in forgone interest (opportunity cost) because of reserve requirements if banks charged 12% on loans and the require reserve ratio was 20%?

    _____

    _____

    d. Use your answers to *b* and *c* above to make a general statement regarding how interest rates and reserve requirements affect the cost to banks of holding required reserves.

    _____

    _____

2. The following questions address trends in banks traditional lines of business.
    a. Has there been an increase or a decrease in banks traditional lines of business of making loans funded by deposits? Why?

    _____

    _____

    b. What factor reduced banks cost advantage in acquiring funds? Explain.

    _____

    _____

    c. What three factors reduced banks income advantages on its assets?

    _____

    _____

    _____

    d. How have banks responded to these events?

    _____

    _____

3. The following questions address bank consolidation and nationwide banking.
    a. From the mid-1980s through the early 1990s, what were the sources of the reduction in the number of banks in the United States?

    _____

    b. After the early 1990s, what were the sources of the reduction in the number of banks?

    _____

    c. Prior to 1994, by what method did banks expand? Why?

    _____

    _____

    d. After 1994, by what method did banks generally expand? Why?

    _____

    _____

SHORT-ANSWER QUESTIONS

1. Has the United States always had a central bank? What are the names and dates of the U.S. central banks?

   _____

   _____

2. What is a dual banking system? How did the United States arrive at such a system?

   _____

   _____

   _____

3. What did the Glass-Steagall Act do? Why was it enacted? Why was it repealed?

   _____

   _____

   _____

4. What did Regulation Q do? When it was repealed, what two effects did it have on the banking system?

   _____

   _____

   _____

5. What did the McFadden Act of 1927 and the Douglas Amendment of 1956 do?

   _____

   _____

6. What two innovations helped banks avoid branching restrictions?

   _____

7. Why has the growth in junk bonds and commercial paper market reduced the demand for bank loans?

   _____

   _____

8. What are thrifts? How do their regulation and structure compare to commercial banks?

   _____

   _____

9. What three factors has caused the rapid growth in international banking?

   _____

   _____

10. What are the three main ways U.S. banks engage in international banking?

    _____

    _____

Critical Thinking

Your roommate is reading an article in the *Wall Street Journal* about trends in banking. It states that there are about half the number of banks in the United States today when compared to 20 years ago. Due to mergers, acquisitions, and interstate branching, the number of banks is expected to continue to drop in the future. Your roommate says, "The drop in the number of banks is clearly reducing competition. Borrowers are surely to be forced to pay higher interest rates in the future. This drop in the number of banks has to be bad for consumers."

1. How many banks does the United States have when compared to other countries? Why the great disparity?

   _____

   _____

2. Which banking system would be more competitive: A banking system where 1,000 banks serve 1,000 towns and each town is served by one bank, or a banking system where ten banks, each with 1,000 offices, serve 1,000 towns so each town has ten banks from which to choose? Why?

   _____

   _____

3. Which are generally more efficient and have lower risk, large banks or community banks? Why?

   _____

   _____

   _____

4. Is the reduction in the number of banks evidence of lack of competition? Explain.

_____

_____

_____

5. Is your roommate's statement correct? That is, is it true that having fewer banks is likely to be bad for the consumer? Explain.

_____

_____

_____

Self-Test

TRUE/FALSE QUESTIONS

_____1. There are many more commercial banks than thrift institutions.

_____2. The average national bank is larger than the average state bank.

_____3. The Federal Reserve System, established in 1791, is the first and only central bank in the United States.

_____4. Bank holding companies are supervised by the Federal Reserve.

_____5. Economic theory suggests that banks will try to skirt regulations that restrict their ability to earn profits.

_____6. The Glass-Steagall Act of 1933 separated the activities of commercial banking from the activities of the securities industry.

_____7. Regulation Q and the McFadden Act were instituted to increase competition within the banking industry.

_____8. The reduction in the number of banks in the United States over the last twenty years is evidence that there is less competition in the banking system today when compared to twenty years ago.

_____9. Growth in the commercial paper market, the junk bond market, and securitization have reduced the return on traditional bank assets and forced banks to seek profits elsewhere.

_____10. Suppose the Fed pays no interest on bank reserves. If the interest rate for bank loans is 10% and the reserve requirement is 10%, a bank loses $1 in interest for each $100 of deposits due to the reserve requirement.

_____11. Most economists think that in the long run, the United States will have only five or ten banks, each with thousands of offices, just like most foreign countries.

_____12. Large banks are less efficient than community banks, and have a greater likelihood of failure.

_____13. The Riegle-Neal Interstate Banking and Branching Efficiency Act of 1994 repealed the Glass-Steagall Act.

_____14. Branching regulations for savings and loans have historically been more liberal than for commercial banks.

_____15. Prior to 1978, foreign banks operating in the United States enjoyed advantages over U.S. banks because foreign banks could branch across state lines and foreign banks were not subject to a reserve requirement.

MULTIPLE-CHOICE QUESTIONS

1. The United States is said to have a dual banking system because
   a. the depository system includes both commercial banks and thrift institutions.
   b. commercial banks offer both banking and securities market services.
   c. state banks and national banks operate side by side.
   d. banks are regulated and examined by both the Federal Reserve and the FDIC.
   e. the banking system includes both bank holding company affiliates and branch banks.

2. The Office of the Comptroller of the Currency charters and supervises
   a. national banks.
   b. state banks.
   c. bank holding companies.
   d. investment banks.

3. At present there are little more than
   a. 5,000 commercial banks in the United States.
   b. 7,000 commercial banks in the United States.
   c. 10,000 commercial banks in the United States.
   d. 15,000 commercial banks in the United States.

4. The Federal Reserve is a
   a. national bank.
   b. dual bank.
   c. state bank.
   d. central bank.
   e. bank holding company.

5. The Glass-Steagall Act of 1933
   a. established the Federal Reserve.
   b. separated the activities of national banks from those of state banks.
   c. separated the activities of commercial banks from those of the securities industry.
   d. separated the activities of commercial banks from those of the thrift industry.

6. Which of the following financial innovations helped banks reduce their interest-rate risk that came from the increased volatility of interest rates since the 1970s?
   a. ATMs
   b. bank holding companies
   c. adjustable-rate mortgages and financial derivatives such as futures contracts
   d. junk bonds and commercial paper

7. Regulation Q
   a. set the ceiling on interest rates that banks could pay on their deposits.
   b. restricted interstate branching.
   c. separated commercial banking and investment banking.
   d. set the ceiling on interest rates that banks could charge on their loans.

8. When depositors fail to deposit funds in banks or withdraw existing deposits because they have found more profitable alternatives, we have observed
   a. securitization.
   b. the effects of economies of scope.
   c. financial innovation
   d. disintermediation.

9. Suppose the Fed pays no interest on bank reserves. For every $1,000 in deposits, how much do banks lose in forgone interest due to the reserve requirement if the reserve requirement is 10% and the rate at which banks lend is 7%?
   a. $7
   b. $10
   c. $70
   d. $100

10. Which of the following is <u>not</u> a source of competition that has reduced the income advantages banks once had on their traditional assets?
   a. growth in the commercial paper market
   b. elimination of Regulation Q
   c. growth in the junk bond market
   d. increasing use of securitization

11. The McFadden Act of 1927
   a. established the FDIC
   b. established the Fed.
   c. eliminated interstate branching.
   d. eliminated bank holding company expansion across state lines.

12. The decline in traditional banking in the United States has led to
    a. a reduction in the profitability of banking.
    b. an increase in riskier bank loans and off-balance-sheet activities of banks.
    c. an increase in the number of banks.
    d. an increase in the number of savings and loans.

13. Historically in the United States, branching laws have been most restrictive in the
    a. Northeast.
    b. Southwest.
    c. West Coast states.
    d. Midwest.
    e. Southeast.

14. The large number of banks in the United States
    a. is evidence that the banking system in the United States is very competitive.
    b. resulted from restrictive branching laws that reduced competition.
    c. are likely to substantially grow in number over the next few decades.
    d. are roughly equal to the number of banks in most developed countries.

15. Which of the following laws established a basis for a nationwide banking system in the United States?
    a. Riegle-Neal Interstate Banking and Branch Efficiency Act of 1994
    b. Gramm-Leach-Bliley Financial Services Modernization Act of 1999
    c. International Banking Act of 1978
    d. Glass-Steagall Act of 1933
    e. McFadden Act of 1927

16. The bundling of a portfolio of mortgage or student loans in to a marketable capital market instrument is know as
    a. computerization.
    b. consolidation.
    c. economies of scope.
    d. securitization.

17. Which of the following innovations helped banks circumvent restrictive branching laws?
    a. financial derivatives
    b. securitization
    c. bank holding companies and ATMs
    d. sweep accounts

18. Which of the following statements about savings and loans is true?
    a. There are more savings and loans than banks.
    b. Savings and loans do not have deposit insurance.
    c. Savings and loans have historically been subject to more restrictive branching laws than banks.
    d. Savings and loans are supervised by the Office of Thrift Supervision.

19. Compared to banks, credit unions
    a. have customers that share some common bond such as employment.
    b. tend to be larger.
    c. have no deposit insurance.
    d. usually lend to commercial enterprises.
    e. All of the above are correct.

20. Which of the following is <u>not</u> true regarding international banking?
    a. International banking has grown in part because of the growth in international trade.
    b. Foreign banks in the U.S. operate at a disadvantage compared to U.S. banks because they have higher reserve requirements and more restrictive branching rules.
    c. Eurodollars are dollar denominated deposits in foreign banks outside the U.S. or foreign branches of U.S. banks.
    d. U.S. banks can engage in international banking by opening branches overseas, creating Edge Act corporations, and opening IBFs in the United States.

Solutions

Terms and Definitions

 8 bank holding companies

 3 branches

10 central bank

16 community banks

 4 deposit rate ceilings

14 disintermediation

 2 dual banking system

12 economies of scope

 9 futures contracts

11 hedge

 5 national banks

 7 securitization

15 shadow banking system

 1 state banks

13 superregional banks

 6 sweep account

Practice Problems

1. a. Changes in demand conditions: interest rate volatility caused lenders to increase the demand for adjustable-rate mortgages and futures contracts.

    Changes in supply conditions: cost reductions from improvements in information technology increased the use of bank credit and debit cards, and electronic banking. It also allowed for expansion of junk bonds, commercial paper, and securitization.

    Avoidance of costly regulations: to avoid reserve requirements and Regulation Q, money market mutual funds and sweep accounts were created.

    b. $1,000 × 0.08 × 0.10 = $8

    c. $1,000 × 0.12 × 0.20 = $24

    d. The greater the interest rate and reserve requirement, the greater the opportunity cost of holding required reserves.

2. a. Decrease. More competition has made traditional banking less profitable.

    b. The elimination of Regulation Q caused banks to have to pay a competitive market rate for their deposits.

    c. Competition from junk bonds, securitization, and commercial paper have reduced the demand for bank loans and reduced profit on bank loans.

    d. Banks made riskier loans and pursued off-balance-sheet activities to earn fee income.

3. a. Bank failures and consolidation.

    b. Bank consolidation.

    c. Bank holding companies, because interstate branching was essentially illegal.

    d. Branching, because the Reigle-Neal Interstate Banking and Branching Efficiency Act was passed, making interstate branching legal.

Short-Answer Questions

1. No. Bank of the United States (1791-1811), Second Bank of the United States (1816-1832), Federal Reserve System (1913-today).

2. Banks supervised by the federal government operating side by side with banks supervised by the state governments. The federal government passes a law taxing state bank notes with the intention of eliminating state banks. State banks avoided the regulation, survived, and operate along side national banks.

3. It separated the activities of banking from those of the securities industry. Investment banking activities of banks were blamed for bank failures during the Depression. To put U.S. banks on an equal footing with foreign banks.

4. It set the maximum interest rate banks could pay on deposits. Repeal allowed banks to compete for deposits to reduce disintermediation, but it made the cost of funds rise to banks so they lost their cost advantage on their source of funds.

5. They made interstate branching illegal and let each state decide branching restrictions within that state.

6. The establishment of bank holding companies and ATMs.

7. It has given less well-known and smaller companies the ability to bypass banks by gaining a direct access to credit.

8. Savings and loans, mutual savings banks, and credit unions. It so closely parallels commercial banking that, in the case of S&Ls, regulating them separately from banks may no longer make sense.

9. The rapid growth of international trade and multinational corporations, increased involvement of American banks in global investment banking, and the expansion of the Eurodollar market.

10. By opening branches overseas, creating Edge Act corporations, and opening international banking facilities (IBFs) in the United States.

Critical Thinking

1. The United States has thousands more than any other country. The United States restricted branch banking to protect the markets of small banks, particularly in the Midwest.

2. Ten banks each with 1,000 offices would be more competitive because each bank customer would have a choice of ten banks rather than just one local bank.

3. Large banks are more efficient because they can take advantage of economies of scale and scope from advances in information technology. Large banks are better diversified so they have lower risk of failure.

4. No. The large number of banks is evidence of a lack of competition in the past due to branching restrictions. As banks compete, many will fail or be acquired by more efficient banks, reducing the number of banks.

5. No. Fewer banks with more branches is likely to offer the bank customer more choices, greater efficiency, and lower risk.

True/False Questions

1. F
2. T
3. F
4. T
5. T
6. T
7. F
8. F
9. T
10. T
11. F
12. F
13. F
14. T
15. T

Multiple-Choice Questions

1. c
2. a
3. b
4. d
5. c
6. c
7. a
8. d
9. a
10. b
11. c
12. b
13. d
14. b
15. a
16. d
17. c
18. d
19. a
20. b

13 Central Banks and the Federal Reserve System

Chapter Review

PREVIEW

This chapter describes the goals and institutional structure of the Federal Reserve, the European Central Bank, and other foreign central banks. Knowing the institutional structure of a central bank will help you to understand who controls the central bank, what motivates its behavior, and who holds the reigns of power within the central bank. A key feature of the institutional structure of a central bank is the degree to which it is independent of political pressures from government officials outside of the central bank. This chapter examines the advantages and disadvantages of central bank independence.

THE PRICE STABILITY GOAL AND THE NOMINAL ANCHOR

Price stability, which is defined as low and stable inflation, is increasingly viewed as the most important goal of monetary policy. Unstable prices (inflation) create uncertainty, which hampers economic growth. Achieving price stability requires the use of a *nominal anchor*, which ties down the price level and limits the *time-inconsistency problem*. The time-inconsistency problem arises when monetary policy is conducted using discretion and re-evaluated on a day-to-day basis without considering the potential long-run consequences of those day-to-day decisions. Policymakers are always tempted to pursue a discretionary policy that is more expansionary than firms or workers expect in order to boost output in the short run. But firms and workers would eventually come to expect such policy and would increase their wages and prices, which would counteract any expansionary effect of monetary policy on output and lead only to higher inflation. Therefore, a central bank is better off if it does not try to surprise people in the first place and instead tries to keep inflation under control. A nominal anchor helps a central bank avoid the time-inconsistency problem by focusing on the long-term goal of controlling inflation.

OTHER GOALS OF MONETARY POLICY

Five additional goals of monetary policy are (1) high employment, (2) economic growth, (3) stability of financial markets, (4) interest-rate stability, and (5) stability in foreign exchange markets. High employment means a level of employment that is consistent with the *natural rate of unemployment*--the unemployment rate that would exist when the demand for labor equals the supply of labor, taking the frictions in the labor market into account. The second goal, economic growth, is consistent with low unemployment. Financial market stability is important in order to avoid financial crises, which interfere with the ability of financial markets to channel funds to people with productive investment opportunities. Interest rate stability is desirable because it makes it easier for firms and households to plan for the future. International trade is increasingly important in both the U.S. economy as well as elsewhere. Stabilizing extreme movements in the value of the dollar in foreign exchange markets is therefore an important goal for monetary policy.

SHOULD PRICE STABILITY BE THE PRIMARY GOAL OF MONETARY POLICY?

In the long run, price stability is consistent with the other five goals mentioned above. But in the short run, price stability often conflicts with these other goals. Central banks such as the European Central Bank, the Bank of England, the Bank of Canada, and the Reserve Bank of New Zealand have a *hierarchical mandate* that states that as long as price stability is achieved, other goals can be pursued by the central bank. The Federal Reserve has a *dual mandate* that states that price stability and maximum employment are co-equal objectives. Both types of mandates can work equally well as long as central banks maintain price stability as their long-run goal.

ORIGINS OF THE FEDERAL RESERVE SYSTEM

Two attempts to establish central banks in the United States during the nineteenth century failed because the American public feared centralization of power and moneyed interests.

After the charter for the Second Bank of the United States expired in 1836, U.S. financial markets experienced periodic bank panics. The widespread bank panic of 1907 convinced the public that there was a need for a central bank to prevent future panics. The Fed was established in 1913 by an act of Congress. To address the public's fear of centralized power and mistrust of moneyed interests, Congress wrote an elaborate system of checks and balances into the Federal Reserve act. An important feature of the act that was meant to ease fear of centralized power is that it created 12 regional Federal Reserve banks spread throughout the country.

STRUCTURE OF THE FEDERAL RESERVE SYSTEM

The Federal Reserve consists of the following entities: *Federal Reserve banks, the Board of Governors* of the Federal Reserve System and the *Federal Open Market Committee*, the Federal Advisory Council and member commercial banks, which are about a third of all commercial banks. There are 12 Federal Reserve banks. The three largest are New York, Chicago, and San Francisco. Each Federal Reserve Bank is part government and part private. The directors of the Federal Reserve banks represent all constituencies of the American public: professional bankers; prominent leaders from industry; labor, agriculture, and the consumer sector; and representatives of the public interest. The 12 Federal Reserve banks perform the following functions:

- Clear checks

- Issue new currency

- Withdraw damaged currency from circulation

- Administer and make discount loans to banks in their districts

- Evaluate proposed mergers and applications for banks to expand their activities

- Act as liaisons between the business community and the Federal Reserve System

- Examine bank holding companies and state-chartered member banks

- Collect data on local business conditions

- Use their staffs of professional economists to research topics related to the conduct of monetary policy

Directors of the 12 Federal Reserve banks "establish" the discount rate and determine which banks get discount loans. The Board of Governors is comprised of seven members who are appointed by the president and confirmed by the senate for 14-year nonrenewable terms. The chairman is one of the seven board members and serves a four-year term.

The Federal Open Market Committee (FOMC) is comprised of the Board of Governors, and 5 of the 12 Federal Reserve Bank presidents. The president of the Federal Reserve Bank of New York is always a member of the FOMC. The remaining four positions on the FOMC rotate annually among the remaining 11 Federal Reserve Bank presidents. The FOMC meets eight times per year. At each FOMC meeting, the Board of Governors' director of Research and Statistics presents the national economic forecast contained in the "green book." The Board's director of Monetary Affairs presents alternative monetary policy scenarios as outlined in the "blue book." The FOMC votes on the direction of monetary policy as well as the monetary policy statement and then directs the open market desk at the Federal Reserve Bank of New York to conduct the appropriate *open market operations* necessary to achieve that policy.

HOW INDEPENDENT IS THE FED?

A Central Bank is *instrument independent* if it has the ability to choose its own monetary policy instruments and *goal independent* if it has the ability to choose its own goals for monetary policy. The Federal Reserve has both types of independence. One important feature of the Fed that makes it independent is that it funds its own operations mainly through interest earned on its holdings of government securities. Congress can influence the Federal Reserve through legislation. The president can influence the Federal Reserve to a limited extent through his appointments to the Board of Governors.

STRUCTURE AND INDEPENDENCE OF THE EUROPEAN CENTRAL BANK

The European Central Bank (ECB) rivals the Federal Reserve in terms of importance in the central banking world. The ECB has a structure similar to the structure of the Federal Reserve, but there are important differences between the two central banks. In contrast to the Federal Reserve, the ECB has less centralized power and is not involved in supervision and regulation of financial institutions.

The Governing Council is the committee within the ECB that plays a role similar to that of the FOMC. The Governing Council decides on monetary policy by consensus rather than by vote as in the FOMC. Another difference is that the Governing Council holds a press conference following each monetary policy meeting while the FOMC simply releases a statement announcing its decision about the course for monetary policy. The ECB is the most independent central bank in the world. The Maastricht Treaty specifies "price stability" as the single goal of the ECB.

STRUCTURE AND INDEPENDENCE OF OTHER FOREIGN CENTRAL BANKS

On paper the Bank of Canada has less instrument independence than the Federal Reserve because the minister of finance can issue a directive that the Bank must follow. But in practice this has not happened. The Bank of Canada has less goal independence than the Fed because it has a single target of low inflation. In 1997 the Bank of England was granted the power to set the interest rate, but the Bank of England does not have complete instrument independence because the government has the power to overrule the Bank's interest rate decisions "for a limited period in extreme economic circumstances." The Bank of England is also less goal independent than the Federal Reserve because it has a single goal of low inflation that is set by the Chancellor of the Exchequer (the equivalent of the Treasury Secretary in the United States). The Bank of Japan was granted greater instrument and goal independence in 1998. Before that time the government had voting members sitting on the monetary policy committee. Representatives from the government still attend monetary policy meetings but no longer have voting rights. There is a worldwide trend towards greater central bank independence. Both theory and experience suggest that more independent central banks produce better monetary policy.

EXPLAINING CENTRAL BANK BEHAVIOR

The theory of bureaucratic behavior suggests that the objective of a bureaucracy is to maximize its own welfare. As predicted by this theory, the Fed has fought vigorously to preserve its autonomy, it avoids conflict by slowly, rather than abruptly increasing interest rates to slow the economy, and it has successfully expanded its jurisdiction to cover all banks thereby increasing its power.

SHOULD THE FED BE INDEPENDENT?

An independent Federal Reserve is less subject to political pressures, which could lead to excessive inflation or a political business cycle. Furthermore, an independent Federal Reserve is more likely to resist pressure to help the Treasury finance deficit spending by purchasing government securities. Opponents of Federal Reserve independence argue that it is undemocratic to have monetary policy controlled by an elite group responsible to no one. Another argument against Fed independence is that by placing the Fed under the control of Congress, fiscal and monetary policy could be better coordinated. Independence does not imply that the Fed will always be successful. Recent research supports the prediction that greater central bank independence is associated with lower inflation rates. Furthermore, those lower inflation rates have not come at the expense of higher unemployment or greater output fluctuations.

Helpful Hints

Price stability is the most important goal of monetary policy. Central banks have successfully achieved price stability using monetary targeting, inflation targeting, dual mandates, and hierarchical mandates. The key point to understand about the institutional structure of the Federal Reserve and other central banks is how institutional structure relates to independence. Independent central banks are less likely to create excessive inflation and a *political business cycle*. On the other hand, an independent central bank is potentially less accountable for its policies. Worldwide there has been a greater movement toward central bank independence in recent years. As predicted by theory, greater central bank independence has been associated with lower inflation.

Terms and Definitions

Choose a definition for each key term.

Key Terms:

_____dual mandate

_____hierarchical mandate

_____natural rate of unemployment

_____nominal anchor

_____price stability

_____time-inconsistency problem

_____Board of Governors of the Federal Reserve System

_____Federal Open Market Committee

_____Federal Reserve banks

_____goal independence

_____instrument independence

_____open market operations

_____political business cycle

Definitions:

1. The committee that is comprised of the Board of Governors, the president of the Federal Reserve Bank of New York, and four other Federal Reserve Bank presidents

2. The problem that occurs when monetary policymakers conduct monetary policy in a discretionary way and pursue expansionary policies that are attractive in the short run but lead to bad long-run outcomes

3. A monetary policy practice that puts priority on one goal above all others

4. A nominal variable such as the inflation rate or the money supply that ties down the price level to achieve price stability

5. The ability of the central bank to set goals of monetary policy

6. The rate of unemployment consistent with full employment at which the demand for labor equals the supply of labor

7. The seven-member board that heads the Federal Reserve System

8. The purchase and sale of government securities by the Federal Reserve that affect both interest rates and the amount of reserves in the banking system

9. A monetary policy practice that aims to achieve two co-equal objectives

10. A situation in which monetary policy is expansionary prior to an election and contractionary after an election

11. Low and stable inflation

12. The ability of the central bank to set monetary policy instruments

13. The 12 banks of the Federal Reserve System

Problems and Short-Answer Questions

PRACTICE PROBLEMS

1. a.   Give an example of a nominal anchor.

   _____

   _____

   b.   Describe the time-inconsistency problem as it applies to monetary policy.

   _____

   _____

   _____

   _____

   c.   Explain how a nominal anchor helps a central bank avoid the time-inconsistency problem.

   _____

   _____

   _____

   _____

2.   The first two attempts at establishing a central bank in the United States failed.
   a.   What characteristics of American politics before the twentieth century resulted in their demise?

   _____

   _____

   b.   What recurring economic problem was attributed to the lack of a central bank in the later half of the nineteenth century?

   _____

   _____

c. When was the Federal Reserve founded?

_____

d. What specific features of the Federal Reserve were a response to the characteristics of American politics at the time of its founding?

_____

_____

_____

3. The authors of the Federal Reserve Act of 1913 designed a decentralized banking system that reflected their fears of centralized financial power. Today, this decentralization is still evident in the allocation of responsibilities and duties among the various Federal Reserve entities. Match the Federal Reserve entity to its responsibilities and duties given on the left by placing the appropriate letter in the space provided.

Responsibilities and Duties	Federal Reserve Entity
____ 1. clears checks	a. Board of Governors
____ 2. "establishes" discount rate	b. Federal Open Market Committee
____ 3. reviews and determines discount rate	c. Federal Reserve banks
____ 4. appointed by the president of the United States	
____ 5. appointed for 14-year terms	
____ 6. meets eight times a year	
____ 7. decides monetary policy	
____ 8. evaluates bank merger applications	
____ 9. determines margin requirements	
____ 10. issues new currency	

4. An important reason to study the institutional structure of central banks is to understand how that institutional structure relates to central bank independence.
a. What are the two types of central bank independence?

_____

b. What institutional features of the Federal Reserve make it independent?

_____

_____

5. The European Central Bank, which was started in January 1999, was patterned after the Federal Reserve, but there are some important differences between the two central banks as well.
   a. In what ways are the ECB and the Federal Reserve similar?

   _____

   _____

   b. In what ways are the ECB and the Federal Reserve different?

   _____

   _____

   c. Is the ECB more independent or less independent than the Federal Reserve? Why?

   _____

   _____

6. On paper, both the Bank of Canada and the Bank of England appear to lack instrument independence.
   a. Explain why both central banks appear on paper to lack instrument independence, and explain why in practice the two central banks essentially do have instrument independence.

   _____

   _____

   b. What institutional feature of the Bank of Canada and the Bank of England make both banks less goal independent than the Federal Reserve?

   _____

   _____

7. When studying the behavior of a central bank, it is important to understand the objectives facing a bureaucracy.
    a. What does the theory of bureaucratic behavior suggest is the objective of a bureaucracy?

    _____

    _____

    b. Name two ways that the Fed has acted that are consistent with the theory of bureaucratic behavior?

    _____

    _____

8. There are arguments for and against Federal Reserve independence.
    a. What are the arguments in favor of an independent Federal Reserve?

    _____

    _____

    b. What are the arguments against an independent Federal Reserve?

    _____

    _____

SHORT-ANSWER QUESTIONS

1. Why is price stability desirable?

    _____

    _____

2. Why is interest rate stability desirable?

    _____

    _____

3. Define the natural rate of unemployment and describe how it relates to a central bank's goals.

    _____

    _____

    _____

    _____

    _____

    _____

4. Does the Fed have a dual mandate or a hierarchical mandate?

    _____

5. Does the European Central Bank have a dual mandate or a hierarchical mandate?

    _____

6. What does it mean for a commercial bank to be a member of the Federal Reserve System?

    _____

    _____

7. What is contained in the "green book?" What is contained in the "blue book?"

    _____

    _____

8. In what ways can the president and Congress influence the Federal Reserve?

    _____

    _____

9. How did the Bank of Japan Law, which took effect in 1998, affect the independence of the Bank of Japan?

    _____

    _____

10. Do countries with greater central bank independence have higher unemployment or greater output fluctuations?

_____

_____

Critical Thinking

Suppose the Senator from your state introduces a bill to Congress that would require the Federal Reserve to establish a single goal of low inflation.

1. How would passage of this bill affect the Fed's goal and instrument independence?

_____

_____

_____

2. Would passage of this bill make the Fed more or less like the European Central Bank? Explain your answer.

_____

_____

_____

3. Would passage of this bill make it more or less likely that the Fed would pursue policies that would lead to a political business cycle? Explain your answer.

_____

_____

_____

Self-Test

TRUE/FALSE QUESTIONS

_____1. Price stability is viewed as the most desirable goal of monetary policy.

_____2. A time-inconsistent plan is a short-term plan that we abandon because doing so has long-term gains.

_____3. The European Central Bank has a dual mandate.

_____4. The Federal Reserve has a dual mandate.

_____5. Price stability is inconsistent with the natural rate of unemployment in the long run.

_____6. The Federal Reserve Act, which created a central bank with regional banks, reflected a compromise between traditional distrust of moneyed interest and concern for elimination of financial panics.

_____7. The president of the Federal Reserve Bank of New York is always a member of the Federal Open Market Committee.

_____8. The Governing Council of the European Central Bank plays a role similar to role played by the Federal Open Market Committee of the Federal Reserve.

_____9. The European Central Bank is less independent than the Federal Reserve.

_____10. The Bank of England has more goal independence than the Federal Reserve.

_____11. The Bank of Japan was granted greater instrument and goal independence in 1998.

_____12. In recent years central banks around the world have moved toward greater independence.

_____13. The theory of bureaucratic behavior may help explain why the Federal Reserve has resisted attempts by Congress to control its budget.

_____14. An independent central bank is less likely to produce a political business cycle.

_____15. A disadvantage of central bank independence is that it tends to result in higher inflation.

MULTIPLE-CHOICE QUESTIONS

1. A nominal anchor
   a. reduces employment and growth.
   b. leads to the time-inconsistency problem.
   c. can limit the time-inconsistency problem.
   d. all of the above

2. If a central bank pursues a time-inconsistent policy, it will eventually lead to
   a. lower inflation and higher output.
   b. lower inflation and no gain in output.
   c. higher inflation and higher output.
   d. higher inflation and no gain in output.

3. Which of the following is not a goal of monetary policy?
    a. high employment
    b. economic growth
    c. low interest rates
    d. stability in foreign exchange markets

4. A central bank that follows a hierarchical mandate
    a. mostly uses open-market operations and occasionally uses the discount rate.
    b. uses open-market operations and discount lending equally.
    c. will first achieve its primary goal before it pursues it secondary goals.
    d. places equal weight on all goals.

5. Price stability
    a. can only be achieved under a hierarchical mandate.
    b. can only be achieved under a dual mandate.
    c. can be achieved under a hierarchical mandate or a dual mandate as long as the primary goal in the short run and the long run is price stability.
    d. can be achieved under a hierarchical mandate or a dual mandate as long as the primary goal is price stability in the long run.

6. The Federal Reserve System is comprised of the following three entities:
    a. Federal Reserve banks, Board of Governors, and the U.S. Treasury.
    b. Federal Reserve banks, the Governing Council, and the U.S. Treasury.
    c. Federal Reserve banks, the Governing Council, and the Federal Open Market Committee.
    d. Federal Reserve banks, the Board of Governors, and the Federal Open Market Committee.

7. The Federal Open Market Committee is comprised of
    a. the five members of the Board of Governors plus seven of the twelve Federal Reserve Bank presidents.
    b. the seven members of the Board of Governors plus five of the twelve Federal Reserve Bank presidents.
    c. the five members of the Board of Governors plus the twelve Federal Reserve Bank presidents.
    d. the seven members of the Board of Governors plus the twelve Federal Reserve Bank presidents.

8. The directors of the Federal Reserve banks
    a. represent all constituencies of the American public.
    b. are all professional bankers.
    c. are appointed by the president of the United States.
    d. are all stockholders of the Federal Reserve Bank.

9. Monetary policy is determined by
    a. the Board of Governors.
    b. the 12 Federal Reserve banks.
    c. the Federal Open Market Committee.
    d. the Federal Reserve Advisory Committee.

10. Which of the following statements concerning the 14-year term for members of the Board of Governors is false?
    a.   The 14-year term is nonrenewable.
    b.   The 14-year term allows great independence from political considerations.
    c.   Members of the Board of Governors are appointed by the president for 14-year terms.
    d.   Most members of the Board of Governors serve out the entire 14-year term.

11. The Federal Reserve is remarkably free from political pressure because
    a.   it has an independent source of revenue.
    b.   its structure cannot be changed by Congress through legislation.
    c.   like members of the Supreme Court, members of the Board of Governors serve lifetime appointments.
    d.   the chairman of the Board of Governors is appointed by the Federal Reserve Bank presidents.

12. The ability of the central bank to set reserve requirements is an example of
    a.   goal independence.
    b.   instrument independence.
    c.   the theory of bureaucratic behavior.
    d.   independent review.

13. While the Fed enjoys a relativity high degree of independence for a government agency, it feels political pressure from the president and Congress because
    a.   Congress must reappoint Fed Governors every three years.
    b.   the Fed must go to Congress each year for operating revenues.
    c.   Congress could limit Fed power through legislation.
    d.   the president can dismiss a Fed Governor at any time.

14. The Bank of Canada is
    a.   less instrument independent than the Federal Reserve on paper and less goal independent than the Federal Reserve.
    b.   more instrument independent than the Federal Reserve on paper and less goal independent than the Federal Reserve.
    c.   less instrument independent than the Federal Reserve on paper and more goal independent than the Federal Reserve.
    d.   more instrument independent than the Federal Reserve on paper and more goal independent than the Federal Reserve.

15. The Bank of Japan
    a.   has two goals: price stability and low unemployment.
    b.   has a single goal: low unemployment.
    c.   has a single goal: price stability.
    d.   is not an independent central bank.

16. The theory of bureaucratic behavior may help explain why the Fed
    a.   is sometimes slow to increase interest rates.
    b.   limits reserve requirements to member banks.
    c.   has moved toward greater transparency in recent years.
    d.   is currently lobbying to give Congress authority over its budget.

17. The principal–agent problem
    a. is greater for an independent central bank than for politicians.
    b. is greater for politicians than for an independent central bank.
    c. explains why the Fed sets reserve requirements.
    d. explains why the Fed is sometimes slow to increase interest rates.

18. An independent Federal Reserve
    a. is more likely to produce higher inflation and less likely to produce a political business cycle.
    b. is more likely to produce higher inflation and more likely to produce a political business cycle.
    c. is less likely to produce higher inflation and less likely to produce a political business cycle.
    d. is less likely to produce higher inflation and more likely to produce a political business cycle.

19. Proponents of a Fed under the control of the president or Congress argue that
    a. greater control would help coordinate fiscal and monetary policies.
    b. the Fed has not always used its independence successfully.
    c. it is undemocratic to have monetary policy controlled by an elite group.
    d. all of the above

20. Greater central bank independence is associated with
    a. lower inflation and lower unemployment.
    b. lower inflation and no change in unemployment.
    c. lower inflation and higher unemployment.
    d. no change in either unemployment or inflation.

Solutions

Terms and Definitions

_9_ dual mandate

_3_ hierarchical mandate

_6_ natural rate of unemployment

_4_ nominal anchor

_11_ price stability

_2_ time-inconsistency problem

_7_ Board of Governors of the Federal Reserve System

_1_ Federal Open Market Committee

_13_ Federal Reserve banks

_5_ goal independence

_12_ instrument independence

_8_ open market operations

_10_ political business cycle

Practice Problems

1. a. The inflation rate and the money supply are both nominal anchors.

    b. The time-inconsistency problem is when policymakers are tempted to pursue a discretionary monetary policy that is more expansionary than expected by firms or people. Monetary policy makers will initially attempt to pursue such policies in order to boost output but once people and firms catch on to this strategy, inflation rises and there is no gain in output.

    c. Nominal anchors such as inflation or the money supply keep the central bank from pursuing overly-expansionary monetary policy and thus help avoid the time-inconsistency problem.

2. a. Before the twentieth century, American politics was characterized by a fear of centralized power and a mistrust of moneyed interests.

    b. Nationwide bank panics

    c. 1913

    d. The Federal Reserve act of 1913 specified an elaborate system of checks and balances and the power of the Federal Reserve was spread throughout the country by establishing 12 regional Federal Reserve banks.

3.

    _c_ 1. clears checks

    _c_ 2. "establishes" discount rate

    _a_ 3. reviews and determines discount rate

    _a_ 4. appointed by the president of the United States

    _a_ 5. appointed for 14-year terms

    _b_ 6. meets 8 times a year

    _b_ 7. decides monetary policy

    _c_ 8. evaluates bank merger applications

    _a_ 9. determines margin requirements

    _c_ 10. issues new currency

4. a. Instrument independence which describes the ability of a central bank to choose its monetary policy instruments and goal independence which describes the ability of a central bank to choose its monetary policy goals.

    b. Institutional features of the Federal Reserve which make it independent are: it has an independent source of revenue, and members of the Board of Governors are appointed for 14-year (technically) non-renewable terms.

5. a. Central banks in each country of the European monetary union which are called National Central Banks, have a similar role to that of the Federal Reserve banks. The ECB has an Executive Board which is similar in structure to the Board of Governors. The ECB's Governing Council which is comprised of the Executive Board and the presidents of the National Central Banks is similar to the FOMC and makes the decisions on monetary policy.

    b. The budgets of the Federal Reserve are controlled by the Board of Governors, while the National Central Banks control their own budgets and the budget of the ECB so the ECB has less power than the Board of Governors. Monetary operations in the Eurosystem are conducted by the National Central Banks in each country. Unlike the Federal Reserve, the ECB is not involved in supervision and regulation of financial institutions.

c. The ECB is more independent than the Federal Reserve. Like the Fed, the ECB controls is own budgets and the governments of the member countries are not allowed to issue instructions to the ECB. But unlike the Federal Reserve, the Eurosystem's charter cannot be changed by legislation; it can be changed only by revision of the Maastricht Treaty, which is a difficult process.

6. a. In both Canada and England, if the bank and the government disagree about the direction of monetary policy, the government can overrule the bank. But economic circumstances would have to be "extreme" and the government's ability to overrule monetary policy is constrained to a limited period of time so in practice it is unlikely that such overruling would occur.

b. The Bank of Canada and the Bank of England have inflation targets which makes them less goal-independent than the Fed.

7. a. According to the theory of bureaucratic behavior, the objective of a bureaucracy is to maximize its own welfare.

b. The Fed continually counterattacks congressional attempts to control its budget. When the Fed raises interest rates to slow the economy it does so slowly in order to minimize conflict with Congress and the president.

8. a. Subjecting the Fed to more political pressure might lead to more inflation in the economy and could possibly lead to a political business cycle. A less independent Fed might also be pressured to help finance deficit spending. Another argument supporting Federal Reserve independence is that the principal-agent problem is worse for politicians than for the Fed because politicians have fewer incentives to act in the public interest.

b. Independence means less accountability which some argue is inconsistent with a democracy. A less independent Fed would be more likely to pursue monetary policy that is consistent with fiscal policy. Finally, the Fed has not always used its independence successfully.

Short-answer Questions

1. Price stability is desirable because a rising price level creates uncertainty in the economy, and uncertainty might hamper economic growth.

2. Interest rate stability is desirable because fluctuations in interest rates create uncertainty in the economy, which makes it harder to plan for the future.

3. The natural rate of unemployment is the rate of unemployment that is consistent with full employment (the demand for labor equals the supply of labor). One of the goals of a central bank is full employment, so achieving an unemployment rate that is near the natural rate of unemployment is consistent with that goal. Another goal of a central bank is price stability. When unemployment is below the natural rate, inflation tends to rise, and when unemployment is above the natural rate, inflation tends to fall. Thus, keeping unemployment near the natural rate is also consistent with the goal of price stability.

4. The Fed has a dual mandate.

5. The European Central Bank has a hierarchical mandate.

6. All national banks are required to be members of the Federal Reserve System. State banks can choose to be members.

7. The "green book" contains the Board staff's national economic forecast. The "blue book" contains different scenarios for monetary policy.

8. The president can influence the Federal Reserve through his appointments to the Board of Governors. Congress can influence the Federal Reserve by passing legislation to make the Fed more accountable for its actions.

9. It increased the independence of the Bank of Japan by giving it more goal and instrument independence.

10. Countries with greater central bank independence do not have higher unemployment or greater output fluctuations.

Critical Thinking

1. Passage of this bill would reduce the Fed's goal independence. Current law does not require the Fed to pursue a specific inflation target. Passage of a bill requiring the Fed to pursue a specific inflation target would

therefore reduce the Fed's goal independence but it would not affect the Fed's instrument independence because the Fed would still have the ability to use any instrument it deems appropriate to achieve the specified inflation goal.

2. This bill would make the Fed more like the ECB. The Maastricht Treaty currently specifies that the overriding, long-term goal of the ECB is price stability.

3. Passage of this bill would make it less likely that the Fed would pursue policies that would lead to a political business cycle because it would make Fed policy more transparent. Both elected officials and the public would be able to evaluate whether the Fed is meeting its goal for inflation. Under current law, the Fed does not have an explicitly stated goal for inflation and so elected officials and the public are less able to evaluate whether the Fed is pursuing policies that would lead to a political business cycle.

8. a
9. c
10. d
11. a
12. b
13. c
14. a
15. c
16. a
17. b
18. c
19. d
20. b

True/False Questions

1. T
2. T
3. F
4. T
5. F
6. T
7. T
8. T
9. F
10. F
11. T
12. T
13. T
14. T
15. F

Multiple-Choice Questions

1. c
2. d
3. c
4. c
5. d
6. d
7. b

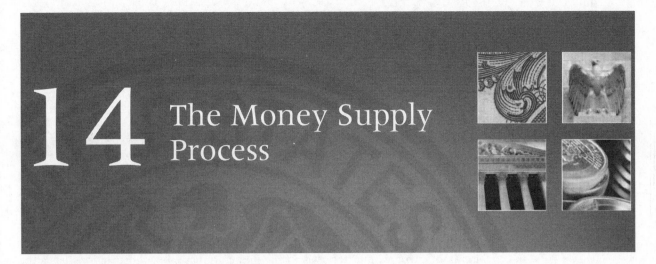

14 The Money Supply Process

Chapter Review

PREVIEW

This chapter describes the money supply process. Bank deposits are by far the largest component of the money supply. This chapter begins by showing how banks create deposits and how deposit creation affects the money supply. It then derives the *money multiplier*. After deriving a more realistic money multiplier, this chapter describes the sources of movement in the monetary base, the money multiplier and the money supply.

Throughout this chapter, money (M) is defined as M1, which is currency plus checkable deposits.

THREE PLAYERS IN THE MONEY SUPPLY PROCESS

The money supply process involves three players: the central bank (the Federal Reserve), banks (depository institutions), and depositors. Of these three players, the central bank--the Federal Reserve System--is the most important.

THE FED'S BALANCE SHEET

The simplified Fed balance sheet is as follows:

Federal Reserve System

Assets	Liabilities
Government securities	Currency in circulation
Discount Loans	Reserves

The sum of the Fed's liabilities, currency in circulation (C) plus *reserves* (R) is called the *monetary base* (MB). Reserves equal *required reserves* plus *excess reserves*. The ratio of required reserves to deposits is called the *required reserve ratio* (r). The required reserve ratio is established by the Federal Reserve and plays an important role in the deposit creation process.

CONTROL OF THE MONETARY BASE

The Federal Reserve exercises control over the monetary base through its buying and selling of securities on the open market, called *open-market operations* and through its extension of discount loans to banks. The Fed has more (but not complete) control over the total of the monetary base than the components of the monetary base (currency and reserves). Actions by the nonbank public can change the mix of currency and reserves in the monetary base, but those actions leave the total monetary base unchanged. When the Fed conducts an *open market purchase* of $100 bond from a bank, reserves, and therefore the monetary base, increase by $100. When the Fed conducts an open market purchase of a $100 bond from the nonbank public, the monetary base again increases by $100. But the increases could take the form of an increase in reserves if the nonbank public deposits the proceeds of the sale into a checking account, or it could take the form of an increase in currency in circulation if the nonbank public decides to hold the proceeds of the sale in currency. Obviously some intermediate case is possible as well; the nonbank public can hold some currency and some deposits, but the main point is that the Fed is able to precisely increase the monetary base by $100, but actions by the nonbank public, not the Fed, determine the mix of reserves and currency in circulation. When the Fed makes a $100 discount loan to a bank, the monetary base increases by $100. When a bank pays off a $100 discount loan from the Fed, the monetary base decreases by $100. The interest rate that the Fed charges on discount loans is called the *discount rate*.

Two sources of change in the monetary base that are outside of the Fed's control are Treasury deposits at the Fed and *float*. When the Treasury moves its deposits from commercial banks to the Fed (it must do this before it can spend the funds), then reserves in the banking system and therefore the monetary base, decline temporarily (reserves move back up once the money is spent by the Treasury). Float occurs when the Fed clears checks. The Fed often credits the account of the bank presenting the check for payment before it debits the account of the bank that the check is drawn on. For that brief period of time before the debit occurs, reserves in the banking system rise. Treasury purchases and float complicate but do not prevent the Fed from accurately controlling the monetary base.

The Fed does not have complete control over the monetary base because banks decide when they want to borrow from the Fed at the discount rate. Bank borrowing from the Fed is called *borrowed reserves* (BR). If we subtract borrowed reserves (BR) from the monetary base we get the *nonborrowed monetary base* (MB$_n$). The nonborrowed monetary base is directly under the control of the Fed and is affected only by open market operations.

MULTIPLE DEPOSIT CREATION: A SIMPLE MODEL

In order to derive the *simple deposit multiplier*, we assume that banks hold no excess reserves (they loan them out as soon as they get them) and the nonbank public holds no currency (only deposits). To illustrate how the deposit multiplier works, suppose the Fed makes an open market purchase of $100 bond from First National Bank. First National Bank will loan out that extra $100 in reserves by creating a $100 checking account deposit for the borrower. By creating that checking account balance, First National Bank has created $100 of new money and the money supply, which includes checking account balances, has increased by $100. This "creation" of money by the bank is key to understanding the *multiple deposit creation* process. But the creation of money does not stop with First National Bank's creation of a deposit. Presumably, the borrower of the $100 will spend that money and by doing so, that money will work its way into some other bank account (the bank account of the store owner where the purchase was made). Assuming that the store owner banks at Bank A, Bank A will now find itself with $100 in new deposits, and assuming the required reserve ratio is 10%, Bank A will keep $10 of that $100 deposit in reserves and loan out the remaining $90 to a new borrower. As was the case with the First National Bank, Bank A will make the loan by creating a checking account deposit for the borrower. Thus, at this stage of the process, Bank A has created an additional $90 of money. That $90 gets spent and the process continues. At the next stage, Bank B will receive a $90 deposit and it will keep 10% or $9 in required reserves and loan out the remaining $81. Thus, Bank B creates $81 of new money. This process continues with Banks C, D, E creating money each time they lend the excess reserves. Once this process is complete, the total amount of deposits (and therefore money) that will have been created by the banking system will be $1,000. In general, the relationship between the initial change in reserves and the total change in deposits in this simple example is given by the simple deposit multiplier $\Delta D = (1/r) \times \Delta R$, where ΔR is the initial change in reserves, r is the required reserve–deposit ratio and ΔD is the total change in deposits by the banking system. Although this formula is helpful for understanding the multiple deposit creation process, the actual creation of deposits is much less mechanical than the simple model indicates. If some of the proceeds from loans are held as currency, or if banks choose to hold all or some of their excess reserves, the money supply will not increase by as much as the simple model of multiple deposit creation tells us.

FACTORS THAT DETERMINE THE MONEY SUPPLY

The money supply is positively related to the *nonborrowed monetary base* (MB_n) as well as the level of *borrowed reserves* (BR) from the Fed. The money supply is negatively related to the required reserve ratio r. The money supply is negatively related to currency holdings as well as the amount of excess reserves.

OVERVIEW OF THE MONEY SUPPLY PROCESS

Three players—the Federal Reserve, depositors and banks—directly influence the money supply. The Federal Reserve influences the money supply by controlling *borrowed reserves*, the *nonborrowed monetary base,* and the required reserve ratio, *r*. Depositors influence the money supply through their decisions about currency holdings, and banks influence the money supply with their decisions about excess reserves. Depositors' behavior also influences bankers' decisions to hold excess reserves.

THE MONEY MULTIPLIER

The relationship between the monetary base and the money supply is $M = m \times MB$, where m denotes the money multiplier. The monetary base is also called *high-powered money* because a \$1 change in the monetary base leads to a more than \$1 change in the money supply. The size of the money multiplier, m, is negatively related to the *required reserve ratio*, *r*. The money multiplier is also negatively related to the *currency ratio*, *c*, which equals the ratio of the publics' holdings of currency to deposits (*C/D*) and the *excess reserves ratio*, *e*, which equals ratio of excess reserves held by banks to deposits (*ER/D*). The formula for the money multiplier is $m = (1 + c)/(r + e + c)$. An important difference between the money multiplier and the deposit multiplier is that the money multiplier is smaller because it is multiplying the monetary base, not just deposits. Although there is multiple expansion of deposits, there is no such expansion for currency. When e is small, as is typically the case, changes in e have a small impact on the money supply and the multiplier. However, during both the subprime financial crisis and the Great Depression, e was much larger and its movements had a substantial effect on the money supply and the money multiplier.

Helpful Hints

The monetary base is the sum of the two Federal Reserve liabilities: reserves and currency in circulation. The two primary ways that the Fed causes changes in the monetary base are through open-market operations and discount lending. The Fed has more precise control over the monetary base than the mix of reserves and currency. The mix of currency and reserves is determined by the nonbank public. The key to understanding the deposit multiplier is to understand that when a bank makes a loan, it creates a deposit, which is part of the money supply. The money multiplier tells us what multiple of the monetary base is transformed into the money supply. Anything that reduces the amount of loans that banks make reduces the size of the multiplier and therefore the money supply. Increases in *r*, *e*, or *c* reduce the quantity of funds that banks have available to lend, which reduces the size of the multiplier and the money supply.

Terms and Definitions

Choose a definition for each key term.

Key Terms:

_____borrowed reserves

_____currency ratio

_____excess reserves ratio

_____money multiplier

_____nonborrowed monetary base

_____discount rate

_____excess reserves

_____float

_____high-powered money

_____monetary base

_____multiple deposit creation

_____open-market operations

_____open-market purchase

_____open-market sale

_____required reserve ratio

_____required reserves

_____reserves

_____simple deposit multiplier

Definitions:

1. The monetary base minus borrowed reserves

2. The ratio of excess reserves to deposits

3. A ratio that relates the change in the money supply to a given change in the monetary base

4. Banks' borrowings from the Fed

5. The ratio of the public's holdings of currency to checkable deposits

6. Deposits at the Fed plus currency that is held by banks

7. The total of Federal Reserve liabilities, which is the sum of currency in circulation and reserves

8. The purchase of a government security by the Fed

9. Reserves that the Fed requires banks to hold

10. The ratio of required reserves to deposits

11. The multiple increase in deposits generated from an increase in the banking system's reserves in a simple model with no excess reserves and no currency holdings

12. Reserves that banks hold in addition to what is required by the Fed

13. The interest rate charged on loans that the Fed makes to banks

14. Another name for the monetary base

15. The temporary net increase in bank reserves occurring from the Fed's check-clearing process

16. The sale of a government security by the Fed

17. The purchase and sale of government securities by the Federal Reserve on the open market

18. The process whereby, when the Fed supplies the banking system with $1 of additional $1 reserves, deposits increase by a multiple of that amount

Problems and Short-Answer Questions

PRACTICE PROBLEMS

1. a. Draw a simplified Fed balance sheet.

    b. Define each of the entries listed in the Fed's balance sheet.

    _____

    _____

    _____

    _____

    c. Which balance sheet entries comprise the monetary base?

    _____

    _____

2. a. Show the T-account entries for the Federal Reserve and a commercial bank that would result from an open market purchase of a $100 government security from the bank.

b.   What was the exact change in the monetary base?

_____

3.   a.   Show the T-account entries for the Federal Reserve, the banking system and the nonbank public that would result from an open market purchase of a $100 government security from the nonbank public. Assume that the nonbank public deposits the proceeds from the sale of the government security in a local bank account.

b.   What was the exact change in the monetary base?

_____

c.   Now assume that the nonbank public cashes the check that it receives from selling the government security to the Federal Reserve and holds currency instead of bank deposits. Show the T-account entries for the Federal Reserve and the nonbank public.

d.   What was the exact change in the monetary base?

_____

e. Compare the change in the composition of the monetary base in *a* and *c*. What does this comparison say about the Fed's ability to control the composition of the monetary base?

_____

_____

_____

_____

4. Suppose the Federal Reserve purchases a $100 government security from First National Bank. Further suppose that banks hold no excess reserves and the nonbank public holds no currency (only deposits).
   a. Show the T-account entries for First National Bank as a result of the sale of the security to the Fed.

   b. Show the T-account entries for First National Bank when it loans out the excess reserves created by the sale of the government security to the Fed.

   c. Show the T-account entries for First National Bank and Bank A when the borrower withdraws their loan from First National Bank and deposits it into Bank A.

d. Show the T-account entries for Bank A when it loans out the excess reserves created by the new deposit.

e. How much "new" money is created by First National Bank and Bank A?

_____

f. Assume this process continues through Bank B, Bank C, and Bank D. How much new money would Banks B, C, and D create?

_____

g. Calculate the total change in deposits resulting from the $100 open market purchase by the Fed.

_____

5. a. Write the formula for the money multiplier.

_____

b. Calculate the currency ratio, the excess reserve ratio, and the money multiplier given the following values:

$r = 0.20$ $C = \$320$ billion

$D = \$1000$ billion $ER = \$60$ billion

$c =$ _____

$e =$ _____

$m =$ _____

c. Calculate the required reserves (RR), total reserves (R), and the monetary base (MB).

$RR = \$$ _____

$R = \$$ _____

$MB = \$$ _____

d. Now assume that the Fed lowers the required reserve ratio to 0.10. Calculate the new money multiplier and the new money supply.

$m =$ _____

$M = \$$ _____

e. Calculate the new level of deposits (D) and currency in circulation (C).

$D = \$$ _____

$C = \$$ _____

f. Calculate the new level of required reserves (RR) and excess reserves (ER).

$RR = \$$ _____

$ER = \$$ _____

6. a. Explain what would happen to the money supply and the money multiplier if there was an increase in the currency ratio. Be sure to describe the intuition behind these changes.

_____

_____

_____

_____

b. Explain what would happen to the money supply and the money multiplier if there was an increase in the excess reserves ratio. Be sure to describe the intuition behind these changes.

_____

_____

_____

_____

7. Assume that the monetary base is $800 billion and borrowed reserves are $5 billion.
a. Calculate the quantity of nonborrowed monetary base.

_____

_____

b. Over which quantity, the monetary base or the nonborrowed monetary base, does the Fed have more precise control?

_____

_____

c. What monetary policy tool does the Fed use to control the quantity of nonborrowed monetary base?

_____

_____

d. What happens to the money supply if the nonborrowed monetary base increases, holding borrowed reserves constant?

_____

e. What happens to the money supply if borrowed reserves increase, holding the nonborrowed monetary base constant?

_____

8. Fill in the missing pieces of information in the table below.

Player	Variable	Change in Variable	Money Supply Response
	r		
Depositors		↓	
	Excess reserves	↑	

SHORT-ANSWER QUESTIONS

1. List the three players in the money supply process. Which of these players is most important?

_____

_____

2. Describe the change in the composition of the monetary base that would result from someone withdrawing $100 in currency from a checking account. Does this withdraw affect the overall monetary base?

_____

_____

3. What happens to the monetary base when the Federal Reserve sells a $100 government security?

_____

_____

4. What happens to the monetary base when the Federal Reserve gives a $100 discount loan to a bank?

_____

_____

5. Use the simple deposit multiplier to show what would happen to total deposits in the banking system as a result of a $100 open market purchase by the Federal Reserve. Assume that the banking system holds no excess reserves, the nonbank public holds no currency, and the required reserve deposit ratio is 10%

_____

_____

_____

6. What is the primary factor that influences banks' decision to hold excess reserves? How will a change in that factor affect excess reserves?

_____

_____

_____

_____

7. How does an increase in the monetary base, which arises from an increase in currency, affect the overall money supply compared to an increase in the monetary base, which arises from an increase in reserves?

_____

_____

8. How does an increase in currency holdings affect the money multiplier and the money supply?

_____

_____

9. Why is it important to distinguish between the nonborrowed monetary base and borrowed reserves?

_____

_____

10. Which of the Fed's monetary policy tools affects the nonborrowed monetary base?

_____

_____

Critical Thinking

Back in the 1950s, economist Milton Friedman proposed setting the required reserve ratio equal to 100%.

1. What would the value of the multiplier be under Friedman's proposal?

_____

_____

2. Describe the roles of banks, depositors, and the Fed in controlling the money supply under Friedman's proposal.

_____

_____

3. Compare the Fed's ability to control the money supply under Friedman's proposal to the current situation in which reserve requirements are much lower.

_____

_____

4. How would Friedman's proposal change the nature of banking?

_____

_____

_____

_____

_____

Self-Test

TRUE/FALSE QUESTIONS

_____1.   Reserves consist of deposits at the Fed plus vault cash.

_____2.   High-powered money is another name for the monetary base.

_____3.   Discount loans are an asset of the banking system.

_____4.   The effect of an open market operation on the monetary base is much more certain than the effect on reserves.

_____5.   If you withdraw $100 from your checking account, deposits in the banking system will fall by $100.

_____6.   If you withdraw $100 from your checking account, the monetary base will fall by $100.

_____7.   Changes in float and Treasury deposits at the Fed prevent the Fed from accurately controlling the monetary base.

_____8.   When a bank chooses to purchase securities instead of making loans, deposit expansion is diminished.

_____9.   The ratio that relates the change in the money supply to a given change in the monetary base is called the money multiplier.

_____10. An increase in the monetary base that goes into currency is multiplied, whereas an increase that goes into supporting deposits is not multiplied.

_____11. An increase in the required reserve ratio causes the multiplier to fall.

_____12. An increase in both the excess reserves ratio and the currency ratio causes the multiplier to rise.

_____13. The money multiplier is smaller than the simple deposit multiplier.

_____14. The excess reserves ratio, e, fell sharply during the Great Depression and the subprime financial crisis.

_____15. The Fed has more precise control over the total monetary base than the nonborrowed monetary base.

MULTIPLE-CHOICE QUESTIONS

1. The three players in the money supply story are
   a. the Federal Reserve, banks, and depositors.
   b. the Federal Reserve, the U.S. Treasury, and commercial banks.
   c. the Federal Reserve, the comptroller of the currency, and depositors.
   d. the comptroller of the currency, the U.S. Treasury, and commercial banks.

2. Which of the following are found on the liability side of the Fed's balance sheet?
   a. government securities
   b. discount loans
   c. reserves
   d. none of the above

3. Which of the following are found on the asset side of the Fed's balance sheet?
   a. government securities
   b. currency in circulation
   c. reserves
   d. none of the above

4. The monetary base is comprised of
   a. discount loans plus government securities held by the Fed.
   b. currency in circulation plus total reserves.
   c. currency in circulation plus deposits in the banking system
   d. discount loans plus excess reserves held by banks.

5. The sum of vault cash and bank deposits at the Fed minus required reserves is called
   a. the monetary base.
   b. the money supply.
   c. excess reserves.
   d. total reserves.

6. When the Federal Reserve sells a government security on the open market, it is called
   a. an open market purchase.
   b. a discount loan.
   c. float.
   d. an open market sale.

7. When the Fed wants to reduce reserves in the banking system, it will
   a. purchase government bonds.
   b. sell government bonds.
   c. extend discount loans to banks.
   d. print more currency.

8. When the Fed gives a discount loan of $100 to a bank,
   a. the Fed's liabilities decrease by $100.
   b. currency in circulation increases by $100.
   c. the monetary base decreases by $100.
   d. the monetary base increases by $100.

9. If Steffi withdraws $400 in cash from her checking account, then
    a. the monetary base declines by $400.
    b. the monetary base rises by $400.
    c. the monetary base stays the same.
    d. it is impossible to tell what happens to the monetary base.

10. When float increases,
    a. currency in circulation falls.
    b. the monetary base rises.
    c. the money supply falls.
    d. none of the above occurs.

11. A bank creates money when it
    a. sells a security to the Fed.
    b. makes a loan and creates a checkable deposit.
    c. borrows reserves from the Fed.
    d. holds excess reserves.

12. On a Bank's balance sheet, a checkable deposit is
    a. an asset.
    b. a liability.
    c. neither an asset nor a liability.
    d. both an asset and a liability.

13. If the nonbank public holds currency in addition to deposits, then an open
    market operation will result in
    a. a smaller change in total deposits than is predicted by the simple deposit
        multiplier.
    b. a larger change in total deposits than is predicted by the simple deposit
        multiplier.
    c. greater control of the monetary base by the Fed.
    d. less control of the monetary base by the Fed.

14. The money multiplier tells us how much the
    a. nonborrowed monetary base changes for a given change in the monetary
        base.
    b. money supply changes for a given change in deposits.
    c. nonborrowed monetary base changes for a given change in deposits.
    d. money supply changes for a given change in the monetary base.

15. A decrease in the excess reserves ratio will cause the money multiplier
    a. to rise and the money supply to fall.
    b. to rise and the money supply to rise.
    c. to fall and the money supply to fall.
    d. to fall and the money supply to rise.

16. The monetary base less borrowed reserves is called
    a. the nonborrowed monetary base.
    b. high-powered money.
    c. reserves.
    d. the borrowed monetary base.

17. If the required reserve ratio is 0.03, currency in circulation is $600 billion, deposits are $700 billion, and excess reserves is $1 billion, then the money multiplier is equal to
    a. 3.09.
    b. 3.29.
    c. 2.29.
    d. 2.09.

18. Which of the following will lead to a decrease in bank reserves?
    a. an increase in the required reserve ratio
    b. an increase in the excess reserve ratio
    c. an increase in the currency ratio
    d. an increase in the monetary base

19. Suppose the required reserve ratio is 0.12, the currency ratio is 0.6, and the excess reserve ratio is 0.03. If the Fed decreases the monetary base by $5 billion, the money supply will fall by
    a. $15.34 billion.
    b. $10.67 billion.
    c. $9.87 billion.
    d. $5.67 billion.

20. The nonborrowed monetary base is controlled by
    a. depositors.
    b. banks.
    c. the Fed.
    d. all of the above

Solutions

Terms and Definitions

_4_ borrowed reserves

_5_ currency ratio

_2_ excess reserves ratio

_3_ money multiplier

_1_ nonborrowed monetary base

_13_ discount rate

_12_ excess reserves

_15_ float

_14_ high-powered money

_7_ monetary base

_18_ multiple deposit creation

_17_ open-market operations

_8_ open-market purchase

_16_ open-market sale

_10_ required reserve ratio

_9_ required reserves

_6_ reserves

_11_ simple deposit multiplier

Practice Problems

1. a.   A simplified Fed balance sheet:

Federal Reserve System

Assets	Liabilities
Government securities	Currency in circulation
Discount loans	Reserves

   b.   Assets: government securities are securities issued by the U.S. Treasury and discount loans are loans that the Fed makes to commercial banks. Liabilities: currency in circulation is the amount of currency in the hands of the public and reserves are bank reserves that are held at the Fed plus vault cash.

   c.   The monetary base is the sum of the Fed's liabilities: reserves and currency in circulation.

2. a.   An open market purchase of $100 government security from a commercial bank results in the following T-account entries.

Federal Reserve System

Assets		Liabilities	
Securities	+$100	Reserves	+$100

Commercial Bank

Assets		Liabilities
Securities	−$100	
Reserves	+100	

   b.   The monetary base increased by $100.

3. a.   An open market purchase of $100 government security from the nonbank public when the nonbank public deposits the proceeds from the sale of the government security in a local bank account results in the following T-account entries.

Federal Reserve System

Assets		Liabilities	
Securities	+$100	Reserves	+$100

Commercial Bank

Assets		Liabilities	
Reserves	+$100	Checkable Deposits	+$100

Nonbank Public

Assets		Liabilities
Securities	−$100	
Checkable Deposits	+100	

   b.   The monetary base increased by $100.

c. If the nonbank public cashes the check that it receives from selling the government security to the Federal Reserve, the T-account entries for the Fed and the nonbank public are as follows.

Federal Reserve System

Assets		Liabilities	
Securities	+$100	Currency in Circulation	+$100

Nonbank Public

Assets		Liabilities
Securities	−$100	
Currency	+100	

d. The monetary base increased by $100.

e. The monetary base increased by $100 in both cases (*a* and *c*). These examples illustrate that the Fed can precisely affect the total monetary base through open market operations, but it cannot affect the mix of currency and reserves in the monetary base. That mix is determined by the nonbank public's desire to hold currency versus deposits.

4. a. First National Bank Sells a $100 government security to the Fed:

First National Bank

Assets		Liabilities
Securities	−$100	
Reserves	+100	

b. First National Bank loans out excess reserves:

First National Bank

Assets		Liabilities	
Securities	−$100	Checkable	
Reserves	+100	Deposits	+100
Loans	+100		

c. Borrower withdraws funds from First National Bank and deposits funds into Bank A:

First National Bank

Assets		Liabilities
Securities	−$100	
Loans	+100	

Bank A

Assets		Liabilities	
Reserves	+$100	Checkable Deposits	+$100

d. Bank A loans out the excess reserves created by the new deposit:

Bank A

Assets		Liabilities	
Reserves	+$100	Checkable	
Loans	+90	Deposits	+$100

e. First National Bank creates $100 in "new" money. Bank A creates $90 in "new" money.

f. Bank B would create $81, Bank C would create $72.90 and Bank D would create $65.60.

g. The total increase in deposits resulting from this $100 open market operation is $1000.

5. a. $m = (1 + c)/(r + e + c)$

b. $c = .32$

$e = .06$

$m = 2.28$

c. $RR = 200 billion

$R = 260 billion

$MB = 580 billion

d. $m = 2.75$

$M = $1,595$ billion

e. $D = $1,208.33$ billion

$C = 386.67 billion

f. $RR = 120.83 billion

$ER = 72.5 billion

6. a. Deposits are subject to the multiplier effect, but currency is not. An increase in the currency ratio means that depositors are holding more of their money in the form of currency rather than deposits, so less of their money is subject to the multiplier effect. As a result, the multiplier declines, and the overall money supply declines as well.

b. Like currency, excess reserves are not subject to the multiplier process because they are held in reserve by banks and are therefore not part of the lending and deposit creation process. An increase in the excess reserves ratio implies that lending and deposit creation will decline, and therefore, the money multiplier and the overall money supply will both decline as well.

7. a. $795 billion
    b. the nonborrowed monetary base
    c. open-market operations
    d. It increases.
    e. It increases.

8.

Player	Variable	Change in Variable	Money Supply Response
Fed	r	↓	↑
Depositors	Currency holdings	↓	↑
Depositors and Banks	Excess reserves	↑	↓

Short-Answer Questions

1. The three players in the money supply process are the central bank (the Fed), banks, and depositors. The Federal Reserve is the most important.

2. When someone withdraws $100 from a checking account, currency in circulation increases by $100, and reserves decrease by $100, but the total monetary base remains unchanged.

3. The monetary base declines by $100.

4. The monetary base increases by $100.

5. According to the simple deposit multiplier, $\Delta D = (1/r)\Delta R$. An open market purchase by the Fed will cause reserves to increase by

$100. Assuming the required reserve deposit ratio is 10%, $\Delta D = (1/.10)100 = \$1,000$.

6. The main factor that influences excess reserve holdings is banks' expectation of deposit outflows. If banks fear that deposit outflows are likely to increase, they will increase their holdings of excess reserves.

7. An increase in the monetary base, which arises from currency, has no multiplier effect while an increase in the monetary base, which arises from reserves, does have a multiplier effect.

8. An increase in currency holdings causes both the money multiplier and the money supply to decline.

9. Because the Fed has precise control over the nonborrowed monetary base but it does not have precise control over borrowed reserves, which are determined by banks.

10. open-market operations

Critical Thinking

1. The multiplier would be 1.

2. Banks and depositors would play no role in the money supply process. Only the Fed would play a role in controlling the money supply under Friedman's proposal.

3. The Fed would have much more control over the money supply under Friedman's proposal because the multiplier would always be equal to 1.

4. Friedman's proposal would completely change how banks earn a profit. Banks currently earn a profit by loaning out a fraction of the funds they receive from depositors. Under Friedman's proposal, banks would have no excess funds to loan out because they would be required to hold 100% of the deposits on reserve. There would be no deposit creation by the banking system, and the money supply would essentially be set by the Fed. Banks would earn a profit by charging depositors a fee for holding their funds and providing check services. Banks would be more like the warehouse banks that existed in the middle ages simply to safeguard depositors' money.

True/False Questions

1. T
2. T

3. F
4. T
5. T
6. F
7. F
8. F
9. T
10. F
11. T
12. F
13. T
14. F
15. F

Multiple-Choice Questions

1. a
2. c
3. a
4. b
5. c
6. d
7. b
8. d
9. c
10. b
11. b
12. b
13. a
14. d
15. b
16. a
17. d
18. c
19. b
20. c

15 Tools of Monetary Policy

Chapter Review

PREVIEW

The Fed uses three tools to manipulate the money supply, and interest rates: open market operations, discount lending and reserve requirements. This chapter looks at how the Fed uses these tools to influence the market for reserves and the *federal funds rate*. The chapter ends with a discussion of the tools of monetary policy used by other central banks besides the Federal Reserve.

THE MARKET FOR RESERVES AND THE FEDERAL FUNDS RATE

The federal funds rate is the interest rate that banks charge each other for overnight lending in the market for reserves. The federal funds rate is determined by the intersection of the demand and supply of reserves. The Federal Reserve's three policy tools (open market operations, discount lending, and reserve requirements) affect the federal funds rate by affecting either the supply of reserves or the demand for reserves. The demand for reserves (R^d in Figure 15.1) is downward sloping until the point that it reaches the interest rate the Fed pays on reserves, i_{er}. After that point, the demand curve for reserves becomes horizontal. Reserve supply (R^s) is a vertical line up to the discount rate (i_d) at which point it becomes a horizontal line. The vertical portion of the reserve supply curve is determined by the quantity of *nonborrwed reserves* (NBR). NBR are the reserves that the Fed controls through its open market operations. When the intersection of the demand and supply of reserves occurs along the vertical part of the reserve supply curve and the downward-sloping part of the reserve demand curve (as shown in Figure 15.1), then the federal funds rate will be determined by the quantity of NBR. In this case, an open-market purchase increases NBR, which reduces the equilibrium federal funds rate, and an open-market sale decreases NBR, which raises the equilibrium federal funds rate. The discount rate places an upper limit on the federal funds rate, and the interest rate paid on reserves places a lower limit on the federal funds rate. Under the Fed's current operating procedures, therefore, fluctuations in the federal funds rate are limited to between i_{er} and i_d.

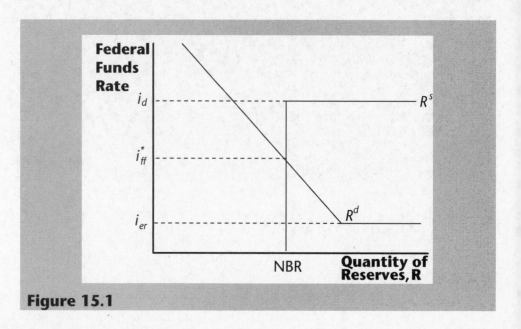

Figure 15.1

OPEN MARKET OPERATIONS

There are two types of open-market operations: *dynamic open-market operations*, which are intended to change the level of reserves and the monetary base, and *defensive open-market operations*, which are intended to offset movements in reserves and the monetary base due to other factors such as Treasury deposits at the Fed and float. Open-market operations are conducted by the trading desk of the Federal Reserve Bank of New York. Early each day the Fed forecasts the demand for reserves for that day. Once the Fed has decided on the appropriate course of action (increase or decrease reserves), they transmit their buy or sell orders to a group of private sector bond dealers called *primary dealers*. To temporarily increase reserves, the Fed uses *repurchase agreements* (also called repos). In a repo, the Fed purchases securities with an agreement that the seller will repurchase them after a short period of time (1 to 15 days). To temporarily reduce the supply of reserves, the Fed uses *matched sale–purchase transactions* (also called reverse repos). Repos and reverse repos are used for defensive open-market operations. Open-market operations are the Fed's main tool for affecting the reserve market and the federal funds rate because they are flexible and precise, they are easily reversed, and they can be implemented quickly. In addition, unlike discount window borrowing, which is initiated by banks, open-market operations are initiated by the Fed.

DISCOUNT POLICY

There are three types of discount loans to banks: primary credit, which healthy banks can borrow from the Fed's *standing lending facility* at the discount rate; secondary credit, which are loans to financially troubled banks at an interest rate 50 basis points above the discount rate; and seasonal credit, which the Fed is considering eliminating in the future. Discount lending allows the Fed to serve as the lender of last resort, which is especially important during financial crises.

RESERVE REQUIREMENTS

Reserve requirements affect the multiplier, so in principle the Fed could manipulate reserve requirements to change the money supply and interest rates. But reserves have become much less important in recent years and for many banks, required reserves are not binding. In addition, raising reserve requirements can cause severe liquidity problems for banks. The Fed no longer uses reserve requirements as a policy tool for changing the money supply and interest rates.

MONETARY POLICY TOOLS
OF THE EUROPEAN CENTRAL BANK

The European Central Bank's target for the overnight lending rate, called the *target financing rate*, and its monetary tools are similar to those used by the Federal Reserve (open-market operations, lending to banks, and reserve requirements). Open-market operations that are reversed within two weeks are called *main refinancing operations*. These operations, which are similar to the Fed's repos and reverse repos, are the ECB's primary tool for targeting the overnight lending rate. The ECB also operates a standing lending facility called the *deposit facility* that pays interest on reserves and is set 100 basis points below the target financing rate. The interest rate paid on reserves places a lower limit on the ECB's target financing rate.

Helpful Hints

The federal funds rate is determined by the demand and supply for reserves. The key to understanding how the Fed's monetary policy tools affect the federal funds rate is to understand how those tools affect the demand and supply for reserves. The Fed mostly uses open market operations to manipulate nonborrowed reserves in order to target the federal funds rate. The discount rate serves as an upper limit on the federal funds rate and allows the Fed to serve its role as lender of last resort. The interest rate the Fed pays on reserves serves as a lower bound on the federal funds rate. Reserve requirements are not used to manipulate the money supply and interest rates.

Terms and Definitions

Choose a definition for each key term.

Key Terms:

_____ defensive open-market operations

_____ deposit facility

_____ discount window

_____ dynamic open-market operations

_____ federal funds rate

_____ lender of last resort

_____ longer-term refinancing operations

_____ main refinancing operations

_____ marginal lending facility

_____ marginal lending rate

_____ matched sale–purchase transaction (reverse repo)

_____ nonborrowed reserves

_____ overnight cash rate

_____ primary dealers

_____ repurchase agreement

_____ reverse transactions

_____ standing lending facility

_____ target financing rate

Definitions:

1. The European Central Bank's standing facility that pays interest on bank reserves

2. The amount of reserves supplied by the Fed's open-market operations

3. The Fed facility from which banks are allowed to borrow all they want

4. The European Central Bank's standing facility that provides loans to banks

5. The interest rate charged on loans by the national central banks of the ECB

6. An agreement whereby the Fed, or another party, purchases securities with the understanding that the seller will repurchase them in a short period of time

7. The overnight interest rate target set by the European Central Bank

8. Open-market operations intended to change the level of reserves and the monetary base

9. Private sector government securities dealers

10. The predominant form of open-market operations used by the European Central Bank

11. An agreement whereby the Fed, or another party, sells securities with the understanding that the buyer will sell them back in a short period of time

12. The Fed facility from which banks borrow reserves

13. The secondary type of open-market operations used by the European Central Bank

14. Provider of reserves to financial institutions when no one else would provide them in order to prevent a financial crisis

15. The interest rate on very short-term interbank loans that is targeted by the European Central Bank

16. The European equivalent to the repurchase agreement

17. The name given in the United States to the interest rate on overnight lending between banks.

18. Open-market operations that are intended to offset movements in other factors that affect reserves and the monetary base

Problems and Short-Answer Questions

PRACTICE PROBLEMS

1. Suppose the demand for reserves is initially R^d_0 in Figure 15.2.
   a. Use Figure 15.2 to determine the following:

   Nonborrowed reserves = $_____

   Borrowed reserves = $_____

   The federal funds rate = _____%

   The discount rate = _____%

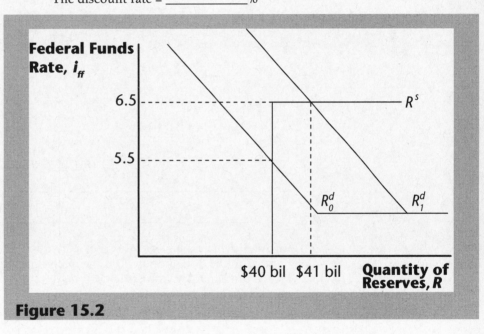

Figure 15.2

   b. Now assume that the demand for reserves increases to R^d_1. Recalculate the following given this new higher demand for reserves:

   Nonborrowed reserves = $_____

   Borrowed reserves = $_____

   The federal funds rate = _____%

   The discount rate = _____%

2. a. Draw the demand and supply diagram for reserves assuming that the equilibrium federal funds rate is below the discount rate and above the interest rate on reserves.

    b. Re-draw the diagram you drew for part *a* and illustrate the effect of an open market purchase by the Fed on the equilibrium federal funds rate. Explain why the federal funds rate changes.

        _____

        _____

        _____

    c. Re-draw the diagram you drew for part *a* and illustrate the effect of an increase in the discount rate. Did the increase in the discount rate affect the federal funds rate? Why or why not?

        _____

        _____

        _____

d. Now draw the demand and supply diagram for reserves assuming that the equilibrium federal funds rate is equal to the discount rate. Illustrate the effect of a reduction in the discount rate on the equilibrium federal funds rate.

e. Explain why a change in the discount rate sometimes causes the federal funds rate to change and sometimes has no effect on the federal funds rate.

_____

_____

_____

_____

_____

f. Re-draw the diagram you drew for part *a* and illustrate the effect of an increase in reserve requirements on the equilibrium federal funds rate. Explain why this happens.

_____

_____

_____

_____

3. Suppose the Fed expects a change in Treasury deposits will cause reserves to decline by $2 billion for a one-week period after which reserves will return to their initial level.

    a. Describe the open market operation that the Fed would use to maintain the level of reserves in the banking system during this one-week decline in reserves due to the change in Treasury deposits.

    _____

    _____

    _____

    _____

    _____

    b. Now assume that bad weather delays the delivery of checks causing float to increase for one day. How will this increase in float affect reserves? Describe the open market operation that the Fed would use to maintain the level of reserves in the banking system during this temporary change in reserves due to the increase in float.

    _____

    _____

    _____

    _____

    _____

    _____

4. a. What is primary credit?

    _____

    b. Where does primary credit lending take place?

    _____

    c. What role does primary credit lending play in the market for federal funds?

    _____

    _____

    _____

    _____

    _____

    d.   What is secondary credit? How does it differ from primary credit?

_____

_____

_____

5. a.   What is the name of the interest rate targeted by the European Central Bank?

_____

    b.   What is the difference between the main refinancing operations and longer-term refinancing operations by the European Central Bank?

_____

_____

_____

_____

    c.   Explain how the ECBs marginal lending facility and deposit facility set limits on how far short-term interest rates can move in relation to the target.

_____

_____

_____

_____

_____

SHORT-ANSWER QUESTIONS

1.   What monetary policy tool does the Fed use to control the amount of nonborrowed reserves?

_____

_____

2. What will happen to nonborrowed reserves and the federal funds rate when the Fed conducts an open market purchase?

   _____

   _____

3. Under what conditions will a change in the discount rate affect the federal funds interest rate?

   _____

   _____

4. Under what conditions would the federal funds rate equal the interest rate paid on reserves?

   _____

   _____

   _____

5. How will a decrease in reserve requirements affect the demand for reserves and the federal funds rate?

   _____

   _____

6. What are the advantages of open market operations?

   _____

   _____

7. Explain why the existence of FDIC insurance does not make the lender-of-last resort function of the Fed superfluous.

   _____

   _____

8. What are the advantages and disadvantages of the Fed's discount policy?

   _____

   _____

   _____

   _____

9. What are the disadvantages of using reserve requirements as a policy tool to change the federal funds rate?

_____

_____

_____

10. What is the Eurosystem's equivalent of the Fed's discount rate?

_____

_____

Critical Thinking

Use the demand and supply diagram for reserves to illustrate and explain how the Fed's current policy with regard to the discount rate and the rate they pay on reserves limits the fluctuations in the federal funds rate.

_____

_____

_____

_____

Self-Test

TRUE/FALSE QUESTIONS

_____ 1. Open market operations are the Fed's most important monetary policy tool.

_____ 2. Changes in the discount rate usually affect the equilibrium federal funds rate.

_____ 3. The federal funds rate can never rise above the interest rate that the Fed pays on reserves.

_____ 4. The Fed controls nonborrowed reserves through open market operations.

_____ 5. Dynamic open market operations are intended to offset movements float.

_____ 6. Defensive open market operations are intended to offset changes in Treasury deposits.

_____ 7. A matched sale-purchase transaction is used by the Fed to conduct a temporary open market purchase.

_____ 8. The Fed's standing lending facility lends to banks that are in financial trouble.

_____ 9. The federal funds rate is usually 100 basis points above the discount rate.

_____10. The secondary credit rate is usually 50 basis points above the discount rate.

_____11. The marginal lending rate provides a ceiling for the overnight market interest rate in the European Monetary Union.

_____12. The Fed frequently changes the reserve requirement in order to influence the money supply.

_____13. The European Central Bank signals its monetary policy stance by setting a target financing rate.

_____14. The European Central Bank's predominant form of open market operations is called longer-term refinancing operations.

_____15. The European Central Bank has no reserve requirements.

MULTIPLE-CHOICE QUESTIONS

1. An open market purchase will cause
    a. nonborrowed reserves to fall and the federal funds rate to rise.
    b. nonborrowed reserves to rise and the federal funds rate to fall.
    c. borrowed reserves to fall and the federal funds rate to rise.
    d. borrowed reserves to rise and the federal funds rate to fall.

2. An increase in reserve requirements
    a. increases nonborrowed reserves and increases the federal funds rate.
    b. decreases nonborrowed reserves and decreases the federal funds rate.
    c. leaves nonborrowed reserves unchanged and increases the federal funds rate.
    d. leaves nonborrowed reserves unchanged and decreases the federal funds rate.

Figure for questions 3-7

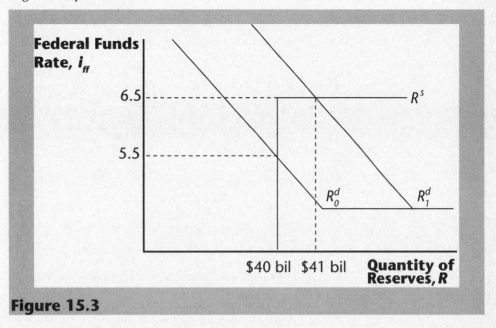

Figure 15.3

3. The rightward shift in reserve demand depicted in Figure 15.3 most likely resulted from
   a. an increase in required reserves.
   b. a decrease in required reserves.
   c. an open market purchase.
   d. an open market sale.

4. When reserve demand is R^d_1 in Figure 15.3, borrowed reserves are
   a. $40 billion.
   b. $41 billion.
   c. $0.
   d. $1 billion.

5. When reserve demand is R^d_0 in Figure 15.3, borrowed reserves are
   a. $40 billion.
   b. $41 billion.
   c. $0.
   d. $1 billion.

6. When reserve demand is R^d_1 in Figure 15.3, nonborrowed reserves are
   a. $40 billion.
   b. $41 billion.
   c. $0.
   d. $1 billion.

7. When reserve demand is R^d_0 in Figure 15.3, nonborrowed reserves are
   a. $40 billion.
   b. $41 billion.
   c. $0.
   d. $1 billion.

8. To lower the federal funds rate, the Fed would
    a. increase the reserve requirement.
    b. increase the discount rate.
    c. conduct an open market purchase.
    d. all of the above

9. Which of the following will shift the supply of reserves to the right?
    a. increase the reserve requirement
    b. increase the discount rate
    c. conduct an open market purchase
    d. all of the above

10. By paying interest on reserves, the Fed is able to keep the federal funds rate
    a. equal to the interest rate on reserves
    b. equal to the discount rate
    c. at or below the interest rate on reserves
    d. at or above the interest rate on reserves

11. An open market operation by the Federal Reserve aimed at maintaining the level of reserves is called a
    a. defensive open market operation.
    b. dynamic open market operation.
    c. longer-term refinancing operation.
    d. reverse transaction.

12. An open market operation by the European Central Bank aimed at maintaining the level of reserves is called a
    a. defensive open market operation.
    b. dynamic open market operation.
    c. longer-term refinancing operation.
    d. reverse transaction.

13. To temporarily raise reserves in the banking sector, the Fed engages in a
    a. repurchase agreement.
    b. reverse repo.
    c. matched sale-purchase transaction.
    d. reverse transaction.

14. Which of the following tools does the Fed use in its role as lender of last resort?
    a. discount lending
    b. reserve requirements
    c. open market operations
    d. FDIC insurance

15. The interest rate on secondary credit is
    a. set below the federal funds rate.
    b. above the discount rate to penalize financially troubled banks.
    c. equal to the federal funds rate.
    d. below the discount rate but above the federal funds rate to help financially troubled banks.

16. The Fed's primary credit lending facility keeps the federal funds rate from rising high above its target because
    a. the Fed routinely sets the discount rate below the federal funds rate.
    b. the Fed will extend unlimited credit to healthy banks at the discount rate, which means that the federal funds rate will not rise above its target.
    c. banks are prohibited by Fed regulators from charging interest rates to other banks above its target rate.
    d. secondary credit lending kicks in whenever the federal funds rate rises too high.

17. The Fed buys and sells government securities through
    a. the U.S. Treasury.
    b. the standing lending facility.
    c. the discount lending facility.
    d. primary dealers.

18. A repurchase agreement by the Fed is
    a. an agreement by the Fed to repurchase securities from the Treasury.
    b. a temporary open market sale that will be reversed shortly.
    c. a temporary open market purchase that will be reversed shortly.
    d. especially desirable way of conducting a dynamic open market operation.

19. Reserve requirements are no longer used by the Fed to manage the money supply and interest rates because
    a. reserve requirements are no longer binding for most banks.
    b. raising reserve requirements can cause immediate liquidity problems for banks.
    c. changing reserve requirements would create uncertainty for banks.
    d. all of the above

20. The European System of Central Banks lends to commercial banks through its
    a. discount window.
    b. marginal lending facility.
    c. standing lending facility.
    d. deposit facility.

Solutions

Terms and Definitions

_18_ defensive open-market operations

_1_ deposit facility

_3_ discount window

_8_ dynamic open-market operations

_17_ federal funds rate

_14_ lender of last resort

_13_ longer-term refinancing operations

_10_ main refinancing operations

_4_ marginal lending facility

_5_ marginal lending rate

_11_ matched sale–purchase transaction (reverse repo)

_2_ nonborrowed reserves

_15_ overnight cash rate

_9_ primary dealers

_6_ repurchase agreement

_16_ reverse transactions

_12_ standing lending facility

_7_ target financing rate

Practice Problems

1. a. Nonborrowed reserves = $ _40_
        Borrowed reserves = $ _0_
        The federal funds rate = _5.5%_
        The discount rate = _6.5%_
    b. Nonborrowed reserves = $ _40 billion_
        Borrowed reserves = $ _1 billion_
        The federal funds rate = _6.5%_
        The discount rate = _6.5%_

2. a. The equilibrium federal funds rate is i_{ff}^0 and the equilibrium quantity of reserves is NBR_0 (because the equilibrium federal funds rate is below the discount rate, the quantity of borrowed reserves equals zero).

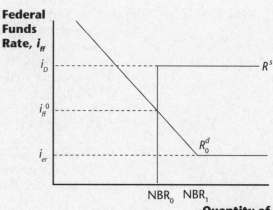

b. An open-market purchase increases nonborrowed reserves from NBR_0 to NBR_1. At the initial equilibrium federal funds rate, i_{ff}^0 there is now an excess supply of reserves, which causes the equilibrium federal funds rate to fall to i_{ff}^1.

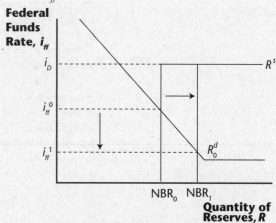

c. An increase in the discount rate as shown below has no effect on the federal funds rate because reserve demand intersects reserve supply below the discount rate.

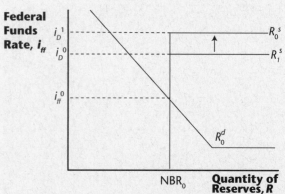

d. In this case, the demand for reserves intersects the supply of reserves along the horizontal portion of the reserve supply curve, which means that the federal funds rate is equal to the discount rate. If the Fed lowers the discount rate from i_D^0 to i_D^1 the federal funds rate will fall from i_{ff}^0 to i_{ff}^1.

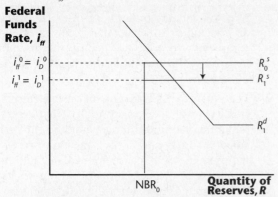

e. The change in the discount rate in problem c did not affect the federal funds rate because the demand for reserves intersected the supply of reserves along the vertical portion of the reserve supply curve. In this case, banks will not borrow from the Fed so changes in the discount rate have no effect on the reserve market or the federal funds rate. The change in the discount rate in problem d did affect the federal funds rate because the demand for reserves intersected the supply of reserves along the horizontal portion of the reserve supply curve. In this case, a portion of total reserves in the banking sector is borrowed from the Fed and the federal funds rate is equal to the discount rate so changes in the discount rate affect the federal funds rate.

f. An increase in reserve requirements causes the demand for reserves to increase from R^d_0 to R^d_1, which leads to an increase in the equilibrium federal funds rate from i_{ff}^0 to i_{ff}^1.

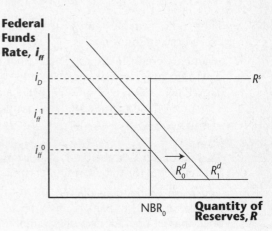

3. a. The Fed would use a repurchase agreement, which is an agreement to purchase securities on the open market (which increases reserves in the banking system) and then resell them to the original owner of the securities (which decreases reserves in the banking system). In this case, the securities would be resold to the original owner after one week, so the net result would be that total reserves in the banking system would remain unchanged.

b. The increase in float will cause reserves to increase. In this case, the Fed would use a matched sale–purchase transaction or reverse repo to offset the temporary increase in reserves. With the reverse repo, the Fed sells securities to a buyer (which decreases reserves in the banking system) and then buys them back (which increases reserves in the banking system) after a short period of time. In this case, the Fed would buy the securities back after one day. This reverse repo would keep reserves in the banking system unchanged in the face of the temporary increase in float.

4. a. Primary credit is the discount lending that the Fed extends to healthy banks.

b. Primary credit takes place at the standing lending facility.

c. The discount rate is the interest rate that the Fed charges on primary credit loans to healthy banks. The discount rate places an upper limit on the federal funds rate. If the demand for reserves rises (unexpectedly, say due to an unexpected increase in deposits) to exceed the quantity of nonborrowed reserves in the banking system, banks will simply borrow from the Fed at the discount rate.

Thus, the federal funds rate cannot exceed the discount rate.

d. Secondary credit loans are given to banks that are in financial trouble and are experiencing severe liquidity problems. The interest rate on secondary credit is 50 basis points higher than the discount rate.

5. a. The European Central Bank sets a target financing rate for the overnight cash rate.

b. The main refinancing operations are the European Central Bank's main form of open market operations and are similar to the Fed's repo transactions. The longer-term refinancing operations are a much smaller source of liquidity in the euro area banking system.

c. The ECB lends to banks at the marginal lending rate, which is set 100 basis points above the target financing rate. Banks can deposit reserves in the ECB and earn interest on reserves. The interest paid on reserves is 100 basis points below the target financing rate. The overnight lending rate will not fall below the rate that the ECB pays on reserves, and it will not rise above the rate that the ECB lends at.

Short-Answer Questions

1. The Fed uses open market operations to control the amount of nonborrowed reserves.

2. An open market purchase increases the quantity of nonborrowed reserves and lowers the federal funds rate.

3. A change in the discount rate will only affect the federal funds rate when the demand for reserves is high enough to be on the horizontal portion of the reserve supply curve.

4. The federal funds rate would equal the interest rate paid on reserves when the vertical portion of the supply for reserves intersects the horizontal portion of the demand for reserves. This could occur as a result of a large decrease in the demand for reserves.

5. A decrease in reserve requirements will decrease the demand for reserves and cause the federal funds rate to fall

6. The main advantages of open market operations are that they occur at the initiative of the Fed, they are flexible and precise, they

are easily reversed, and they can be implemented quickly.

7. FDIC insurance amounts to only about 1% of deposits outstanding. In addition, accounts over $100,000 are not covered by FDIC insurance.

8. The most important advantage of discount lending is that it allows the Fed to play the role of lender of last resort. The main disadvantage is that the Fed does not completely control the quantity of discount loans since borrowing at the discount rate is initiated by banks.

9. The main disadvantage of using reserve requirements as a policy tool is that reserve requirements are no longer binding for most banks. In addition, raising reserve requirements can cause immediate liquidity problems for banks, and fluctuating reserve requirements create uncertainty for banks.

10. The Eurosystem's equivalent to the Fed's discount rate is called the marginal lending rate.

Critical Thinking

The Fed currently pays interest on reserves equal to i_{er} and discount loans are made at interest rate i_D. The federal funds interest rate is limited to fluctuating between these two rates as illustrated below. If the demand for reserves rises from R^d_0 to R^d_1, the federal funds interest rate will be equal to i_D. If the demand for reserves falls from R^d_0 to R^d_2, the federal funds interest rate will fall to i_{er}.

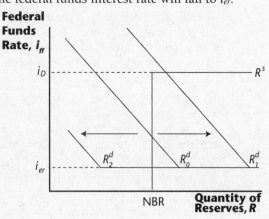

True/False Questions

1. T

2. F

3. F

4. T

5. F
6. T
7. F
8. F
9. F
10. T
11. T
12. F
13. T
14. F
15. F

Multiple-Choice Questions

1. b
2. c
3. a
4. d
5. c
6. a
7. a
8. c
9. c
10. d
11. a
12. d
13. a
14. a
15. b
16. b
17. d
18. c
19. d
20. b

16 The Conduct of Monetary Policy: Strategy and Tactics

Chapter Review

PREVIEW

The last chapter described how the tools of monetary policy affect the market for reserves and the interest rate. This chapter looks at the strategies and tactics central banks use to conduct monetary policy and evaluates the Fed's conduct of monetary policy in the past.

MONETARY TARGETING

Monetary targeting means the central bank is responsible for achieving a stated growth rate of a monetary aggregate (M1 or M2 for example). During the 1970s the Fed committed itself to monetary targets but in practice never really achieved them either because of shocks to the economy, rapid financial innovations, or a lack of commitment on the part of the Fed under Paul Volcker who some analysts believe was interested in raising interest rates enough to wring inflation out of the economy rather than hitting the stated monetary aggregate targets. The Fed decreased its emphasis on monetary targets in 1982 and abandoned them altogether in 1993.The Bank of Canada and the Bank of England experimented with monetary targeting in the 1970s but abandoned them in the 1980s.

The Bank of Japan, while committed to inflation targeting, started to pay more attention to the growth rate of monetary aggregates starting in the 1970s. Concern over an appreciating yen led the Bank of Japan to allow the money supply to grow rapidly during the late 1980s, which helped fuel speculation in land and the stock market. When Japan switched to slower monetary growth in 1989, stock and land prices collapsed. The Bank of Japan has maintained tight (some analysts say overly tight) monetary policy since that time, which has hampered Japan's recovery.

Germany's central bank, the Budesbank, adopted inflation targeting in the 1970s. The Bundesbank frequently (about 50% of the time) missed its stated money growth targets. Nonetheless, they were successful in keeping inflation low because they clearly communicated the strategy of monetary policy focused on long-run considerations and the control of inflation. The European Central Bank has borrowed some elements of monetary targeting from the Bundesbank but has elements of inflation targeting as well.

An advantage of monetary targeting is that policymakers and the public get quick feedback on whether the targets are being achieved because monetary aggregates are reported with a short (few week) lag. However, these advantages can only be achieved if there is a strong and reliable relationship between the monetary aggregate and the goal variable (growth, employment, inflation). The relationship between monetary aggregates and goal variables has broken down since the 1980s.

INFLATION TARGETING

The breakdown in the relationship between monetary aggregates and goals has led several countries to adopt inflation targeting. New Zealand, Canada, and the United Kingdom adopted inflation targeting in the early 1990s. Inflation targeting has the advantage that it does not rely on the relationship between monetary aggregates and inflation. Inflation targeting is more transparent and more readily understood by the public than monetary targeting, and inflation targeting has the potential to reduce the likelihood that the central bank will fall into the time-inconsistency trap. Inflation-targeting countries also place great emphasis on communication and transparency. There are four claimed disadvantages of inflation targeting: delayed signaling, too much rigidity, potential for increased output fluctuations, and low economic growth. But there is little evidence to support these claimed disadvantages.

MONETARY POLICY WITH AN IMPLICIT NOMINAL ANCHOR

Monetary policy affects real output and inflation with a substantial lag. As a result, to prevent inflation from getting started, monetary policy needs to be forward-looking and preemptive. Under Federal Reserve Chairmen Alan Greenspan and Ben Bernanke, the Fed has pursued preemptive monetary policy. The Fed has no nominal anchor but it has some of the same elements of inflation targeting and some of the same advantages as well. A disadvantage of the Fed's "just do it" monetary policy strategy is that it is less transparent than inflation targeting and therefore leads to more volatility in financial markets because financial markets are left to guess what the Fed is going to do in any particular situation. Another disadvantage of the "just do it" approach is that its success is highly dependent the skills of the Fed chair. Thus, continued success is not guaranteed when a new chair takes over the Fed. A final disadvantage of the Fed's approach is that it is inconsistent with democratic principles. Inflation targeting would make the Fed more accountable to elected officials and therefore inflation targeting would be more consistent with democratic principles.

TACTICS: CHOOSING THE POLICY INSTRUMENT

Central banks use tools such as open market operations, reserve requirements, and the discount rate to achieve their goals. But the connection between tools and goals is not direct and immediate so central banks use the tools of monetary policy to affect *policy instruments* (also called *operating instruments*) to indicate whether monetary policy is tight or easy. Operating instruments give more immediate feedback to the central bank about whether it is moving toward its goals. Examples of policy instruments are reserve aggregates or interest rates. The policy instrument might be linked to an intermediate target, which is more directly related to the goals of monetary policy but less related to the actual tools of monetary policy than the operating instruments. A central bank can choose either a reserve aggregate or an interest rate as its policy instrument but it cannot choose both because targeting one implies that the central bank must be free to move the other. There are three criteria for choosing a policy instrument: (1) It must be observable and measurable; (2) it must be controllable by the central bank; (3) and it must have a predictable effect on the goals.

TACTICS: THE TAYLOR RULE

The *Taylor rule* is a mathematical equation which describes how the Fed sets the federal funds target. According to the Taylor rule, the federal funds rate equals an "equilibrium" real fed funds rate plus a weighted average of the inflation and output gaps. The output gap appears in the Taylor rule because the Fed is concerned about stabilizing output fluctuations in addition to maintaining low and stable inflation. Another possible reason that the output gap appears in the Taylor rule is that it indicates future inflationary pressures. When the monetary authority responds to an increase in inflation by raising the nominal interest rate by more than the rise in inflation, it is said to follow the *Taylor principle*. Failure to follow the Taylor principle results in unstable inflation. According to the *Phillips curve theory*, when output is above potential (the gap is positive), inflationary pressures rise, and when output is below potential (the gap is negative), inflationary pressures fall. The Taylor rule does a pretty good job of describing the Fed's setting of the federal funds rate under Chairmen Greenspan and Bernanke. But there are several reasons why the Fed should not set monetary policy solely based on a mechanical Taylor rule formula.

CENTRAL BANKS' RESPONSE TO ASSET PRICE BUBBLES: LESSONS FROM THE SUBPRIME CRISIS

There are two types of asset-price bubbles: those driven by credit and those driven solely by irrational exuberance. Credit driven bubbles pose a greater threat to the financial system than bubbles driven solely by irrational exuberance. Policymakers will likely recognize a credit-driven bubble that is in progress but not a bubble driven solely by irrational exuberance. There are strong arguments against using monetary policy to prick an asset-price bubble. *Macroprudential regulation* appears to be the right tool for reining in credit-driven bubbles.

FED POLICY PROCEDURES: HISTORICAL PERSPECTIVE

When the Fed was founded, the discount rate was the primary tool for monetary policy and monetary policy was guided by the *real bills doctrine*. By the end of World War I, rising inflation caused the Fed to abandon the real bills doctrine because it was inconsistent with the goal of price stability. During the Great Depression, the Fed failed to engage in its role as lender-of-last-resort, and the money supply fell by 25%. Between 1936 and 1937, the Fed raised reserve requirements, which pushed the economy into a severe recession.

During World War II, the Fed agreed to keep interest rates low to aid the Treasury in financing the war. But by the early 1950s inflation had reached unacceptable levels. In 1951, the Fed and Treasury reached an agreement called the Accord, which reasserted the Fed's control over monetary policy. During the 1950s and 1960s, the Fed targeted money market conditions, which led to a procyclical monetary policy. The Fed committed to monetary aggregate targeting in the 1970s, but its commitment was not strong and monetary policy remained procyclical. In October 1979, the Fed changed its primary operating instrument to nonborrwed reserves and it de-emphasized the federal funds rate. In October 1982, the Fed switched to targeting borrowed reserves in order to smooth interest rates. Starting in 1994, the Fed began announcing its target for the federal funds rate immediately following its FOMC meetings.

INTERNATIONAL CONSIDERATIONS

International considerations are likely to be a major factor in the conduct of future U.S. monetary policy. The recognition that monetary policy needs to be more forward looking prompted the Fed to be more preemptive. The preemptive strike against rising inflation in the mid-1990s was successful. The Fed's attempt to preemptively reduce inflation in 2008 was less successful. The Fed has also responded preemptively to negative shocks to aggregate demand. Those preemptive strikes were particularly successful during the Greenspan era in keeping fluctuations very mild. The preemptive strike during the subprime financial crisis, however, was not enough to contain the crisis.

Helpful Hints

Monetary policy strategies and tactics vary across countries and over time. It is important to keep in mind that each strategy has advantages and disadvantages. Moreover, as illustrated in the discussion of the Fed's past policies, sometimes the disadvantages are discovered only after the policy has resulted in a recession or excessive inflation.

Terms and Definitions

Choose a definition for each key term.

Key Terms:

_____operating instrument

_____real bills doctrine

_____inflation targeting

_____asset price bubble

_____intermediate target

_____monetary targeting

_____Phillips curve theory

_____policy instrument

_____international policy coordination

_____Taylor rule

_____Taylor principle

_____NAIRU

_____macroprudential regulation

Definitions:

1. A monetary policy rule that describes the setting of the federal funds rate target under Chairmen Greenspan and Bernanke

2. Any of a set of variables such as reserve aggregates or interest rates that the Fed seeks to influence and that are responsive to its policy tools

3. The rate of unemployment when demand for labor equals supply, consequently eliminating the tendency for the inflation rate to change

4. Monetary policy aimed at achieving a certain inflation rate

5. Any of a set of variables, such as monetary aggregates or interest rates, that have a direct effect on employment and the price level and that the Fed seeks to influence

6. Monetary policy that aims to achieve a certain value of the annual growth of a monetary aggregate

7. A theory suggesting that changes in inflation are influenced by the state of the economy relative to its production capacity, as well as other factors

8. An alternative term used to describe a policy instrument

9. The practice of conducting monetary policy so that the nominal interest changes by more than changes in the inflation rate

10. The practice of conducting monetary policy to facilitate the production and sale of goods and services

11. The practice of countries agreeing to enact policies cooperatively

12. Pronounced increases in asset prices that depart from fundamental values

13. Regulatory policy to affect what is happening in credit markets in the aggregate

Problems and Short-Answer Questions

PRACTICE PROBLEMS

1. a. What is monetary targeting?

   _____

   _____

   b. What are the advantages of monetary targeting?

   _____

   _____

   _____

   _____

   c. What are the disadvantages of monetary targeting?

   _____

   _____

   _____

   _____

   d. When did the Fed commit itself to monetary targeting?

   _____

   e. What factors account for the Fed's inability to achieve its monetary growth targets?

   _____

   _____

   _____

   _____

2. a. Why have central banks around the world moved from monetary targeting to inflation targeting since the early 1990s?

   _____

   _____

   b. What are the advantages of inflation targeting?

   _____

   _____

   c. What are the disadvantages of inflation targeting?

   _____

   _____

3. a. Describe the Fed's "just do it" approach to monetary policy.

   _____

   _____

   _____

   b. What are the advantages of the Fed's approach?

   _____

   _____

   c. What are the disadvantages of the Fed's approach?

   _____

   _____

   _____

   _____

   _____

4. a. Draw the demand and supply for reserves and show what happens to the federal fund rate when the Fed targets nonborrowed reserves.

b.   Draw the demand and supply for reserves and show what happens to the quantity of nonborrowed reserves when the Fed targets the federal funds rate.

c.   Use your answers in a and b to explain why the Fed cannot target both the federal funds rate and the quantity of nonborrowed reserves at the same time.

_____

_____

_____

_____

_____

_____

5.   Suppose the inflation rate is 2%, the equilibrium real federal funds rate is 2%, the output gap is –1.5%, and the target inflation rate is 2.5%.
   a.   Use the Taylor Rule to predict the target federal funds rate given the above data.

_____

_____

   b.   According to the data given above, is the unemployment rate at, above, or below NAIRU? Does this mean that inflation is expected to rise, fall, or remain unchanged in the future?

_____

_____

   c.   Based on your Taylor rule calculation, is monetary policy neutral, contractionary, or expansionary?

_____

_____

6. a. List and describe the two types of bubbles.

    _____

    _____

    b. Which type of bubble poses a larger risk to the financial system?

    _____

    _____

    c. What are the arguments against using monetary policy to burst an asset-price bubble that is driven solely by irrational exuberance?

    _____

    _____

    d. What are the appropriate policy responses to a credit-driven bubble?

    _____

    _____

    _____

7. a. Explain how the policy of targeting money market interest rates during the 1960s and 1970s resulted in procyclical monetary policy.

    _____

    _____

    _____

    _____

    b. Explain how the policy of targeting borrowed reserves during the 1980s resulted in a procyclical monetary policy.

    _____

    _____

    _____

    _____

SHORT-ANSWER QUESTIONS

1. Explain why the Bundesbank's monetary targeting regime was deemed a success despite the fact that they frequently missed their monetary aggregate growth targets.

   _____

   _____

2. What are the three criteria that a central bank uses to choose a policy instrument?

   _____

   _____

3. Explain why a central bank must choose either a reserve aggregate or an interest rate as its policy instrument, but it cannot choose both at once.

   _____

   _____

   _____

   _____

   _____

4. What is the difference between an operating instrument and an intermediate target?

   _____

   _____

   _____

5. Which type of bubble are policymakers more likely to identify while it is happening?

   _____

   _____

   _____

6. What was the Fed's primary policy tool during its early years?

_____

_____

_____

7. What is the real bills doctrine and why was it abandoned by the Fed in the early 1920s?

_____

_____

_____

8. What two monetary policy mistakes did the Fed make during the 1930s?

_____

_____

_____

9. What was the Accord between the Fed and the Treasury? How did the Accord change the way the Fed conducted monetary policy?

_____

_____

_____

10. Describe a time when the Fed was successful in preempting a rise in inflation. Describe a time when the Fed was not as successful in preempting a rise in inflation.

_____

_____

_____

Critical Thinking

Suppose the central bank's goal for inflation is 2%, and the equilibrium federal funds rate is 2%.

1. Assume that GDP is currently at potential and inflation is 2%. Use the Taylor rule to calculate the target federal funds rate and the value of the *real* federal funds rate that is implied by that target rate. Is monetary policy expansionary, contractionary, or neutral? How will GDP growth and inflation be effected by this monetary policy?

    _____

    _____

    _____

    _____

    _____

    _____

2. Now assume that GDP is 1% below potential and inflation is 1%. Use the Taylor rule to calculate the target federal funds rate and the value of the *real* federal funds rate that is implied by that target rate. Is monetary policy expansionary, contractionary, or neutral? How will GDP growth and inflation be effected by this monetary policy?

    _____

    _____

    _____

    _____

    _____

    _____

3. Now assume that GDP is 1% above potential and inflation is 3%. Use the Taylor rule to calculate the target federal funds rate and the value of the *real* federal funds rate that is implied by that target rate. Is monetary policy expansionary, contractionary, or neutral? How will GDP growth and inflation be effected by this monetary policy?

_____

_____

_____

_____

_____

_____

Self-Test

TRUE/FALSE QUESTIONS

_____1. The Bank of Japan's monetary policy performance during the 1978-1987 period was much better than the Fed's.

_____2. Inflation targeting is less transparent than monetary targeting.

_____3. Inflation targeting reduces the likelihood that a central bank will fall into the time-inconsistency trap.

_____4. An advantage of the Fed's "just do it" strategy is that it relies on a stable money-inflation relationship.

_____5. The Fed's "just do it" strategy is consistent with democratic principles.

_____6. Following the Taylor principle will result in more stable inflation.

_____7. A central bank can target either the federal funds rate or nonborrowed reserves but not both.

_____8. Both interest rates and reserve aggregates have observability and measurability problems.

_____9. Bubbles driven solely by irrational exuberance pose a much larger risk to the financial system than bubbles driven by credit.

_____10. Monetary policymakers are more likely to identify a bubble driven by irrational exuberance than a bubble driven by credit.

_____11. The Fed continues to use the real bills doctrine to guide monetary policy.

_____12. After the Fed's Accord with the Treasury, the Fed began pegging interest rates at low levels.

_____13. The Fed's policy of targeting money market interest rates during the 1950s and 1960s led to a countercyclical monetary policy.

_____14. Since February 1994, the Fed has announced its federal funds interest rate targets immediately after each FOMC meeting.

_____15. The Fed was particularly successful in keeping economic fluctuations very mild during the Greenspan era.

MULTIPLE-CHOICE QUESTIONS

1. During the period of 1979–1982, the Fed frequently missed its stated monetary targets for all except which of the following reasons?
   a. The economy was exposed to shocks which made monetary targeting difficult.
   b. Financial innovation and deregulation accelerated during the 1970s
   c. The Fed was officially targeting inflation during that time period
   d. Fed chairman Volcker was more interested in wringing inflation out of the economy than in hitting monetary targets.

2. During the period of monetary targeting, which started in the 1970s and lasted 20 years, the German Bundesbank
   a. always met its target goals for money growth.
   b. was secretive about its goals and intentions.
   c. was transparent about its goals and intentions.
   d. placed greater emphasis on it short-term money growth targets and less emphasis on its long-term inflation goals.

3. Monetary aggregate targeting has fallen out of favor because
   a. figures for monetary aggregates are reported with a substantial lag.
   b. the relationship between monetary aggregates and goal variables has broken down.
   c. the relationship between monetary policy tools and monetary aggregates has broken down.
   d. monetary aggregate targeting is more likely to lead to the time-inconsistency trap than inflation targeting.

4. Which of the following is not an essential element of inflation targeting?
   a. public announcement of a numerical target for inflation
   b. an institutional commitment to price stability as the primary, long-run goal of monetary policy
   c. increased transparency of monetary policy
   d. a mechanism for firing the head of the central bank if the inflation target is not achieved

5. Which of the following is a disadvantage of inflation targeting?
   a. There is a long lag between monetary policy actions and inflation.
   b. Inflation targeting is more likely to result in the time-inconsistency problem than monetary targeting is.
   c. Inflation targeting leads to increased exchange rate fluctuations.
   d. Inflation targeting is less transparent than monetary targeting.

6. If the Fed follows the Taylor principle, it will
   a. increase the nominal interest rate by less than an increase in inflation.
   b. increase the nominal interest rate by more than an increase in inflation.
   c. follow the Taylor rule when inflation is below the nominal interest rate.
   d. follow the Taylor rule when inflation is above the nominal interest rate.

7. The Fed should not base monetary policy solely on the Taylor rule conducted in a mechanical fashion because
   a. the Fed looks at a much wider range of information than is contained in the Taylor rule.
   b. no one knows what the true model of the economy is.
   c. times of economic crisis may require very different monetary policy.
   d. all of the above

8. Under Fed Chairmen Greenspan and Bernanke, the Fed has followed
   a. an inflation target.
   b. a money target.
   c. a explicit nominal anchor.
   d. an implicit nominal anchor.

9. Which of the following is a disadvantage of the Fed's "just do it" strategy?
   a. It lacks transparency.
   b. It does not rely on a stable money-inflation relationship.
   c. It uses many sources of information.
   d. It has performed poorly over the past 20 years.

10. Which of the following is a policy instrument?
    a. open market operations
    b. reserve aggregates
    c. inflation
    d. discount rate

11. Intermediate targets
    a. stand between policy tools and policy instruments.
    b. stand between policy instruments and policy goals.
    c. indicate whether policy is tight or easy.
    d. are inconsistent with inflation targeting.

12. The most important characteristic of a policy instrument is that it
    a. is observable and measurable.
    b. is controllable.
    c. has a predictable impact on goals.
    d. is a nominal anchor.

13. According to the Taylor rule, if the equilibrium real federal funds rate is 2%, the inflation rate is 3%, the target inflation rate is 2%, and the output gap is 1%, the federal funds rate target will be
    a. 2.
    b. 4.
    c. 5.
    d. 6.

14. When the unemployment rate rises above NAIRU,
    a. output is below potential and inflation rises.
    b. output is below potential and inflation falls.
    c. output is above potential and inflation rises.
    d. output is above potential and inflation falls.

15. According to the Taylor rule, if inflation falls below its target and output falls below potential,
    a. the federal funds target will decrease.
    b. the federal funds target will increase
    c. the equilibrium real federal funds rate will decrease.
    d. the equilibrium real federal funds rate will increase.

16. Credit-driven bubbles are ____ to identify and pose a ____threat to the financial system compared to bubbles driven solely by irrational exuberance.
    a. easier; smaller
    b. easier; larger
    c. harder; smaller
    d. harder; larger

17. In the presence of a credit-driven asset price bubble, the appropriate policy is
    a. monetary policy tightening.
    b. monetary policy easing.
    c. macroprudential regulation.
    d. nothing; it is best to let the bubble run its course.

18. During the period from October 1979 to October 1982, fluctuations in money supply growth _____ and fluctuations in the federal funds rate _____.
    a. increased; decreased
    b. increased; increased
    c. decreased; decreased
    d. decreased; increased

19. The Fed no longer uses monetary aggregate targets to guide monetary policy because
    a. the rapid pace of financial innovation has made the measurement of money difficult.
    b. it leads to procyclical monetary policy.
    c. it is inconsistent with the real bills doctrine.
    d. it is inconsistent with a federal funds target.

20. The Fed's decision to slow money growth in 1987 after the dollar had declined in value is an example of
    a. a preemptive strike against inflation.
    b. a preemptive strike against a negative aggregate demand shock.
    c. international policy coordination.
    d. the real bills doctrine.

Solutions

Terms and Definitions

_8_ operating instrument

_10_ real bills doctrine

_4_ inflation targeting

_12_ asset price bubble

_5_ intermediate target

_6_ monetary targeting

_7_ Phillips curve theory

_2_ policy instrument

_11_ international policy coordination

_1_ Taylor rule

_9_ Taylor principle

_3_ NAIRU

_13_ macroprudential regulation

Practice Problems

1. a. Monetary targeting is a strategy in which the central bank announces that it will achieve a certain value of the annual growth rate of a monetary aggregate.

    b. One advantage of monetary targeting is that it provides almost immediate feedback to policymakers because monetary aggregate measures are available with only a few week lag. Another advantage of monetary targeting is that it helps constrain monetary policymakers from falling into the time-inconsistency trap.

    c. The biggest disadvantage of monetary targeting is that it only works as long as monetary aggregates and goal variables such as inflation or nominal income growth are closely related. Since the early 1990s many central banks have found that the relationship between monetary aggregates and goals has broken down, thus making monetary aggregate targeting less desirable.

    d. The Fed committed itself to monetary targeting between 1979 and 1982.

    e. Several shocks to the economy such as increased financial innovation and back-to-back recessions might account for the Fed's inability to hit its targets. Some analysts believe, however, that Fed Chairman Volcker was more interested in

wringing inflation out of the economy than achieving money growth targets.

2. a. Because the relationship between monetary aggregates and inflation and nominal income growth has broken down since the early 1990s.

    b. The advantages of inflation targeting are: It is highly transparent; it increases accountability; and it reduces the likelihood of a central bank falling into the time-inconsistency trap.

    c. The disadvantages of inflation targeting are: delayed signaling, too much rigidity, potential for increased output fluctuations, low economic growth.

3. a. The Fed has an implicit rather than explicit inflation target. The Fed is forward-looking in the sense that they continuously monitor the economy for signs of future inflation. The Fed is also pre-emptive, tightening monetary policy before inflation rises.

    b. The main advantage of the Fed's approach is that it has been highly successful. Another advantage is that it does not rely on a stable money-inflation relationship.

    c. A disadvantage of the Fed's approach is that it lacks transparency, which might lead to excess volatility in financial markets. The Fed's current policy relies heavily on the skills of the chair of the Fed. Finally, the Fed's current system lacks accountability and therefore may be inconsistent with democratic principles.

4. a. If the Fed targets nonborrowed reserves, *NBR* is held constant at *NBR**. As illustrated in the figure below, changes in the demand for reserves (R^d) will therefore cause the federal funds rate (i_{ff}) to fluctuate when nonborrowed reserves is held constant.

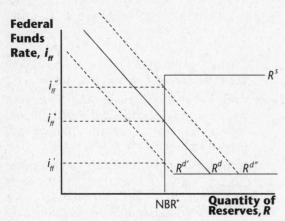

b. If the Fed targets the federal funds rate, i_{ff} is held constant at $i_{ff}*$. As illustrated in Figure 2, changes in the demand for reserves (R^d) will therefore cause nonborrowed reserves (NBR) to fluctuate when the federal funds rate is held constant.

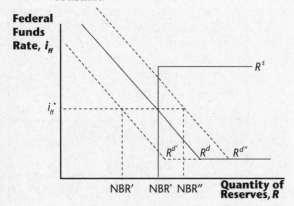

c. The answers to *a* and *b* illustrate how the Fed can target either the federal funds rate (i_{ff}) or nonborrowed reserves (NBR), but it cannot target both at the same time. The reason the Fed cannot target both at the same time is that the demand for reserves fluctuates daily. So if the Fed targets (holds constant) NBR, fluctuations in the demand for reserves (R^d) will cause the federal funds rate to move up and down. And if the Fed targets (holds constant) i_{ff}, fluctuations in the demand for reserves (R^d) will cause NBR to move up and down.

5. a. According to the Taylor-rule, the target federal fund rate = 2 + 2 + .5× (−.5) + .5× (−1.5) = 3%.

    b. The output gap is negative, which means that the unemployment rate is above NAIRU, which means that there is a tendency for inflation to fall.

c. Monetary policy is expansionary. Neutral policy would be achieved when the inflation rate is at the target inflation rate and the output gap is zero.

6. a. The two types of asset price bubbles are credit-driven bubbles and bubbles driven solely by irrational exuberance.

    b. Credit-driven bubbles pose a larger risk to the financial system.

    c. The argument against bursting a bubble driven solely by irrational exuberance is that they are nearly impossible to identify.

    d. The appropriate policy response is macroprudential regulation.

7. a. As the economy expands, money market interest rates rise. During the 1960s and 1970s, the Fed targeted money market interest rates, which means that when the money market interest rates started to rise, they expanded the money supply to push interest rates back down. Economic expansions therefore resulted in an increase in the money supply.

    b. As the economy expands, market interest rates rise, which gives banks a greater incentive to borrow more from the Fed. During the 1980s the Fed targeted borrowed reserves, which means that when a rise in market interest rates caused discount window borrowing rise, the Fed responded by lowering market interest rates to push discount window borrowing back down to its target level. Economic expansions therefore resulted in an increase in the money supply.

Short-Answer Questions

1. The Bundesbank's monetary targeting is best viewed as a mechanism for transparently communicating how monetary policy is being directed to achieve long-term inflation goals.

2. The three criteria that a central bank uses to choose a policy instrument are: (1) observability and measurability; (2) controllability; and (3) predictable effect on goals.

3. The overnight interest rate is determined by the demand and supply for reserves. The central bank controls the supply of reserves but the demand for reserves moves around in response to the reserve needs of banks. If the central bank targets the quantity of reserves,

fluctuations in the demand for reserves will move the interest rate. If the central bank wishes to target the interest rate, it must be willing to move the supply of reserves to match movements in demand in order to keep the interest rate at its target.

4. An operating instrument is directly affected by the central bank's tools. An intermediate target is less directly affected by the central bank's tools but more directly related to the goals of monetary policy.

5. The Fed is more likely to recognize a credit-driven asset price bubble while it is happening.

6. The Fed's primary tool during its early years of operation was discount lending.

7. The real bills doctrine was doctrine that the Fed would make loans to facilitate the production and sale of goods and services. Rising inflation by the end of World War I caused the Fed to abandon the real bills doctrine because it was inconsistent with the goal of price stability.

8. During the Great Depression the Fed failed to engage in its role as lender-of-last-resort, and the money supply fell by 25%. Between 1936 and 1937, the Fed raised reserve requirements, which pushed the economy into a severe recession.

9. In 1951, the Fed and Treasury reached an agreement called the Accord, which reasserted the Fed's control over monetary policy by allowing the Fed to stop pegging the interest rate at low levels.

10. The Fed was successful in preempting the rise in inflation in the mid-1990s. The Fed was less successful in preempting the rise in inflation in 2008.

Critical Thinking

1. According to the Taylor rule, $i_{ff}{}^* = 2 + 2 + .5 \times (2 - 2) + .5 \times 0 = 4$. If the economy is operating at potential and inflation is at its target of 2%, the Taylor rule calls for a federal funds rate target ($i_{ff}{}^*$) of 4%. This target rate for the nominal federal funds rate implies a real federal funds rate that is equal to 2% (real federal funds rate equals nominal federal funds rate − inflation). This would be neutral monetary policy because the real federal funds rate implied by the Fed's target is equal to the equilibrium federal funds rate. Under neutral monetary policy, monetary policy is

neither stimulating or dampening GDP growth nor inflation.

2. According to the Taylor rule, $i_{ff}{}^* = 2 + 1 + .5 \times (1-2) + .5 \times (-1) = 2$. If the economy is operating below potential and inflation is below its target of 2%, the Taylor rule calls for a federal funds rate target ($i_{ff}{}^*$) of 2%. This target rate for the nominal federal funds rate implies a real federal funds rate that is equal to 1%. This would be expansionary monetary policy because the real federal funds rate implied by the Fed's target is less than the equilibrium federal funds rate. Under expansionary monetary policy, GDP growth and inflation will tend to rise.

3. According to the Taylor rule, $i_{ff}{}^* = 2 + 3 + .5 \times (3 - 2) + .5 \times (1) = 6$. If the economy is operating above potential and inflation is above its target of 2%, the Taylor rule calls for a federal funds rate target ($i_{ff}{}^*$) of 6%. This target rate for the nominal federal funds rate implies a real federal funds rate that is equal to 3%. This would be contractionary monetary policy because the real federal funds rate implied by the Fed's target is greater than the equilibrium federal funds rate. Under contractionary monetary policy, GDP growth and inflation will tend to fall.

True/False Questions

1. T
2. F
3. T
4. F
5. F
6. T
7. T
8. T
9. F
10. F
11. F
12. F
13. F
14. T
15. T

Multiple-Choice Questions

1. c
2. c
3. b
4. d
5. a
6. b
7. d
8. d
9. a
10. b
11. b
12. c
13. d
14. b
15. a
16. b
17. c
18. b
19. a
20. c

17 The Foreign Exchange Market

Chapter Review

This is the first chapter in a two chapter sequence on international finance and monetary policy. This chapter looks at the foreign exchange market. The next chapter looks at the International Financial System.

PREVIEW

The price of one currency in terms of another is called the *exchange rate*. Fluctuations in the exchange rate affect both inflation and output and are an important concern for monetary policymakers. This chapter looks at how the exchange rate is determined in the *foreign exchange market*.

FOREIGN EXCHANGE MARKET

When a U.S. firm buys a foreign good or asset, it first must exchange dollars (or dollar denominated deposits) for the foreign currency (or foreign denominated deposits). That exchange takes place in the foreign exchange market. Two kinds of transactions take place in that market: *spot transactions*, which involve the immediate exchange of bank deposits and *forward transactions*, which involve the exchange of bank deposits at some specified future date. The *spot exchange rate* is the exchange rate on spot transactions, and the *forward exchange rate* is the exchange rate on forward transactions. When a currency increases in value, it experiences an *appreciation*; when it falls in value, it experiences a *depreciation*. When a country's currency appreciates, its goods become more expensive for foreign buyers and foreign goods become less expensive for domestic buyers. When a country's currency depreciates, its goods become less expensive for foreign buyers and foreign goods become more expensive for domestic buyers.

EXCHANGE RATES IN THE LONG RUN

According to the *law of one price*, if transportation costs and trade barriers are low, the price of identical goods should be the same throughout the world. If a candy bar costs $1 in the United States and the same candy bar costs 10 pesos in Mexico, then according to the law of one price, the exchange rate between pesos and dollars should be 10 pesos per dollar. The law of one price applied to national price levels (rather than prices of individual goods such as candy bars) is called the *theory of purchasing power parity (PPP)*. According to PPP, if the Mexican price level rises 10% relative to the U.S. price level, the dollar will appreciate 10% relative to the peso. Another way to think about purchasing power parity is through the concept called the real exchange rate, which is the price of domestic goods relative to the price of foreign goods denominated in the domestic currency. PPP does not fully explain movements in exchange rates, even in the long run. Trade barriers, preferences for domestic versus foreign goods, and differences in productivity across countries also influence exchange rates in the long run.

EXCHANGE RATES IN THE SHORT RUN:
A SUPPLY AND DEMAND ANALYSIS

In the short run, exchange rates are determined mainly by the demand and supply for domestic assets. The supply of assets is fixed. The quantity of assets demanded depends on the relative expected return on domestic assets. To understand the demand for domestic assets, think about starting at a point on the demand curve where the euro/dollar exchange rate is 1 and future euro/dollar exchange rate (E^e_{t+1}) is expected to remain constant at 1 as well. A decrease in the current exchange rate to .8 will increase the return on dollar assets relative to European assets and lead to a rise in the quantity of dollar assets demanded. The demand for dollar assets will shift when there is a change in the expected future exchange rate E^e_{t+1}, domestic interest rate i^D, or foreign interest rate i^F. An increase in the expected future exchange rate E^e_{t+1} causes the demand curve to shift right, causing the dollar to appreciate and E to rise. An increase in domestic interest rates, i^D, causes the demand for dollar assets to shift right as well. An increase in foreign interest rates i^F causes the demand curve to shift left, causing the dollar to depreciate and E to fall.

The above analysis assumes that changes in the interest rate arise from changes in the real interest rate. If the increase in interest rates is due to an increase in the expected inflation rate instead of the real interest rate then the dollar will depreciate. A higher domestic money supply causes the exchange rate to depreciate because the price level rises and the interest rate declines. Eventually the interest rate returns to its original level and the exchange rate appreciates, but only partially, leaving it lower than it was before the increase in the money supply. Thus, the exchange rate depreciates more in the short run than in the long run. This phenomenon is called *exchange rate overshooting* and it helps explain why exchange rates are volatile.

Earlier models of exchange rate fluctuations were based on the goods market and did not predict substantial movements in exchange rates because they did not emphasize changing expectations as a source of exchange rate movements. The weakness of the dollar in the late 1970s and the strength of the dollar in the early 1980s can both be explained by movements in real interest rates but not movements in nominal interest rates. As the subprime crisis spread to the rest of the world in 2008, the dollar increased in value relative to a wider basket of currencies. This occurred because foreign central banks began reducing their interest rates and there was a "flight to quality" which increased the demand for U.S. Treasury securities.

Helpful Hints

In the long run, movements in exchange rates are mainly driven by relative inflation rates between countries. In the short run, movements in exchange rates are mainly driven by relative rates of returns on assets between countries.

Terms and Definitions

Choose a definition for each key term.

Key Terms:

_____ appreciation

_____ capital mobility

_____ depreciation

_____ effective exchange rate index

_____ exchange rate

_____ exchange rate overshooting

_____ foreign exchange market

_____ forward exchange rate

_____ real exchange rate

_____ forward transaction

_____ law of one price

_____ monetary neutrality

_____ quotas

_____ spot exchange rate

_____ spot transaction

_____ theory of purchasing power parity

_____ tariffs

Definitions:

1. The immediate exchange of bank deposits in the foreign exchange market

2. A fall in the value of a currency

3. The situation in which foreigners can easily purchase American assets and Americans can easily purchase foreign assets

4. The proposition that a one-time percentage rise in the money supply is matched by the same one-time percentage rise in the price level in the long run

5. The idea that the prices of identical goods should be identical throughout the world

6. The price of one currency in terms of another

7. The exchange rate for forward transactions

8. Taxes on imported goods

9. The exchange of bank deposits in the foreign exchange market at some future specified date

10. An increase in the value of a currency

11. The theory that exchange rates between any two countries will adjust to reflect changes in the price levels of the two countries

12. The term used to describe the phenomenon in which the exchange rate falls by more in the short run than it does in the long run when the money supply increases

13. The value of the dollar in terms of a basket of foreign currencies

14. The market in which the exchange rate is determined

15. The exchange rate for spot transactions

16. Restrictions on the quantity of foreign goods that can be imported

17. The price of domestic goods relative to the price of foreign goods denominated in the domestic currency

Problems and Short-Answer Questions

PRACTICE PROBLEMS

1. Suppose the dollar/euro exchange rate is 1.20.
   a. What is the euro/dollar exchange rate?

   _____

   b. What would the new euro/dollar exchange rate be if the euro appreciated by 5% relative to the dollar?

   _____

   c. Starting from the original exchange rate you calculated in <u>a</u>, what would the new euro/dollar exchange rate be if the euro depreciated by 5% against the dollar?

   _____

2. a. Suppose the law of one price holds for wheat and the price of wheat is $4.50 per bushel in the United States, and the peso/dollar exchange rate is 10. Calculate the price of wheat in terms of pesos.

   _____

   b. Now suppose that purchasing power parity holds between the United States and Mexico. Calculate the new peso/dollar exchange rate if the price level in Mexico rises 10% relative to the price level in the United States.

   _____

   c. Now suppose a basket of goods in the United States costs $100, while the cost of the same basket of goods in Mexico costs 950 pesos. Calculate the real exchange rate assuming the peso/dollar exchange rate is 15.

   _____

3. In the second column of the following table, indicate with an arrow whether the exchange rate will rise (↑) or fall (↓) as a result of the change in the factor. (Recall that a rise in the exchange rate is viewed as an appreciation of the domestic currency).

Change in Factor	Response of the Exchange Rate
Domestic interest rate ↓	_____
Foreign interest rate ↓	_____
Domestic price level ↓	_____
Tariffs and quotas ↓	_____
Import demand ↓	_____
Export demand ↓	_____
Domestic productivity ↓	_____

4. Use the demand–and–supply diagram for domestic assets to demonstrate the following.
   a. Show what happens to the exchange rate E_t when the domestic interest rate i^D decreases.

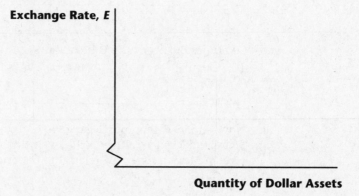

   b. Show what happens to the exchange rate E_t when the foreign interest rate i^F increases.

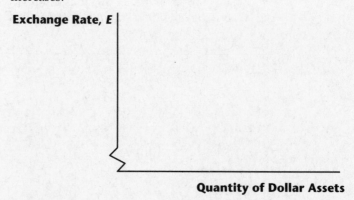

c. Show what happens to the exchange rate E_t when the expected future exchange rate E_{t+1} increases.

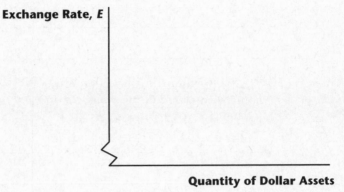

Exchange Rate, *E*

Quantity of Dollar Assets

SHORT-ANSWER QUESTIONS

1. What happens to the price of foreign imports into the United States when the dollar depreciates?

   _____

   _____

2. What is likely to happen to the quantity of imports demanded by Americans as a result of the dollar depreciating?

   _____

   _____

3. What happens to a country's currency if that country increases its trade barriers and becomes more productive relative to other countries?

   _____

   _____

4. What determines the demand for domestic assets?

   _____

   _____

5. What will happen to the exchange rate today if the expected future exchange rate declines?

   _____

   _____

6. What will happen to the value of the domestic currency when the domestic real interest rate rises?

_____

_____

7. What will happen to the value of the domestic currency when the domestic nominal interest rate rises and the increase is due to an increase in expected inflation?

_____

_____

8. What will happen to the value of the domestic currency when the money supply rises?

_____

_____

9. What is exchange rate overshooting and how does it happen?

_____

_____

_____

_____

_____

10. Why did the dollar appreciate during the subprime financial crisis?

_____

_____

Critical Thinking

Most of the analysis in this chapter looks at how a single factor, such as a change in domestic interest rates, affects the exchange rate, holding all other factors constant. But in the real world, many factors change at once and so sometimes it is not possible to predict the impact on exchange rates. For each of the following combinations of factors, state whether it is possible to predict the direction of the effect on the domestic exchange rate. For the cases where it is possible to predict the direction of effect, state what that direction is.

a. The domestic interest rate rises, foreign interest rate falls, and expected import demand falls as well.

_____

_____

_____

b. The domestic price level rises, quotas are placed on imports, and productivity is expected to rise.

_____

_____

_____

c. Export demand is expected to rise, the domestic price level is expected to fall, and foreign interest rates are expected to fall as well.

_____

_____

_____

Self-Test

TRUE/FALSE QUESTIONS

_____1. Most trades in the foreign exchange market involve the buying and selling of bank deposits.

_____2. When a country's currency appreciates, its goods abroad become less expensive and foreign goods in that country become more expensive, all else constant.

_____3. Forward exchange rates involve the immediate exchange of bank deposits.

_____4. The theory of purchasing power parity explains most of the movements in exchange rates in the short run.

_____5. If purchasing power parity holds, the real exchange rate equals 1.

_____6. The quantity of domestic assets supplied increases as the exchange rate E_t rises.

_____7. The quantity of domestic assets demanded increases as the exchange rate E_t falls.

_____8. If the price level in the United States rises relative to the price levels in other countries, the dollar will appreciate.

_____9. Increasing trade barriers causes a country's currency to appreciate in the long run.

_____10. In the long run, as a country becomes more productive relative to other countries, its currency appreciates.

_____11. When export demand rises, the domestic currency appreciates.

_____12. When the domestic real interest rate rises, the domestic currency depreciates.

_____13. When the domestic interest rate rises because of an expected increase in inflation, the domestic currency depreciates.

_____14. Exchange rate overshooting occurs when an increase in the money supply causes the exchange rate to fall more in the long run than in the short run.

_____15. The weakness of the dollar in the late 1970s and the strength of the dollar in the early 1980s can be explained by movements in nominal interest rates but not movements in real interest rates.

MULTIPLE-CHOICE QUESTIONS

1. When the euro appreciates (holding everything else constant), then
    a. European chocolate sold in the United States becomes more expensive.
    b. American computers sold in Europe become more expensive.
    c. European watches sold in the United States become less expensive.
    d. American toothpaste sold in Europe becomes less expensive.
    e. a and c
    f. a and d

2. If the Mexican peso depreciates against the dollar, then
    a. it takes more dollars to buy a peso.
    b. it takes fewer pesos to buy a dollar.
    c. the dollar has appreciated against the peso.
    d. U.S. goods are less expensive in Mexico.

3. If transportation costs and trade barriers are low, and the exchange rate is .80 euros per dollar, then according to the law of one price, a computer that costs $1,000 in the United States will cost
    a. 1,000 euros in Europe.
    b. 1,250 euros in Europe.
    c. 800 euros in Europe.
    d. 1,800 euros in Europe.

4. According to the theory of purchasing power parity, if the price level in the United States rises by 5% while the price level in Mexico rises by 6%, then the dollar will
    a. appreciate 1% relative to the peso.
    b. depreciate 1% relative to the peso.
    c. appreciate 5% relative to the peso.
    d. depreciate 5% relative to the peso.

5. Reasons why the theory of purchasing power parity might not fully explain exchange rate movements include
    a. differing monetary policies in different countries.
    b. changes in the prices of goods and services not traded internationally.
    c. changes in the domestic price level that exceed changes in the foreign price level.
    d. changes in foreign price levels that exceed changes in the domestic price level.

6. If the cost of a market basket of goods in the United States is $80, the cost of that same market basket in France is 90 euros, and the euro/dollar exchange rate is .77, the real exchange rate will be
    a. .68.
    b. 1.46.
    c. 1.
    d. .77.

7. If, in retaliation for "unfair" trade practices, Congress imposes a tariff on Chinese imports, but at the same time Chinese demand for American goods increases, then in the long run
    a. the Chinese yuan will appreciate relative to the dollar.
    b. the Chinese yuan will depreciate relative to the dollar.
    c. the dollar will depreciate relative to the yuan.
    d. it is not clear whether the dollar will appreciate or depreciate relative to the yuan.

8. If U.S. products become popular in Europe and exports of U.S. products to Europe increase, then in the long run,
    a. the euro per dollar exchange rate will fall.
    b. European goods will become more expensive in the United States.
    c. U.S. goods will become less expensive in Europe.
    d. the euro per dollar exchange rate will rise.

9. Holding everything else constant, an increase in the expected future exchange rate will cause the
    a. expected return on dollar assets in terms of foreign currency to rise.
    b. expected return on dollar assets in terms of foreign currency to fall.
    c. expected return on foreign assets in terms of dollars to rise.
    d. expected return on foreign assets in terms of dollars to fall.
    e. a and c
    f. a and d

10. All else held constant, an increase in the exchange rate E_t will lead to
    a. a rightward shift in the demand for domestic assets.
    b. a leftward shift in the demand for domestic assets.
    c. an increase in the quantity of domestic assets demanded.
    d. a decrease in the quantity of domestic assets demanded.

11. If the exchange rate is above the equilibrium exchange rate, then
    a. the quantity of domestic assets supplied is greater than the quantity of domestic assets demanded, and the domestic currency will appreciate.
    b. the quantity of domestic assets supplied is less than the quantity of domestic assets demanded, and the domestic currency will appreciate.
    c. the quantity of domestic assets supplied is greater than the quantity of domestic assets demanded, and the domestic currency will depreciate.
    d. the quantity of domestic assets supplied is less than the quantity of domestic assets demanded, and the domestic currency will depreciate.

12. A rise in the expected future exchange rate shifts the demand for domestic assets to the _____ and causes the domestic currency to_____.
    a. right; appreciate
    b. right; depreciate
    c. left; appreciate
    d. left; depreciate

13. A rise in the domestic interest rate shifts the demand for domestic assets to the _____ and causes the domestic currency to_____.
    a. right; appreciate
    b. right; depreciate
    c. left; appreciate
    d. left; depreciate

14. A rise in the foreign interest rate shifts the demand for domestic assets to the _____ and causes the domestic currency to_____.
    a. right; appreciate
    b. right; depreciate
    c. left; appreciate
    d. left; depreciate

15. If the domestic real interest rate rises, then
    a. the nominal interest rate will rise if there is no change in expected inflation.
    b. the return on domestic assets falls.
    c. the return on foreign deposits rises.
    d. the domestic currency depreciates.

16. Lowering the domestic money supply causes the domestic currency to
    a. depreciate more in the short run than in the long run.
    b. depreciate more in the long run than in the short run.
    c. appreciate more in the short run than in the long run.
    d. appreciate more in the long run than in the short run.

17. Exchange rates are volatile because
    a. central banks are constantly manipulating the value of foreign exchange.
    b. inflation rates are volatile.
    c. expectations about the variables that influence exchange rates change frequently.
    d. real interest rates are volatile.

18. According to the theory of monetary neutrality, a 10% increase in the money supply
    a. leads to a 10% increase in the price level in the long run.
    b. leads to less than a 10% increase in the price level in the long run.
    c. does not affect the price level in the long run.
    d. leads to a greater than 10% increase in the price level in the long run.

19. The rise in nominal interest rates in the United States in the 1970s caused the dollar to
    a. appreciate because the increase in nominal interest rates was due mainly to an increase in the real interest rate.
    b. appreciate because the increase in nominal interest rates was due mainly to an increase in expected inflation.
    c. depreciate because the increase in nominal interest rates was due mainly to an increase in the real interest rate.
    d. depreciate because the increase in nominal interest rates was due mainly to an increase in expected inflation.

20. Early models of exchange rate behavior could not predict substantial fluctuations in exchange rates because
    a. they assumed purchasing power parity always holds.
    b. they did not emphasize changing expectations.
    c. they assumed the supply of domestic assets is fixed.
    d. they did not take into account monetary neutrality.

Solutions

Terms and Definitions

<u>10</u> appreciation

<u>3</u> capital mobility

<u>2</u> depreciation

<u>13</u> effective exchange rate index

<u>6</u> exchange rate

<u>12</u> exchange rate overshooting

<u>14</u> foreign exchange market

<u>7</u> forward exchange rate

<u>17</u> real exchange rate

<u>9</u> forward transaction

<u>5</u> law of one price

<u>4</u> monetary neutrality

<u>16</u> quotas

<u>15</u> spot exchange rate

<u>1</u> spot transaction

<u>8</u> tariffs

<u>11</u> theory of purchasing power parity

Practice Problems

1. a. 0.83
   b. 0.79
   c. 0.875

2. a. 45 pesos per bushel.
   b. 11 pesos per dollar.
   c. real exchange rate = 1.58

3.

Change in Factor	Response of the Exchange Rate
Domestic interest rate ↓	↓
Foreign interest rate ↓	↑
Domestic price level ↓	↑
Tariffs and quotas ↓	↓
Import demand ↓	↑
Export demand ↓	↓
Domestic productivity ↓	↓

4. a. A decrease in the domestic interest rate i^D causes the demand for dollar assets to shift left and the exchange rate to fall from E_1 to E_2.

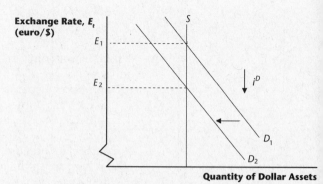

b. An increase in the foreign interest rate i^F causes the demand for dollar assets to shift left and the exchange rate to fall from E_1 to E_2.

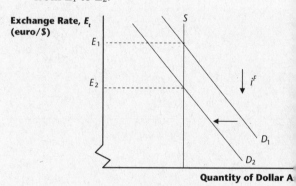

c. An increase in the expected future exchange rate E_{t+1} causes the demand for dollar assets to shift right and the exchange rate to rise from E_1 to E_2.

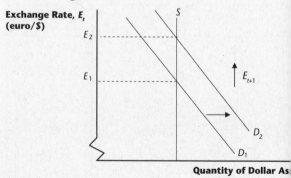

Short-Answer Questions

1. When the dollar depreciates, the price of imports (into the United States) rises.

2. When the dollar depreciates, the quantity of imports demanded by Americans will decline.

3. Both an increase in trade barriers and an increase in productivity will cause a country's currency to appreciate.

4. The demand for domestic assets is determined by the relative expected return of domestic assets.

5. A fall in the expected future exchange rate E^e_{t+1} will cause a depreciation of the currency.

6. When domestic real interest rates rise, the domestic currency appreciates.

7. When domestic interest rates rise due to an expected increase in inflation, the domestic currency depreciates.

8. A higher domestic money supply causes the domestic currency to depreciate.

9. Overshooting is when a one-time increase in the money supply causes the exchange rate to depreciate more in the short run than in the long run. In the short run there are two forces causing the exchange rate to depreciate: the increase in inflation and the increase in the price level. In the long run, once the new higher price level is reached, the effect of inflation on the exchange rate disappears but the effect of the higher price level remains.

10. Two reasons: Foreign central banks cut their interest rates, which reduced the return on foreign assets, and there was a "flight to quality" as foreign investors bought U.S. Treasury securities.

Critical Thinking

a. An increase in domestic interest rates will cause the exchange rate to rise. A decrease in foreign interest rates will cause the exchange rate to rise and a decrease in expected import demand will cause the exchange rate to rise. Since all three factors cause the exchange rate to rise, their combined effect is unambiguous.

b. An increase in the domestic price level will cause the exchange rate to fall. Quotas will cause the exchange rate to rise, and an expected rise in productivity will cause the exchange rate to rise as well. Since the impact of a rise in the domestic price level has the opposite effect as quotas and productivity, the overall effect of these changes is ambiguous.

c. An increase in export demand will cause the exchange rate to rise. A fall in the expected domestic price level will cause the exchange rate to rise and a fall in foreign interest rates will cause the exchange rate to rise as well. Since all three factors cause the exchange rate to rise, their combined effect is unambiguous.

True/False Questions

1. T
2. F
3. F
4. F
5. T
6. F
7. T
8. F
9. T
10. T
11. T
12. F
13. T
14. F
15. F

Multiple-Choice Questions

1. f
2. c
3. c
4. a
5. b
6. a.
7. b
8. d
9. f
10. d
11. c
12. a
13. a
14. d
15. a
16. c
17. c
18. a
19. d
20. b

18

The International Financial System

Chapter Review

PREVIEW

This is the second chapter in a two chapter sequence on international finance and monetary policy. The last chapter looked at the foreign exchange market. This chapter looks at the structure of the international financial system and how that structure affects monetary policy. This chapter also looks at the evolution of the international financial system during the past half century.

INTERVENTION IN THE FOREIGN EXCHANGE MARKET

Central banks regularly engage in *foreign exchange interventions* in order to influence exchange rates. Central banks hold *international reserves*, which are holdings of assets denominated in a foreign currency. When a central bank sells $1 billion of its international reserves, the monetary base declines by $1 billion, and when it buys $1 billion of foreign assets in order to add to its international reserves, the monetary base increases by $1 billion. A central bank can either allow the monetary base to change when it intervenes in the foreign exchange market (this is called an *unsterilized foreign exchange intervention*), or it can offset the effect of the intervention on the monetary base by conducting an offsetting open market operation (this is called a *sterilized foreign exchange intervention*). An unsterilized intervention in which the central bank sells domestic currency to purchase foreign assets leads to a depreciation of the domestic currency. An unsterilized intervention in which the central bank sells foreign assets to purchase domestic currency leads to an appreciation of the domestic currency. A sterilized intervention leaves the monetary base unchanged and therefore has almost no effect on the exchange rate.

BALANCE OF PAYMENTS

The *balance of payments* is the bookkeeping system for the movements of funds between a nation and foreign countries. It is comprised of three main parts: the *current account*, the *capital account* and the *official reserve transactions balance*. The current account records the movements of funds in exchange for currently produced goods and services. The capital account records the movements of funds in exchange for capital transactions, and the official reserve transactions balance records the net change in international reserves. The sum of the current account and the capital account equals the official reserve transactions balance.

EXCHANGE RATE REGIMES IN THE INTERNATIONAL FINANCIAL SYSTEM

In a *fixed exchange rate regime* the central bank pegs its currency to another currency (called the *anchor currency*). In a *floating exchange rate regime* the value of a currency is allowed to fluctuate in value relative to all other currencies. In a *managed* (or *dirty*) *float regime* a country influences (but does not strictly peg) the value of its currency relative to another currency. Prior to World War I the world economy operated under a *gold standard*, which is a type of fixed exchange rate regime in which currencies are convertible into gold at a fixed rate. From 1945 until 1971, exchange rates between countries were fixed under the *Bretton Woods system* fixed exchange rates. Under a fixed exchange rate regime, the central bank offsets shifts in the demand for domestic assets in order to keep the exchange rate fixed, at some desired level called the par value of the exchange rate. Under a fixed exchange rate regime, smaller economies have to follow the same monetary policy as the larger economy. The Bretton Woods system collapsed in 1971 because many smaller economies refused to follow the inflationary monetary policy of the United States.

One risk of maintaining a fixed exchange rate is a *balance of payments crisis*. A balance of payments crisis occurs when there is a decline in the demand for a country's currency that is large enough to make currency speculators believe that the central bank will deplete its international reserves. The expectation that the central bank will eventually allow the currency to depreciate leads to an even greater decline in the demand for the country's currency (as currency speculators sell assets denominated in the country's currency), which speeds the depletion of international reserves.

CAPITAL CONTROLS

Some politicians in emerging market countries have recently found capital controls particularly attractive. But controls on capital outflows suffer from several disadvantages. Economists are more supportive of controls on capital inflows.

THE ROLE OF THE IMF

The *International Monetary Fund* (IMF) was originally established to make loans to countries participating in the Bretton Woods exchange rate system. That system was abandoned in 1971 and since then the IMF has taken on new roles. The IMF has served as the lender of last resort for countries experiencing balance of payments crisis. Central banks in emerging markets sometimes lack credibility and are therefore unable to function as a lender of last resort. The IMF, serving as an international lender of last resort, has the credibility to prevent a balance of payments crisis from getting worse or spreading to other countries. But the IMF may also create a moral hazard problem. Countries may take on too much risk if they believe that the IMF will ultimately bail them out if they get into financial trouble. Countries have avoided borrowing from the IMF in recent years because they did not want to be subjected to harsh austerity programs. The IMF was at risk of becoming irrelevant—until the subprime crisis.

TO PEG OR NOT TO PEG: EXCHANGE-RATE TARGETING AS AN ALTERNATIVE MONETARY POLICY STRATEGY

Exchange rate targeting is an alternative to either monetary targeting or inflation targeting. Advantages of exchange rate targeting are that it ties the inflation expectations to the inflation rate in the anchor country, it helps reduce the time-inconsistency problem, and it is highly transparent. Disadvantages are that the targeting country can no longer pursue its own monetary policy and may suffer a speculative attack on its currency. Emerging market economies with weak political and monetary institutions sometimes opt for a stricter form of fixed exchange rates by either adopting a *currency board* or *dollarization*. A currency board is a monetary policy strategy in which the domestic currency is backed 100% by a foreign currency. Dollarization is when a country adopts the dollar as its official currency.

Helpful Hints

Unsterilized exchange rate interventions have exactly the same effect on the monetary base as open market operations. International reserves and government securities are both assets on the Fed's balance sheet. When the Fed conducts an open market purchase of securities, the monetary base increases. When the Fed purchases international reserves, the monetary base increases. When the Fed conducts an open market sale of government securities, the monetary base decreases. And when the Fed sells international reserves, the monetary base decreases as well.

Terms and Definitions

Choose a definition for each key term.

Key Terms:

_____anchor currency

_____balance of payments

_____balance-of-payments crisis

_____Bretton Woods System

_____capital account

_____currency board

_____current account

_____dollarization

_____fixed exchange rate regime

_____floating exchange rate regime

_____foreign exchange intervention

_____gold standard

_____International Monetary Fund (IMF)

_____international reserves

_____managed float regime (dirty float)

_____official reserve transactions balance

_____seignorage

_____sterilized foreign exchange intervention

_____trade balance

_____unsterilized foreign exchange intervention

Definitions:

1. The difference between merchandise exports and imports

2. A regime in which central banks buy and sell their own currencies to keep their exchange rate fixed at a certain level

3. An account that shows international transactions involving currently produced goods and services

4. The term used to describe the currency that another currency is pegged to in a fixed exchange rate regime

5. Central Bank holdings of assets denominated in foreign currencies

6. The bookkeeping system for recording all payments that have a direct bearing on the movement of funds between a country and foreign countries

7. A regime in which central banks allow their currencies to fluctuate in value against all other currencies

8. A regime under which currency is directly convertible into gold

9. The current account balance plus items in the capital account

10. A foreign exchange intervention that leads to a change in the monetary base

11. A regime in which central banks buy and sell their own currencies to influence (but not fix) the value of their currency relative to another country's currency

12. The international monetary system in use from 1945 to 1971 in which exchange rates were fixed and the U.S. dollar was freely convertible into gold

13. A foreign exchange crisis stemming from problems in a country's balance of payments

14. The adoption of a sound currency, like the U.S. dollar, as a country's money

15. A foreign exchange intervention that is offset by a domestic open market operation, which keeps the monetary base unchanged

16. The international organization created by the Bretton Woods agreement whose objective is to promote growth of world trade by making loans to countries experiencing balance-of-payments difficulties

17. A monetary regime in which the domestic currency is backed 100% by a foreign currency

18. The revenue a government receives by issuing money

19. An account that describes the flow of capital between the United States and other countries

20. An international financial transaction in which a central bank buys or sells currency to influence foreign exchange rates

Problems and Short-Answer Questions

PRACTICE PROBLEMS

1. a. Show the T-account transactions for the case where the Federal Reserve buys $1 billion in foreign assets in exchange for $1 billion in currency.

    Federal Reserve System

Assets	Liabilities

    b. What is the impact of this transaction on the monetary base?

    _____

    _____

    c. Show the T-account transactions for the case where the Federal Reserve buys $1 billion in foreign assets in exchange for $1 billion in deposits.

    Federal Reserve System

Assets	Liabilities

    d. What is the impact of this transaction on the monetary base?

    _____

    _____

e. Show the T-account transactions for the case where the Federal Reserve buys $1 billion in foreign assets in exchange for $1 billion in deposits. Assume that the Fed sterilizes this exchange rate intervention by selling $1 billion in government bonds.

Federal Reserve System

Assets	Liabilities

f. What is the impact of these transactions on the monetary base?

_____

_____

2. a. Draw the demand and supply curves for dollar assets and show what happens to the exchange rate in the short run and the long run when the Fed conducts an unsterilized sale of foreign assets.

Exchange Rate, *E*

Quantity of Dollar Assets

b. Explain why there is exchange rate overshooting in response to this exchange rate intervention.

_____

_____

_____

_____

_____

_____

c. Draw the demand and supply curves for dollar assets and show what happens to the exchange rate in the short run and the long run when the Fed conducts a sterilized sale of foreign assets.

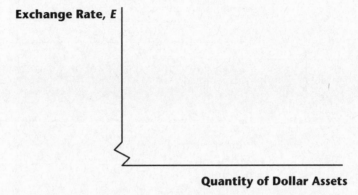

3. a. Draw the demand and supply for dollar assets and show what happens to the exchange rate if the return on foreign assets increases, everything else held constant.

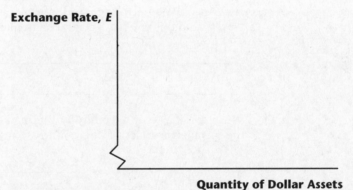

b. Now assume that the central bank wishes to fix the exchange rate at its original level (the level it was at before the return on foreign assets increased). Describe the type of foreign exchange intervention that the central bank would undertake and use the diagram you constructed for part a to show the effect of this intervention on the exchange rate.

_____

_____

_____

_____

4. Consider an emerging market country with a fixed exchange rate that experiences a sudden decrease in the demand for its domestic assets. Despite the decrease in demand, the central bank continues to keep the exchange rate at its original value (its value before the decrease in demand for its assets).
    a. Is this country's currency overvalued or undervalued?

    _____

b. Describe the exchange rate intervention that this country would undertake in order to keep its exchange rate at par.

_____

_____

c. What will happen to this country's international reserves as a result of this intervention?

_____

d. Under what circumstances would this country likely experience a speculative attack on its currency as a result of the decrease in demand for its domestic assets?

_____

_____

e. How would a speculative attack affect this county's balance of payments? How would this country's central bank likely respond to such an attack?

_____

_____

f. What possible action would the International Monetary Fund take to halt the speculative attack on this country's currency?

_____

_____

g. Explain how that action by the IMF might create a moral hazard problem for emerging market economies.

_____

_____

SHORT-ANSWER QUESTIONS

1. What is the difference between a sterilized exchange rate intervention and an unsterilized exchange rate intervention?

_____

_____

2. What is the difference between the current account and the trade balance?

    _____

    _____

3. Suppose the current account balance is –$725 billion and the capital account balance is $720 billion. Calculate the net change in government international reserves.

    _____

4. What role does an anchor currency play in a fixed exchange rate regime?

    _____

    _____

5. What is a dirty float exchange rate regime?

    _____

    _____

6. Under the Bretton Woods system, the U.S. dollar was the reserve currency. What did that mean?

    _____

    _____

    _____

7. When did the Bretton Woods system collapse? Why did the Bretton Woods system collapse?

    _____

    _____

    _____

    _____

    _____

8. Explain why economists are more likely to support controls on capital inflows rather than controls on capital outflows.

    _____

    _____

    _____

    _____

    _____

    _____

9. What are the advantages and disadvantages of using an exchange rate target to promote price stability?

    _____

    _____

    _____

    _____

10. Why might a country choose to dollarize instead of adopting a currency board? What is the main disadvantage of dollarization relative to a currency board?

    _____

    _____

Critical Thinking

The U.S. current account deficit has approached nearly $1 trillion in recent years.

1. What does a current account deficit of nearly $1 trillion dollars imply about foreign claims on U.S. wealth?

    _____

    _____

2. Is the U.S. increasing or decreasing its claims on foreign wealth?

    _____

    _____

3. How will the U.S. current account deficit affect the wealth of future Americans? Why?

_____

_____

Self-Test

TRUE/FALSE QUESTIONS

_____1. When the Fed sells international reserves in exchange for currency the monetary base increases by more than if it sells international reserves in exchange for funds drawn from a checking account.

_____2. Sterilized exchange rate interventions leave the monetary base unchanged.

_____3. An unsterilized intervention in which domestic currency is purchased by selling foreign assets leads to a drop in international reserves, a decrease in the money supply, and a depreciation of the domestic currency.

_____4. The U.S. current account deficit implies that foreigners' claims on U.S. assets are falling.

_____5. One disadvantage of the gold standard was that monetary policy was greatly influenced by the production of gold and discoveries of gold.

_____6. The Bretton Woods system was a managed float regime.

_____7. When the domestic currency is undervalued, the central bank must sell domestic currency to keep the exchange rate fixed, but as a result it gains international reserves.

_____8. The importance of gold in international financial transactions has grown in recent years.

_____9. Great Britain pulled out of the exchange rate mechanism in 1992 because it did not want to follow the same inflationary monetary policy as Germany.

_____10. Economists are more likely to favor controls on the outflow of capital rather than controls on the inflow of capital.

_____11. In recent years countries have avoided borrowing from the IMF because they did not want to be subjected to harsh austerity programs.

_____12. Under the current managed float exchange rate system, balance of payments considerations have a larger influence on monetary policy than do exchange rate considerations.

_____13. Special drawing rights are a paper substitute for gold that serve as international reserves.

_____14. Exchange rate targeting is sometimes used as a monetary policy strategy to achieve price stability.

_____15. An advantage of dollarization over a currency board is that it completely eliminates the possibility of a speculative attack on a country's currency.

MULTIPLE-CHOICE QUESTIONS

1. When a central bank buys its currency in the foreign exchange market,
   a. it loses international reserves.
   b. it acquires international reserves.
   c. the money supply increases.
   d. the quantity of international reserves remains unchanged.

2. An unsterilized intervention in which domestic currency is sold to purchase foreign assets leads to a
   a. loss of international reserves and a depreciation of the domestic currency.
   b. gain of international reserves and a depreciation of the domestic currency.
   d. loss of international reserves and an appreciation of the domestic currency.
   e. gain of international reserves and an appreciation of the domestic currency.

3. A sterilized intervention in which domestic currency is sold to purchase foreign assets leads to a
   a. loss of international reserves and a depreciation of the domestic currency.
   b. gain of international reserves and a depreciation of the domestic currency.
   c. loss of international reserves and almost no change in the exchange rate.
   d. gain of international reserves and almost no change in the exchange rate.

4. Which of the following will most likely lead to an increase in the exchange rate from 3.5 Brazilian real per dollar to 3.7 Brazilian real per dollar?
   a. The Brazilian central bank sells Brazilian government bonds.
   b. The Brazilian central bank buys international reserves.
   c. The U.S. Federal Reserve sells dollars.
   d. The U.S. Federal Reserve buys U.S. Treasury bonds.

5. Which of the following appears in the current account part of the balance of payments?
   a. a German's purchase of a share of Google stock
   b. a loan by a Swiss bank to an American corporation
   c. income earned by Barclay's Bank of London England, from subsidiaries in the United States
   d. a purchase by the Federal Reserve System of an English Treasury bond

6. If the current account balance is -$530 billion and the official reserve transactions balance is $10 billion, then the capital account balance is
   a. -$540 billion.
   b. $540 billion.
   c. -$520 billion.
   d. $520 billion.

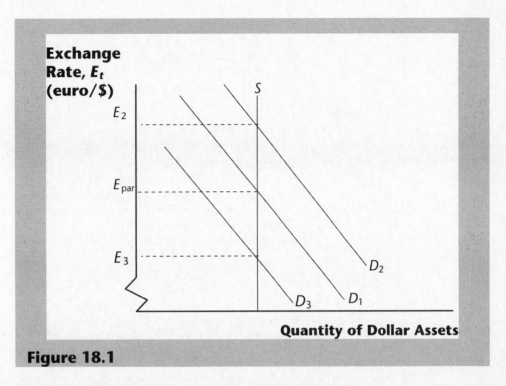

Figure 18.1

7. Starting from exchange rate E_{par} in Figure 18.1, an increase in the foreign interest rate, holding everything else constant, will
   a. shift the demand for domestic assets right causing the exchange rate to become overvalued.
   b. shift the demand curve for domestic assets right causing the exchange rate to become undervalued.
   c. shift the demand for domestic assets left causing the exchange rate to become overvalued.
   d. shift the demand curve for domestic assets left causing the exchange rate to become undervalued.

8. Starting from exchange rate E_{par} in Figure 18.1, an increase in the domestic interest rate, holding everything else constant, will
   a. shift the demand for domestic assets right, causing the exchange rate to become overvalued.
   b. shift the demand curve for domestic assets right, causing the exchange rate to become undervalued.
   c. shift the demand for domestic assets left, causing the exchange rate to become overvalued.
   d. shift the demand curve for domestic assets left, causing the exchange rate to become undervalued.

9. In a fixed exchange rate regime, when the domestic currency becomes overvalued, in order to keep the exchange rate at par the central bank must
   a. sell domestic currency, which leads to a gain of international reserves.
   b. sell domestic currency, which leads to a loss of international reserves.
   c. buy domestic currency, which leads to a gain of international reserves.
   d. buy domestic currency, which leads to a loss of international reserves.

10. If there is perfect capital mobility, then a sterilized exchange rate intervention
    a. can only be used for devaluation.
    b. can only be used for revaluation.
    c. is much more effective than an unsterilized exchange rate intervention.
    d. cannot keep the exchange rate at par.

11. The Bretton Woods system of fixed exchange rates collapsed because
    a. inflationary U.S. monetary policy forced other countries to lose international reserves, which led to inflation in those countries as well.
    b. inflationary U.S. monetary policy forced other countries to gain international reserves, which led to inflation as those countries as well.
    c. inflationary U.S. monetary policy forced other countries to lose international reserves, which led to recession in those countries.
    d. inflationary U.S. monetary policy forced other countries to gain international reserves, which led to recession in those countries.

12. An important advantage for a reserve currency country is that
    a. it has more control of its monetary policy than nonreserve currency countries.
    b. it will always have a balance of payments surplus.
    c. it has more control over its exchange rate than nonreserve countries.
    d. it will experience lower inflation than nonreserve currency countries.

13. When a country experiences a speculative attack on its currency, it
    a. loses international reserves and may be forced to revalue its currency.
    b. gains international reserves and may be forced to revalue its currency.
    c. loses international reserves and may be forced to devalue its currency.
    d. gains international reserves and may be forced to devalue its currency.

14. A central bank that wants to _____ its currency is likely to adopt a _____ monetary policy.
    a. strengthen; more contractionary
    b. strengthen; less contractionary
    c. weaken; less expansionary
    d. weaken; neutral

15. When a currency depreciates, then exports become
    a. more expensive for foreigners to purchase, and imports become less expensive for domestic consumers to purchase.
    b. less expensive for foreigners to purchase, and imports become less expensive for domestic consumers to purchase.
    c. more expensive for foreigners to purchase, and imports become more expensive for domestic consumers to purchase.
    d. less expensive for foreigners to purchase, and imports become more expensive for domestic consumers to purchase.

16. Countries experiencing a foreign exchange crisis, such as Mexico, Brazil, and Thailand did in the 1990s,
    a. are also experiencing a balance of payments crisis.
    b. may turn to the World Bank for help.
    c. are gaining international reserves.
    d. can revalue their currencies to end the crisis.

17. Since 1994, the IMF has stepped into the role of lender-of-last-resort because
    a. central banks in emerging markets lack experience with open market operations.
    b. it has been authorized by the world trade organization to perform this function.
    c. it is less likely to create a moral hazard problem than the World Bank.
    d. central banks in emerging markets often lack credibility as inflation fighters.

18. A case can be made for controls on capital inflows because capital inflows
    a. can lead to a lending boom and encourage excessive risk taking.
    b. never go to financing productive investments.
    c. do more harm than good.
    d. are easier to control than capital outflows.

19. A disadvantage of exchange rate targeting is that
    a. it is likely to cause monetary policy to be time-inconsistent.
    b. the exchange rate is not a nominal anchor.
    c. the central bank loses the ability to conduct independent monetary policy.
    d. the exchange rate is more difficult to target than either inflation or the money supply.

20. The main difference between a currency board and dollarization is that
    a. with a currency board a country gives up seignorage, but with dollarization it does not.
    b. with dollarization a country gives up seignorage, but with a currency board it does not.
    c. with dollarization a country's currency is 100% backed by the dollar, but with a currency board it is less than 100% backed by the dollar.
    d. a currency board is a firmer commitment to a fixed exchange rate than dollarization.

Solutions

Terms and Definitions

_4_ anchor currency

_6_ balance of payments

_13_ balance-of-payments crisis

_12_ Bretton Woods System

_19_ capital account

_17_ currency board

_3_ current account

_14_ dollarization

_2_ fixed exchange rate regime

_7_ floating exchange rate regime

_20_ foreign exchange intervention

_8_ gold standard

_16_ International Monetary Fund (IMF)

_5_ international reserves

_11_ managed float regime (dirty float)

_9_ official reserve transactions balance

_18_ seignorage

_15_ sterilized foreign exchange intervention

_1_ trade balance

_10_ unsterilized foreign exchange intervention

Practice Problems

1. a. The T-account when the Fed buys $1 billion in foreign assets in exchange for $1 billion in currency:

Federal Reserve System

Assets	Liabilities
Foreign assets (international reserves) +$1 billion	Currency in circulation +$1 billion

b. The monetary base will increase by $1 billion as a result of this foreign exchange transaction.

c. The T-account when the Fed buys $1 billion in foreign assets in exchange for $1 billion in deposits:

Federal Reserve System

Assets	Liabilities
Foreign assets (international reserves) +$1 billion	Deposits with the Fed (reserves) +$1 billion

d. The monetary base will increase by $1 billion as a result of this foreign exchange transaction.

e. The T-account when the Fed buys $1 billion in foreign assets in exchange for $1 billion in deposits, and then sells $1 billion in government bonds to sterilize the exchange rate intervention:

Federal Reserve System

Assets	Liabilities
Foreign assets (international reserves) +$1 billion	Monetary base (reserves) +$1 billion
Government bonds −$1 billion	

f. Sterilized exchange rate interventions leave the monetary base unchanged.

2. a. The long-run and short-run effects of an unsterilized sale of foreign assets.

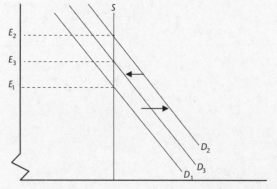

Quantity of Dollar Assets

b. An unsterilized sale of foreign assets reduces the monetary base, which leads to a rise in the domestic interest rate in the short run and a decline in the domestic price level in the long run. The increase in the domestic interest rate and the decline in the domestic price level both act to push the exchange rate up (from E_1 to E_2) in the short run. In the long run, the interest rate returns to its original level but the price level remains at its lower level. Thus, the exchange rate depreciates part way back to its original level because the interest rate effect disappears but the price level effect remains.

c. A sterilized intervention in the foreign exchange market leaves the monetary base unchanged and so the interest rate and price level remain unchanged as well. As a consequence, the demand for dollar assets remains unchanged and the exchange rate remains unchanged as shown below.

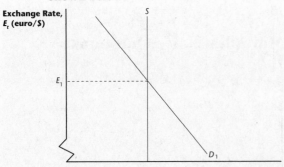

3. a. An increase in the return on foreign assets will shift the demand curve for dollar assets to the left and the exchange rate will fall from E_1 to E_2.

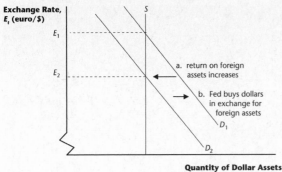

b. To keep the exchange rate at its original level (E_1) the Fed would buy dollars in exchange for foreign assets. This transaction would reduce the monetary base, which would cause the domestic interest rate to rise, which would in turn cause the exchange rate to rise back to E_1

as the demand for dollar assets shifts back to D_1.

4. a. overvalued

b. The central bank would need to purchase domestic currency to keep the exchange rate fixed at par.

c. It would lose international reserves.

d. If currency traders fear that the central bank will run out of foreign assets, then they may mount a speculative attack on the currency.

e. A speculative attack on a country's currency will lead to a balance of payments deficit. The central bank will respond by raising interest rates.

f. The IMF may provide loans to the country in order to shore up its foreign reserves.

g. Countries may come to expect that the IMF will bail them out and as a result they may use macroeconomic policies that are more likely to lead to a balance of payments deficit.

Short-answer Questions

1. In the case of a sterilized exchange rate intervention, the central bank offsets the intervention with an open market operation so that the monetary base remains unchanged. In the case of an unsterilized intervention, the central bank does not offset the intervention with an open market operation, and so the monetary base does change.

2. The current account balance includes everything that is included in the trade balance plus three additional categories of net receipts: investment income, service transactions, and unilateral transfers.

3. The net change in government international reserves = −$5 billion.

4. The anchor currency is the currency that other currencies are pegged to.

5. A dirty float (also called a managed float) is an exchange rate regime in which the central bank intervenes to keep the exchange rate within a certain range (rather than keeping the exchange rate fixed at a particular value).

6. The other countries (other than the United States) that fixed their exchange rates under the Bretton Woods System held international reserves denominated in dollars.

7. The Bretton Woods System broke down in 1971 when the United States pursued inflationary monetary policies. In order to maintain fixed exchange rates with the United States, other countries would have had to pursue inflationary policies as well. Countries with balance of payments surpluses refused to adopt inflationary policies and so they abandoned the fixed exchange rate system.

8. Evidence suggests that controls on capital outflows are seldom effective during a crisis and may even increase capital flight. Controls on capital outflows often lead to corruption and controls on capital outflows may keep the government from undertaking meaningful reforms, which would prevent capital outflows. Economists are more likely to support controls on capital inflows reasoning that if speculative capital cannot come in then it cannot go out quickly.

9. The advantages of an exchange rate target are: The exchange rate is a nominal anchor; an exchange rate target provides an automatic rule for conducting monetary policy; and an exchange rate target is simple, clear and easily understood by the public. The disadvantages of exchange rate targeting are: The country loses of independent monetary policy; economic shocks in the anchor-currency country are easily transmitted to the domestic economy; and it opens the country to the possibility of a speculative-attack on its currency.

10. Dollarization is a firmer commitment to a fixed exchange rate than a currency board because a currency board can be abandoned. Countries that suffer credibility problems may therefore choose dollarization because it sends a strong signal that the country is committed to low inflation. The main disadvantage of dollarization is that the country gives up the opportunity to earn revenue from money creation, which is called seignorage.

Critical Thinking

1. Foreign clams on U.S. wealth are increasing.
2. U.S. claims on foreign wealth are decreasing.
3. At some point, America will have to pay back those claims on its wealth and that will make Americans poorer.

True/False Questions

1. F
2. T
3. F
4. F
5. T
6. F
7. T
8. F
9. F
10. F
11. T
12. F
13. T
14. T
15. T

Multiple-Choice Questions

1. a
2. b
3. d
4. b
5. c
6. b
7. c
8. b
9. d
10. d
11. b
12. a
13. c
14. a
15. d
16. a
17. d
18. a
19. c
20. b

19

The Demand for Money

Chapter Review

PREVIEW

Earlier chapters looked at how the Federal Reserve, the public, and commercial banks all influence the money supply. This chapter looks at what determines money demand. Later in the text you will put money supply and demand together in order to study *monetary theory,* which is the study of how money affects the economy. The central question in monetary theory is whether or to what extent money demand is affected by interest rates.

QUANTITY THEORY OF MONEY

The quantity theory of money is based on the *equation of exchange*: $M \times V = P \times Y$, where M is the quantity of money, P is the price level, Y is aggregate income and V is the *velocity of money*. The velocity of money is the average number of times per year a dollar is spent in buying the total amount of goods and services in the economy. The equation of exchange is simply an identity that the total amount of spending in a year ($P \times Y$) equals the total amount of money (M) multiplied times the number of times that money is spent (V). Irving Fisher, an early twentieth century economist, reasoned that velocity was constant in the short run. With the assumption that velocity is reasonably constant in the short run, the equation of exchange becomes the *quantity theory of money*, which states that nominal income is determined solely by movements in the quantity of money. If V is fixed and M doubles, $P \times Y$ will double as well. The early classical economists went one step further with this theory by assuming that wages and prices were perfectly flexible, implying that the level of output Y was always at full-employment. This assumption implies that movements in the price level result solely from changes in the quantity of money. The quantity theory of money is not only a theory about how money affects the economy, it is also a theory of money demand. If we rearrange the equation:

$$M = (1/V) \times PY \text{ or } M^d = k \times PY$$

Since V is assumed constant, k is constant as well, so nominal income determines money demand. According to the quantity theory of money, interest rates play no role in determining the quantity of money demanded.

IS VELOCITY A CONSTANT?

Contrary to the assumption by early classical economists, velocity is not constant. It was not until the Great Depression in the 1930s that economists realized that velocity declines sharply during severe economic contractions. After World War II, the government began collecting consistent data on the economy. Economists now recognize that velocity fluctuates considerably.

KEYNES'S LIQUIDITY PREFERENCE THEORY

Keynes assumed that there are three motives for holding money: the transactions motive, the precautionary motive, and the speculative motive. The transactions and precautionary motives are both positively related to income. The more income you earn, the more money you will hold for transactions (the transactions motive), and the more money you will hold to make unexpected purchases (the precautionary motive). These two motives for holding money alone are not too different from the classical view of money demand because they are both related to income. But Keynes went one step further by assuming that there is a third motive for holding money called the speculative motive. The speculative motive assumes that people also hold money as a store of wealth, which simply means that people treat money as an asset in their financial portfolio. Here's how that works. To keep things simple, Keynes assumed that there are only two types of assets that people can choose from: bonds and money. Bonds earn interest, and money does not. At first you might think, why would anyone ever hold money when bonds pay interest? But recall from earlier in the text that the total return on a bond is comprised of the interest payment and the capital gain or loss. When the interest rate is below normal, people naturally expect it to rise, and so they will hold money because if they purchased a bond, they would experience a capital loss once the interest rate does rise (which would cause the price of the bond to fall). When the interest rate is above normal, the opposite happens. People will expect the interest rate to fall, so they will hold bonds and not money (at least for this purpose, they will still hold money for transactions and as a precaution against unexpected purchases). In sum, according to the speculative motive for holding money, the demand for money is negatively related to the interest rate. When the interest rate falls, people hold more money. When the interest rate rises, people hold less money. This was an important innovation in the theory of money demand because, unlike the classical theory, it provided a rationale for why the demand for money depends on the interest rate. Combing all three motives for holding money, the Keynesian money demand function is $M^d/P = f(i,Y)$, where M^d/P represents *real money balances*. If we substitute Keynes's money demand function into the equation of exchange, we get the following expression for the velocity of money: $V = Y/f(i,Y)$. This equation demonstrates how the Keynesian money demand function can be used to explain why velocity is not constant. When the interest rate rises, $f(i,Y)$ falls and velocity rises. Since interest rates experience substantial fluctuations, velocity experiences substantial fluctuations. Because interest rates are procyclical, velocity will be procyclical as well. Keynes's theory of money demand is called *liquidity preference theory*.

FURTHER DEVELOPMENTS IN THE KEYNESIAN APPROACH

Economists William Baumol and James Tobin demonstrated that money held for transactions also depends on the interest rate. Baumol and Tobin assumed that when a person receives income (say, at the beginning of the month), he decides how much to hold in the form of money and how much of his income he will use to purchase bonds. The advantage of holding bonds is that bonds earn interest. The disadvantage of holding bonds is that buying and selling bonds involves transaction costs (brokerage fees, time). When a person is deciding how much money to hold for transaction purposes, she weighs the costs of holding bonds (the transaction costs) against the benefits of holding bonds (interest). When the interest rate rises, a person will hold more bonds and less money because it is worthwhile to incur the higher transaction costs at a higher interest rate.

FRIEDMAN'S MODERN QUANTITY THEORY OF MONEY

Milton Friedman's money demand function differs from the classical and Keynesian money demand functions in two respects. First, Friedman assumed that money demand depends on permanent, not current income. Permanent income fluctuates less than current income because some of the movements in current income are transitory. Second, Friedman assumed that the demand for money depends on the return on other assets in addition to bonds (the only alternative to money considered by Keynes). When the rate of return on bonds, equities, or goods rises relative to the return on money, the demand for money falls. Even though Friedman included these relative returns in his money demand function, he argued that competition among banks to attract deposits would cause the rate of return on money to move up and down with the rates of return on other assets. Relative rates of return would remain unchanged and therefore money demand will depend only on permanent income. Friedman's money demand function can also be used to explain why velocity is procyclical. Friedman's money demand function implies that velocity is predictable.

DISTINGUISHING BETWEEN FRIEDMAN AND KEYNESIAN THEORIES

Two major differences exist between Friedman's theory of money demand and Keynes's theory of money demand. First, according to Friedman's theory, money demand is insensitive to interest rates while Keynes's theory holds that money demand is sensitive to interest rates. Second, according to Friedman's theory, money demand is stable, while Keynes's theory money holds that demand is not stable. Friedman's theory implies that the velocity of money is predictable, which leads to the conclusion that money is the primary determinant of aggregate spending, which is the basis for *monetarism*.

EMPIRICAL EVIDENCE ON THE DEMAND FOR MONEY

The more sensitive money demand is to the interest rate, the less aggregate demand is determined by the quantity of money. The extreme case, where money demand is infinitely responsive to changes in interest rates is called a liquidity trap. When the economy is in a liquidity trap, changes in the quantity of money have no effect on aggregate spending. The empirical evidence suggests that money demand is somewhat, but not infinitely responsive to interest rates. There is no evidence of a liquidity trap where money demand is infinitely responsive to interest rates; however, there is evidence of a liquidity trap of a different sort. When the interest rate hits zero, monetary policy becomes ineffective because interest rates cannot go below zero. Japan experienced this type of liquidity trap in recent years.

The demand for money appeared to be stable through the early 1970s. Since that time, money demand has become unstable and velocity is hard to predict, which implies that setting rigid money supply targets in order to control aggregate spending may not be an effective way to conduct monetary policy.

Helpful Hints

Does money demand depend on the interest rate? The early classical economists said no. Keynes said yes. Friedman said yes, but no. Why does it matter? The more sensitive the demand for money is to the interest rate, the less influence the Fed has over aggregate spending. What is the evidence? Interest rates do influence money demand, but the demand for money is not extremely (or infinitely) sensitive to interest rates, which means the Fed can influence, but not completely control, aggregate spending.

Terms and Definitions

Choose a definition for each key term.

Key Terms:

_____ equation of exchange

_____ liquidity preference theory

_____ real money balances

_____ quantity theory of money

_____ monetary theory

_____ velocity of money

_____ monetarism

Definitions:

1. The equation $MV = PY$ which relates nominal income to the quantity of money

2. The theory that nominal income is determined solely by movements in the quantity of money

3. The rate of turnover of money

4. The view that the money supply is the primary source of movements in the price level and aggregate output

5. The theory that relates changes in the quantity of money to changes in economic activity

6. The quantity of money in real terms

7. John Maynard Keynes's theory of the demand for money

Problems and Short-Answer Questions

PRACTICE PROBLEMS

1. a. Suppose nominal GDP is $15 trillion and the quantity of money is $5 trillion. Calculate the velocity of money.

   _____

   b. Now suppose that velocity is 5 and nominal GDP is $25 trillion. Calculate the quantity of money.

   _____

   c. What assumption transforms the equation of exchange into the quantity theory of money?

   _____

   d. According to the quantity theory of money, what will happen to the price level if the money supply increases from $1 trillion to $1.3 trillion?

   _____

e.   According to the quantity theory of money, what will the demand for money be if nominal income is $20 trillion and velocity is 2?

_____

2.   Suppose that people have come to expect that interest rates are normally 2%, but interest rates are currently 4%.

a.   What will people expect to happen to the price of bonds as the interest rate returns to normal?

_____

b.   What will happen to the return on bonds as the interest rate returns to normal?

_____

c.   According to Keynes, what will happen to the demand for money if interest rates are above normal? Why?

_____

_____

3.   Suppose you earn $1,800 at the beginning of each month from your part-time job. Initially you cash your entire paycheck and spend your money evenly throughout the month.

a.   What are your average cash balances?

_____

b.   What is your velocity of money?

_____

c.   Now suppose the interest rate increases and you decide to cash half of your paycheck at the beginning of the month, putting the remainder in bonds. Half way through the month you convert the bonds to cash. What are your average cash balances in this case?

_____

d.   What is your velocity of money?

_____

e. What are the costs and benefits of holding money? Why did you decide to reduce you average cash balances when the interest rate rose?

_____

_____

_____

_____

4. a. What are the two major differences between Friedman's money demand function and the Keynesian money demand function?

_____

_____

b. Suppose the rate of return on bonds rises. According to Friedman, what will happen to the rate of return on money? Explain how the rate of return on money changes even when money does not pay an explicit interest rate.

_____

_____

c. Use Friedman's money demand function to explain why velocity is procyclical.

_____

_____

_____

_____

SHORT-ANSWER QUESTIONS

1. What reasoning did Irving Fisher use to argue that the velocity of money is constant?

_____

_____

2. Why do classical economists believe that the level of output in the economy in normal times is at full employment?

_____

_____

3. Is the velocity of money constant?

_____

_____

4. According to Keynes, what are the three motives for holding money? Which of these motives is related to the interest rate?

_____

_____

5. What is the difference between nominal money balances and real money balances and what was Keynes's argument for why people desire to hold a certain level of real money balances?

_____

_____

6. Why do people hold precautionary money balances and how are those money balances related to income?

_____

_____

7. What does Keynes's liquidity preference theory predict about the relationship between interest rates and the velocity of money?

_____

_____

8. Explain why Keynes's liquidity preference theory predicts that the velocity of money is procyclical.

_____

_____

9. Why is it still unclear whether a speculative demand for money even exists?

_____

_____

10. What is permanent income and how does it differ from current income?

_____

_____

Critical Thinking

Suppose you read in the paper that the Fed just increased the money supply by 20%. You decide to figure out what this means for the economy but having just learned about three possible money demand functions you know that your answer will depend on how money demand responds to the interest rate.

1. Analyze how this increase in the supply of money will affect the economy if the demand for money is the
    a. quantity theory of money demand.

    _____

    _____

    b. Keynesian liquidity preference function when there is a liquidity trap.

    _____

    _____

    c. Keynesian liquidity preference function but the interest sensitivity of money demand is somewhere between ultrasensative and completely insensitive.

    _____

    _____

    d. Friedman's money demand.

    _____

    _____

2. Which one of your descriptions of the effect of the increase in the money supply on the economy is closest to what would likely happen in the real world? Why?

    _____

    _____

    _____

    _____

3. What does you answer to question 2 imply about the Fed's ability to influence nominal income?

_____

_____

_____

_____

Self-Test

TRUE/FALSE QUESTIONS

_____1. A central question in monetary theory is whether, and to what extent the quantity of money demanded is affected by changes in interest rates.

_____2. Classical economists believed that wages and prices were inflexible.

_____3. The most important implication of the quantity theory of money is that interest rates affect the demand for money.

_____4. Irving Fisher reasoned that velocity is constant after looking at the historical data.

_____5. The velocity of money remained constant throughout the Great Depression.

_____6. The demand for money and the velocity of money are positively related.

_____7. According to the speculative demand for money, people will hold money instead of bonds when the interest rate is above normal.

_____8. The velocity of money has become more volatile since the early 1970s.

_____9. It is not clear whether the speculative demand for money even exists because Treasury securities pay interest and are risk free.

_____10. The expected return on money is influenced by the services that banks provide to depositors.

_____11. Friedman's theory of money demand implies that interest rates should have little effect on the demand for money.

_____12. In a boom, permanent income rises more than current income.

_____13. The more sensitive the demand for money is to interest rates, the more predictable velocity will be.

_____14. A liquidity trap exists when the demand for money is ultrasensitive to interest rates.

_____15. The fact that money demand has become unstable implies that setting rigid money supply targets to control aggregate spending in the economy may be an effective way to conduct monetary policy.

MULTIPLE-CHOICE QUESTIONS

1. The velocity of money is best defined as
   a. the average real money balances that are held in a month.
   b. the average number of times per year that a dollar is spent buying aggregate output.
   c. the average amount of money that a person spends over one year.
   d. the average number of months that a currency bill circulates.

2. According to the quantity theory of money, if the quantity of money falls by one-third,
   a. output will decline by one-third.
   b. velocity will decline by one-third.
   c. the price level will decline by one-third.
   d. output will decline by one-sixth and the price level will decline by one-sixth.

3. Classical economists believed that velocity could be regarded as constant in the short run because
   a. the opportunity cost of holding money was close to zero.
   b. the historical data on velocity showed that it was constant.
   c. financial innovation tended to offset changes in interest rates.
   d. institutions that affect the way individuals conduct transactions change slowly over time.

4. If real income is $5 trillion, the price level is 2, and the velocity of money is 4, then the quantity of money is
   a. $8 trillion.
   b. $2 trillion.
   c. $2.5 trillion.
   d. $20 trillion.

5. The classical economists made the following two assumptions in order to transform the equation of exchange into the quantity theory of money:
   a. velocity is constant, and wages and prices are sticky.
   b. velocity is variable, and wages and prices are sticky.
   c. velocity is constant, and wages and prices are flexible.
   d. velocity is variable, and wages and prices are flexible.

6. According to the quantity theory of money, movements in _____ result solely from changes in _____.
   a. the price level; interest rates
   b. real output; interest rates
   c. the price level; the quantity of money
   d. real output; the quantity of money

7. According to the quantity theory of money demand, if the price level is 1.2, real income is $8 trillion, and velocity is 2, then the demand for money will be _____.
   a. $6.67 trillion.
   b. $16 trillion.
   c. $4 trillion.
   d. $4.8 trillion.

8. According to Keynes's liquidity preference theory, the three motives for holding money are
   a. unit of account, store of value, and medium of exchange.
   b. transactions, precautionary, and speculative.
   c. positive, normative, and speculative.
   d. transactions, precautionary, and liquidity.

9. Keynes's _____ motive states that people hold real money balances as a cushion against unexpected need.
   a. quantity
   b. speculative
   c. precautionary
   d. transactions

10. Keynes's liquidity preference theory explains why velocity is expected to rise when
    a. income increases.
    b. wealth increases.
    c. brokerage commissions increase.
    d. interest rates increase.

11. Keynes's liquidity preference theory implies that velocity
    a. has substantial fluctuations and is procyclical.
    b. has substantial fluctuations and is countercyclical.
    c. is constant.
    d. is not constant but is predictable.

12. According to Keynes's speculative demand for money, if the interest rate is above normal, people will hold
    a. money because they anticipate capital losses on bonds.
    b. bonds because they anticipate capital gains on bonds.
    c. money because they anticipate capital gains on bonds.
    d. bonds because the anticipate capital losses on bonds.

The following figures are for multiple choice questions 13 and 14.

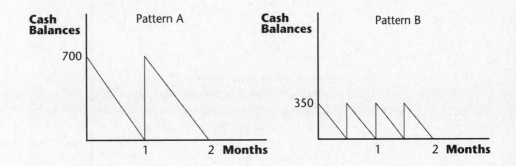

13. The figures show two different patterns of money holdings. You are likely to move from pattern A to pattern B when
    a. the interest rate on T-bills rises, and brokerage fees rise.
    b. the interest rate on T-bills falls, and brokerage fees rise.
    c. the interest rate on T-bills rises, and brokerage fees fall.
    d. the interest rate on T-bills falls, and brokerage fees fall.

14. Average cash balances in pattern A are _____ and average cash balances in pattern B are _____.
    a. 700; 350
    b. 350; 700
    c. 175; 350
    d. 350; 175

15. Friedman's theory of money demand implies that velocity is
    a. undefined.
    b. not constant and therefore unpredictable.
    c. not constant but predictable.
    d. countercyclclical.

16. According to Friedman's theory of money demand, the expected return on money _____ when the expected return on other assets _____ because _____.
    a. falls; rises; it is required by law
    b. rises; rises; it is required by law
    c. falls; rises; of competition among banks to attract deposits
    d. rises; rises; of competition among banks to attract deposits

17. According to Friedman's theory of money demand, the demand for money ultimately depends on
    a. permanent income.
    b. the ratio of current income to permanent income.
    c. permanent income and the return on bonds.
    d. permanent income and the return on money.

18. In Friedman's view, during a business cycle contraction income falls _____ than permanent income, which causes velocity to _____.
    a. more; rise
    b. less; rise
    c. more; fall
    d. less; fall

19. Empirical evidence on money demand shows that money demand is
    a. ultrasensitive to interest rates.
    b. unaffected by changes in interest rates.
    c. highly volatile but predictable.
    d. somewhere in between ultrasensitive and unresponsive to changes in interest rates.

20. Since the early 1970s, money demand has become _____, which implies that the best way to conduct monetary policy is by targeting _____.
    a. stable; interest rates
    b. unstable; interest rates.
    c. stable; the quantity of money
    d. unstable; the quantity of money

Solutions

Terms and Definitions

_1_ equation of exchange

_7_ liquidity preference theory

_6_ real money balances

_2_ quantity theory of money

_5_ monetary theory

_3_ velocity of money

_4_ monetarism

Practice Problems

1. a. Velocity = 3

    b. The quantity of money = 5 trillion

    c. Velocity is constant.

    d. The price level will rise by 30%.

    e. The demand for money will be $10 trillion.

2. a. The price of bonds will rise as the interest rate falls back to normal.

    b. The return on bonds will increase.

    c. If interest rates are above normal, people will hold bonds instead of money because they will expect the interest rate to fall back to normal in the future, and as interest rates fall back to normal, the return on bonds will increase.

3. a. Average cash balances = $900

    b. Velocity = $1,800x12/$900 = 24

    c. Average cash balances = $450

    d. Velocity = $1,800x12/$450 = 48

    e. The cost of holding money is the forgone interest that you could earn by holding bonds. The benefit of holding money is that it reduces the transaction costs that you would have to incur by holding bonds. As the interest rate rose, the cost of holding money increased, and so you were willing to incur more transaction costs to hold bonds.

4. a. Freidman believed that changes in interest rates have little effect on the expected return on other assets relative to money, and as a result, money demand is insensitive to changes in the interest rate. In addition, Friedman believed that money demand is stable.

    b. According to Friedman, if the rate of return on assets other than money increases, the rate of return on money will increase as well. Even if money does not pay interest, banks compete to provide services to attract checking account balances. These services might include convenient banking hours, free checking, or a free toaster when you open up a checking account.

    c. By substituting Friedman's money demand equation into the equation of exchange we get the following expression for the velocity of money: $V = Y/f(Y_P)$. In a business cycle expansion, permanent income (Y_P) rises by less than income (Y). As a result, Y rises by more than $f(Y_P)$ and V increases. The opposite happens in a business cycle contraction (Y falls by more than Y_P). Therefore V is procyclical—rises in a business cycle expansion and falls in a business cycle contraction.

Short-answer Questions

1. Irving Fisher reasoned that velocity is determined by the institutions in an economy that affect the way individuals conduct transactions, and those institutions evolve slowly over time. Therefore, velocity is roughly constant.

2. Classical economists believed that wages and prices were perfectly flexible, and as a result, the economy will remain at full employment.

3. No, velocity is not constant.

4. Keynes postulated three motives for holding money, the transactions motive, the precautionary motive, and the speculative motive. Keynes reasoned that the speculative motive is related to the interest rate.

5. Nominal money balances refers to the actual dollars that you hold. Real money balances equal the dollars you hold divided by the price level. Keynes reasoned that people desire to hold a certain amount of real money balances because real money balances measure how much a person can buy with their money. If prices in the economy double,

the same nominal quantity of money will buy only half as many goods.

6. People hold precautionary money balances in order to make unexpected purchases. Precautionary money balances are positively related to income.

7. As interest rates rise, people will reduce their money holdings (because of the speculative motive) and therefore velocity will rise. Interest rates and velocity will be positively related.

8. Earlier in the text you learned that interest rates are procyclical. In a business cycle expansion, interest rates, and velocity rise. In a business cycle contraction, interest rates, and velocity fall. Velocity is procyclical.

9. James Tobin formulated a theory for why people hold money even when it pays no interest, but that theory relied on the fact that money is risk free. The fact that government securities are also risk free and at the same time do pay interest presents a challenge for this theory. Why do people hold money for speculative purposes when they could simply hold government securities?

10. Permanent income is expected average, long-run income. Permanent income has much smaller short-run fluctuations than current income.

Critical Thinking

1. a. The quantity theory of money implies that a 20% increase in the money supply will result in a 20% increase in nominal income, and if prices and wages are flexible, a 20% increase in the price level and no change in real output.

   b. If there is a liquidity trap, a 20% increase in the money supply will have no impact on real income, the price level or nominal income.

   c. If the Keynesian liquidity preference function best describes money demand, but the interest sensitivity of money demand is somewhere between ultrasensitive and completely insensitive, then the increase in the money supply will lead to an increase in nominal income. However the increase in nominal income will be something less than the 20% increase in the money supply because there is some interest sensitivity of money demand. One again, the split

between a change in real income and the price level depends on whether prices and wages are flexible.

   d. With Friedman's money demand function, the increase in the money supply causes interest rates in the economy to fall, which according to Keynes would make the demand for money rise. But in the Friedman theory, competition among banks would cause the return on money to fall along with market interest rates, and so people would not change their money demand in response to the decline in interest rates. As a result, the increase in the money supply would lead to a 20% increase in nominal income.

2. The Keynesian money demand function in part *c* best describes the real world. Neither extreme case (ultrasensitive or completely insensitive) are consistent with the data.

3. Since money demand is a function of interest rates, the Fed does not have precise control over nominal income. Nonetheless, the interest sensitivity of money demand also does not appear to be ultrasensitive, and so the Fed does have some, but not complete, influence over nominal income.

True/False Questions

1. T
2. F
3. F
4. F
5. F
6. F
7. F
8. T
9. T
10. T
11. T
12. F
13. F
14. T
15. F

Multiple-Choice Questions

1. b
2. c

3. d
4. c
5. c
6. c
7. d
8. b
9. c
10. d
11. a
12. b
13. c
14. d
15. c
16. d
17. a
18. c
19. d
20. b

20 The *ISLM* Model

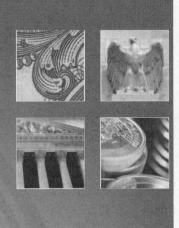

Chapter Review

PREVIEW

This chapter develops the *ISLM* model. The *ISLM* model explains how interest rates and total output produced in the economy are determined given a fixed price level. It is sometimes called the Keynesian *ISLM* model because it is based on the work of John Maynard Keynesian during the 1930s. In the next chapter we use the *ISLM* model to evaluate the effects of monetary and fiscal policy.

DETERMINATION OF AGGREGATE OUTPUT

Total quantity demanded in the economy is the sum of four types of spending: (1) *consumer expenditures* (C); (2) *planned investment spending* (I); (3) *government spending* (G); and (4) *net exports* (NX). The total quantity demanded of an economy's output is called *aggregate demand* (Y^{ad}):

$$Y^{ad} = C + I + G + NX.$$

Equilibrium is where total output supplied (Y) equals total output demanded (Y^{ad}): $Y = Y^{ad}$. Keynes assumed that the price level is fixed, so changes in nominal variables are equivalent to changes in real variables. To keep the analysis simple, we begin by assuming that G and NX are both zero, which means that $Y^{ad} = C + I$.

Consumption spending is based on *disposable income*, which equals aggregate income (Y) minus taxes (T). This relationship is described by the *consumption function*: $C = a + (mpc \times Y_D)$. The slope of the consumption function, $\Delta C/\Delta Y = mpc$ which stands for *marginal propensity to consume*. The *mpc* is a constant between 0 and 1 which measures the change in consumer expenditures, which result from an additional dollar of disposable income. The "*a*" in the consumption function represents autonomous consumer expenditures; consumer expenditures that are unrelated to disposable income. Investment spending is the sum of two types of investment: (1) fixed investment, which is spending on structures and equipment by firms and; (2) inventory investment, which is the change in inventories held by firms in a given time period. Inventory investment plays an important role in the adjustment story of the *ISLM* model. Since prices are assumed to be fixed, unexpected changes in demand cause inventories to fluctuate. If demand is less than expected, unplanned inventory investment will be positive. If firms sell more than expected, unplanned inventory investment will be negative. Planned investment spending, which equals planned fixed investment plus planned inventory investment, is a component of aggregate demand. To begin, we assume that planned investment is a known value. For example, assume that $I = 200$. Further, assume that $C = 100 + 0.8Y$. Adding together planned investment and consumption, we get the *aggregate demand function*, $Y^{ad} = 200 + 100 + .8Y = 300 + 0.80Y$. Figure 1 shows a plot of aggregate demand along with the 45^0 line, which shows the points where $Y = Y^{ad}$. Equilibrium is point A where Y^{ad} intersects the 45^0 line.

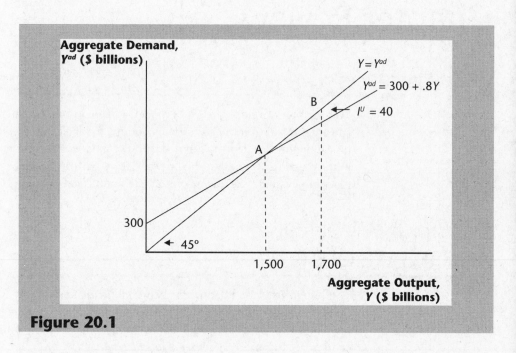

Figure 20.1

To solve for equilibrium mathematically, set aggregate supply (Y) equal to aggregate demand Y^{ad} and solve for Y: $Y = 300 + .8Y$, $Y^* = 1,500$. If the economy starts off away from equilibrium, it will automatically adjust back to equilibrium. For example, at point B, output produced, $Y = 1,700$, which is greater than $Y^{ad} = 300 + .8(1,700) = 1,660$. Since output exceeds aggregate demand by 40, firms have positive unplanned inventory investment, $I^U = 40$ (which equals the vertical distance between Y^{ad} and Y at point B). Firms will reduce production until equilibrium is reached at point A. If the economy starts out below equilibrium, firms have negative unplanned inventory investment, which causes them to increase production until the economy reaches point A.

If either autonomous consumer expenditure (the "*a*" in the consumption function) or planned investment expenditures increases, aggregate output (Y) will increase by a multiple of that change. The ratio of the change in aggregate output to the change in planned expenditures, $\Delta Y/\Delta I$, is called the *expenditures multiplier*, which is equal to $1/(1 - mpc)$. Any change in autonomous spending $(a + I)$ has a multiplier effect. Keynes believed that most changes in autonomous spending were due to unstable fluctuations in I, which he labeled "*animal spirits.*" Keynes viewed the economy as inherently unstable (due to animal spirits), and he reasoned that government spending and taxes should be used to offset decreases in autonomous spending (particularly investment spending) and therefore restore the economy to full-employment equilibrium. Changes in government spending have the same multiplier effect as changes in autonomous spending: $\Delta Y/\Delta G = 1/(1 - mpc)$. Changes in taxes have a slightly different effect. When taxes are reduced by \$1, consumer spending rises by $\$1 \times (mpc)$ [consumers save the remaining $\$1 \times (1-mpc)$]. Therefore, $\Delta Y/\Delta T = -mpc/(1-mpc)$. The minus sign appears because decreases in taxes increase consumer spending. Changes in net exports also have a multiplier effect as well: $\Delta Y/\Delta NX = 1/(1-mpc)$.

THE *ISLM* MODEL

In the model presented above, both planned investment spending and net exports were given. In the real world, however, both of these components of aggregate demand depend on the interest rate. Both planned investment spending and net exports are negatively related to the interest rate. The inverse relationship between aggregate expenditures and the interest rate is called the *IS curve* which is shown in Figure 2.

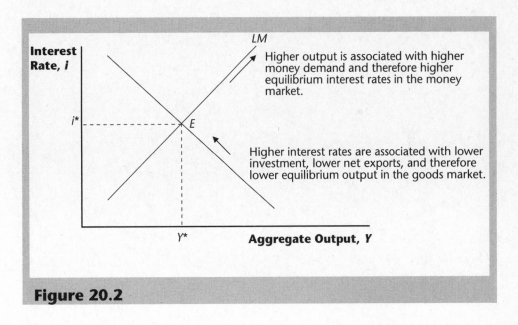

Figure 20.2

At each point along the *IS* curve, the goods market is in equilibrium. Low interest rates are associated with equilibrium in the goods market in which aggregate expenditures are high. High interest rates are associated with equilibrium in the goods market in which aggregate expenditures are low. The *IS* curve tells us that equilibrium in the goods market depends on the interest rate so a natural question arises: What determines the interest rate? The interest rate is determined by equilibrium in the money market. The demand for money is described by the

Keynesian liquidity preference theory, which tells us that the demand for money is positively related to income and negatively related to the interest rate. The intersection of the downward-sloping money demand function and the vertical money supply function determines the interest rate. As aggregate income rises, money demand shifts right, which moves the interest rate to a higher level along the vertical money supply curve. Therefore, higher levels of aggregate income are associated with higher interest rates along the *LM curve* as shown in Figure 2. At point E, both the goods market and the money market are in equilibrium.

Helpful Hints

Changes in autonomous spending have a multiplier effect on aggregate output. Movements along the *IS* curve happen because an increase in the interest rate causes planned investment spending and net exports to decline, which leads to lower aggregate output (Y). Movements along the *LM* curve happen because higher aggregate output (Y) causes the demand for money to increase, which leads to higher interest rates. The equilibrium point is the point where both the goods market (described by the IS curve) and the money market (described by the LM curve) are in equilibrium at the same time.

Terms and Definitions

Choose a definition for each key term.

Key Terms:

_____ aggregate demand

_____ aggregate demand function

_____ "animal spirits"

_____ autonomous consumer expenditure

_____ consumer expenditure

_____ consumption function

_____ disposable income

_____ expenditure multiplier

_____ fixed investment

_____ government spending

_____ inventory investment

_____ *IS* curve

_____ *LM* curve

_____ marginal propensity to consume

_____ net exports

Definitions:

1. The total quantity demanded of an economy's output

2. Net foreign spending on domestic goods and services

3. The relationship between disposable income and consumer expenditures

4. Spending by firms on equipment and structures and planned spending on residential homes

5. The slope of the consumption function line that measures the change in consumer expenditures resulting from an additional dollar of disposable income

6. Combinations of aggregate output and interest rates for which the goods market is in equilibrium

7. Total spending on consumer goods and services

8. Spending by all levels of government on goods and services

9. Spending by firms on additional holdings of raw materials, parts, and finished goods

10. The relationship between aggregate output and aggregate demand that shows the quantity of aggregate demand at any given level of aggregate output

11. Waves of optimism and pessimism that affect consumers' and businesses' willingness to spend

12. Total income available for spending (aggregate income minus taxes)

13. Combinations of aggregate output and interest rates for which the money market is in equilibrium

14. The ratio of a change in aggregate output to a change in investment spending (or autonomous spending)

15. The amount of consumer expenditure that is independent of disposable income

Problems and Short-Answer Questions

PRACTICE PROBLEMS

1. Suppose that autonomous consumer expenditures are $300 billion and the marginal propensity to consume is 0.80.
   a. Fill in the missing values in the table below using the information about consumption given above.

Point in Figure 3	Disposable Income, Y_D	Consumer Expenditure, C	Change in Disposable Income, ΔY_D	Change in Consumer Expenditure, ΔC
E	0	_____	_____	_____
F	200	_____	_____	_____
G	400	_____	_____	_____
H	800	_____	_____	_____

   b. Use the data from the table you completed in part *a* to construct a consumption function graph. Label the points on the graph with the letters in the far left column (E through H).

2. Assume that the marginal propensity to consume is 0.90, and autonomous consumer expenditures equal $100 billion. Further, assume that planned investment spending is $300 billion, and government spending and net exports are zero.
   a. Calculate equilibrium output.

   _____

   _____

b. Plot the aggregate demand function along with the 45^0 line and mark the equilibrium point on your graph.

c. Now suppose that autonomous consumer expenditures drop by $50 billion to $50 billion. Calculate the new equilibrium output.

d. Calculate the expenditure multiplier for this economy.

e. Now consider an economy with government spending and taxes. Assume that the marginal propensity to consume is 0.90. Calculate the change in equilibrium output that would result from a $10 billion increase in government spending.

f. Consider the same economy as in part *d* above. Calculate change in equilibrium output that would results from a $10 billion decrease in government spending.

3. Use the Keynesian cross diagram to illustrate the effect of each of the following on aggregate output, *Y*.
    a. A decrease in autonomous consumer expenditure, *a*.

    b. A decrease in planned investment spending, *I*.

    c. A decrease in taxes, *T*.

d. A decrease in net exports, *NX*.

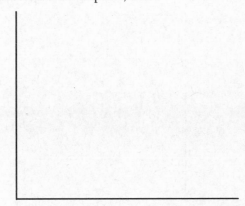

4. a. Match each interest rate with the corresponding level of investment spending, aggregate demand, and equilibrium output:

i	I	Y^{ad}	Y^*
3%	100	$700 + .75Y$	4,000
8%	200	$800 + .75Y$	2,800
2%	400	$1,000 + .75Y$	3,200

b. Label the points in the figure below using the numbers from part *a*.

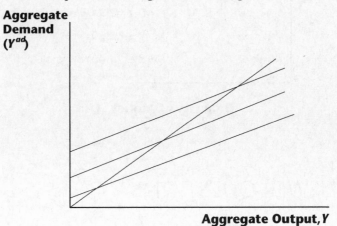

c.   Use the numbers from part a to construct an *IS* curve.

5.   Panel a in the figure below shows equilibriums in the money market corresponding to three different levels of aggregate income. Use the data from panel a to construct an *LM* curve in panel b.

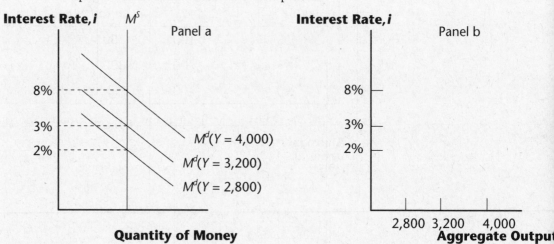

SHORT-ANSWER QUESTIONS

1.   What are the four types of spending that sum to total quantity demanded of the economy's output?

_____

_____

2.   Explain why, in the Keynesian model, an increase in nominal output is the same as an increase in real output.

_____

_____

3. Suppose that aggregate demand is $900 billion and aggregate output is $850 billion. What is the value of unplanned inventory investment in this economy, and what will happen to bring this economy back to equilibrium?

    _____

    _____

4. According to Keynes, what is the dominant source of instability in autonomous expenditures?

    _____

    _____

5. Suppose the *mpc* is 0.80 and net exports falls by $20 billion. Calculate the change in aggregate output.

    _____

    _____

6. Why does a change in taxes have a smaller impact on aggregate output than a change in government spending?

    _____

    _____

7. Why are interest rates and aggregate output negatively related along the *IS* curve?

    _____

    _____

8. Why are interest rates and aggregate output positively related along the *LM* curve?

    _____

    _____

9   Suppose the economy is to the left of the *IS* curve. Is there an excess supply or an excess demand for goods? Describe the adjustment of the economy back to the *IS* curve.

    _____

    _____

10. Suppose the economy is to the left of the *LM* curve. Is there an excess supply or excess demand for money? Describe the adjustment of the economy back to the *LM* curve.

_____

_____

Critical Thinking

Suppose you get a job working for one of your Senators. The economy has just entered a recession, and she asks you to propose three different plans for increasing aggregate output by $200 billion. Under plan 1, government spending would increase holding taxes constant. Under plan 2, taxes would decrease, holding government spending constant, and under plan 3, government spending would increase, but taxes would increase by the same amount in order to keep the budget deficit unchanged. Assume that the *mpc* is 0.80.

1. How much would government spending have to rise by under plan 1?

    _____

    _____

2. How much would taxes have to fall by under plan 2?

    _____

    _____

3. How much would government spending and taxes both have to rise by under plan 3?

    _____

    _____

Self-Test

TRUE/FALSE QUESTIONS

_____1.   The Keynesian model assumes that the price level is fixed, which implies that changes in nominal variables are the same as changes in real variables.

_____2.   Autonomous consumer expenditure is positively related to income.

_____3.   Planned investment spending includes purchases of stock by a corporation.

_____4.   In contrast to fixed investment, which is always planned, some inventory investment is unplanned.

_____5. The expenditure multiplier is identical to the money supply multiplier developed in Chapter 14.

_____6. The larger the *mpc*, the smaller the expenditure multiplier.

_____7. Keynes believed that changes in autonomous spending are dominated by unstable fluctuations in planned investment spending, which are influenced by "animal spirits."

_____8. The Great Depression, 1929–1933, was caused by a sharp decline in autonomous consumer expenditure.

_____9. A $100 billion increase in government spending has a smaller impact on aggregate output than a $100 billion decrease in taxes.

_____10. If foreigners suddenly get an urge to buy $100 billion more American goods, aggregate output will increase by $100 billion.

_____11. The *IS* curve shows the combinations of interest rates and aggregate output for which the goods market is in equilibrium.

_____12. If a company uses surplus funds instead of borrowed funds to undertake investment in physical capital, then the interest rate has no impact on investment spending.

_____13. A higher interest rate causes the dollar to depreciate, which leads to an increase in net exports and therefore aggregate output.

_____14. Keynes's liquidity preference theory states that the demand for money in real terms depends only on the interest rate.

_____15. Equilibrium in the goods market produces a unique equilibrium level of aggregate output.

MULTIPLE-CHOICE QUESTIONS

1. The four components of aggregate demand are
   a. consumer expenditure, planned investment spending, government spending, and net exports.
   b. consumer expenditure, unplanned inventory investment, government spending, and net exports.
   c. consumer expenditure, planned inventory investment, government spending, and exports.
   d. consumer expenditure, unplanned inventory investment, government spending, and imports.

2. A marginal propensity to consume of 0.50 means that
   a. people spend half of their income.
   b. the expenditure multiplier is 0.50.
   c. people spend half of their disposable income.
   d. people spend half of each additional dollar of disposable income.

3. If autonomous consumer expenditure is $100 billion, the marginal propensity to consume is 0.90, aggregate income is $1,000 billion and taxes are $200 billion, consumer expenditures will equal
   a. $1,000 billion.
   b. $100 billion.
   c. $280 billion.
   d. $820 billion.

4. Suppose that Dell Computer Company starts the year with $20 million in inventory and ends the year with $14 million in inventory. Inventory investment for the year for Dell will be
   a. −$14 million.
   b. $14 million.
   c. −$6 million.
   d. $6 million.

5. If aggregate demand is $875 billion and aggregate supply is $900 billion, then
   a. unplanned inventory investment = −$25 billion, and firms will increase production.
   b. unplanned inventory investment = $25 billion, and firms will increase production.
   c. unplanned inventory investment = −$25 billion, and firms will decrease production.
   d. unplanned inventory investment = $25 billion, and firms will decrease production.

6. An increase in planned investment spending leads to an even larger change in aggregate output because
   a. it causes interest rates to fall, which raises investment spending further.
   b. it leads to further consumer expenditure, which raises aggregate demand.
   c. it leads to a depreciation of the exchange rate, which raises net exports.
   d. it leads to an increase in autonomous consumer expenditure.

7. If the *mpc* is 0.80, then the expenditure multiplier is
   a. 5.
   b. 4.
   c. 3.
   d. 0.80.

8. If the marginal propensity to consumer is 0.75 and autonomous spending, *A*, increases by $25 billion, then aggregate output will increase by
   a. $25 billion.
   b. $75 billion.
   c. $100 billion.
   d. $125 billion.

9. If the government reduces taxes by $120 billion and the marginal propensity to consume is 0.50, then aggregate output will
   a. rise by $120 billion.
   b. rise by $240 billion.
   c. fall by $120 billion.
   d. fall by $240 billion.

10. If the government raises taxes and government spending by $20 billion, and the marginal propensity to consume is 0.80, aggregate output will
    a. rise by $100 billion.
    b. rise by $20 billion.
    c. remain unchanged.
    d. fall by $20 billion.

11. An increase in the interest rate will cause
    a. investment spending to rise and net exports to fall.
    b. investment spending to fall and net exports to fall.
    c. investment spending to rise and net exports to rise.
    d. investment spending to fall and net exports to rise.

12. The *IS* curve slopes downward because the higher _____ lead to lower _____ and _____.
    a. government spending; consumption; investment spending
    b. interest rates; money demand; investment spending
    c. government spending; money demand; net exports
    d. interest rates; investment spending; net exports

13. In the money market, an increase in aggregate output leads to _____ in money demand and _____ in the interest rate.
    a. an increase; a decrease
    b. a decrease; an increase
    c. an increase; an increase
    d. a decrease; a decrease

14. The *IS* curve shows combinations of interest rates and levels of income for which
    a. government spending equals taxes.
    b. the money market is in equilibrium.
    c. net exports and government spending both equal zero.
    d. the goods market is in equilibrium.

15. The *LM* curve shows combinations of interest rates and levels of income for which
    a. government spending equals taxes.
    b. the money market is in equilibrium.
    c. net exports and government spending both equal zero.
    d. the goods market is in equilibrium.

16. When the supply of money is greater than the demand for money, people will
    a. spend the excess money causing interest rates to rise.
    b. sell bonds causing interest rates to fall.
    c. buy bonds causing the interest rate to rise.
    d. buy bonds causing the price of bonds to rise.

17. At points to the left of the *IS* curve
    a. there is an excess demand for goods, which leads to an unplanned decrease in inventories.
    b. there is an excess supply of goods, which leads to an unplanned decrease in inventories.
    c. there is an excess demand for goods, which leads to an unplanned increase in inventories.
    d. there is an excess supply of goods, which leads to an unplanned increase in inventories.

18. At points to the right of the *LM* curve
    a. there is an excess supply of money, which will cause interest rates to fall.
    b. there is an excess supply of money, which will cause interest rates to rise.
    c. there is an excess demand for money, which will cause interest rates to fall.
    d. there is an excess demand for money, which will cause interest rates to rise.

19. The intersection of the *IS* and *LM* curves shows
    a. the only combination of interest rates and aggregate output for which the goods market is in equilibrium.
    b. the only combination of interest rates and aggregate output for which the money market is in equilibrium.
    c. one of many possible combinations of interest rates and aggregate output for which both the goods market and the money market are in equilibrium.
    d. the only combination of interest rates and aggregate output for which both the goods market and the money market are in equilibrium.

20. At point B in Figure 20.3, there is excess
    a. demand for goods and excess supply of money.
    b. supply of goods and excess supply of money.
    c. demand for goods and excess demand for money.
    d. supply of goods and excess demand for money.

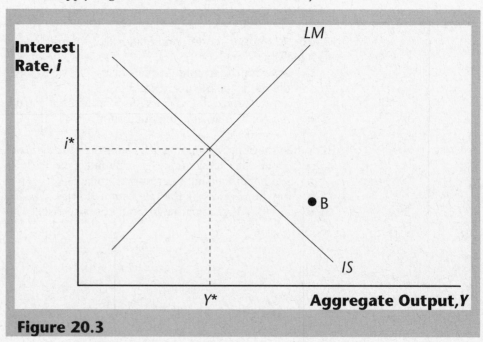

Figure 20.3

Solutions

Terms and Definitions

_1_ aggregate demand

_10_ aggregate demand function

_11_ "animal spirits"

_15_ autonomous consumer expenditure

_7_ consumer expenditures

_3_ consumption function

_12_ disposable income

_14_ expenditure multiplier

_4_ fixed investment

_8_ government spending

_9_ inventory investment

_6_ *IS* curve

_13_ *LM* curve

_5_ marginal propensity to consume

_2_ net exports

Practice Problems

1. a.

Point in Figure 3	Disposable Income, Y_D	Consumer Expenditure, C	Change in Disposable Income, ΔY_D	Change in Consumer Expenditure, ΔC
E	0	300	--	--
F	200	460	200	160
G	400	620	200	160
H	800	940	400	320

b.

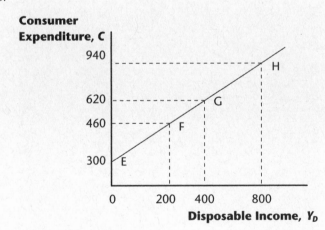

2. a. $Y^* = \$4,000$ billion.

b.

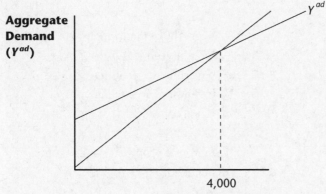

c. $Y^* = \$3,500$ billion.

d. $\Delta Y/\Delta a = 1/(1-mpc) = 10$.

e. $\Delta Y = [1/(1-mpc)]\Delta G = \$1,000$ billion.

f. $\Delta Y = -\$1,000$ billion.

3.   a.   A decrease in autonomous consumer expenditure, *a*.

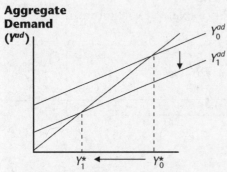

b.   A decrease in planned investment spending, *I*.

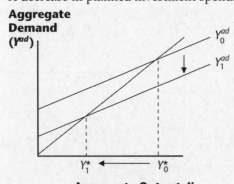

c. A decrease in taxes, *T*.

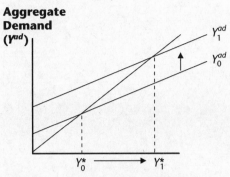

d. A decrease in net exports, *NX*.

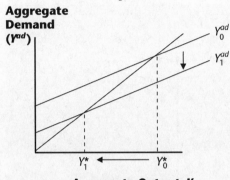

4. a.

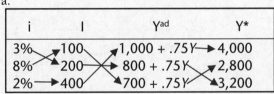

i	I	Y^{ad}	Y^*
3%	100	$1{,}000 + .75Y$	4,000
8%	200	$800 + .75Y$	2,800
2%	400	$700 + .75Y$	3,200

b.

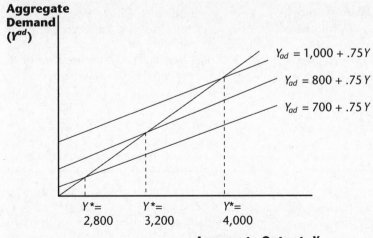

c. Use the numbers from part *a* to construct an *IS* curve.

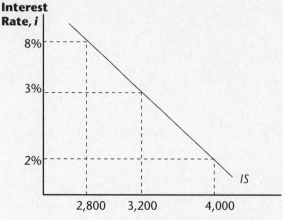

5.

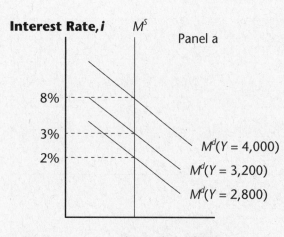

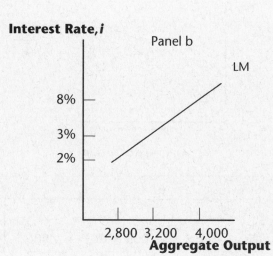

Short-Answer Questions

1. Consumer expenditure, planned investment spending, government spending, net exports.

2. In the Keynesian model, an increase in nominal output is the same as an increase in real output because the price level is assumed to be fixed.

3. $I^U = -50$, unplanned inventory investment is –50. Firms will respond by increasing production until the economy reaches equilibrium.

4. According to Keynes, changes in autonomous spending are dominated by unstable fluctuations in planned investment spending, which is influenced by "animal spirits."

5. $\Delta Y = [1/(1-mpc)]\Delta NX = -\$100$ billion.

6. A change in taxes has a smaller impact on aggregate output than a change in government spending because when taxes are reduced, part of the increase in disposable income is saved. And when taxes are increased, part of the decrease in disposable income is paid out of saving.

7. Interest rates and aggregate output are negatively related along the IS curve because as interest rates rise, investment spending and net exports decline and as investment spending and net exports decline, so does aggregate output.

8. Interest rates and aggregate output positively related along the *LM* curve because as aggregate income rises, the demand for money increases, which causes the interest rate to rise.

9. If the economy is to the left of the *IS* curve, there is excess demand for goods, which results in an unplanned decrease in inventory. Firms will respond by increasing production until equilibrium in the goods market is restored, and the economy returns to the IS curve.

10. If the economy is to the left of the *LM* curve, there is an excess supply of money. People will purchase bonds with their excess money holdings. The increased demand for bonds will cause the price of bonds to rise, and the interest rate to fall until equilibrium is restored along the *LM* curve.

10. b
11. b
12. d
13. c
14. d
15. b
16. c
17. a
18. d
19. d
20. d

Critical Thinking

1. ΔG = $40 billion
2. ΔT = −$50 billion
3. $\Delta G = \Delta T$ = $200 billion

True/False Questions

1. T
2. F
3. F
4. T
5. F
6. F
7. T
8. F
9. F
10. F
11. T
12. F
13. F
14. F
15. F

Multiple-Choice Questions

1. a
2. d
3. d
4. c
5. d
6. b
7. a
8. c
9. a

21

Monetary and Fiscal Policy in the *ISLM* Model

Chapter Review

PREVIEW

The last chapter developed the *ISLM* model. This chapter uses the *ISLM* model to show how monetary and fiscal policies affect aggregate economic activity.

FACTORS THAT CAUSE THE *IS* CURVE TO SHIFT

The *IS* curve shifts whenever there is a change in an autonomous factor that is unrelated to the interest rate. There are five factors that shift the *IS* curve:

- changes in autonomous consumer expenditure;
- changes in investment spending unrelated to the interest rate;
- changes in government spending;
- changes in taxes;
- changes in net exports unrelated to the interest rate.

It is important to differentiate between changes in investment spending and net exports that are related to the interest rate and changes in investment spending and net exports that are unrelated to the interest rate. In Chapter 20 you learned that an increase in the interest rate causes both investment spending and net exports to decline. These changes in investment spending and net exports are represented by movements along the *IS* curve because they are both caused by changes in the interest rate. But suppose companies become more optimistic about future sales and decide to increase investment spending. This change in investment spending is represented as a rightward shift in the *IS* curve because it is independent of the interest rate. Similarly, suppose foreign buyers decide U.S. goods are fashionable and decide to buy more of them. This change in net exports is represented as a rightward shift in the *IS* curve because it is independent of the interest rate. Increases in each of the five factors except for taxes will shift the *IS* curve to the right. Decreases in each of the five factors except for taxes will shift the *IS* curve to the left. An increase in taxes will shift the *IS* curve to the left because it reduces spending. A decrease in taxes shifts the *IS* curve to the right because it increases spending.

FACTORS THAT CAUSE THE *LM* CURVE TO SHIFT

Two factors cause the *LM* curve to shift:

- changes in the money supply;

- autonomous changes in money demand.

An increase in the money supply shifts the *LM* curve right. A decrease in the money supply shifts the *LM* curve left. Autonomous changes in money demand are any changes that are not caused by a change in the price level, aggregate output or the interest rate. For example, if bonds suddenly become a riskier asset, the demand for money will rise. Because this increase in demand for money is independent of a change in the price level aggregate output or interest rates, it causes a leftward shift in the *LM* curve. A decrease in autonomous money demand causes the *LM* curve to shift right.

CHANGES IN EQUILIBRIUM LEVEL OF THE INTEREST RATE AND AGGREGATE OUTPUT

Figure 21.1, Panel a, shows the response of output and interest rates to an increase in the money supply. The increase in the money supply shifts the *LM* curve right, which causes the interest rate to fall and aggregate output to rise. A decrease in the money supply shifts the *LM* curve to the left, which causes the interest rate to rise and aggregate output to fall. Aggregate output is positively related to the money supply. Panel b shows the response of output and interest rates to expansionary fiscal policy. Expansionary fiscal policy (either an increase in government spending or a reduction in taxes) shifts the *IS* curve to the right, which causes interest rates to rise and aggregate output to rise as well. Contractionary fiscal policy shifts the *IS* curve to the left, which causes interest rates to fall and aggregate output to fall. Aggregate output is positively related to government spending and negatively related to taxes.

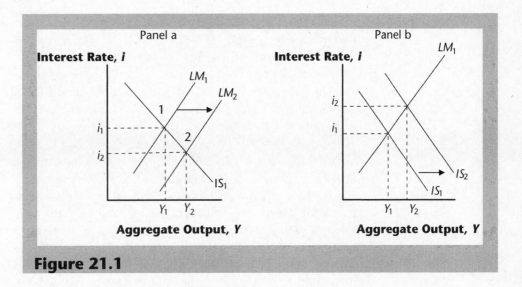

Figure 21.1

EFFECTIVENESS OF MONETARY VERSUS FISCAL POLICY

When money demand is unaffected by the interest rate, the *LM* curve is vertical, and monetary policy affects output, but fiscal policy does not. Expansionary fiscal policy (either increasing government spending or decreasing taxes) shifts the *IS* curve to the right, but because the *LM* curve is vertical, the interest rate rises causing investment spending and net exports to decline enough to completely offset the effects of the expansionary fiscal policy. This special case, when expansionary fiscal policy has no effect on output, is called *complete crowding out*. Expansionary monetary policy does lead to an increase in aggregate output when the *LM* curve is vertical. In general, the less interest-sensitive money demand is, the more effective monetary policy is relative to fiscal policy.

APPLICATION: TARGETING MONEY SUPPLY VERSUS INTEREST RATES

In the real world, unanticipated changes in autonomous spending and money demand cause the *IS* and *LM* curves to shift. Because of these shifts, the positions of the *IS* and *LM* curves are uncertain. The Fed's choice of whether to target the interest rate or the money supply depends on which of these curves, the *IS* curve or the *LM* curve, is more unstable. If the *IS* curve is more unstable than the *LM* curve, a money supply target is preferred. If the *LM* curve is more unstable than the *IS* curve, an interest-rate target is preferred.

ISLM MODEL IN THE LONG RUN

So far in the *ISLM* model we have assumed that the price level is fixed. But in the long run, the price level does change, so when we use the *ISLM* model to analyze the effect of monetary or fiscal policy in the long run, we need to consider changes in the price level. Changes in the price level do not affect the *IS* curve. Recall that changes in the real money supply (*M/P*) shift the *LM* curve. So far we have only considered changes in the real money supply that arise from changes in the nominal money supply (M). Changes in the money supply can arise from changes in the price level (P) as well. Holding the nominal money supply constant, an increase in the price level reduces the real money supply and causes the LM curve to shift left. A decrease in the price level increases the real money supply and causes the LM curve to shift right. The natural rate level of output (Y_n) is the level of output at which the price level has no tendency to rise or fall. Suppose the economy begins at the natural rate level of output and expansionary monetary policy shifts the LM curve to the right. In the short run, aggregate output will rise above the natural rate level of output. In the long run, the price level will rise, the real money supply will fall back to its original level, the LM curve will shift back to its original position, aggregate output will return to the natural rate and the interest rate will return to its original value as well. The fact that the increase in the money supply has left output and interest rates unchanged in the long run is referred to as *long-run monetary neutrality*. Expansionary fiscal policy also has no long-run effect on output, but it does leave the interest rate at a higher level.

ISLM MODEL AND THE AGGREGATE DEMAND CURVE

In the short run, when the price level rises, the real money supply falls, the LM curve shifts left and aggregate output declines. When the price level falls, the real money supply increases, the LM curve shifts right and aggregate output increases. The negative relationship between the price level and aggregate output is called the *aggregate demand curve*. Points on the aggregate demand curve are combinations of the price level and aggregate output for which both the goods market and the money market are in equilibrium. Any factor that shifts the IS curve shifts the aggregate demand curve in the same direction. Holding the price level constant, any factor that shifts the LM curve shifts the aggregate demand curve in the same direction.

Helpful Hints

Fiscal policy (changes in government spending and taxes) shifts the IS curve. Monetary policy (changes in the money supply) shifts the LM curve. In the long run, aggregate output returns to the natural rate level of output. If output is above the natural rate level, the price level rises, the real money supply declines, and the LM curve shifts left until aggregate output returns to the natural rate level of output. If output is below the natural rate level, the price level falls, the real money supply increases, and the LM curve shifts right until aggregate output returns to the natural rate level of output. Fiscal and monetary policy both shift the aggregate demand curve in the same direction. Expansionary policy shifts the aggregate demand curve to the right. Contractionary policy shifts the aggregate demand curve to the left.

Terms and Definitions

Choose a definition for each key term.

Key Terms:

_____aggregate demand curve

_____complete crowding out

_____long-run monetary neutrality

_____natural rate level of output

Definitions:

1. The proposition that in the long run, a percentage rise in the money supply is matched by the same percentage rise in the price level, leaving unchanged the real money supply and all other economic variables such as interest rates

2. The relationship between aggregate output and the price level when the goods and money markets are in equilibrium

3. The situation in which expansionary fiscal policy does not lead to a rise in output because there is an exactly offsetting movement in private spending

4. The level of output produced at the natural rate of unemployment at which there is no tendency for wages or prices to change

Problems and Short-Answer Questions

PRACTICE PROBLEMS

1. Assume the economy is initially at the natural rate level of output (Y_n).
    a. Show what happens in the short run to the interest rate and aggregate output when the Fed increases the money supply.

b. On the same graph you used to illustrate your answer to part *a* show what will happen in the long run. Explain your result.

_____

_____

_____

c. Assume the economy is once again at the natural rate level of output (Y_n). Show what happens in the short run to the interest rate and aggregate output when government increases spending.

d. On the same graph you used to illustrate your answer to part *c* show what will happen in the long run. Explain your result.

_____

_____

_____

e. Now assume the economy is at the natural rate level of output (Y_n), but this time also assume that money demand is unaffected by the interest rate. Show what happens in the short run and the long run to the interest rate and aggregate output when government increases spending. Explain your result.

_____

_____

_____

2. Complete the table by indicating whether each shift factor listed in the far left column shifts the *IS* or *LM* curve right (right), left (left) or not at all (no shift), and whether the resulting shift in *IS* or *LM* causes interest rates and aggregate output to rise (+), fall (–) or remain unchanged (0).

Shift factor	Direction of change	IS curve shifts...	LM curve shifts...	Effect on Interest rate	Effect on Aggregate Output
Autonomous consumer expenditure	+				
Autonomous investment spending	–				
Government spending	+				
Taxes	+				
Net exports	–				
Money supply	–				
Autonomous money demand	–				

3. a. Suppose the *IS* curve is stable, and the *LM* curve is unstable. In the graph below, panel a, illustrate the effect on aggregate output of following an

interest rate target. In panel b, illustrate the effect on aggregate output of following a money supply target.

Interest Rate, *i*   Panel a   **Interest Rate, *i***   Panel b

Aggregate Output, *Y*   **Aggregate Output, *Y***

b. Based on your analysis in part *a*, which type of policy would you recommend for an economy with a stable *IS* curve and an unstable *LM* curve? Why?

———————————————————————————————

———————————————————————————————

———————————————————————————————

c. Suppose the *IS* curve is unstable, and the *LM* curve is stable. In panel a below, illustrate the effect on aggregate output of following an interest rate target. In panel b illustrate the effect on aggregate output of following a money supply target.

Interest Rate, *i*   Panel a   **Interest Rate, *i***   Panel b

Aggregate Output, *Y*   **Aggregate Output, *Y***

d. Based on your analysis in part *c,* which type of policy would you recommend for an economy with an unstable *IS* curve and a stable *LM* curve? Why?

_____

_____

_____

4. Consider the following data on interest rates, aggregate output, and the price level.

i	P	Y
2%	100	$1.0 trillion
7%	98	$1.5 trillion
4%	72	$1.8 trillion

a. Label both axes in panel a of the graph below.
b. Use the data from the table to complete the *ISLM* graph in panel a.
c. Use the data from the table to draw the aggregate demand curve in panel b that corresponds to the *ISLM* graph in panel a.
d. Label both axes in panel b.

Panel b

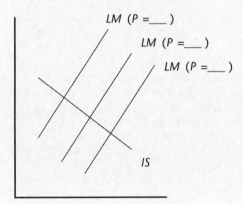

LM (P =___)

LM (P =___)

LM (P =___)

IS

SHORT-ANSWER QUESTIONS

1. List the factors that shift the *IS* curve.

_____

_____

_____

2. List the factors that shift the *LM* curve.

    _____

    _____

3. Give an example of a change in investment spending that would cause a shift in the *IS* curve. Give an example of a change in investment spending that would cause a movement along the *IS* curve.

    _____

    _____

4. Give an example of a change in net exports that would cause a shift in the *IS* curve. Give an example of a change in net exports that would cause a movement along the *IS* curve.

    _____

    _____

5. Give an example of change in money demand that would cause a shift in the *LM* curve. Give an example of a change in money demand that would cause a movement along the *LM* curve.

    _____

    _____

6. Suppose the economy is currently below the natural rate level of output and the demand for money is unaffected by the interest rate. What type of policy, monetary or fiscal, would you recommend to move the economy back to the natural rate level of output? Why?

    _____

    _____

7. Describe the adjustment of prices that will occur when the economy is above the natural rate level of output. Explain how the economy returns to the natural rate level of output as a result of the price adjustment you described.

    _____

    _____

8. Describe the adjustment of prices that will occur when the economy is below the natural rate level of output. Explain how the economy returns to the natural rate level of output as a result of the price adjustment you described.

    _____

    _____

9. Explain why the aggregate demand curve is downward sloping.

   _____

   _____

10. List the shift factors for aggregate demand.

   _____

   _____

Critical Thinking

Most of the analysis of fiscal and monetary policy in this chapter considers one type of policy at a time, holding the other type of policy constant. But in the real world, both monetary policy and fiscal policy are changing all of the time. Consider the combinations of monetary and fiscal policy listed in the table on the following page. Fill in the missing columns in the table by indicating whether the given combination of monetary and fiscal policy has a positive (+), negative (–), or ambiguous (?) impact on interest rates and aggregate output.

Fiscal Policy	Monetary Policy	Interest Rates	Aggregate Output
Expansionary	Expansionary	_____	_____
Contractionary	Contractionary	_____	_____
Expansionary	Contractionary	_____	_____
Contractionary	Expansionary	_____	_____

Self-Test

TRUE/FALSE QUESTIONS

_____1. An increase in investment spending that is caused by a decrease in the interest rate is represented as a rightward shift in the *IS* curve.

_____2. An increase in net exports that is caused by a decrease in the interest rate, which leads to a depreciation of the dollar, is represented as a movement (down and to the right) along the *IS* curve.

_____3. If bonds become less risky, people will decrease their demand for money, which will cause the *LM* curve to shift right.

_____4. Complete crowding out occurs when the demand for money is ultrasensitive to changes in the interest rate.

_____5. An increase in the money supply caused by an open market purchase of bonds by the Federal Reserve causes the *LM* curve to shift right.

_____6. When the *LM* curve is more unstable than the *IS* curve, the Fed should target the interest rate to minimize fluctuations in aggregate output.

_____7. Although monetary and fiscal policy can affect output in the long run, neither affects output in the short run.

_____8. Fiscal policy affects the interest rate in the long run; monetary policy does not affect the interest rate in the long run.

_____9. When aggregate output is below the natural rate level of output, the price level rises.

_____10. When aggregate output is at the natural rate level of output, the price level remains unchanged.

_____11. Long-run monetary neutrality refers to the fact that in the long run, an increase in the money supply has no effect on the price level.

_____12. The aggregate demand curve is the relationship between the price level and quantity of aggregate output for which only the money market is in equilibrium.

_____13. Any factor that shifts the *IS* curve shifts the aggregate demand curve in the opposite direction.

_____14. Any factor that shifts the *IS* curve shifts the *LM* curve in the same direction.

_____15. Holding the price level constant, any factor that shifts the *LM* curve shifts the aggregate demand curve in the same direction.

MULTIPLE-CHOICE QUESTIONS

1. Which of the following causes the *IS* curve to shift left?
   a. increase in taxes
   b. increase in government spending
   c. increase in the money supply
   d. increase in autonomous money demand

2. In the short run, an increase in government spending will lead to
   a. higher interest rates and higher aggregate output.
   b. lower interest rates and higher aggregate output.
   c. no change in interest rates and higher aggregate output.
   d. higher interest rates but no change in aggregate output.

3. In the short run, an increase in taxes will lead to
    a. lower interest rates and lower aggregate output.
    b. higher interest rates and lower aggregate output.
    c. no change in interest rates and lower aggregate output.
    d. higher interest rates but no change in aggregate output.

4. In the short run, an increase in the money supply will lead to
    a. higher interest rates and higher aggregate output.
    b. lower interest rates and higher aggregate output.
    c. no change in interest rates and higher aggregate output.
    d. higher interest rates but no change in aggregate output.

5. Complete crowding out implies that
    a. an increase in the money supply has no long-run impact on aggregate output.
    b. an increase in government spending has no long-run impact on aggregate output. c.   an increase in the money supply has no impact on output, even in the short run.
    d. an increase in government spending has no impact on output, even in the short run.

Figure 21.2 is for multiple choice questions 6, 7 and 8.

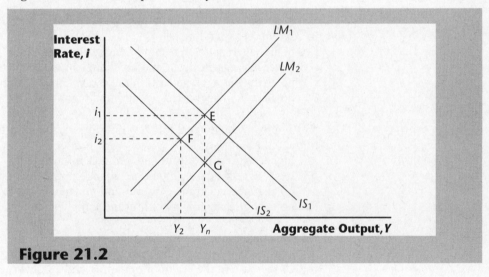

Figure 21.2

6. A possible reason that the economy moved from equilibrium point E to equilibrium point F in Figure 21.2 is
    a. a decrease in the money supply.
    b. an increase in autonomous money demand.
    c. a decrease in autonomous consumer expenditure.
    d. an increase in autonomous consumer expenditure.

7. If policymakers are interested in moving the economy from point F back to the natural rate level of output at point E, they could
    a. increase in the money supply.
    b. decrease the money supply.
    c. increase government spending.
    d. decrease government spending.

8. If policymakers decided to do nothing in response to the economy moving to point F from point E, then in the long run the price level would
   a. fall, and the economy would return to point E.
   b. rise, and the economy would return to point E.
   c. fall, and the economy would move to point G.
   d. rise, and the economy would move to point G.

9. If the *IS* curve is relatively more unstable than the *LM* curve, then the optimal monetary policy is
   a. target the money supply.
   b. target the inflation rate.
   c. target unemployment.
   d. target the interest rate.

10. When the *LM* curve is completely stable, targeting the interest rate results in
    a. smaller fluctuations in aggregate output than would occur with a money supply target.
    b. larger fluctuations in aggregate output than would occur with a money supply target.
    c. no fluctuations in aggregate output.
    d. the same fluctuations in aggregate output as would occur with a money supply target.

11. Starting from the natural rate level of output, the long-run effect of an increase in government spending is
    a. higher aggregate output and a higher interest rate.
    b. lower aggregate output and no change in the interest rate.
    c. no change in aggregate output and no change in the interest rate.
    d. no change in aggregate output but a higher interest rate.

12. Starting from the natural rate level of output, the long-run effect of an increase in the money supply is
    a. higher aggregate output and a higher interest rate.
    b. lower aggregate output and no change in the interest rate.
    c. no change in aggregate output and no change in the interest rate.
    d. no change in aggregate output but a higher interest rate.

13. An increase in the price level leads to
    a. a decrease in the real money supply and a rightward shift in the *LM* curve.
    b. an increase in the real money supply and a leftward shift in the *LM* curve.
    c. a decrease in the real money supply and a leftward shift in the *LM* curve.
    d. an increase in the real money supply and a rightward shift in the *LM* curve.

14. An increase in investment spending that is unrelated to the interest rate will cause
    a. movement along the *IS* curve and a shift in the aggregate demand curve.
    b. a shift in the *IS* curve and a movement along the aggregate demand curve.
    c. movement along the *IS* curve and a movement along the aggregate demand curve.
    d. a shift in the *IS* curve and a shift in the aggregate demand curve.

15. In terms of its effect on the *LM* curve, which of the following has the same effect as an increase in the money supply?
    a. an increase in the price level
    b. an increase in autonomous money demand
    c. a decrease in autonomous money demand
    d. an increase in autonomous consumer expenditure

16. Other things equal, an increase in the price level shifts the LM curve _____ and leads to a _____ the aggregate demand curve.
    a. right; rightward shift in
    b. right; movement down and to the right along
    c. left; leftward shift in
    d. left; movement up and to the left along

17. Other things equal, an increase in the price level
    a. shifts the *IS* curve to the right.
    b. shifts the *IS* curve to the left.
    c. has no effect on the *IS* curve.
    d. shifts the *IS* curve to the right in the short run but not in the long run.

18. Other things equal, an increase in the price level
    a. reduces the interest rate and increases aggregate output.
    b. increases the interest rate and increases aggregate output.
    c. reduces the interest rate and reduces aggregate output.
    d. increases the interest rate and reduces aggregate output.

19. The difference between the long-run effect of an increase in the money supply and the long-run effect of an increase in government spending is that
    a. an increase in government spending results in a higher interest rate in the long run while an increase in the money supply does not.
    b. an increase in the money supply results in a higher interest rate in the long run while an increase in government spending does not.
    a. an increase in government spending results in a higher aggregate output in the long run while an increase in the money supply does not.
    b. an increase in the money supply results in a higher aggregate output in the long run while an increase in government spending does not.

20. Beginning from the natural rate level of output, if the Fed increases the money supply and Congress and the president increase government spending, then
    a. aggregate output will rise but the effect on interest rates will be ambiguous.
    b. interest rates will rise but the effect on output will be ambiguous.
    c. aggregate output will fall but the effect on interest rates will be ambiguous.
    d. interest rates will fall but the effect on output will be ambiguous.

Solutions

Terms and Definitions

<u>2</u> aggregate demand curve

<u>3</u> complete crowding out

<u>1</u> long-run monetary neutrality

<u>4</u> natural rate level of output

Practice Problems

1. a. and b. The short-run (a) and long-run (b) effects of an increase in the money supply.

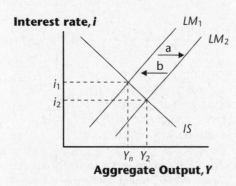

An increase in the money supply shifts the *LM* curve to the right in the short run (a). In the long run, the price level rises because aggregate output is above the natural rate level. As the price level rises, the real money supply falls causing the *LM* curve to shift back to LM_1 (b). In the long run, aggregate output returns to the natural rate level Y_n.

c. and d. The short-run (c) and long-run (d) effects of an increase in government spending.

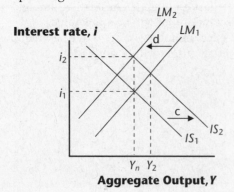

An increase in government spending shifts the *IS* curve to the right in the short run (c). In the long run the price level rises because the aggregate output is above the natural rate level. As the price level rises, the real money supply falls causing the *LM* curve to shift left to LM_2 (d). In the long run, aggregate output returns to the natural rate level Y_n.

e. The short-run and long-run effects of an increase in government spending, when the demand for money is unaffected by the interest rate;

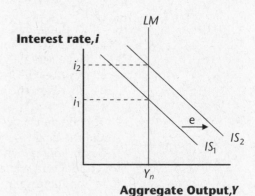

In the short run, an increase in government spending shifts the *IS* curve to the right (e). Since the demand for money is unaffected by interest rates there is complete crowding out and aggregate output remains at Y_n. Since aggregate output remains at Y_n, the price level remains unchanged and the long-run response of interest rates and aggregate output is the same as the short-run response.

2.

Shift factor	Direction of change	*IS* curve shifts...	*LM* curve shifts...	Effect on Interest rate	Effect on Aggregate Output
Autonomous consumer expenditure	+	right	no shift	+	+
Autonomous investment spending	–	left	no shift	–	–
Government spending	+	right	no shift	+	+
Taxes	+	left	no shift	–	–
Net exports	–	left	no shift	–	–
Money supply	–	no shift	left	+	–
Autonomous money demand	–	no shift	right	–	+

3. a.

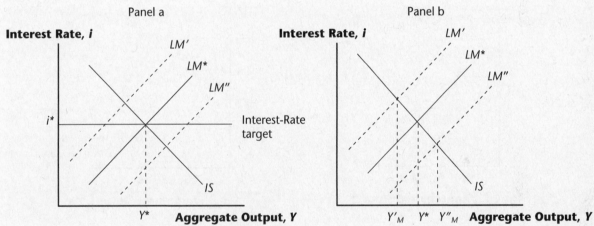

Panel a

Panel b

b. If the *LM* curve is unstable and the *IS* curve is stable (or more generally, if the *LM* curve is relatively more unstable than the *IS* curve), then a policy that targets the interest rate is preferred because it will keep aggregate output closer to *Y** as shown in panel a.

c.

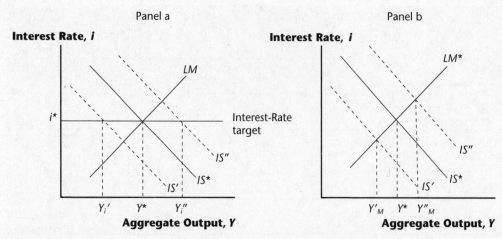

Panel a

Panel b

d. If the *IS* curve is unstable and the *LM* curve is stable (or more generally, if the *IS* curve is relatively more unstable than the *LM* curve), then a policy that targets the money supply is preferred because it will keep aggregate output closer to Y* as shown in panel b.

4. a. through d.

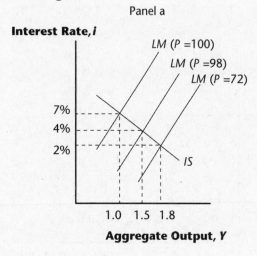

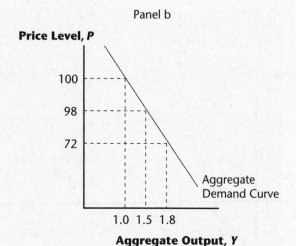

Panel a

Panel b

Short-Answer Questions

1. Five factors shift the *IS* curve: changes in autonomous consumer expenditure, changes in investment spending unrelated to the interest rate, changes in government spending, changes in taxes, and changes in net exports unrelated to the interest rate.

2. Two factors shift the *LM* curve: changes in the money supply and autonomous changes in money demand.

3. If firms become optimistic about the future of the economy and increase investment spending, then the *IS* curve will shift right. If the interest rate declines and firms increase investment spending because new investment

projects are now profitable at the lower interest rate, then the economy moves along the *IS* curve.

4. If foreign buyers decide that U.S.-produced goods are fashionable, then exports will increase and the *IS* curve will shift right. If the interest rate declines, the dollar will depreciate relative to foreign currencies causing exports to rise and imports to fall, which will cause the economy to move along the *IS* curve.

5. If the rate of return on bonds becomes more volatile and therefore riskier people will increase their demand for money, which will cause the *LM* curve to shift left. If income rises, people will increase their demand for

money, which will cause the economy to move along the *LM* curve.

6. Since money demand is unaffected by the interest rate, the *LM* curve is vertical and fiscal policy is ineffective because there is complete crowding out. The only type of policy that can be used to bring the economy back to the natural rate level of output is expansionary monetary policy.

7. When the economy is above the natural rate of output, the price level rises (in the long run). As the price level rises, the real money supply declines, which causes the *LM* curve to shift left until the economy returns to the natural rate level of output.

8. When the economy is below the natural rate of output, the price level falls (in the long run). As the price level falls, the real money supply increases, which causes the *LM* curve to shift right until the economy returns to the natural rate level of output.

9. The aggregate demand curve slopes downward because as the price level increases, the real money supply declines, which causes the *LM* curve to shift left, which leads to a lower level of aggregate output.

10. Any factor that shifts the *IS* curve shifts the aggregate demand curve in the same direction. Therefore, changes in autonomous consumer expenditures, changes in investment spending unrelated to the interest rate, changes in government spending, changes in taxes, and changes in net exports unrelated to the interest rate all shift the aggregate demand curve. Holding the price level constant, any factor that shifts the *LM* curve shifts the aggregate demand curve in the same direction. Therefore, changes in the money supply and autonomous changes in money demand both shift the aggregate demand curve.

Critical Thinking

Fiscal Policy	Monetary Policy	Interest Rates	Aggregate Output
Expansionary	Expansionary	?	+
Contractionary	Contractionary	?	-
Expansionary	Contractionary	+	?
Contractionary	Expansionary	-	?

True/False Questions

1. F
2. T
3. T
4. F
5. T
6. T
7. F
8. T
9. F
10. T
11. F
12. F
13. F
14. F
15. T

Multiple-Choice Questions

1. a
2. a
3. a
4. b
5. d
6. c
7. c
8. c
9. a
10. c
11. d
12. c
13. c
14. d
15. c
16. d

17. c
18. d
19. a
20. a

22 Aggregate Demand and Supply Analysis

Chapter Review

PREVIEW

This chapter develops and applies the tools of aggregate demand and aggregate supply analysis. Those tools are used to illustrate the effects of changes in the money supply, government spending and taxes, animal spirits and supply shocks on output and the price level.

AGGREGATE DEMAND

Aggregate demand is made up of four component parts: consumer expenditure, planned investment spending, government spending and net exports. The *aggregate demand curve* describes the inverse relationship between the quantity of aggregate output demanded and the price level when all other variables are held constant. The aggregate demand curve slopes downward because as the price level falls, the real quantity of money rises, which causes the interest rate to fall. Lower interest rates cause investment expenditures and therefore aggregate demand to rise. Additionally, as the interest rate falls the dollar depreciates, which causes net exports and therefore aggregate demand to rise. The fact that the aggregate demand curve is downward sloping can also be derived from the quantity theory of money analysis discussed in Chapter 19. According to the quantity theory of money, for a given velocity and a given money supply (M), the price level (P) and aggregate real output (Y) are inversely related—as the price level falls, the quantity of aggregate demand rises; as the price level rises, the quantity of aggregate demand falls.

According to the quantity theory of money approach, aggregate demand is determined solely by the real quantity of money and the only factor that shifts the aggregate demand curve is a change in the money supply. According to the components approach, in addition to changes in the quantity of money (M), changes in *government spending* (G), taxes (T), and *net exports* (NX) shift the aggregate demand curve. John Maynard Keynes thought that waves of optimism and pessimism called "*animal spirits,*" which affect *consumer expenditure* (C) and *planned investment spending* (I), also cause the aggregate demand curve to shift. Taken together, these two approaches suggest that there are six factors, often referred to as *demand shocks* that shift the aggregate demand curve: M, G, T, NX, C and I.

AGGREGATE SUPPLY

The *aggregate supply curve* describes the relationship between the price level and the quantity of output supplied when all other variables are held constant. Because prices and wages take time to adjust fully to their long-run levels, there are two different aggregate supply curves: a long-run aggregate supply curve and a short-run aggregate supply curve. In the long run, output in the economy is determined by the amount of capital, labor, and technology, which means that the long-run aggregate supply curve is vertical at the *natural rate of output*. The natural rate of output is the level of output produced when the unemployment rate is at the *natural rate of unemployment*. When the economy is at the natural rate level of output, it is also at full employment where the demand for labor equals the supply of labor.

The short-run aggregate supply curve is upward sloping because some costs of production (wages for example) are sticky. So when the price of output rises, profits rise and firms increase production. When costs of production increase, the aggregate supply curve shifts left. When costs of production decrease, the aggregate supply curve shifts right. Four factors cause the cost of production to change: tightness in the labor market, expectation of inflation, workers' attempt to push up their real wages, and *supply shocks,* which are changes in the cost of production that are unrelated to wages (such as energy costs).

EQUILIBRIUM IN AGGREGATE SUPPLY AND DEMAND ANALYSIS

There are two types of equilibrium in aggregate demand and supply analysis: short run and long run. Short-run equilibrium is at the intersection of the aggregate demand curve and the aggregate supply curve. Long-run equilibrium occurs when aggregate demand and supply intersect at the long-run aggregate supply curve.

The economy has a *self-correcting mechanism,* which means that it returns to the natural rate of output in the long run. When aggregate demand and aggregate supply intersect below the natural rate level of output, slack in the labor market causes wages to fall. As wages (a cost of production) fall, the aggregate supply curve shifts right until it intersects the long-run aggregate supply curve at the natural rate level of output. When aggregate demand and aggregate supply intersect above the natural rate level of output, tightness in the labor market causes wages to rise. As wages rise, the aggregate supply curve shifts left until it intersects the long-run aggregate supply curve at the long-run equilibrium.

Keynesians believe that the self-correcting mechanism is slow, and therefore active government policy is needed to restore the economy to the natural rate levels of output and unemployment. Other economists, including *monetarists*, believe that the self-correcting mechanism is quick, and therefore they see much less need for active government policy to restore the economy to the natural rate levels of output and unemployment.

Combining aggregate demand and supply with the long-run aggregate supply curve allows us to analyze the effects of various shifts on output and prices. Starting from long-run equilibrium, an increase in the money supply (M), government spending (G), net exports (NX), consumer optimism (C) or business optimism (I), or decreases in taxes (T) shifts the aggregate demand curve right, which causes output and the price level to rise in the short run. Eventually through the self-correcting mechanism the economy adjusts back to the long-run equilibrium. The ultimate long-run effect of any of these shifts is only a rise in the price level.

Shifts in the aggregate supply curve also can be a source of fluctuations in aggregate output. Tightness in the labor market, a rise in the expected price level, an increase in wages, or an increase in the price of raw material used for production all shift the aggregate supply curve left, which causes output to fall and the price level to rise. Improvements in technology that lower the cost of production cause the aggregate supply curve to shift right, which causes output to rise and the price level to fall. Starting from long-run equilibrium, an increase in the price of raw materials will cause the aggregate supply curve to shift left, which will cause output to fall and the price level to rise. The combination of falling output and rising prices is called stagflation. In this short-run equilibrium, the labor market is slack and so wages will decline, which will cause the aggregate supply curve to shift back to the right (the self-correcting mechanism) until the economy adjusts back to the long-run equilibrium. The ultimate long-run effect of the increase in raw material prices is that output and the price level are unchanged.

The usual assumption in aggregate demand and supply analysis is that the natural rate level of output grows steadily over time and shifts in aggregate demand and supply have no effect on the natural rate level of output. According to *real business cycle theory*, the natural rate level of output does not grow steadily over time. Instead, changes in tastes (worker's willingness to work, for example) and technology cause the long-run aggregate supply curve to fluctuate and are therefore major sources of fluctuation in aggregate output. According to this theory, there is very little role for discretionary policy to reduce business cycle fluctuations. According to *hysteresis*, changes in aggregate demand affect the natural rate of unemployment. When aggregate demand falls, unemployment rises above the full employment level, which causes the natural rate of unemployment to rise as well.

SUMMARY

- Shifts in aggregate demand affect the price level and output in the short run.

- Shifts in aggregate demand affect only the price level in the long run.

- Shifts in aggregate supply affect output and the price level only in the short run.

- Shifts in aggregate supply have no affect on output and prices in the long run.

- The economy has a self-correcting mechanism that will return it to the natural rate levels of unemployment and aggregate output over time.

Helpful Hints

The key to understanding the aggregate demand and supply model is to understand that there are two types of equilibrium. Equilibrium means a position of rest. The short-run equilibrium is a position of temporary rest. Short-run equilibrium is where the aggregate supply curve intersects the aggregate demand curve. This intersection can occur below, at, or above the long-run aggregate supply curve, which is the vertical line at the natural rate level of output. When this equilibrium occurs below (to the left of) the natural rate level of output, slack in the labor market will push wages down and cause the aggregate supply curve to shift downward and to the right until it intersects the long-run aggregate supply curve at the natural rate level of output. When the short-run equilibrium is above (to the right) of the natural rate level of output, tightness in the labor market will push wages up and cause the aggregate supply curve to shift upward and to the left until it intersects the long-run aggregate supply curve at the natural rate level of output. When the short-run aggregate supply curve intersects the aggregate demand curve at the long-run aggregate supply curve, the economy is in long-run equilibrium and there is no tendency for the economy to move from that position unless some "shock" causes either the aggregate supply curve or the aggregate demand curve to shift.

Terms and Definitions

Choose a definition for each key term.

Key Terms:

_____aggregate demand curve

_____aggregate supply curve

_____"animal spirits"

_____consumer expenditure

_____demand shocks

_____equation of exchange

_____government spending

_____hysteresis

_____Keynesians

_____monetarists

_____natural rate of output

_____natural rate of unemployment

_____net exports

_____planned investment spending

_____quantity theory of money

_____real business cycle theory

_____self-correcting mechanism

_____supply shocks

_____velocity of money

Definitions:

1. A characteristic of the economy that causes output to return to the natural rate level of output regardless of where output is initially

2. A theory that views real shocks to tastes and technology as the major driving force behind short-run fluctuations in the business cycle

3. Changes in technology and the supply of raw materials

4. Followers of Milton Friedman who advocate the use of a rule whereby the monetary base grows at a constant rate

5. Followers of Keynes who see the need for active government policy to restore the economy to full employment

6. Net foreign spending on domestic goods and services, equal to exports minus imports

7. Spending by all levels of government on goods and services

8. The average number of times per year that a dollar is spent on final goods and services

9. The equation $M \times V = P \times Y$, which relates nominal income to the money supply

10. The level of aggregate output produced at the natural rate of unemployment

11. The rate of unemployment consistent with full employment at which the demand for labor equals the supply of labor

12. The relationship between the quantity of aggregate output demanded and the price level

13. The relationship between the quantity of aggregate output supplied in the short run and the price level

14. The term used to describe the six factors that shift aggregate demand.

15. The theory that nominal income is determined solely by changes in the quantity of money

16. The theory that departures from full employment levels result from past high unemployment

17. Total demand for consumer goods and services

18. Total planned spending by business firms on new machines, factories, and other inputs to production plus planned spending on new homes

19. Waves of optimism and pessimism that affect business and consumer spending

Problems and Short-Answer Questions

PRACTICE PROBLEMS

1. Suppose aggregate output is measured in trillions of dollars with the price level in 1996 having a value of 1.0. Further suppose that velocity is 3, and the money supply is $2 trillion.

   a. Use the information given above along with modern quantity theory of money to calculate the values of aggregate output that correspond to each of the following price levels:

P	Y	P	Y
.5		1.5	
1		2	

   b. Use the values you generated in part (a) to plot the aggregate demand curve on Figure 22.1:

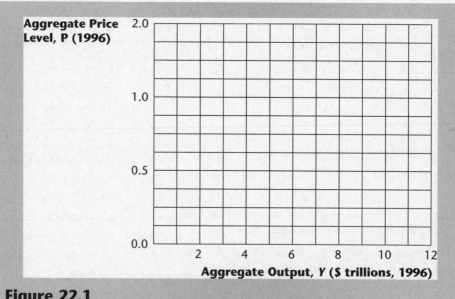

Figure 22.1

   c. Now assume that the money supply decreases to $1 trillion. Generate the new corresponding values of output and plot them on the graph above.

P	Y	P	Y
.5		1.5	
1		2	

2. Use Figure 22.2 to answer parts *a* and *b*.

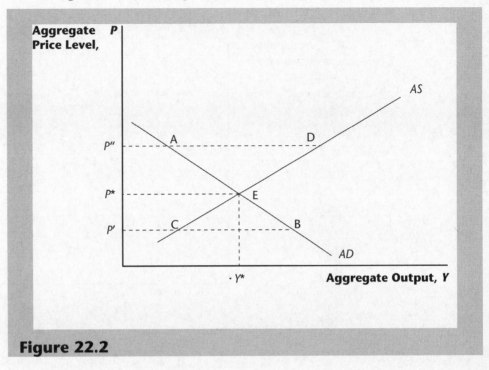

Figure 22.2

a. At which price level is there excess supply? Describe how the economy adjusts back to short-run equilibrium starting from a situation of excess supply.

_____

_____

_____

b. At which price level is there excess demand? Describe how the economy adjusts back to short-run equilibrium starting from a situation of excess demand.

_____

_____

_____

3. Suppose the economy is initially in long-run equilibrium at point 1 as shown in the Figure 3.

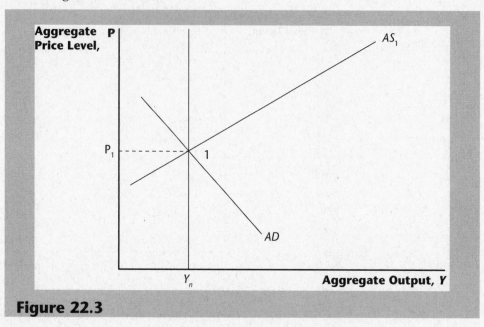

Figure 22.3

a. Use Figure 22.3 to illustrate the effect of an increase in the money supply on the price level (*P*) and aggregate output (*Y*) in the short run.
b. Use Figure 22.3 to illustrate the adjustment back to the long-run equilibrium starting from the short-run equilibrium you illustrated for part *a*.
c. Describe the self-correcting mechanism that brings the economy back to long-run equilibrium.

_____

_____

_____

d. What is the effect of the change in the money supply on aggregate output (*Y*) and the price level (*P*) in the short run?

_____

e. What is the effect of the change in the money supply on aggregate output (*Y*) and the price level (*P*) in the long run?

_____

_____

_____

_____

4. Suppose the economy is initially in long-run equilibrium at point 1 as shown in the Figure 22.4.

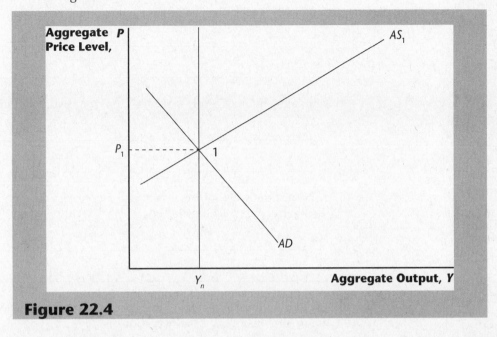

Figure 22.4

a. Use Figure 22.4 to illustrate the effect of a supply shock such as a reduction in the availability of oil on the price level (P) and aggregate output (Y) in the short run.
b. Use Figure 22.4 to illustrate the adjustment back to the long-run equilibrium starting from the short-run equilibrium you illustrated for part (a). Describe the adjustment process back to the long-run equilibrium.

_____

_____

SHORT-ANSWER QUESTIONS

1. According to the component parts approach to deriving aggregate demand, why does the aggregate demand curve slope downward?

_____

_____

2. According to the component parts approach to deriving aggregate demand, what factors cause the aggregate demand curve to shift?

_____

_____

3. According to the quantity theory of money approach to deriving aggregate demand, how does a decrease in the price level lead to an increase in the aggregate quantity demanded?

_____

_____

4. Explain why the aggregate supply curve slopes upward in the short run.

_____

_____

5. Contrast the views of Keynesian and monetarist economists on the speed of the self-correcting mechanism.

_____

_____

6. According to real business cycle theory, what is the major driving force behind short-run business cycle fluctuations?

_____

_____

7. What is hysteresis? How does it account for high unemployment?

_____

_____

8. Describe the movements in aggregate demand and supply that resulted in the rise in inflation and the increase in unemployment during the Vietnam War buildup, 1964–1970.

_____

_____

9. Describe the movements in aggregate demand and supply that resulted in the rise in inflation and the increase in unemployment during the periods of negative supply shocks, 1964–1970 and 1978–1980.

_____

_____

10. Describe the movements in aggregate demand and supply that resulted in the rise in aggregate output, the decrease in unemployment, and the decrease in inflation during the period of favorable supply shocks, 1995–1999.

_____

_____

Critical Thinking

You read in the newspaper that government spending is expected to rise by $30 billion this year and one of the Senators from your state is touting how this increase in spending will lead to an increase in employment and aggregate output. The economy is currently in long-run equilibrium at the natural rate of output.

1. Will the increase in government spending increase employment and aggregate output in the short run?

    _____

    _____

2. Will the increase in government spending increase employment and aggregate output in the long run?

    _____

    _____

3. What will happen to the price level in the long run and the short run as a result of the increase in government spending?

    _____

    _____

4. Now assume that the economy is below the natural rate level of output and your Senator is a follower of Keynes. What policy action, if any, would your Senator likely favor? Why?

    _____

    _____

5. Now assume that the economy is below the natural rate level of output and your Senator is a follower of Milton Freidman. What policy action, if any, would your Senator likely favor? Why?

    _____

    _____

Self-Test

TRUE/FALSE QUESTIONS

_____1.   According to the components approach to deriving aggregate demand, the one primary factor that causes aggregate demand to shift is changes in the quantity of money.

_____2.   The velocity of money measures how quickly consumer expenditures rise following a tax cut.

_____3.   The equation of exchange relates the money supply to aggregate spending.

_____4.   The equation of exchange is transformed into the modern quantity theory of money by assuming that the price level and aggregate output are inversely related.

_____5.   According to the quantity theory of money approach, aggregate demand is comprised of component parts: consumer expenditure, planned investment spending, government spending, and net exports.

_____6.   According to the quantity theory of money approach to deriving aggregate demand, a decrease in the price level leads to an increase in the real money supply, which leads to a decrease in the interest rate and an increase in aggregate demand.

_____7.   A decrease in the price level causes the exchange rate to rise, which leads to a decline in the quantity of aggregate demand.

_____8.   "Animal spirits" refers to waves of consumer and business optimism and pessimism.

_____9.   Keynesian economists believe that the self-correcting mechanism is relatively fast.

_____10.   The natural rate of unemployment is the rate of unemployment that the economy gravitates to in the long run.

_____11.   Inflation rises when the unemployment rate is equal to the natural rate of unemployment.

_____12.   Starting from the natural rate level of output, an increase in consumer expenditure caused by "animal spirits" has no impact on the price level in the long run.

_____13.   The self-correcting mechanism describes how the economy eventually returns to the natural rate level of output regardless of where output is initially.

_____14. When aggregate output is above the natural level of output, the aggregate supply curve shifts to the right; when aggregate output is below the natural rate level of output, the aggregate supply curve shifts to the left.

_____15. During the period 2001–2004, the aggregate supply curve shifted right causing unemployment and inflation to fall.

MULTIPLE-CHOICE QUESTIONS

1. The aggregate demand curve describes the relationship between
   a. the money supply and the interest rate.
   b. the interest rate and the quantity of aggregate output demanded.
   c. the price level and the quantity of aggregate output demanded.
   d. the money supply and the quantity of aggregate output demanded.

2. The aggregate supply curve describes the relationship between
   a. the money supply and the interest rate.
   b. the interest rate and the quantity of aggregate output supplied.
   c. the price level and the quantity of aggregate output supplied.
   d. the money supply and the quantity of aggregate output supplied.

3. According to quantity theory of money approach to deriving aggregate demand, the one primary factor that causes the aggregate demand curve to shift is
   a. changes in the quantity of money.
   b. changes in government spending.
   c. "animal spirits."
   d. All of the above are true.

4. If the money supply is $2 trillion and total nominal spending is $2 trillion, the velocity of money will be
   a. 2.
   b. 1.
   c. 3.
   d. 0.

5. A tightening of the labor market will cause
   a. the aggregate demand curve to shift left.
   b. the aggregate supply curve to shift left.
   c. the aggregate demand curve to shift right.
   d. the aggregate supply curve to shift right.

6. The aggregate supply curve slopes upward because as the overall price level rises,
   a. the price of a unit of output will rise relative to the cost of producing it, which leads to higher profits and higher production.
   b. the price of a unit of output will fall relative to the cost of producing it, which leads to higher profits and higher production.
   c. the price of a unit of output will rise relative to the cost of producing it, which leads to lower profits and higher production.
   d. the price of a unit of output will fall relative to the cost of producing it, which leads to lower profits and higher production.

7. When the price level is above the equilibrium price level, there is
    a. excess supply, and the price level will fall.
    b. excess demand, and the price level will fall.
    c. excess supply, and the price level will rise.
    d. excess demand, and the price level will rise.

8. When the labor market is tight,
    a. wages fall, and the aggregate supply curve shifts left.
    b. wages rise, and the aggregate supply curve shifts left.
    c. wages fall, and the aggregate supply curve shifts right.
    d. wages rise, and the aggregate supply curve shifts right.

9. Keynesian economists
    a. are less likely to see the need for government policy to restore the economy to full employment.
    b. are more likely to see the need for government policy to restore the economy to full employment.
    c. believe that the wage and price adjustment process is reasonably rapid.
    d. are also called monetarist economists.

10. Which of the following will not cause the aggregate demand curve to shift?
    a. a change in government spending
    b. "animal spirits"
    c. a change in the money supply
    d. tightness in the labor market

11. In the short run, a rightward shift in the aggregate demand curve will cause
    a. the price level to rise and output to rise.
    b. the price level to rise and output to fall.
    c. the price level to fall and output to rise.
    d. the price level to fall and output to fall.

12. In the long run, a rightward shift in aggregate demand will cause
    a. the price level to fall and output to rise.
    b. the price level to rise and output to rise.
    c. the price level to rise and output to remain unchanged.
    d. the price level to remain unchanged and output to rise.

13. A rise in the expected price level will cause
    a. aggregate supply curve to shift left.
    b. aggregate demand curve to shift left.
    c. aggregate supply curve to shift right.
    d. aggregate demand curve to shift right.

14. A successful wage push by workers will cause the
    a. aggregate supply curve to shift left.
    b. aggregate demand curve to shift left.
    c. aggregate supply curve to shift right.
    d. aggregate demand curve to shift right.

15. A negative supply shock that raises production costs will cause the
    a. aggregate supply curve to shift left.
    b. aggregate demand curve to shift left.
    c. aggregate supply curve to shift right.
    c. aggregate demand curve to shift right.

16. A leftward shift in aggregate supply *initially* causes
    a. the price level to rise and output to rise.
    b. the price level to rise and output to fall.
    c. the price level to fall and output to rise.
    d. the price level to fall and output to fall.

17. A leftward shift in aggregate supply *ultimately* causes
    a. the price level to fall and output to rise.
    b. the price level to rise and output to rise.
    c. the price level to rise and output to remain unchanged.
    d. the price level to remain unchanged and output to remain unchanged.

18. According to real business cycle theory, short-run business cycle fluctuations are caused by
    a. "animal spirits."
    b. changes in the money supply.
    c. changes in tastes and technology.
    d. changes in net exports.

19. Rising inflation and falling unemployment during the Vietnam War buildup is best described by
    a. a rightward shift in the aggregate demand curve.
    b. a leftward shift in the aggregate demand curve.
    c. a rightward shift in the aggregate supply curve.
    d. a leftward shift in the aggregate supply curve.

20. During the periods of negative supply shocks, 1973–1975 and 1978–1980,
    a. inflation rose and unemployment declined.
    b. inflation declined and unemployment rose.
    c. inflation rose and unemployment rose.
    d. inflation declined and unemployment declined.

Solutions

Definitions:

<u>12</u> aggregate demand curve

<u>13</u> aggregate supply curve

<u>19</u> "animal spirits"

<u>17</u> consumer expenditure

<u>14</u> demand shocks

<u>9</u> equation of exchange

<u>7</u> government spending

<u>16</u> hysteresis

<u>5</u> Keynesians

<u>4</u> monetarists

<u>10</u> natural rate of output

<u>11</u> natural rate of unemployment

<u>6</u> net exports

<u>18</u> planned investment spending

<u>15</u> quantity theory of money

<u>2</u> real business cycle theory

<u>1</u> self-correcting mechanism

<u>3</u> supply shocks

<u>8</u> velocity of money

Practice Problems

1. a.

P	Y
0.5	12
1	6
1.5	4
2	3

b. These points are plotted as *AD* (a) in Figure 22.5.

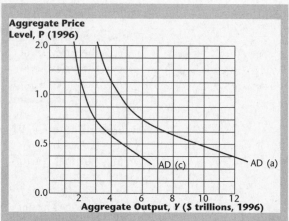

Figure 22.5

c.

P	Y
0.5	6
1	3
1.5	2
2	1.5

These points are plotted as *AD* (c) in Figure 22.5.

2. a. There is excess supply at *P″*. At *P″* the quantity of aggregate output supplied at point D is greater than the quantity of output demanded at point A. Because people want to sell more goods and services than others want to buy, the prices of goods and services will fall and the aggregate price level will drop until equilibrium is reached at *P** (point E).

b. There is excess demand at *P′*. At *P′* the quantity of output demanded is greater than the quantity of output supplied. Because people want to buy more goods and services than others want to sell, the prices of goods and services will rise and the aggregate price level will rise until equilibrium is reached at *P** (point E).

3. a. In the short run, an increase in the money supply will move the economy to 1' in Figure 22.6. The aggregate price level rises to $P_{1'}$ and aggregate output rises to $Y_{1'}$.

    b. Eventually the aggregate supply curve shifts from AS_1 to AS_2 and the economy returns to long-run equilibrium at point 2 in Figure 22.6, where the aggregate price level is P_2 and aggregate output is Y_n.

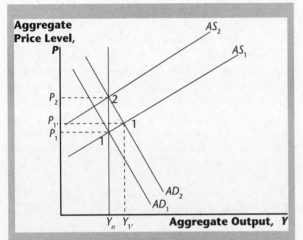

Figure 22.6

    c. At point 1' output is $Y_{1'}$, which is above the natural rate level. Wages will rise eventually shifting the aggregate supply curve leftward to AS_2 where the economy finally comes to rest.

    d. The initial short-run effect of the rightward shift in the aggregate demand curve is a rise in both the price level and output.

    e. The ultimate long-run effect of the rightward shift in the aggregate demand curve is only a rise in the price level. In the long run, aggregate output remains unchanged at Y_n.

4. a. A reduction in the availability of oil causes the aggregate supply curve to shift left from AS_1 to AS_2 in Figure 22.7. The economy initially moves from point 1 to point 2. The aggregate price level rises to P_2 and aggregate output falls to Y_2.

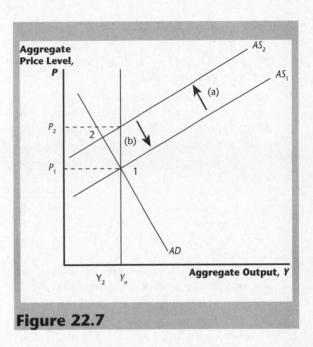

Figure 22.7

    b. At point 2, output is below the natural rate level so wages fall and the aggregate supply curve shifts back to where it was initially at AS_1.

Short-Answer Questions

1. According to the components approach, the aggregate demand curve slopes downward because an increase in the price level reduces the real money supply and leads to a higher interest rate and an appreciation of the domestic currency. The higher interest rate reduces investment spending and the appreciation of the domestic currency reduces net exports, both of which reduce aggregate output.

2. According to the components approach, changes in the money supply, changes in government spending, taxes, investment, consumer expenditures, and net exports shift the aggregate demand curve.

3. Holding the nominal money supply and velocity constant, the equation of exchange implies that a higher price level is associated with a lower level of aggregate output and a lower price level is associated with a higher level of aggregate output.

4. In the short run, the costs of many factors of production are fixed, so when the overall price level rises, the price of a unit of output will rise relative to the cost of producing it, and profit per unit will rise. Firms respond by increasing production.

5. Keyneisan economists believe that the self-correcting mechanism is slow while monetarists believe the self-correcting mechanism is reasonably rapid.

6. According to real business cycle theory, shocks to tastes and technology are the major driving forces behind short-run fluctuations in the business cycle.

7. Hysteresis is said to occur when a departure from full employment levels are a result of past high unemployment. When unemployment rises as a result of a reduction in aggregate demand, the natural rate of unemployment rises above the full employment level. This could occur because the unemployed become discouraged and do not look hard for work or because employers may be reluctant to hire workers who have been unemployed for a long time.

8. Increased spending on the Vietnam War as well as faster money growth shifted the aggregate demand curve right, which resulted in higher aggregate output, lower unemployment, and a rise in the price level.

9. In 1973 the OPEC oil embargo caused oil prices to quadruple. In addition, crop failures caused food prices to rise, and removal of wage and price controls caused wages to rise. These three factors caused the aggregate supply curve to shift left, which led to a rise in both the price level and the unemployment rate. Oil and food prices once again rose sharply in 1978, causing the aggregate supply curve to shift left. As a result, the price level and unemployment rate both shot upwards.

10. Over the period 1995–1999 medical costs fell and productivity rose. These two factors caused the aggregate supply curve to shift right. As a result aggregate output rose and unemployment and inflation both fell.

Critical Thinking

1. The increase in government spending will shift the aggregate demand curve to the right, which will cause employment and aggregate output to rise in the short run.

2. No. In the long run aggregate output returns to the natural rate level of output but at a higher price level.

3. The increase in government spending shifts the aggregate demand curve right and leads to an increase in the price level in the short run. In the long run, wages increase and the

aggregate supply curve shifts left causing the price level to rise further.

4. If your Senator is a follower of Keynes, he would likely favor an activist approach, which means that if the economy is below the natural rate level of output he would advocate boosting government spending, cutting taxes, or increasing the money supply in order to shift the aggregate demand curve back to the natural rate level of output. He believes that the automatic adjustment mechanism is relatively slow.

5. If your Senator is a follower of Friedman, he would likely favor an nonactivist approach, which means that if the economy is below the natural rate level of output he would advocate leaving government spending, taxes, and the money supply unchanged. He believes that the automatic adjustment mechanism is relatively quick and the economy will adjust back to the natural rate level of output if left alone.

True/False Questions

1. F
2. F
3. T
4. F
5. F
6. F
7. F
8. T
9. F
10. T
11. F
12. T
13. T
14. F
15. F

Multiple-Choice Questions

1. c
2. c
3. a
4. b
5. b
6. a
7. a

8. b
9. b
10. d
11. a
12. c
13. a
14. a
15. a
16. b
17. d
18. c
19. a
20. c

23

Transmission Mechanisms of Monetary Policy: The Evidence

Chapter Review

PREVIEW

Aggregate output, the unemployment rate, and inflation fluctuate constantly. Policymakers face the question of what policy or policies, if any, they should use to reduce those fluctuations. To answer that question, monetary policymakers must have an accurate assessment of the effect of their policies on the economy. This chapter looks at the empirical evidence on the effect of monetary policy on the economy.

FRAMEWORK FOR EVALUATING EMPIRICAL EVIDENCE

There are two types of empirical evidence on the affect of changes in the quantity of money on the economy. The first, called *structural model evidence,* looks at the channels through which money affects the economy. The second, called *reduced-form evidence,* looks directly at the relationship between money and the economy. These two different types of empirical evidence lead to different conclusions about the importance of monetary policy to economic fluctuations. Aggregate demand (described in the previous chapter) is an example of a structural model because it describes the channels through which monetary policy affects the economy. According to the aggregate demand model, an increase in the quantity of money leads to a decrease in interest rates, which leads to an increase in investment spending and an increase in aggregate output. The channels through which money affects the economy are called the *transmission mechanisms of monetary policy*. The quantity theory of money approach to aggregate demand is an example of a reduced-form model because it suggests that money and aggregate output are highly correlated, but it does not specify the channels or mechanisms through which money affects the economy.

If the particular structural model we are analyzing is correct and contains all of the channels through which money affects the economy, then there are three major advantages of a structural model over a reduced-form model. Those advantages are:

It provides evidence on the direction of causation (from money to aggregate output rather than the other way around); it provides more accurate predictions of the effect of money on the economy; it helps us understand how changes in institutions will affect the transmission mechanisms. All of these advantages assume that we know the correct structure of the economy. The main advantage of reduced-form evidence is that by not specifying a channel through which money affects the economy, it allows for many possible channels including channels that are not yet discovered. But a disadvantage of reduced-form evidence is that it only shows correlation and not causation, so it cannot rule out the possibility of *reverse causation* whereby changes in aggregate output cause changes in money.

Monetarists focused on reduced-form evidence and believed that changes in the money supply were very important to economic fluctuations. *Keynesians* focused on structural model evidence and were less likely to find that monetary policy is important. Keynesians believed that monetary policy was ineffective during the Great Depression for three reasons: Treasury bill rates were extremely low; empirical studies showed very little relationship between interest rates and investment spending; surveys of business people suggested that interest rates were not important to investment decisions. The Keynesians interpreted low, short-term interest rates to mean that monetary policy was expansionary yet ineffective during the Great Depression. Monetarists Milton Friedman and Anna Schwartz showed that monetary policy was actually contractionary during the Great Depression. Keynesians had focused on low nominal interest rates to claim that monetary policy had been expansionary. Monetarists showed that real interest rates were actually quite high. Monetarists also claimed that the interest-rate effect on investment spending is only one of many channels through which money affects the economy.

In the early 1960s, Milton Freidman and other monetarists published articles based on reduced-form evidence that showed that money has a strong effect on economic activity. This early monetarist evidence can be grouped into three categories: timing, statistical, and historical. The historical evidence combined with the timing evidence and statistical evidence suggests that monetary policy does matter. Most Keynesians currently believe that monetary policy has important effects on economic activity.

TRANSMISSION MECHANISMS OF MONETARY POLICY

Following the monetarists–Keynesian debate in the early 1960s, economists identified additional channels through which lower interest rates lead to higher expenditures. Lower interest rates stimulate *consumer durable expenditures* as well as net exports. Expansionary monetary policy leads to higher stock, land, and housing prices. Higher stock prices boost investment spending by raising Tobin's q (the market value of a firm divided by the replacement cost of capital). Higher stock prices (as well as higher land and housing prices) boost consumer wealth and lead to higher *consumption*.

In addition to these channels, which operate through interest rates, economists have identified a set of channels termed the *credit view*. According to the credit view, monetary policy operates by affecting bank lending as well as firm and household balance sheets. Recall from earlier in the text that banks are especially well suited to solve asymmetric information problems in credit markets. If banks provide lending services to firms that otherwise would not have access to credit markets (small firms for example), then expansionary monetary policy will lead to increased lending, increased investment spending, and increased aggregate output. The balance sheet channel also arises from the presence of asymmetric information problems in credit markets. Expansionary monetary policy improves firm and household balance sheets. As balance sheets improve, asymmetric information and moral hazard problems are reduced and banks are more willing to lend to firms and households, which lead to increased spending.

In response to the subprime financial crisis, the Fed eased monetary policy aggressively starting in September of 2007. Despite the Fed's rapid response, the economy continued to weaken. One reason was that adverse selection and moral hazard problems increased in credit markets, which in turn led to a slowdown in the economy. Another reason was that declines in stock market and housing prices lowered household wealth, which led to restrained consumer spending and weaker investment because of the resulting drop in Tobin's q.

LESSONS FOR MONETARY POLICY

The analysis of this chapter implies the following four basic policy lessons.

1. It is dangerous always to associate the easing or the tightening of monetary policy with a fall or a rise in short-term nominal interest rates.

2. Other asset prices besides those on short-term debt instruments contain important information about the stance of monetary policy because they are important elements in various monetary policy transmission mechanisms.

3. Monetary policy can be highly effective in reviving a weak economy even if short-term interest rates are already near zero.

4. Avoiding unanticipated fluctuations in the price level is an important objective of monetary policy, thus providing a rationale for price stability as the primary long-run goal for monetary policy.

Since 1990 the Japanese economy has suffered from deflation and low growth. The Bank of Japan (Japan's central bank) took the view that monetary policy was sufficiently expansionary when nominal interest rates fell to near zero levels. But Japan suffered from deflation, which means that real interest rates were actually high and monetary policy was tight. Another indication that Japanese monetary policy was not expansionary was that stock and real estate prices collapsed. Officials at the Bank of Japan claimed that monetary policy became ineffective when interest rates fell to near zero. According to the third lesson, above, monetary policy can still be effective even when interest rates are near zero. Japan might have had far more success if it had heeded the advice from these four basic lessons.

Helpful Hints

The early reduced-form evidence suggested that changes in money were related to changes in aggregate economic activity. The early structural model evidence suggested that the link between changes in money and the economy was weak. These conflicting pieces of evidence led economists to search for additional channels through which money effects the economy. Economists have identified several additional channels.

Terms and Definitions

Choose a definition for each key term.

Key Terms:

_____consumer durable expenditure

_____consumption

_____credit view

_____Keynesians

_____monetarists

_____reduced-form evidence

_____reverse causation

_____structural model evidence

_____transmission mechanisms of monetary
policy

Definitions:

1. Followers of Milton Friedman, who tend to focus on reduced-form evidence on the importance of monetary policy to economic fluctuations

2. A situation in which one variable is said to cause another variable when in reality the reverse is true

3. Spending by consumers on durable items such as automobiles and household appliances

4. Monetary transmission operating through asymmetric information effects on credit markets

5. Evidence that examines whether one variable has an affect on another by simply looking directly at the relationship between the two variables

6. Spending by consumers on nondurable goods and services

7. The channel through which the money supply affects economic activity

8. Followers of John Maynard Keynes who tend to focus on structural evidence on the importance of monetary policy to economic fluctuations

9. Evidence that examines whether one variable affects another by using data to build a model illustrating the channels through which this variable affects the other

Problems and Short-Answer Questions

PRACTICE PROBLEMS

1. For each of the following statements, indicate whether reduced form evidence or structural model evidence is being presented by writing in the space provided an **R** for reduced-form evidence or an **S** for structural model evidence.

   ____a. An increase in the money supply is followed by an increase in aggregate output.

   ____b. Happy people earn higher incomes.

   ____c. Drinking one ounce of alcohol per day appears to reduce cholesterol levels in the bloodstream, reducing the likelihood of coronary heart disease and heart attack.

   ____d. A reduction in the money supply causes the volume of loans to fall, which causes investment to fall as banks ration credit. This in turn causes aggregate output to fall.

   ____e. Medical research has found that men who take one aspirin per day following a heart attack significantly reduce the probability of a second heart attack.

____f. An increase in the money supply causes interest rates to fall, which causes an increase in consumer durable expenditures and an increase in aggregate output.

____g. An increase in the price of oil is followed by a reduction in aggregate output.

____h. An increase in the money supply leads to an increase in stock prices, a rise in Tobin's q, and an increase in investment spending by firms.

2. Describe the reverse causation story for each of the following statements.
   a. Increased police patrolling leads to higher crime rates.
   b. Happier people earn more income.
   c. A decrease in the money supply leads to a decline in aggregate output.
   d. Drinking coffee causes heart attacks.
   e. Going to the hospital increases the chance of death.
   f. Children who read do better in school.

3. a. What three pieces of evidence led early Keynesian economists to believe that monetary policy was ineffective?

   _____

   _____

   _____

   _____

   b. Was early Keynesian evidence structural model evidence or reduced-form evidence?

   _____

   c. What three types of evidence did early monetarists present that showed a strong effect of money on economic activity?

   _____

   _____

   _____

   d. Was the early monetarist evidence structural model evidence or reduced-form evidence?

   _____

   e. What are the three objections to the Friedman–Meiselman evidence on the importance of money for economic activity?

   _____

   _____

   _____

f.   Where do Keynesians currently stand on the debate over the importance of money for economic activity?

_____

_____

4.   Consider the following hypothetical data on the supply of money and aggregate output. Assume that the direction of causation runs from output to money in this hypothetical economy.

a.   Calculate the rate of money growth for years 2 through 5 to complete the table.

Year	Output, Y	Money Supply, M	Rate of Money Supply Growth, $\Delta M/M$
1	510	90	_____
2	525	100	_____
3	550	125	_____
4	550	125	_____
5	510	90	_____
6	510	90	_____
7	525	100	_____

b.   Plot the three data series Y, M and $\Delta M/M$ onto Figures 23.1, 23.2, and 23.3 below; label the peaks and troughs for each data series.

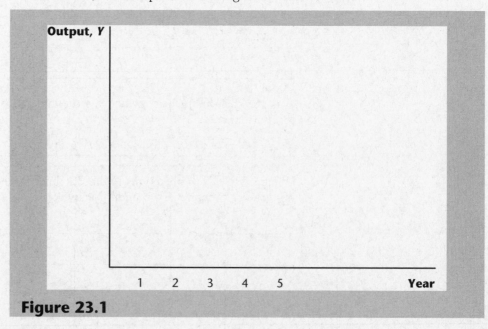

Figure 23.1

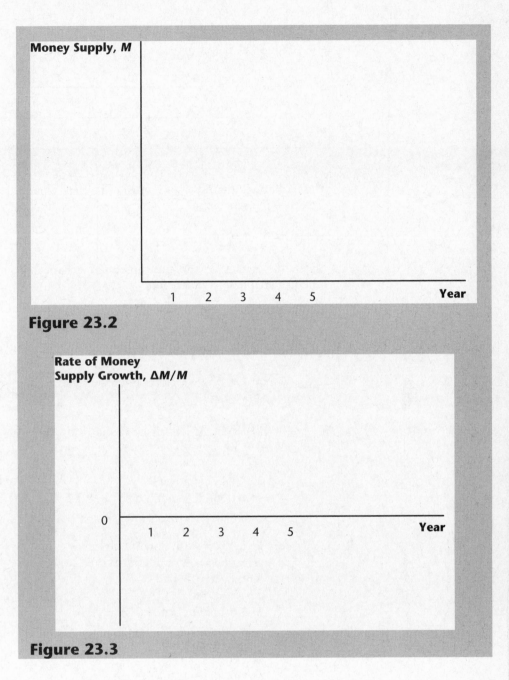

Figure 23.2

Figure 23.3

c. What is the principle of *post hoc, ergo propter hoc,* and what does it imply about the direction of causation between the rate of money supply growth and aggregate output in Figures 23.1 and 23.3?

_____

_____

_____

d. Explain why timing evidence can be a dangerous tool for deciding on the direction of causation.

_____

_____

_____

5. The traditional interest rate channel of monetary policy can be characterized by the following schematic

$M \uparrow \rightarrow i_r \downarrow \rightarrow I \uparrow \rightarrow Y \uparrow$

Match the names of the transmission mechanisms on the right with their schematic depictions on the left.

_____1. $M \uparrow \rightarrow i_r \downarrow \rightarrow E \downarrow \rightarrow NX \uparrow \rightarrow Y \uparrow$

_____2. $M \uparrow \rightarrow P_S \uparrow \rightarrow q \uparrow \rightarrow I \uparrow \rightarrow Y \uparrow$

_____3. $M \uparrow \rightarrow P_S \uparrow \rightarrow$ wealth $\uparrow \rightarrow$ consumption $\uparrow \rightarrow Y \uparrow$

_____4. $M \uparrow \rightarrow$ bank deposits $\uparrow \rightarrow$ bank loans $\uparrow \rightarrow I \uparrow \rightarrow Y \uparrow$

_____5. $M \uparrow \rightarrow P_S \uparrow \rightarrow$ adverse selection $\downarrow \rightarrow$ moral hazard $\downarrow \rightarrow I \uparrow \rightarrow Y \uparrow$

a. Tobin's q theory

b. household liquidity effect channel

c. cash flow channel

d. unanticipated price level

e. exchange rate effect

f. balance sheet channel

g. bank lending channel

h. wealth effects channel

_____6. $M \uparrow \rightarrow i \downarrow \rightarrow$ cash flow $\uparrow \rightarrow$ adverse selection $\downarrow \rightarrow$ moral hazard $\downarrow \rightarrow$ lending $\uparrow \rightarrow I \uparrow \rightarrow Y \uparrow$

_____7. $M \uparrow \rightarrow$ unanticipated $P \uparrow \rightarrow$ adverse selection $\downarrow \rightarrow$ moral hazard $\downarrow \rightarrow$ lending $\uparrow \rightarrow I \uparrow \rightarrow Y \uparrow$

_____8. $M \uparrow \rightarrow P_S \uparrow \rightarrow$ value of financial assets $\uparrow \rightarrow$ likelihood of financial distress $\downarrow \rightarrow$ consumer durable and housing expenditure $\uparrow \rightarrow Y \uparrow$

6. a. List the four basic lessons about monetary policy from this chapter.

_____

_____

_____

_____

b. Explain how heeding the advice from each of these four lessons might have led to a far more successful conduct of monetary policy in Japan in recent years.

_____

_____

_____

SHORT-ANSWER QUESTIONS

1. What are the advantages of structural model evidence?

_____

_____

2. What is the main disadvantage of structural model evidence?

_____

_____

3. What is the main advantage of reduced-form evidence?

_____

_____

4. Explain how monetary policy can stimulate the economy, even if nominal interest rates hit a floor of zero during a deflationary episode.

_____

_____

5. What does real business cycle theory imply about the direction of causation between monetary policy on the economy?

_____

_____

6. What argument, based on the distinction between real and nominal interest rates, did Friedman and Schwartz use to argue that monetary policy was contractionary during the Great Depression?

_____

_____

7. Why might the bank lending channel not be as powerful in the United States as it once was?

   _____

   _____

8. Which transmission mechanism suggests that the nominal interest rate matters for investment spending and aggregate output? Why?

   _____

   _____

9. Why are credit channels likely to be important?

   _____

   _____

10. Why did the economy continue to slow in 2008 despite the Fed's very aggressive easing starting in late 2007?

    _____

    _____

Critical Thinking

Suppose you are hired as an economic adviser to the Central Bank of Causation (a fictitious country). The head of the central bank shows you a graph indicating that the growth rate of money rises about three months before aggregate output rises and falls about three months before aggregate output falls.

1. Explain to the head of the central bank why it would be dangerous to base monetary policy decisions on the evidence presented in this graph.

   _____

   _____

   _____

   _____

2. Suppose after careful research you have discovered that the direction of causation runs from money to aggregate output. The economy of Causation has just entered a recession in which the nominal interest rate is near zero and there is deflation. What policy would you recommend to bring the economy out of recession?

_____

_____

_____

_____

3. Suppose after implementing the policy you described in your answer to question 2, the economy experienced a subprime financial crisis like the one that hit the U.S. economy in the summer of 2007. Explain to the head of the central bank why the policy you recommended to bring the economy out of recession will likely result in a slow recovery.

_____

_____

_____

_____

Self-Test

TRUE/FALSE QUESTIONS

_____1. Reduced-form evidence looks at the channels through which monetary policy affects the economy.

_____2. Correlation does not imply causation.

_____3. A disadvantage of structural models is that they may ignore the transmission mechanisms for monetary policy that are most important.

_____4. Monetarists tended to focus on structural model evidence while Keynesians tended to focus on reduced-form evidence.

_____5. Early Keynesians thought monetary policy was ineffective.

_____6. During periods of deflation, the real interest rate is lower than the nominal interest rate.

_____7. According to the principle of *post hoc, ergo propter hoc,* if event A occurs before event B, event A must have caused event B.

_____8. The timing evidence on the link between the quantity of money and economic activity does not eliminate the possibility of reverse causation.

_____9. According to the interest rate channel, expansionary monetary policy reduces the real interest rate, which stimulates investment spending and leads to an increase in aggregate output.

_____10. Consumption is spending on all goods and services including durable goods.

_____11. An increase in housing prices, which raises the price of housing relative to the replacement cost, leads to a rise in Tobin's q for housing and an increase in the production of housing as well.

_____12. Since the mid-1980s, the bank lending channel in the United States has become more powerful.

_____13. When expansionary monetary policy lowers interest rates, high-risk borrowers make up a greater fraction of those demanding loans.

_____14. Asset prices besides those on short-term debt instruments contain no information about the stance of monetary policy.

_____15. Monetary policy is ineffective in economies with deflation and short-term interest rates near zero.

MULTIPLE-CHOICE QUESTIONS

1. An advantage of structural model evidence over reduced-form evidence is that
   a. it helps researchers determine the direction of causation.
   b. it helps researchers predict the effect of changes in M on Y more accurately.
   c. it helps researchers to anticipate how changes in institutions will affect the link between M and Y.
   d. All of the above are true.

2. An advantage of reduced-form evidence over structural evidence is that
   a. it helps determine the direction of causation.
   b. it helps researchers identify the relationship between money and output when we are not sure of the transmission mechanism.
   c. it helps researchers to anticipate how changes in institutions will affect the link between M and Y.
   d. All of the above are true.

3. The early Keynesians' belief that monetary policy was _____ was based on the fact that _____.
   a. ineffective; nominal interest rates fell below 1% during the Great Depression
   b. effective; nominal interest rates fell below 1% during the Great Depression
   c. ineffective; real interest rates fell below 1% during the Great Depression
   d. effective; real interest rates fell below 1% during the Great Depression

4. Friedman and Schwartz's evidence that monetary policy was contractionary during the Great Depression was based on the fact that
   a. the money supply contracted and nominal interest rates rose.
   b. the money supply contracted and real interest rates rose.
   c. the money supply expanded and nominal interest rates declined.
   d. the money supply expanded and real interest rates declined.

5. Early monetarists presented the following three types of evidence to demonstrate the importance of money in determining aggregate economic activity:
   a. timing evidence, reduced-form evidence, and structural model evidence.
   b. timing evidence, reduced-form evidence, and historical evidence.
   c. timing evidence, statistical evidence, and structural evidence.
   d. timing evidence, statistical evidence, and historical evidence.

6. The statistical evidence presented by Friedman and Meiselman suggested that
   a. monetary policy and autonomous spending are equally important in explaining movements in aggregate output.
   b. neither monetary policy nor autonomous spending are important in explaining movements in aggregate output.
   c. monetary policy is more important than autonomous spending in explaining movements in aggregate output.
   d. autonomous spending is more important than monetary policy in explaining movements in aggregate output.

7. When nominal interest rates hit a floor of zero during a deflationary episode,
   a. monetary policy can no longer stimulate the economy.
   b. monetary policy can stimulate the economy by pushing nominal interest rates below zero.
   c. monetary policy can stimulate the economy by raising the expected inflation rate.
   d. monetary policy can stimulate the economy by reducing the expected inflation rate.

8. According to the exchange rate effect, expansionary monetary policy will cause
   a. domestic interest rates to rise, the dollar to appreciate, and net exports to fall.
   b. domestic interest rates to fall, the dollar to depreciate, and net exports to fall.
   c. domestic interest rates to rise, the dollar to depreciate, and net exports to rise.
   d. domestic interest rates to fall, the dollar to depreciate, and net exports to rise.

9. According to Tobin's q theory, expansionary monetary policy will lead to an increase in investment spending because
   a. the market value of firms rises relative to the replacement cost of capital.
   b. the replacement cost of capital rises relative to the market value of firms.
   c. firms' balance sheets improve, which reduces adverse selection and moral hazard.
   d. the likelihood of financial distress falls, which leads to an increase in bank lending.

10. According to the bank lending channel, lending by banks rises when the money supply expands because
    a. the interest rate falls and the quantity of loans demanded rises.
    b. Tobin's q for banks rises.
    c. bank deposits increase, which leads to an increase in the quantity of bank loans available.
    d. stock prices rise, causing consumer wealth to rise, which increases the demand for bank loans.

11. Because of asymmetric information problems in credit markets, monetary policy may affect economic activity through the balance sheet channel, which holds that an increase in the money supply
    a. raises equity prices, which lowers the cost of new capital relative to the market value of firms, thereby increasing investment spending.
    b. raises the net worth of firms, decreasing adverse selection and moral hazard problems, thereby increasing banks' willingness to lend to finance investment spending.
    c. raises the level of bank reserves, deposits, and the quantity of bank loans available, which raises the spending by those individuals who do not have access to credit markets.
    d. reduces the real interest rate, which leads to an increase in the quantity of bank loans demanded.

12. According to the cash flow channel, a 1 percentage point rise in both the nominal interest rate and expected inflation will
    a. leave the cash flow of firms unchanged.
    b. decrease the cash flow of firms, increasing the moral hazard and adverse selection problem, which makes banks less willing to lend to firms.
    c. decrease the cash flow of firms, decreasing the moral hazard and adverse selection problem, which makes banks less willing to lend to firms.
    d. increase the cash flow of firms, decreasing the moral hazard and adverse selection problem, which makes banks more willing to lend to firms.

13. When the price level rises unexpectedly, a firm's debt burdens _____ and net worth increases. The effect is to _____ adverse selection and moral hazard problems, which results in increased lending.
    a. increase; increase
    b. increase; decrease
    c. decrease; increase
    d. decrease; decrease

14. Because of asymmetric information about their quality, consumer durables and housing are _____ to sell compared to liquid assets and therefore _____ to hold in periods of financial distress.
    a. more difficult; less desirable
    b. less difficult; less desirable
    c. more difficult; more desirable
    d. less difficult; more desirable

15. Expansionary monetary policy _____ the likelihood of financial distress, which _____ consumer durable and housing expenditures.
    a. increases; increases
    b. increases; decreases
    c. decreases; increases
    d. decreases; decreases

16. Credit channels are likely to be important monetary transmission mechanisms because
    a. asymmetric information, which forms the core of credit channel theory, does a good job of explaining why financial institutions exist.
    b. credit market imperfections do appear to affect firm spending and employment decisions.
    c. small firms, which are more likely to be credit constrained, appear to be most affected by monetary policy.
    d. All of the above are true.

17. One reason the economy continued to weaken in 2008 was
    a. the Fed was slow to react by lowering interest rates.
    b. adverse selection and moral hazard problems increased.
    c. credit spreads narrowed.
    d. stock prices fell, which led to an increase in Tobin's q.

18. It is dangerous always to associate the easing or tightening of monetary policy with a fall or a rise in short-term nominal interest rates because
    a. central banks often target the money supply rather than interest rates.
    b. stock prices are a better indicator of whether monetary policy is tight or easy.
    c. movements in nominal interest rates do not always correspond to movements in real interest rates.
    d. short-term interest rates have very little impact on borrowing and lending.

19. If short-term interest rates are low, stock prices and land prices are _____, and the value of the domestic currency is _____, then monetary policy is clearly _____.
    a. low; low; easy
    b. high; high; easy
    c. low; high; tight
    d. high; low; easy

20. In the late 1990s in Japan, short-term nominal interest rates _____ while short-term real interest rates _____, indicating that monetary policy was _____.
    a. increased; decreased; tight
    b. increased; decreased; easy
    c. decreased; increased; tight
    d. decreased; increased; easy

Solutions

Definitions:

_3_ consumer durable expenditure

_6_ consumption

_4_ credit view

_8_ Keynesians

_1_ monetarists

_5_ reduced-form evidence

_2_ reverse causation

_9_ structural model evidence

_7_ transmission mechanisms of monetary policy

Practice Problems

1.

    _R_ a.

    _R_ b.

    _S_ c.

    _S_ d.

    _R_ e.

    _S_ f.

    _R_ g.

    _S_ h.

2. a. More police are hired to patrol in areas where there is a high crime rate.

    b. People who earn more income are happier.

    c. A decline in aggregate output leads to a decline in the money supply.

    d. People who are stressed and therefore prone to heart attacks drink more coffee.

    e. People who are close to death go to the hospital.

    f. Children who do well in school like to read.

3. a. (1) During the Great Depression, interest rates on U.S. Treasury securities fell to extremely low levels, suggesting that monetary policy was easy but aggregate output still contracted sharply. (2) Early empirical evidence found no link between nominal interest rates and investment spending. (3) Surveys of businesspeople revealed that investment decisions were not influenced by interest rates.

    b. Early Keynesian evidence was structural model evidence.

    c. (1) Timing evidence: The money supply tends to decline prior to the decline in aggregate output. (2) Statistical evidence: Changes in the quantity of money are correlated with changes in aggregate output. (3) Historical evidence: Historical episodes in which decreases in the money supply were clearly exogenous were followed by a decline in aggregate output.

    d. Early monetarist evidence was reduced-form evidence.

    e. (1) Reduced-form evidence is subject to the reverse-causation problem. (2) The Keynesian model was characterized too simplistically in the Friedman–Meiselman tests. (3) The Freidman–Meiselmen measure of autonomous expenditure might have been constructed poorly.

    f. Many Keynesians have shifted their views toward the monetarist position, but not all the way.

4. a.

Year	Output, Y	Money Supply, M	Rate of Money Supply Growth, $\Delta M/M$
1	510	90	--
2	525	100	11%
3	550	125	25%
4	550	125	0%
5	510	90	−28%
6	510	90	0
7	525	100	11%

b.

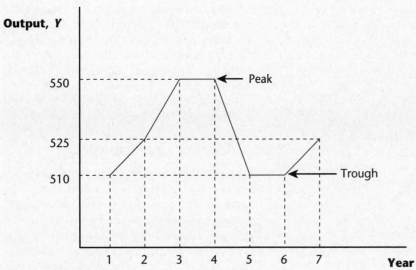

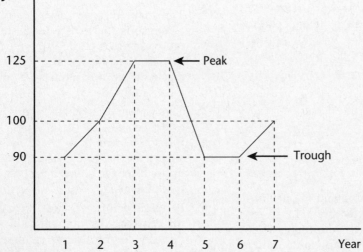

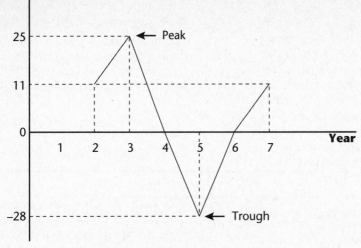

c. The principle of *post hoc, ergo propter hoc* is that if event A occurs before event B, event A must have caused event B. The growth rate of money reaches a peak in period 3 and then turns downward in period 4. Aggregate output turns downward in period 5. The growth rate of the money supply reaches a trough in period 5 and then turns upward in period 6. Aggregate output turns upward in period 7. Thus, the growth rate of the money supply appears to "lead" aggregate output even though the money supply and aggregate output move up and down in unison.

d. As the above example illustrates, by comparing the growth rate of the money supply to aggregate output, we might incorrectly infer that money causes output even through (as was assumed) the direction of causation is the opposite.

5. _e_ 1.
   _a_ 2.
   _h_ 3.
   _g_ 4.
   _f_ 5.
   _c_ 6.
   _d_ 7.
   _b_ 8.

6. a. The four basic lessons about monetary policy from this chapter are: (1) It is dangerous always to associate the easing or the tightening of monetary policy with a fall or a rise in short-term nominal interest rates. (2) Other asset prices besides those on short-term debt instruments contain important information about the stance of monetary policy. (3) Monetary policy can be highly effective in reviving a weak economy even when short-term interest rates are already near zero. (4) Avoiding unanticipated fluctuation in the price level is an important objective of monetary policy, thus providing a rationale for price stability as the primary long-run goal for monetary policy.

b. Japan thought monetary policy was expansionary because nominal interest rates were near zero, but in fact, real interest rates were quite high. The Bank of Japan claimed that it had no ability to

stimulate the economy because interest rates were near zero, but it could have reduced real interest rates by raising expected inflation. The Bank of Japan could have seen that monetary policy was tight by looking at falling stock and real estate prices. The Bank of Japan would have been more successful if it had prevented deflation.

Short-Answer Questions

1. The advantages of structural model evidence are: It provides clearer evidence on the direction of causation; it is helpful in predicting the effect of changes in M on Y; it helps us to understand and predict how changes in institutions (such as the elimination of Regulation Q) will effect the link between M and Y.

2. The main disadvantage of structural model evidence is that it is only useful if we know the correct structure of the model. Structural models may ignore the transmission mechanisms for monetary policy that are most important.

3. The main advantage of reduced-form evidence is that it does not impose restrictions on the way monetary policy affects the economy. As a result, it may help us to discover some unknown transmission mechanisms.

4. If nominal interest rates hit a floor of zero, the central bank can still reduce real interest rates by committing to increase the inflation rate.

5. Real business cycle theory implies that the direction of causation runs from the business cycle (aggregate output) to money.

6. Friedman and Schwartz showed that even though nominal interest rates were low, real interest rates were high indicating that monetary policy was actually tight during the Great Depression.

7. The bank lending channel may not be as powerful in the United States as it once was because current U.S. regulation no longer imposes restrictions on banks' ability to raise funds.

8. The cash flow channel suggests that the nominal interest rate matters for investment spending. As nominal interest rates fall, firms' balance sheets improve, which makes it easier for lenders to assess whether the firm or

household will be able to pay its bills. As a result, adverse selection and moral hazard decline and lending increases.

9. Credit channels are likely to be important monetary transmission mechanisms because (1) asymmetric information, which forms the core of credit channel theory, does a good job of explaining why financial institutions exist; (2) credit market imperfections do appear to affect firm spending and employment decisions; and (3) small firms, which are more likely to be credit-constrained, appear to be most affected by monetary policy.

10. One reason was that adverse selection and moral hazard problems increased in credit markets, leading to a slowdown in the economy. Another reason was that declines in stock market and housing prices lowered household wealth, which led to restrained consumer spending and weaker investment because of the resulting drop in Tobin's q.

Critical Thinking

1. The fact that changes in money growth occur before changes in output does not necessarily imply that money causes output. In fact, if the quantity of money and aggregate output move in unison, simply by converting the quantity of money to a growth rate will make it appear as if changes in money growth lead changes in aggregate output.

2. Even when nominal interest rates are near zero and there is deflation, the central bank can stimulate aggregate output by committing to raising inflationary expectations, which will reduce the real interest rate.

3. A subprime financial crisis will make it more difficult for lenders to separate good credit risks from bad credit risks so the potential for adverse selection and moral hazard has increased. As a result, lending has slowed which will slow the recovery from recession even if the real interest rate has declined because of an increase in expected inflation.

True/False Questions

1. F
2. T
3. T
4. F
5. T
6. F
7. T
8. T
9. T
10. F
11. T
12. F
13. F
14. F
15. F

Multiple-Choice Questions

1. d
2. b
3. a
4. b
5. d
6. c
7. c
8. d
9. a
10. c
11. b
12. d
13. d
14. a
15. c
16. d
17. b
18. c
19. d
20. c

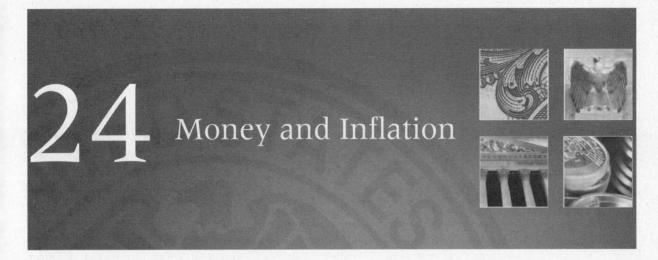

24 Money and Inflation

Chapter Review

PREVIEW

Inflation is caused by high growth rates of the money supply. This chapter applies aggregate demand and supply analysis to show that inflationary monetary policy is an offshoot of large government deficits or policies aimed at hitting high-employment targets.

MONEY AND INFLATION: EVIDENCE

Countries with extremely high rates of money supply growth also have high inflation. Such reduced-form evidence is subject to the reverse causality problem (discussed last chapter). But historical evidence in which high money growth is clearly exogenous rules out reverse causality.

MEANING OF INFLATION

Inflation is a continual and rapid rise in the price level that is persistent. Inflation, as typically reported in the popular press, is simply a one-month percentage change in the price level. It is only when that one-month percentage change in the price level is persistently repeated over a substantial period of time that it becomes inflation. By this definition, almost all economists agree with Milton Friedman's proposition that "inflation is always and everywhere a monetary phenomenon."

VIEWS OF INFLATION

According to aggregate demand and supply analysis, a one-time increase in the money supply, a one-time increase in government spending, or a one-time negative supply shock such as an increase in the price of oil will all lead to a one-time increase in the price level. But inflation is a persistent, not one-time, increase in the price level. In order for any of these three aggregate demand shift factors to cause inflation, they must persistently increase as well. Of these three shift factors, only the money supply is capable of persistent increase.

ORIGINS OF INFLATIONARY MONETARY POLICY

Inflation is the result of a persistent increase in the money supply. A persistent increase in the money supply is represented as a continual rightward shift in the aggregate demand curve. If a central bank starts a continual rise in the money supply in response to a negative supply shock, the resulting inflation is called *cost-push inflation*. If a central bank starts a continual rise in the money supply in an effort to push employment and output above the full-employment level, the resulting inflation is called *demand-pull inflation*. Beginning from long-run equilibrium, if workers demand higher wages, the aggregate supply curve will shift left causing the price level to rise and real output to fall. If left alone, the price level would decline and real output would return to its full-employment level. But if policymakers try to increase employment back to full employment before it returns on its own, the aggregate demand curve will shift right and the price level will rise even further. Even though the price level has increased two times (the first time because of the negative supply shock and the second time because of the *accommodating policy*), we still don't have inflation. But if workers respond by asking for even higher wages, the aggregate supply curve will again shift to the right and the process begins again. If the central bank continues to accommodate the increased wage demands by workers by increasing the money supply, then cost-push inflation will result.

If policymakers try to push the unemployment rate below the natural rate by increasing the money supply, shifting the aggregate demand curve to the right causing the price level and aggregate output to rise. As wages adjust, the aggregate supply curve shifts back, and the economy returns to full employment but at a higher price level. If the central bank tries to push the unemployment rate below the natural rate again (and again, and again, and again…) by continually pursuing a target for the unemployment rate that is below the natural rate, then demand-pull inflation will result.

Another possible source of inflation is government budget deficits. The government faces a budget constraint: $DEF = G - T = \Delta MB + \Delta B$, where DEF is the government budget deficit, G is government spending, T is tax revenue, ΔMB is the change in the monetary base and ΔB is the change in government bonds held by the public. According to this *government budget constraint*, the government can finance a deficit by increasing bonds (borrowing from the public) or increasing the monetary base. In the United States as well as many other countries, the government (Congress, the president and the U.S. Treasury) cannot simply increase the monetary base to finance the deficit. The only option for the government is to issue bonds to finance the deficit. If the central bank decides to conduct an open market purchase of those bonds, then bonds are removed from the hands of the public and the monetary base increases. This method of financing the deficit is called *monetizing the debt*. Budget deficits in and of themselves do not lead to persistent inflation. But persistent budget deficits that are financed by money creation will lead to a sustained inflation. Countries generally resort to monetizing their debt when they do not have sufficient access to capital markets or they face huge budget deficits. Neither describes the United States.

An increase in the government budget deficit leads to an increase in the interest rate. If the central bank wishes to keep interest rates low, it will purchase the new bonds through open market operations thus monetizing the debt. Economist Robert Barro contends that issuing bonds to finance a budget deficit does not cause the interest rate to rise and therefore does not lead to an increase in the money supply. Barro's argument is based on the theory of *Ricardian equivalence,* which says that when the government issues bonds to finance a deficit, the public recognizes that taxes will be raised in the future to pay off those bonds, and so the public increases its demand for bonds (to save for the future taxes) to match the increased supply and the interest rate remains unchanged.

The rise in inflation from 1960 to 1980 can be attributed to the rise in money growth over this period. After 1980, velocity gyrated substantially and the relationship between money growth and inflation broke down. The increase in money growth cannot be blamed on rising budget deficits because U.S. government debt actually declined as a percent of GDP over this period. Over the period 1965–1973 the unemployment rate was mostly below the natural rate of unemployment which suggests that persistent inflation during that period was demand-pull inflation. After 1975, the unemployment rate was mostly above the natural rate of unemployment, which suggests that persistent inflation during that time period was cost-push inflation.

THE DISCRETIONARY/ NONDISCRETIONARY POLICY DEBATE

Advocates of *discretionary policy* regard the self-correcting mechanism through wage and price adjustment as very slow and hence see the need for the government to pursue discretionary policy to eliminate high unemployment whenever it develops. Advocates of nondiscretionary policy, by contrast, believe that the performance of the economy would be improved if the government avoided using policy to eliminate unemployment. If the economy is below full employment, policymakers must decide whether to leave aggregate demand alone and allow the economy to shift back to full employment on its own or increase aggregate demand in order bring the economy back to full employment. The decision about whether to pursue discretionary government policy to eliminate high unemployment is complicated by several types of lags:

1. The data lag: data measuring the health of the economy is available with a lag making it difficult to tell how the economy is doing at the present time.

2. The recognition lag: it takes time for policymakers to be sure of what the data are signaling about the future course of the economy.

3. The legislative lag: It takes time to pass legislation to implement a particular policy. This lag applies to fiscal but not monetary policy.

4. The implementation lag: it takes time to implement the policy once a decision has been made to take a policy action. This lag applies to fiscal but not monetary policy.

5. The effectiveness lag: it takes time for a policy to impact the economy once it has been implemented. Advocates of *discretionary policy* believe that the effectiveness lag is long and variable.

Advocates of *discretionary policy* believe that the wage and price adjustment is extremely slow and therefore policy can move the aggregate demand curve before the economy adjusts on its own. Nonactivists believe that the wage and price adjustment process is rapid. Advocates of nondiscretionary policy argue that by the time policymakers can move the aggregate demand curve to return the economy to full employment, it will have moved back on its own and therefore the policy-induced change in aggregate demand will cause the economy to overshoot full-employment and fluctuate excessively. If workers take account of the type of policy (discretionary vs. nondiscretionary) when setting wages, then the case for nondiscretionary policy is much stronger. Workers are much more likely to push for higher wages if they believe that policymakers will accommodate the resulting leftward shift in aggregate supply.

Helpful Hints

1. A leftward shift in aggregate supply or a rightward shift in aggregate demand will cause the price level to rise. But persistent inflation is not a one-time increase in the price level--it is a continuous increase in the price level. Therefore, when we look for causes of persistent inflation, we must look for factors that can lead to either a persistent rightward shift in aggregate demand or a persistent leftward shift in aggregate supply. The only factor that is capable of generating persistent shifts is persistent increases in the money supply, which shifts the aggregate demand curve. A rise in the budget deficit, an increase in wages and a negative supply shocks all lead to a rise in the price level. These shift factors will only lead to persistent inflation if they cause the Fed to initiate a persistent increase in the supply of money.

Terms and Definitions

Choose a definition for each key term.

Key Terms:

_____accommodating policy

_____constant-money-growth-rate rule

_____cost-push inflation

_____demand-pull inflation

_____government budget constraint

_____monetizing the debt

_____ discretionary policy

_____printing money

_____Ricardian equivalence

Definitions:

1. Inflation that results when policymakers pursue policies to shift the aggregate demand curve to the right

2. A method of financing government spending whereby the government debt issued to finance government spending is removed from the hands of the public and is replaced by high-powered money

3. Policy aimed at eliminating high unemployment whenever it happens.

4. A policy rule advocated by monetarists, whereby the Federal Reserve keeps the money supply growing at a constant rate

5. Another term used to describe monetizing the debt

6. The requirement that the government budget deficit equal the sum of the change in the monetary base and the change in government bonds held by the public

7. Policy aimed at achieving a high employment target

8. The idea that when the government runs deficits and issues bonds, the public recognizes that it will be subject to higher taxes in the future to pay off these bonds

9. Inflation that occurs because of the push by workers to obtain higher wages

Problems and Short-Answer Questions

PRACTICE PROBLEMS

1. a. What caused hyperinflation in Germany after World War I?

_____

_____

b. Why did the German government pursue the policy you described in your answer to part *a*?

_____

_____

_____

c. How does the evidence you described in your answers to parts *a* and *b* rule out the possibility of reverse causation?

_____

_____

2. Suppose the economy is initially in equilibrium at point 1 in Figure 24.1 where aggregate output is equal to the natural rate level of output (Y_n).
    a. Use Figure 24.1 to demonstrate the effect of a one-shot permanent increase in government expenditures.

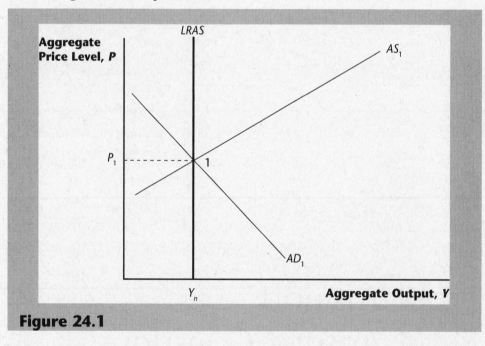

Figure 24.1

b. Did the one-shot permanent increase in government expenditures cause persistent inflation? Why or why not?

_____

_____

c.   Use Figure 24.2 to demonstrate the effect of a negative supply shock.

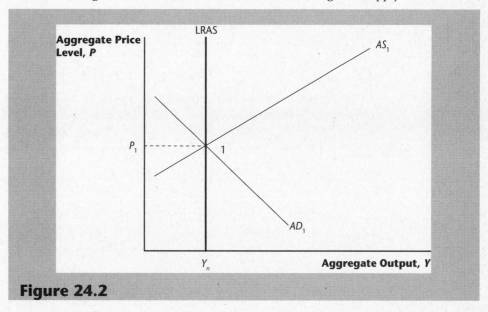

Figure 24.2

d.   Did the negative supply shock cause persistent inflation? Why or why not?

_____

_____

3.   Suppose the economy is initially in equilibrium at point 1 in Figure 24.3 where aggregate output is equal to the natural rate level of output (Y_n).
a.   Now suppose that workers decide to seek higher wages because they expect inflation to be high. Use Figure 24.3 to show what happens to aggregate output and the price level as a result of an increase in wages.
b.   Use Figure 24.3 to show what advocates of discretionary policy with a high employment target would do if this situation developed.

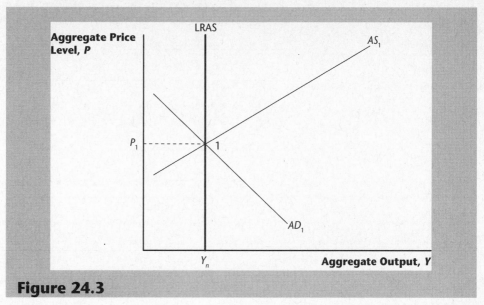

Figure 24.3

c. Did the increase in wages and the resulting accommodating policy cause persistent inflation? Why or why not?

_____

_____

d. Under what circumstances would an increase in wages lead to persistent inflation?

_____

_____

4. Suppose that government spending is $500 billion, tax revenue is $300 billion, and the change in government bonds held by the public is $150 billion.

a. Calculate the government budget deficit and the change in the monetary base.

_____

_____

b. Explain why your calculation in part *a* does not imply that Congress and the president can simply print money to finance the government budget deficit.

_____

_____

c. Under what circumstances are government budget deficits inflationary?

_____

_____

d. Were government deficits the likely cause of inflation in the United States between 1960 and 1980? Why or why not?

_____

_____

e. Did the American economy experience demand-pull or cost-push inflation between 1965 and 1973? What evidence supports your answer?

_____

_____

f. Did the American economy experience demand-pull or cost-push inflation between 1975 and 1980? What evidence supports your answer?

_____

_____

5. Suppose that policymakers are faced with the situation depicted in Figure 24.4 where the economy has moved below the natural rate level of output.

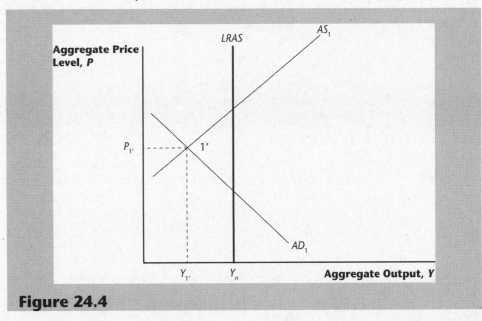

Figure 24.4

a. Describe what would happen if policymakers are proponents of nondiscretionary policy and illustrate the effect of nondiscretionary policy in Figure 24.4.

    _____

    _____

    _____

    _____

b. Describe what would happen if policymakers are advocates of discretionary policy and illustrate the effect of discretionary policy in Figure 24.4. Assume that the discretionary policy takes affect before wages and prices have time to adjust.

    _____

    _____

    _____

    _____

c. Describe what would happen if policymakers are advocates of discretionary policy and illustrate the effect of discretionary policy in Figure 24.4. Assume that the discretionary policy takes affect after wages and prices have time to adjust.

_____

_____

_____

_____

d. Under what circumstances would discretionary be preferable? Why?

_____

_____

_____

e. Under what circumstances would a nondiscretionary policy be preferable? Why?

_____

_____

_____

SHORT-ANSWER QUESTIONS

1. What is the difference between a one-time increase in the price level and persistent inflation?

_____

_____

2. Why is it not possible for continual increases in government spending or continual tax cuts to cause persistent inflation?

_____

_____

3. What causes persistent high inflation?

_____

_____

4. Under what circumstances will the pursuit of an employment target by policymakers lead to persistent inflation?

   _____

   _____

5. How would you distinguish between cost-push and demand-pull inflation by looking at the unemployment rate?

   _____

   _____

6. Why do governments frequently finance persistent deficits by creating money?

   _____

   _____

7. What is Ricardian equivalence and what does it imply about the effect of government deficits on the monetary base?

   _____

   _____

8. Of the five lags that prevent policymakers from moving the economy immediately back to full employment, which ones do not apply to monetary policy? Why?

   _____

   _____

9. Under what circumstances will discretionary policy cause output to overshoot and lead to excess volatility in aggregate output?

   _____

   _____

10. Explain why the case for nondiscretionary policy is much stronger if workers' opinions about whether policy is accommodating or nonaccommodating matter to the wage-setting process.

   _____

   _____

   _____

   _____

Critical Thinking

The popular press is often incorrect or misleading about its description of inflation and its description of the causes of persistent inflation. Below are three examples of newspaper headlines. For each example, state what is incorrect and/or misleading.

1.   "Increasing Oil Prices Caused Inflation to Rise Last Month"

   _____

   _____

   _____

   _____

2.   "Congress Tries to Reign in Spending Fearing That Deficits Will Cause Inflation"

   _____

   _____

   _____

   _____

3.   "Unions Push For Higher Wages, Policymakers Fear Rising Inflation"

   _____

   _____

   _____

   _____

Self-Test

TRUE/FALSE QUESTIONS

_____1.   Historical evidence on inflation and money growth is useful because it can help rule out the possibility of reverse causation.

_____2.   High money growth produces high inflation.

_____3.   If the price level rises 1% in a given month, then the inflation rate is 1%.

_____4.   Persistent high inflation cannot be driven by fiscal policy alone.

_____5. Supply-side phenomena are a source of persistent high inflation.

_____6. When inflation is accompanied by an unemployment rate that is below the natural rate of unemployment, the inflation is cost-push inflation.

_____7. Cost-push inflation is unrelated to money growth.

_____8. The United States government, as well as the governments of many other countries, has the right to issue currency to pay its bills.

_____9. From 1960–1980, debt relative to GDP increased in the United States.

_____10. Proponents of nondiscretionary policy believe that the effectiveness lag is long and variable.

_____11. In the past, Monetarists advocated discretionary monetary policy.

_____12. Advocates of discretionary policy favor the use of a constant-money-growth-rate rule.

_____13. Monetarists now favor rules that adjust for changes in velocity.

_____14. Both cost-push and demand-pull inflation can result from discretionary policy to promote high employment.

_____15. In all episodes of hyperinflation, huge government budget deficits are the ultimate reason for high money growth and persistent high inflation.

MULTIPLE-CHOICE QUESTIONS

1. After World War I, the German economy experienced hyperinflation because
   a. the German government increased the money supply to pay for reparations and reconstruction.
   b. destruction of the German economy during the war caused a shortage of goods.
   c. German workers demanded higher wages.
   d. crop failures and increasing oil prices caused prices to rise.

2. "Inflation is always and everywhere a monetary phenomenon" applies when
   a. there is a one-shot permanent increase in government spending.
   b. there is a one-shot increase in the price of oil.
   c. there is a one-time increase in workers' wages.
   d. there is high money growth.

3. Cost-push inflation occurs when
   a. policymakers attempt to target the unemployment rate below the natural rate of unemployment.
   b. policymakers attempt to target the unemployment rate above the natural rate of unemployment.
   c. workers demand higher wages.
   d. demands by workers to increase wages are accommodated by continual increases in the money supply.

4. Demand-pull inflation occurs when
   a. policymakers attempt to target the unemployment rate below the natural rate of unemployment.
   b. policymakers attempt to target the unemployment rate above the natural rate of unemployment.
   c. workers demand higher wages.
   d. demands by workers to increase wages are accommodated by continual increases in the money supply.

5. According to Ricardian equivalence,
   a. inflation is always and everywhere a monetary phenomena.
   b. budget deficits do not influence the monetary base.
   c. an increase in oil prices is equivalent to an increase in wages.
   d. budget deficits cause persistent inflation.

6. According to the government budget constraint, the deficit equals
   a. tax revenue.
   b. the change in the monetary base.
   c. the change in the quantity of bonds held by the public.
   d. the change in the monetary base plus the change in the quantity of bonds held by the public.

7. Monetizing the debt occurs
   a. whenever the government runs a deficit.
   b. when debt issued by the government has been removed from the hands of the public and replaced by high-powered money.
   c. when Ricardian equivalence holds.
   d. only in developing countries.

8. A deficit is
   a. always a source of persistent inflation.
   b. only a source of persistent inflation if it is temporary.
   c. only a source of persistent inflation if it is persistent and is financed by issuing bonds.
   d. only a source of persistent inflation if it is persistent and is financed by creating money.

9. Deficits can lead to persistent inflation if
   a. Ricardian equivalence does not hold and the Fed pursues a goal of preventing high interest rates.
   b. Ricardian equivalence holds and the Fed pursues a goal of preventing high interest rates.
   c. Ricardian equivalence does not hold and the Fed does not pursue a goal of preventing high interest rates.
   d. Ricardian equivalence holds and the Fed does not pursue a goal of preventing high interest rates.

10. Inflation in the United States between 1960 and 1980 is best described as
    a. cost-push inflation.
    b. demand-pull inflation.
    c. cost-push inflation in the early part of this period and demand-pull inflation in the later part.
    d. demand-pull inflation in the early part of this period and cost-push inflation in the later part.

11. The time it takes for policymakers to be sure of what the data are signaling about the course of the economy is called the
    a. data lag.
    b. recognition lag.
    c. legislative lag.
    d. implementation lag.

12. Which two types of lags are unimportant for monetary policy?
    a. data lag and recognition lag
    b. legislative lag and implementation lag
    c. recognition lag and effectiveness lag
    d. implementation lag and effectiveness lag

Use Figure 24.5 for questions 13-15.

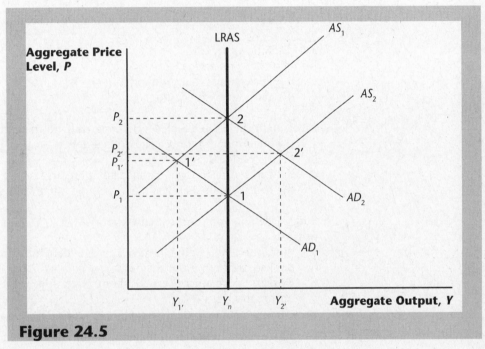

Figure 24.5

13. Suppose the economy has moved to point 1' in Figure 24.5. If policymakers pursue discretionary policy, and the wage and price adjustment is very slow, the economy will
    a. move back to point 1.
    b. move to point 2.
    c. move to point 2' then back to point 1.
    d. move to point 2' then back to point 2.

14. Suppose the economy has moved to point 1' in Figure 24.5. If policymakers pursue nondiscretionary policy, the economy will
    a. move back to point 1.
    b. move to point 2.
    c. move to point 2' then back to point 1.
    d. move to point 2' then back to point 2.

15. Suppose the economy has moved to point 1' in Figure 24.5. If policymakers pursue discretionary policy, and the wage and price adjustment is rapid, the economy will
    a. move back to point 1.
    b. move to point 2.
    c. move to point 2' then back to point 1.
    d. move to point 2' then back to point 2.

16. If workers' opinions about whether policy is accommodating or nonaccommodating matter to the wage setting process,
    a. the case for discretionary policy is much stronger
    b. the case for nondiscretionary policy is much stronger.
    c. Ricardian equivalence holds.
    d. deficits cause persistent inflation.

17. Advocates of _____ policy tend to recommend the use of policy _____.
    a. discretionary; rules
    b. nondiscretionary; rules
    c. nondiscretionary; accommodation
    d. discretionary; expectations

18. Inflation in the United States fell dramatically in the early 1980s because
    a. the government reduced the budget deficit.
    b. oil prices declined.
    c. the Fed switched to an explicit inflation target.
    d. the Fed reestablished itself as a credible inflation fighter.

19. Budget deficits do not explain the rise in U.S. inflation from 1960–1980 because
    a. the United States did not have a budget deficit during this period.
    b. the Fed did not pursue discretionary policy during this period.
    c. workers were unconcerned about what type of policy the Fed pursued during this period.
    d. U.S. government debt as a percent of GDP actually declined over this period.

20. If the wage and price adjustment process is rapid and policymakers use discretionary policy, then
    a. aggregate output will remain close to the natural rate level of output at all times.
    b. aggregate output will be more volatile than it would be under nondiscretionary policy.
    c. aggregate output will be less volatile than it would be under nondiscretionary policy.
    d. aggregate output will be just as volatile as it would be under nondiscretionary policy.

Solutions

Terms and Definitions

<u>7</u> accommodating policy

<u>4</u> constant-money-growth-rate rule

<u>9</u> cost-push inflation

<u>1</u> demand-pull inflation

<u>6</u> government budget constraint

<u>2</u> monetizing the debt

<u>4</u> discretionary policy

<u>5</u> printing money

<u>8</u> Ricardian equivalence

Practice Problems

1. a. Rapid money supply growth.

    b. The German government needed to make large reparation payments, and it was burdened by large reconstruction costs following World War I. It was politically unpopular to raise taxes and the amount of revenue needed exceeded the German government's capacity to borrow.

    c. The rapid money growth in Germany was clearly a response to exogenous events.

2. a. A one-shot permanent increase in government expenditures:

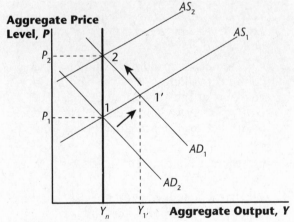

    b. No, the one-shot permanent increase in government expenditures caused the price level to rise to P_2 but did not result in persistent inflation which is a continuous rise in the price level.

    c. A negative supply shock:

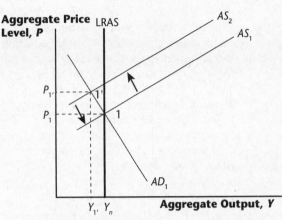

    d. In response to the negative aggregate supply shock the economy moves from 1 to 1' and then back to 1 again. A negative aggregate supply shock does not cause persistent inflation because it does not lead to a continuous increase in the price level.

3. a. The economy moves from 1 to 1' as wages rise.

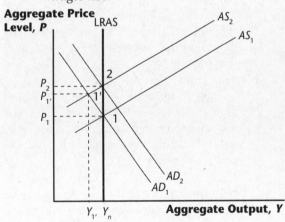

    b. The economy moves from 1' to 2 as activist policymakers pursue policies to shift the aggregate demand curve to the right.

    c. The increase in wages and the resulting discretionary policy did not cause persistent inflation because the price level stopped increasing after it reached P_2.

    d. If workers continue to ask for higher wages and monetary policymakers continue to accommodate the decline in aggregate output by increasing the money supply, then persistent inflation will result.

4. DEF = \$200 billion, ΔMB = \$50 billion.

    b. The change in the monetary base to finance the deficit is a two-step process. First Congress and the president (through the Treasury) issue bonds to finance the deficit. Then the Fed buys those bonds from the public increasing the monetary base. In the United States as well as many other countries, the decision by the central bank to purchase bonds from the public (and therefore monetize the debt) is independent of the decision of Congress and the president to run a budget deficit.

    c. A deficit can be the source of a persistent inflation only if it is persistent rather than temporary and if the government finances it by creating money rather than by issuing bonds to the public.

    d. Government budget deficits were not the likely cause of persistent inflation because government debt relative to GDP was actually declining between 1960 and 1980.

    e. The American economy experienced demand-pull inflation between 1965 and 1973. This is supported by the fact that the unemployment rate was below the natural rate of unemployment for most of that time period.

    f. The American economy experienced cost-push inflation between 1975 and 1980. This is supported by the fact that the unemployment rate was above the natural rate of unemployment for most of that time period.

5. a. Under the nondiscretionary approach, policymakers would leave aggregate demand unchanged and wages and prices would adjust downward because the economy is below the natural rate level of output at 1'. As wages and prices adjust downward, the AS curve shifts to AS_2 and the economy returns to point 1.

    b. Under a discretionary approach, policymakers would pursue policies to shift the aggregate demand curve to the right. If those policies take affect before wages and prices have time to adjust downward, the economy will move to point 2.

    c. If discretionary policies take affect after wages and prices have adjusted downward, the economy will move to point 2'.

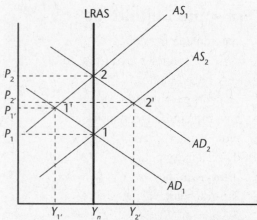

Aggregate Output, Y

    d. Discretionary policy is preferable if the wage and price adjustment process is extremely slow because it would keep the economy closer to the natural rate level of output Y_n.

    e. Nondiscretionary policy is preferable if the wage and price adjustment process is rapid because discretionary policy in this situation would create excess volatility (aggregate output would swing from $Y_{1'}$ to $Y_{2'}$).

Short-Answer Questions

1. Persistent inflation is when changes in the price level are repeated for a substantial period of time.

2. Government spending cannot increase continually--there is a natural limit; government spending cannot exceed 100% of GDP. Similarly, taxes cannot be reduced indefinitely because eventually they would hit zero.

3. Persistent high money growth causes persistent high inflation.

4. When the employment target is too high, meaning that policymakers attempt to push unemployment below the natural rate, persistent inflation results.

5. With cost-push inflation, the unemployment rate is above the natural rate of unemployment. With demand-pull inflation, the unemployment rate is below the natural rate of unemployment.

6. Because it is politically unpopular to increase taxes to finance government expenditures and/or the government does not have access to well-developed money and capital markets.

7. Ricardian equivalence is the idea that when the government issues bonds to finance a deficit the public recognizes that taxes will increase in the future, and so they save for those taxes by buying the newly issued bonds from the government. Since bond demand increases along with bond supply, the interest rate remains unchanged and there is no incentive for the Fed to increase the monetary base in order to keep the interest rate from rising.

8. The legislative lag and the implementation lag do not apply to monetary policy because the Fed does not have to pass legislation in order to pursue a policy change and once a policy change has been decided on the Fed can immediately notify the Fed's trading desk to undertake the appropriate open market operations.

9. When wages and prices adjust faster than policymakers can shift the aggregate demand curve, discretionary policy will lead to excess volatility in aggregate output.

10. If workers' expectations about the type of policy matter, and the Fed follows an accommodating policy, workers will come to expect that their wage demands will be met. As a result, workers will continue to ask for higher wages and the aggregate supply curve will continue to shift leftward, which sets up a situation where the Fed will continue to react to the higher wage demands by continually increasing the money supply, which leads to persistent inflation. If expectations matter, following a nonaccommodating, nondiscretionary policy will lead to lower inflation.

Critical Thinking

1. "Increasing Oil Prices Caused Inflation to Rise Last Month": This headline incorrectly identifies a one-time increase in the price level (last month) as inflation. In addition, it also attributes inflation to a negative supply shock (the increase in oil prices), which is also incorrect since persistent inflation is caused by money growth.

2. "Congress Tries to Reign in Spending Fearing That Deficits Will Cause Inflation": This headline is misleading because deficits in and of themselves do not cause persistent inflation. If the deficits are persistent and the Fed monetizes the deficits, then persistent inflation can results. But it is not inevitable that deficits are inflationary.

3. "Unions Push for Higher Wages, Policymakers Fear Rising Inflation": Unions pushing for higher wages can lead to persistent higher inflation if the Fed follows an discretionary, accommodating policy, which sets up the expectations on the part of workers that their wage demands will always be met by an increase in the money supply. But again, it is important to distinguish between a one-shot increase in wages (which is not inflation) from a continual increase in wages that is accommodated by higher money growth (which is inflationary).

True/False Questions

1. T
2. T
3. F
4. T
5. F
6. F
7. F
8. F
9. F
10. T
11. F
12. F
13. T
14. T
15. T

Multiple-Choice Questions

1. a
2. d
3. d
4. a
5. b
6. d
7. b
8. d
9. a
10. d
11. b

12. b
13. b
14. a
15. d
16. b
17. b
18. d
19. d
20. b

25 Rational Expectations: Implications for Policy

Chapter Review

PREVIEW

In previous chapters you learned how government policy could, in principle, be used to steer output toward full employment. But in practice (especially during the 1960s and 1970s) discretionary policies have not been successful. The theory of rational expectations was developed in the 1970s and 1980s to examine why discretionary policies performed so poorly. This chapter examines the analysis behind the rational expectations revolution. The existence of rational expectations makes discretionary policies less likely to be successful and raises the issue of credibility as an important element affecting policy outcomes.

THE LUCAS CRITIQUE OF POLICY EVALUATION

Econometric models are models whose equations are estimated with statistical procedures. Those statistical procedures measure the relationship between variables that existed in the past. For example, suppose that in the past, increases in short-term interest rates were usually temporary and therefore had very little impact on long-term interest rates. The econometric model will therefore show very little relationship between short- and long-term interest rates. Now suppose that policymakers wish to use that econometric model to evaluate the effect of a permanent increase in short-term interest rates. The econometric model will give a misleading result. It will show that an increase in short-term interest rates will have very little effect on long-term interest rates. But in reality, if the increase in interest rates is expected to be permanent rather than temporary, then the response of long-term interest rates will be greater than predicted by the model.

The reason for this misleading prediction is that people will change the way in which they form expectations about a variable when the behavior of that variable changes. The past relationship between short-term and long-term interest rates was based on the expectation that increases in short-term interest rates are temporary. But if the behavior of short-term interest rates changes so that increases in short-term interest rates are permanent, then people will change their expectations and the relationship between short-term interest rates and long-term interest rates will change. This critique of econometric models (called the Lucas critique after economist Robert Lucas) implies not only that conventional econometric models cannot be used for policy evaluation, but also that the public's expectations about a policy will influence the response to that policy.

NEW CLASSICAL MACROECONOMIC MODEL

The new classical macroeconomic model views expectations as rational. In the new classical model, all wages and prices are completely flexible with respect to expected changes in the price level. If the Fed increases the money supply unexpectedly the expected price level will remain at P_1 and the economy will move to 2' as the aggregate demand curve shifts right in Figure 25.1. But if the increase in the money supply is anticipated, workers and firms will recognize that the increase in the money supply will cause the price level will rise to P_2. As a consequence, the aggregate supply curve will shift left just as aggregate demand is shifting right. The conclusion from this model is that anticipated policy has no effect on the business cycle; only unanticipated policy matters. This conclusion is called the *policy ineffectiveness proposition*.

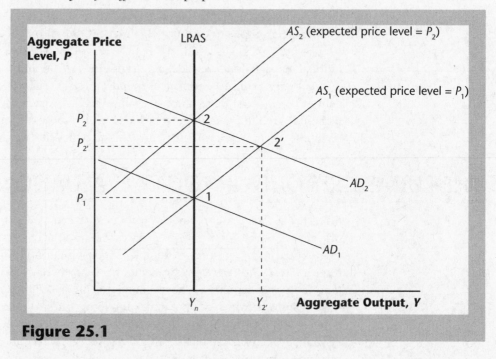

Figure 25.1

There are two important lessons of the new classical model for policymakers. First, it shows that the effect of policy depends on whether it is anticipated or unanticipated, and second, it shows that policymakers cannot know the outcome of their decisions without knowing the public's expectations regarding them. This model implies that the Fed and other policymaking agencies should abandon discretionary policy and generate as few policy surprises as possible.

NEW KEYNESIAN MODEL

The new Keynesian model assumes expectations are rational, but wages and prices are sticky for various reasons (long-term contracts for example). *Wage-price stickiness* means that wages and prices do not respond fully to changes in the expected price level. An unanticipated increase in the money supply will cause aggregate output to rise to Y_U in Figure 25.2. This is the identical effect that an unanticipated increase in the money supply has in the new classical model. An anticipated increase in the money supply will cause aggregate output to rise to Y_A in Figure 25.2. This result differs from the new classical result because wage and price stickiness prevent wages and prices from fully adjusting the anticipated change in the price level, and therefore the aggregate supply curve does not shift all the way back to AS_2.

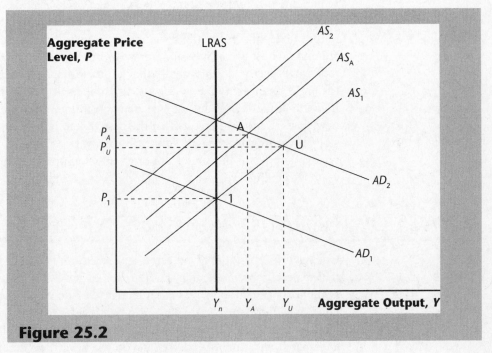

Figure 25.2

COMPARISON OF THE TWO NEW MODELS WITH THE TRADITIONAL MODEL

The traditional model assumes expectations are adaptive, which implies that there is no distinction between anticipated and unanticipated policy. The new classical, the new Keynesian, and the traditional model all predict that an unanticipated increase in the money supply will cause aggregate output to increase from Y_n to Y_U in Figure 25.2. According to the traditional model, an anticipated increase in the money supply will cause aggregate output to rise to Y_U as well. According to the new Keynesian model, an anticipated increase in the money supply will cause aggregate output to rise to Y_A. And according to the new classical model, an anticipated increase in the money supply will have no impact on aggregate output (it will remain at Y_n).

The three models differ in terms of their recommendations about stabilization policy. In the traditional model, it is possible for discretionary policy to stabilize output fluctuations. In the new classical model, it is not possible for discretionary policy to stabilize output fluctuations. The new Keynesian model takes an intermediate position and therefore raises the possibility that a discretionary policy could be beneficial, but designing such a beneficial policy is extremely difficult.

The three models also differ in terms of their recommendations about anti-inflation policy. In the traditional model, both an anticipated and an unanticipated halt in aggregate demand stimulus will cause aggregate output to decline. Thus, according to the traditional model, reducing inflation is costly. In the new classical and new Keynesian models, an unanticipated halt in aggregate demand stimulus will have the same effect as in the traditional model: Output declines making it costly to reduce inflation. According to the new classical model, inflation reduction, if anticipated, is costless. The new Keynesian model again takes an intermediate position. An anticipated halt in aggregate demand stimulus will cause output to decline but not by as much as an unanticipated halt in aggregate demand stimulus. Thus, according to the new Keynesian model, an anticipated reduction in inflation is costly, but less costly than an unanticipated reduction in inflation. Both the new classical and new Keynesian models indicate that in order to reduce inflation at the lowest output cost, the anti-inflation policies must be credible. The new classical model suggests that the best way to reduce inflation is to immediately stop the aggregate demand stimulus. The new Keynesian model suggests a more gradual approach. But under a more gradual approach, it may be more difficult to establish credibility.

IMPACT OF THE RATIONAL EXPECTATIONS REVOLUTION

One result of the rational expectations revolution is that economists now recognize that expectations matter for the outcome of policy. Because of the Lucas critique, economists are no longer as confident in the success of discretionary stabilization policies as they once were. The empirical evidence on whether anticipated policy matters is mixed. Thus, many economists recognize the distinction between anticipated and unanticipated policy but believe that anticipated policy can affect output. Because of the rational expectations revolution, economists now recognize the importance of credibility to the success of anti-inflation policies.

Helpful Hints

According to the theory of rational expectations, it is important to distinguish between anticipated and unanticipated policy. New classical and new Keynesian models both assume that people form expectations rationally but differ on the speed at which wages and prices can adjust to changes in expectations. New classical models assume the adjustment is immediate. New Keynesians models assume the adjustment takes time. As a result, new classical models predict that anticipated policy has no affect on aggregate output. New Keynesian models predict that anticipated policy does have some affect on aggregate output. Both new Keynesian and new classical models agree that establishing credibility is important for minimizing the output cost of reducing inflation.

Terms and Definitions

Choose a definition for each key term.

Key Terms:

_____econometric models

_____policy ineffectiveness proposition

_____wage-price stickiness

Definitions:

1. When wages and prices do not respond fully to changes in the expected price level

2. Models whose equations are estimated using statistical procedures

3. The conclusion from the new classical model that anticipated policy has no effect on output fluctuations

Problems and Short-Answer Questions

PRACTICE PROBLEMS

1. Suppose your roommate studies late in the library each night, returning to your room after you have gone to bed and turned out the light. In an effort not to disturb you, he leaves the light off but ends up bumping into things in the dark and making so much noise that you wake up anyway. Fortunately your roommate is fairly quick about it, and after 5 minutes or so he is usually in bed. In an effort to remedy this situation, you decide to leave the light on to reduce the noise. Your experiment fails. Not only does your roommate still make noise, but seeing that the light is on, he makes noise for 10 minutes instead of 5 minutes.

   a. How does your experiment with your dorm light relate to the Lucas critique?

   _____

   _____

   _____

   b. How does your experiment with your dorm light relate to policymakers' ability to predict the effect of a change in policy on the economy?

   _____

   _____

   _____

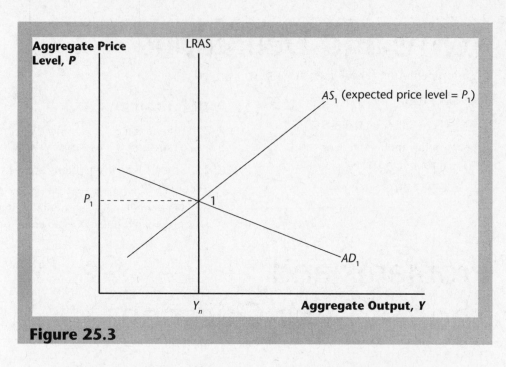

Figure 25.3

2. a. Use Figure 25.3 to show the effect of an unanticipated increase in the money supply in the new classical model. Explain what happened.

    _____

    _____

    _____

    b. Use Figure 25.3 to show the effect of an anticipated increase in the money supply in the new classical model. Explain what happened.

    _____

    _____

    _____

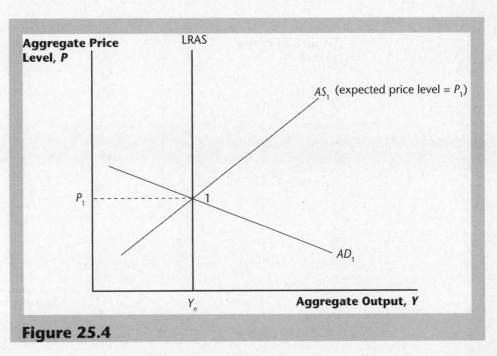

Aggregate Price Level, P

LRAS

AS_1 (expected price level = P_1)

P_1 -------------- 1

AD_1

Y_n

Aggregate Output, Y

Figure 25.4

c. Now suppose that workers and firms have come to expect that the Fed will increase the money supply by 10% each year. Use Figure 25.4 to show what would happen if the Fed unexpectedly increased the money supply by only 5%. Explain what happened.

_____

_____

_____

d. Based on your answers to parts *a* through *c*, what are the implications of the new classical model for policymakers?

_____

_____

_____

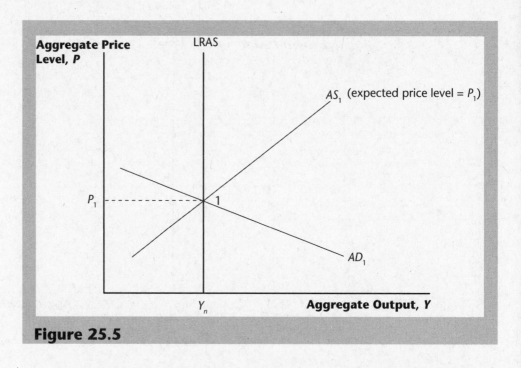

Figure 25.5

3. a. Use Figure 25.5 to show the effect of an unanticipated increase in the money supply in the new Keynesian model. Explain what happened.

    _____

    _____

    _____

    b. Use Figure 25.5 to show the effect of an anticipated increase in the money supply in the new Keynesian model. Explain what happened.

    _____

    _____

    _____

    c. What are the implications of the new Keynesian model for policymakers?

    _____

    _____

    _____

4. Listed below are statements about stabilization policy. If the statement is consistent with the new classical model, write NC in the space provided. If the statement is consistent with the new Keynesian model, write NK in the space provided. And if the statement is consistent with the traditional model, write T in the space provided. Each statement may be consistent with more than one model. List all of the models that are consistent with each statement.

____a. An unanticipated increase in the money supply leads to an increase in aggregate output.

____b. An anticipated increase in the money supply leads to an increase in aggregate output.

____c. A credible, anticipated reduction in money growth will lead to a reduction in inflation without causing aggregate output to fall.

____d. A credible, anticipated reduction in money growth will lead to a reduction in inflation and aggregate output.

____e. Expectations and credibility matter for the affect of policy on the economy.

____f. It is possible for discretionary stabilization policy to stabilize output fluctuations.

____g. Discretionary policy could be beneficial, but uncertainty about the outcome of policies may make the design of such a beneficial policy extremely difficult.

____h. The best anti-inflation policy is to go "cold turkey."

____i. Anticipated policy has no effect on the business cycle.

SHORT-ANSWER QUESTIONS

1. Suppose that temporary increases in the budget deficit in the past have not caused interest rates to rise. Explain why it would be dangerous to infer that a permanent increase in the budget deficit will not cause interest rates to rise.

2. According to the new classical model, how can an increase in the money supply lead to a reduction in aggregate output?

3. In the new classical model, only unanticipated policy changes have an effect on the business cycle. Does it follow that the Fed should randomly change policy so that people don't catch on to what it is doing? Explain.

4. Why are wages and prices sticky?

_____

_____

5. The new Keynesian model predicts that anticipated policy has an effect on output. Does it follow that policymakers should pursue discretionary policy? Explain.

_____

_____

6. What are adaptive expectations and what do they imply about the effects of predictions of future policy on the aggregate supply curve?

_____

_____

7. Which of the three models (new classical, new Keynesian, and traditional) implies that the best way to fight inflation is a policy of "cold turkey?" Explain why.

_____

_____

8. Why is credibility important for the effectiveness of anti-inflation policy?

_____

_____

9. What might have been the outcome of the anti-inflation policy during the Reagan administration if the government had actively tried to reduce the budget deficit?

_____

_____

10. Has the rational expectations revolution convinced economists that there is no role for discretionary stabilization policy? Explain.

_____

_____

Critical Thinking

The policy recommendations of the three models presented in this chapter are sometimes contradictory. Suppose you are an economic advisor to the president.

The inflation rate is currently 10%, and the president asks you for recommendations to bring the inflation rate down to 5% without causing excessive unemployment.

1. What policy would you recommend based on the new classical model? Explain.

   _____

   _____

   _____

2. What policy would you recommend based on the new Keynesian model? Explain.

   _____

   _____

   _____

3. Of course the president wants just one recommendation. What is the common element in both the new classical and new Keynesian models that you would recommend as part of any policy to reduce inflation? Explain.

   _____

   _____

   _____

Self-Test

TRUE/FALSE QUESTIONS

_____1. The Lucas critique implies that econometric models are not useful for evaluating the effects of alternative policies on the economy.

_____2. The new classical model predicts that neither anticipated nor unanticipated policies affect output.

_____3. The new Keynesian model predicts that both anticipated and unanticipated policies affect output.

_____4. The new classical model predicts that an expansion in the money supply that is smaller than anticipated will cause output to rise.

_____5. According to the new classical model, wages and prices rise fully in response to an increase in the expected price level.

_____6. Firms might be reluctant to decrease wages when demand falls because it might result in poorer work performance on the part of workers.

_____7. An anticipated increase in the money supply will lead to a larger increase in output in the new Keynesian model than in the traditional model.

_____8. An anticipated decrease in the money supply will lead to a larger decrease in the price level in the new Keynesian model than in the traditional model.

_____9. The new classical model predicts that stabilization may be beneficial but difficult to design.

_____10. According to the new Keynesian model, discretionary stabilization policy will aggravate output fluctuations.

_____11. The traditional model assumes that the effect of anticipated and unanticipated policy is the same.

_____12. The new classical model predicts that the most effective way to reduce inflation is by a policy of "cold turkey."

_____13. Both the new classical and new Keynesian models predict that a credible anti-inflation policy is less costly (in terms of lost output) than a policy that is not credible.

_____14. The conclusion that the Reagan budget deficits helped create a more severe recession in 1981–1982 is widely accepted by most economists.

_____15. The rational expectations revolution has caused a major rethinking about the way economic policy should be conducted.

MULTIPLE-CHOICE QUESTIONS

1. Which of the following statements is true?
    a. Lucas's econometric policy critique suggests that econometric models are useless for forecasting.
    b. Lucas's econometric policy critique suggests that econometric models are useful for forecasting.
    c. Lucas's econometric policy critique suggests that econometric models are useful for evaluating the impact of alternative policies on the economy.
    d. Lucas's econometric policy critique says nothing about the usefulness of econometric models as forecasting tools.

2. An important difference between the new classical and new Keynesian models is
    a. the new classical model assumes rational expectations and the new Keynesian model does not.
    b. the new Keynesian model assumes rational expectations and the new classical model does not.
    c. the new classical model assumes wages and prices are sticky and the new Keynesian model does not.
    d. the new Keynesian model assumes wages and prices are sticky and the new classical model does not.

3. According to the new classical model, an anticipated increase in the money supply will
   a. cause the price level to rise, leaving aggregate output unchanged.
   b. cause aggregate output to rise, leaving the price level unchanged.
   c. cause both aggregate output and the price level to rise.
   d. have no affect on either aggregate output or the price level.

4. According to the new Keynesian model, an anticipated increase in the money supply will
   a. cause the price level to rise, leaving aggregate output unchanged.
   b. cause aggregate output to rise, leaving the price level unchanged.
   c. cause both aggregate output and the price level to rise.
   d. have no affect on either aggregate output or the price level.

5. According to the new classical model, an unanticipated increase in the money supply will
   a. cause the price level to rise, leaving aggregate output unchanged.
   b. cause aggregate output to rise, leaving the price level unchanged.
   c. cause both aggregate output and the price level to rise.
   d. have no affect on either aggregate output or the price level.

6. According to the new Keynesian model, an unanticipated increase in the money supply will
   a. cause the price level to rise, leaving aggregate output unchanged.
   b. cause aggregate output to rise, leaving the price level unchanged.
   c. cause both aggregate output and the price level to rise.
   d. have no affect on either aggregate output or the price level.

7. The policy ineffectiveness proposition states that
   a. anticipated policy has no effect on the business cycle, only unanticipated policy matters.
   b. unanticipated policy has no effect on the business cycle, only anticipated policy matters.
   c. anticipated policy has no effect on the price level, only unanticipated policy matters.
   d. unanticipated policy has no effect on the price level, only anticipated policy matters.

8. The reason the aggregate supply curve shifts leftward in response to an anticipated increase in aggregate demand is
   a. the increase in output demanded raises the cost of production.
   b. tax revenues increase in response to an increase in aggregate demand.
   c. the Fed typically raises interest rates, which makes investment expenditures more costly.
   d. workers will demand higher wages in order to keep real earnings unchanged when the price level rises.

9. Expansionary policy can lead to a decline in aggregate output if
   a. the public expects a less expansionary policy than the one that is actually implemented.
   b. the public expects a more expansionary policy than the one that is actually implemented.
   c. wages are sticky because of long-term labor contracts.
   d. workers and firms have adaptive expectations.

10. The new classical model supports _____ policy and suggests that policy be based on _____.
    a. discretionary; rules
    b. nondiscretionary; rational expectations
    c. discretionary; adaptive expectations
    d. nondiscretionary; rules

11. The new Keynesian model
    a. suggests that designing successful discretionary policies is a straightforward task.
    b. does not rule out the potential benefits of discretionary policy but recognizes that such policies are difficult to design.
    c. clearly rules out the possibility of improving the economy through discretionary policy.
    d. says nothing regarding the benefits of discretionary policy.

Use Figure 25.6 to answer questions 12 through 17.

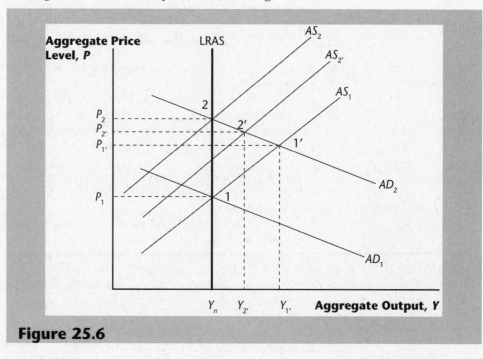

Figure 25.6

12. Suppose the economy is initially at point 1 in Figure 25.6. According to the traditional model, an unanticipated increase in the money supply will cause the economy to
    a. remain at point 1.
    b. move to point 1'.
    c. move to point 2.
    d. move to point 2'.

13. Suppose the economy is initially at point 1 in Figure 25.6. According to the new classical model, an unanticipated increase in the money supply will cause the economy to
    a.   remain at point 1.
    b.   move to point 1'.
    c.   move to point 2.
    d.   move to point 2'.

14. Suppose the economy is initially at point 1 in Figure 25.6. According to the new Keynesian model, an unanticipated increase in the money supply will cause the economy to
    a.   remain at point 1.
    b.   move to point 1'.
    c.   move to point 2.
    d.   move to point 2'.

15. Suppose the economy is initially at point 1 in Figure 25.6. According to the traditional model, an anticipated increase in the money supply will cause the economy to
    a.   remain at point 1.
    b.   move to point 1'.
    c.   move to point 2.
    d.   move to point 2'.

16. Suppose the economy is initially at point 1 in Figure 25.6. According to the new classical model, an anticipated increase in the money supply will cause the economy to
    a.   remain at point 1.
    b.   move to point 1'.
    c.   move to point 2.
    d.   move to point 2'.

17. Suppose the economy is initially at point 1 in Figure 25.6. According to the new Keynesian model, an anticipated increase in the money supply will cause the economy to
    a.   remain at point 1.
    b.   move to point 1'.
    c.   move to point 2.
    d.   move to point 2'.

18. According to the new classical model, a credible, anticipated reduction in aggregate demand designed to reduce inflation
    a.   is costly in terms of lost output.
    b.   is costly in terms of lost output, but the cost is less than it would be under the traditional model.
    c.   is costly in terms of lost output, but the cost is greater than it would be under the traditional model.
    d.   is costless in terms of lost output.

19. According to the new Keynesian model, a credible, anticipated reduction in aggregate demand designed to reduce inflation
    a.   is costly in terms of lost output.
    b.   is costly in terms of lost output, but the cost is less than it would be under the traditional model.
    c.   is costly in terms of lost output, but the cost is greater than it would be under the traditional model.
    d.   is costless in terms of lost output.

20. Both the new classical and new Keynesian models agree that any anti-inflation policy must be _____ in order to minimize the loss in output.
    a.   credible
    b.   quick
    c.   gradual
    d.   unanticipated

Solutions

Terms and Definitions

_2_   econometric models

_3_   policy ineffectiveness proposition

_1_   wage-price stickiness

Practice Problems

1. a. Your prediction was based on your past observations of what happened when the light was out. You assumed that when you turned the light on your roommate's behavior would not change--he would not make as much noise because he would not be bumping into things in the dark, but he also would not change the length of time he bumped around the room before going to bed. According to the Lucas critique, econometric models assume this same type of unchanging behavior because they are based on past data. Your experiment failed because your roommate changed his behavior by staying awake for longer with the lights on.

    b. When policymakers use an econometric model to predict the outcome of a change in policy, they fail to take account of the fact that by changing policy, people will change their behavior. The change in behavior (staying awake longer with the lights on) invalidates the prediction based on past data.

2. a. In response to an unanticipated increase in the money supply the economy will move from point 1 to 2' and output will rise to $Y_{2'}$. With an unanticipated increase in the money supply, the expected price level remains at P_1 so wages and prices remain unchanged and the economy moves along AS_1.

    b. In response to an anticipated increase in the money supply the economy will move from point 1 to 2, and output will remain at Y_n. With an anticipated increase in the money supply, the expected price level increases along with the increase in the money supply and so the aggregate supply curve shifts left as the aggregate demand curve is shifting right.

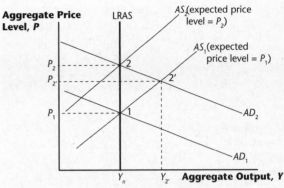

c. If workers and firms expect the Fed to increase the money supply by 10%, then the aggregate demand curve to shift rightward to AD_2. If the Fed unexpectedly increases the money supply by only 5%, then aggregate demand will shift by less than expected (to $AD_{2'}$) but aggregate supply will still shift back to AS_2 based on an expected price level of P_2. Output will decrease to $Y_{2'}$.

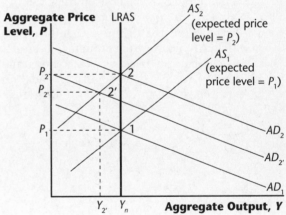

d. The policy recommendation that follows from the analysis in parts (a) through (c) is that policymakers should strive to minimize unanticipated changes in aggregate demand.

3. a. In response to an unanticipated increase in the money supply, the economy will move from point 1 to point U and output will rise to Y_U. With an unanticipated increase in the money supply, the expected price level remains at P_1, so wages and prices remain unchanged, and the economy moves along AS_1.

b. In response to an anticipated increase in the money supply, the economy will move from point 1 to point A, and output will remain at Y_A. With an anticipated increase in the money supply, the expected price level increases along with the increase in the money supply, but prices and wages are sticky and do not fully adjust to the new expected price level, so the *AS* curve shifts leftward partially to AS_A.

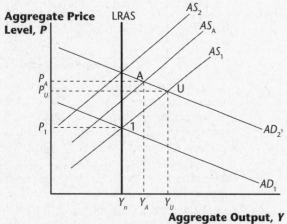

c. According to the analysis in parts *a* and *b*, anticipated policy can affect output. However, it is still a challenge to design policy to improve the economy because it is difficult to measure expectations and the effect of policy still depends on expectations in the new Keynesian model.

4. <u>NC, NK, T</u>   a.

    <u>NK, T</u>   b.

    <u>NC</u>   c.

    <u>NK, T</u>   d.

    <u>NC, NK</u>   e.

    <u>T</u>   f.

    <u>NK</u>   g.

    <u>NC</u>   h.

    <u>NC</u>   i.

Short-Answer Questions

1. The Lucas econometric critique implies that when the behavior of a variable changes, the expectation of that variable changes as well. Using past data on the relationship between budget deficits and interest rates will provide misleading predictions of the effect of a permanent increase in budget deficits on interest rates.

2. If the increase in the money supply is less than expected, the leftward shift in the aggregate supply curve will more than offset the rightward shift in aggregate demand and aggregate output will decrease.

3. No. Random policy changes would cause undesirable fluctuations around the natural rate level of aggregate output.

4. Wages and prices are sticky for three reasons: (1) long-term contracts, (2) reducing wages when demand declines may adversely affect worker productivity, and (3) changing prices is costly.

5. Not necessarily. Although discretionary policy has an effect on output according to the Keynesian model, the effect of discretionary policy is still difficult to predict (because expectations are difficult to measure).

6. Adaptive expectations are expectations based solely on past experience. If people form expectations adaptively, then predictions of future policy have no effect on the aggregate supply curve.

7. The new classical model implies that the best way to fight inflation is a policy of "cold turkey" because wages and prices will adjust immediately and fully to a decrease in aggregate demand so there will not be a decline in output.

8. When an anti-inflation policy is credible, people believe that policymakers will follow through with their commitment to decrease aggregate demand. As a result they will adjust their expectations to a lower price level, which will shift the aggregate supply rightward, which minimizes the decline in output resulting from the leftward shift in aggregate demand.

9. It is possible (but controversial) that the recession of 1981–1982 might have been less severe if the Reagan administration had raised taxes to reduce budget deficits. The failure of the Reagan administration to raise taxes lessened the credibility of policymakers to reduce inflation.

10. New classical economists say yes, the rational expectations revolution has convinced economists that there is no role for discretionary stabilization policy. But such a position is not accepted by many economists because the empirical evidence on the policy ineffectiveness proposition is mixed.

Critical Thinking

1. Based on the new classical model, the policy recommendation is to immediately announce that the Fed will reduce money growth to achieve a reduction in inflation to 5%. If the announced reduction in money growth is credible (and the Fed follows through with the intended policy), inflation will fall without causing unemployment to rise.

2. A new Keynesian might recommend a more gradual approach because wages and prices are sticky, so even though workers and firms will immediately adjust their expectations to the new inflation rate, they will not fully adjust their wages and prices. The challenge of this policy recommendation is that a gradual reduction in inflation may compromise the ability of policymakers to convince the public that their policy is credible.

3. The common element of both theories is credibility. If the president decides to follow a gradual approach, he (or she) must overcome the fact that a gradual policy will tend to be less credible. If the president decides to follow a "cold turkey" approach, it is equally important that the policy is credible.

True/False Questions

1. T
2. F
3. T
4. F
5. T
6. T
7. F
8. T
9. F
10. F
11. T
12. T
13. T
14. F
15. T

Multiple-Choice Questions

1. d
2. d
3. a
4. c
5. c
6. c
7. a
8. d
9. b
10. d
11. b
12. b
13. b
14. b
15. b
16. c
17. d
18. d
19. b
20. a